PRACTICAL

Firewalls

Terry William

Ogletree

Contents at a Glance

Introduction   1

I Understanding Firewalls and Internet Security   7

1 Firewall Basics 9
2 Introduction to the TCP/IP Protocol Suite 25
3 Security and the Internet 63
4 Firewall Security Policy and Firewall Design Strategies 85
5 Packet Filtering 109
6 Using a Bastion Host 131
7 Application Gateways and Proxy Servers 157
8 Operating System Monitoring and Auditing Techniques 177

II Encryption and Secure Communication on the Internet   197

9 Encryption Technology 199
10 Virtual Private Networks (VPNs) and Tunneling 211
11 Using Pretty Good Privacy (PGP) for Encryption 227

III Firewall Installation and Configuration   239

12 Firewall Tools Available on the Internet 241
13 Using TCP Wrappers 253
14 Using the TIS Firewall Toolkit (FWTK) 263
15 SOCKS 291
16 SQUID 301
17 Using ipfwadm and ipchains on Linux 313
18 Microsoft Proxy Server 333
19 The Elron Commander Firewall 357
20 Firewall Appliances 371
21 Firewalls and Beyond 381

IV Appendixes   393

A TCP and UDP Common Ports 395
B Other Security Tools You Can Use 445
C Additional Resources 455

Index 463

A Division of Macmillan Computer Publishing, USA
201 W. 103rd Street
Indianapolis, Indiana 46290

Practical Firewalls

International Standard Book Number: 0-7897-2416-2

Library of Congress Catalog Card Number: 00-101765

Printed in the United States of America

First Printing: June 2000

01   00   4   3   2   1

Trademarks

Warning and Disclaimer

Associate Publisher
Tracy Dunkelberger

Senior Acquisitions Editor
Jenny Watson

Development Editor
Todd Brakke

Managing Editor
Thomas Hayes

Project Editor
Pamela Woolf

Copy Editor
Kelly Talbot

Indexer
Mary SeRine

Proofreader
Benjamin Berg

Technical Editors
Amol Kabe
Frank Gleason
Gary Krakow
Brian Tanaka
Vern Hart

Interior Design
Anne Jones

Cover Design
Rader Design

Layout Technician
Darin Crone

Formatter
Mandie Rowell

Contents

Introduction 1

I Understanding Firewalls and Internet Security 7

1 Firewall Basics 9

Why You Need a Firewall 10
    What Is a Firewall? 10
    It's a Jungle Out There! 12

Use Your Site's Security Policy to Design the Firewall 12
    New Security Threats to Consider 13
    Decide Which Services You Will Provide for Your Users 14
    Firewall Policy 16

Firewall Technologies 16
    The First Firewalls: Packet Filtering 17
    Using Application Gateways 17
    Other Firewall Components 18

Hardware or Software Firewalls? Build or Buy? 18
    Operating System Concerns 19

What a Firewall Can Do 21

What a Firewall Cannot Protect You From 21
    Maintaining a Firewall 23

Summary 24

2 Introduction to the TCP/IP Protocol Suite 25

The OSI Networking Model 26
    Physical Layer 28
    Data Link Layer 28
    Network Layer 28
    Transport Layer 29

    Session Layer 29
    Presentation Layer 30
    Application Layer 30
    How Does TCP/IP Fit into the OSI Model? 30

TCP/IP Protocols 31
    The Internet Protocol (IP) 31
    The Transmission Control Protocol (TCP) 32
    Other Related Protocols 33

IP Addressing 36
    IP Address Classes 36
    Class A Addresses 38
    Class B Addresses 39
    Class C Addresses 39
    Broadcast and Multicast Addresses 40
    What Are Subnets? 41

Examining the Contents of an IP Datagram 45
    Important Packet Header Information 47

What Are TCP and UDP Ports? 49
    Well-Known Ports 49
    Registered Ports 50

Common TCP/IP Services 50
    Telnet 50
    The File Transfer Protocol (FTP) 51
    The Trivial File Transfer Protocol (TFTP) 52
    The Domain Name Service (DNS) 52
    Primary, Secondary, and Caching-Only Name Servers 54
    The Simple Mail Transport Protocol (SMTP) 60
    The r Utilities 60

Other Network Services 62

Summary 62

3 Security and the Internet   63

LANS and WANS   64

Security in the Local Area Network   64
   User Authentication   64
   Resource Protections   66
   Physical Safeguards   67

Security in Wide Area Networks   67
   Network Protocol Backdoors and
   Holes   68
   What Is Source Routing and Why Is It
   Not a Good Idea?   69
   Denial-of-Service Attacks   69
   SYN Flooding   70
   ICMP Redirects and Other ICMP
   Problems   72
   Ping of Death   74
   Distributed Denial-of-Service
   Attacks   74
   Packet Fragmentation   76
   Viruses and Trojan Horses   78
   Forged Email   78
   Break-Ins   79
   Password Theft   80
   Friendly Customer Service (Social
   Engineering)   80
   Backdoors   81
   Snooping: Monitoring Network
   Traffic   81
   IP Spoofing and Impersonation   82

Summary   83

**4 Firewall Security Policy and Firewall
Design Strategies   85**

The Design Comes Before the
Firewall   86
   Your Company's Security Policy   86
   The Firewall Policy   91

Firewall Strategies   93
   Using a Packet Filter   94
   Using an Application Proxy Gateway   96
   Combinations   97
   Using a Screened Subnet to Create a
   Demilitarized Zone (DMZ)   101
   Using Bastion Hosts and Sacrificial Hosts   104

Incident Reporting and Response   105

Keeping Up-to-date on Security Advisories   106

Summary   107

5 Packet Filtering   109

The First Line of Defense   110
   Where to Use Packet Filters   110
   Creating Packet Filtering Rules   113
   Dangerous Services   115

IP Header Information That Can Be Used to
Filter Packets   116

TCP and UDP Header Information   117
   Ports and Sockets   120
   The SYN Bit   123
   The ACK Bit   123

ICMP Packets   124

Stateless Operation Versus Stateful
Inspection   125

Hardware and Software Packet Filters   126
   Using a Router to Restrict Access   126
   Using a Dual-Homed Host to Restrict
   Access   127

Advantages and Disadvantages of Packet
Filters   128

Summary   129

6 Using a Bastion Host 131

Configuring a Bastion Host   132

Installing a Secure Operating System from
Scratch   133

Eliminating Unnecessary Services and
Applications   134
   UNIX   135
   Other UNIX Network Files to
   Review   138
   Windows NT   139

Removing Unnecessary Applications
and Files   141

Resource Protections and Access
Control   142
   UNIX Resource Permissions   142
   Windows NT   147

Configuring Auditing and Logging   152

Running Proxy Software on the Bastion
Host   153

When the Bastion Host Is
Compromised   154

Summary   155

7 Application Gateways and Proxy Servers   157

   Disable Routing on the Proxy
   Server   160
   Advantages and Disadvantages of Proxy
   Servers   161

Classical and Transparent Proxies   162
   Classical Proxies   162
   Transparent Proxies   163
   Classical Proxies Can Hide DNS
   Information About Your Network   165
   Creating a Custom Proxy
   Application   166

Network Address Translators (NATs)   166
   Basic NAT   167
   Network Address Port Translation
   (NAPT)   168
   Using NAT to Hide Information About the
   LAN   169
   Using NAT to Increase the LAN Address
   Space   170
   What Is Address Vectoring?   170

Content Screening and Blocking   171

Logging and Alerting Facilities   173

Client Considerations   174

Summary   175

8 Operating System Monitoring and Auditing Techniques   177
   What Is Auditing?   178
   Reviewing Those Log Files!   178
   The Front End of Auditing: Resource
   Protections   181

UNIX   181
   Using the syslog Utility   181
   Miscellaneous UNIX Log Files   185

Windows NT   188
   Setting Up Auditing Events   189
   Using the Event Viewer to Review Log
   Files   193
   Managing Event Log Files   195

Application-Specific Log Files   196

Other Considerations   196

Summary   196

II Encryption and Secure Communications on the Internet 197

9 Encryption Technology 199

Protecting Sensitive Information 200

What Is Encryption? 201
Single Key Encryption 201
Public Key Encryption 202
Hybrids 203

Practical Applications for Cryptography on the Internet 204
What Are Digital Signatures? 204
Digital Certificates 206
The Secure Sockets Layer (SSL) Protocol 207
Is That Web Page Using Encryption? 209

Summary 210

10 Virtual Private Networks (VPNs) and Tunneling 211

Secure Communications on the Internet 212
What Is a Virtual Private Network (VPN)? 212
What Can a VPN Do? 214
Disadvantages of VPNs 215

The IPSec Protocol Suite 216
Internet Key Exchange (IKE) 217
The Authentication Header (AH) 219
Encapsulation Security Payload (ESP) 221
AH and ESP 221

The Point-to-Point Tunneling Protocol (PPTP) 222
The PPTP Control Connection 223

Data Transmission Using PPTP Tunnel 224
Layer Two Tunneling Protocol (L2TP) 225

Summary 225

11 Using Pretty Good Privacy (PGP) for Encryption 227

Securing Information Transfers on the Internet 228

Installing PGP 229
Installing PGP on UNIX Systems 229
Installing PGP on Windows NT 233

Summary 238

III Firewall Installation and Configuration 239

12 Firewall Tools Available on the Internet 241

Using Freeware and Shareware Products 242

TCP Wrappers 242

The TIS Firewall Toolkit 244

SOCKS 246

SQUID 247

Drawbridge 248

SATAN 250

Other Handy Security Software 252

Summary 252

13 Using TCP Wrappers 253

Introduction to TCP Wrappers 254
How TCP Wrappers Works 255
Logging via syslogd 255

Obtaining TCP Wrappers   256

Configuring TCP Wrappers   256
Configuring the inetd.conf File   257
The hosts.allow and hosts.deny
Files   258

Limitations of TCP Wrappers   261

Summary   262

**14   Using the TIS Firewall Toolkit
(FWTK)   263**

Building a Firewall Using the Toolkit   264
A Short History of the Toolkit   264
Obtaining FWTK   264
How Does Gauntlet Firewall Differ
from FWTK?   265

FWTK Components   266
netacl   267
The Configuration File:
/usr/local/etc/netperm-table   272

Configuring Proxy Services   275
FTP: ftp-gw   275
Remote Logins and Telnet: tn-gw and
rlogin-gw   279
SMTP: smap   282
Configuring Other Services:
plug-gw   285
Other FWTK Components   289

Installing the Toolkit on a Bastion
Host   289

Summary   290

15   SOCKS   291

SOCKS V4 and SOCKS V5   292
Version 4   292
Version 5   296

SOCKSified Applications   298

SocksCap   298

How to Get SOCKS   299

SOCKS Support   299

Summary   300

16   SQUID   301

What Is SQUID?   302

Where to Get SQUID   303

Installing and Configuring SQUID   303
Choosing a SQUID Server   303
Installing the Software   304

Managing SQUID   305
The squid.conf file   305
The squid Command   306
SQUID Log Files   308
What Is the SQUID Cache Hierarchy?   309

Configuring Clients to Use SQUID   310

Summary   311

**17   Using ipfwadm and ipchains
on Linux   313**

What Are ipfwadm and ipchains?   314

Installing and Configuring ipfwadm   315
Obtaining ipfwadm   315
Installing ipfwadm   316
Using ipfwadm Commands   316
Place ipfwadm Rules in a Startup File   321

Installing and Configuring ipchains   321
Obtaining ipchains   322
How ipchains Differs from ipfwadm   322
Creating and Deleting Chains   323

Summary   331

18 Microsoft Proxy Server   333

Overview of Microsoft Proxy Server   334

Installing and Configuring Microsoft
Proxy Server 2.0   335
   Running Setup   336
   Using the Internet Service
   Manager.   340
   Packet Filter Properties   341
   Web Proxy Service Properties   343
   Configuration Management on the
   Service Property Page   346
   Managing Permissions For the Web
   Proxy Services   346
   Managing the Caching Properties of the
   Service   347
   Routing Within Proxy Arrays   350
   Using the Publishing Property Page
   350
   Setting Real Time Alerts and Logging
   Options   351

Client Software Configuration
Issues   353

Summary   355

**19 The Elron CammandView Firewall
357**

Overview   358

Installing CommandView Firewall   358
   Running the Setup Program   360

The CommandView Firewall Manager
Application   364
   File Menu and View Menu   365
   Firewall Menu Options   367
   Logs Menu Options   368

Managing User Services   368

Where to Go from Here   369

Summary   370

20 Firewall Appliances   371

What Is a Firewall Appliance?   372
   Quick, Easy Installation   373
   Simple Management Interface   373
   Self-Contained Device   374
   Multiple Network Interfaces   374
   Default Security Policies   375
   Packet Filtering and Application Proxies   376
   Network Address Translation (NAT)   376
   Reporting and Alerting   377
   Virtual Private Networking (VPN)   378

Pricing a Firewall Appliance   378

Summary   379

21 Firewalls and Beyond   381

New Functionality   382
   Firewall Integration   383
   Firewall Testing   384

Home Computers   384

Virtual Private Network Clients   385

IPv6: The Next Generation IP Protocol   386
   The IPv6 Header   386
   Extension Headers   389
   IPv6 Addressing   391
   The Transition to IPv6   391

Summary   392

   395

IV Appendixes   393

A TCP and UDP Common Ports   395

B Other Security Tools You Can Use   445

C Additional Resources   455

About the Author

Terry Ogletree is a consultant currently working in New Jersey. He has worked with networked computer systems since 1980, starting out on Digital Equipment PDP computers and OpenVMS-based VAX and AlphaServer systems. He has worked with UNIX and TCP/IP since 1985 and has been involved with Windows NT since it first appeared. He is the author of *Upgrading and Repairing Networks, Second Edition*, also published by Que, and *Windows NT Server 4.0 Networking*, which is volume 4 of Sams's *Windows NT Server 4 Resource Library*, published by Sams. In addition, he has contributed chapters to many other books published by Macmillan, including *Windows NT Server Unleashed* (and the *Professional Reference Edition*), as well as *Special Edition Using UNIX, Third Edition*, published by Que.

You can email him at ogletree@bellsouth.net or two@twoinc.com, or visit his home page at www.twoinc.com.

Dedication

Dedicated to my parents, Gordon Charles Ogletree and Billie Jean Ogletree.

Acknowledgments

Once again, I must acknowledge the help I have received in the writing of this book from the editors at Macmillan—Jenny Watson, the senior acquisitions editor, and Todd Brakke, the development editor for this book. Both made many useful suggestions to help improve this book. Also deserving mention is Vicki Harding, the team coordinator responsible for keeping track of much of the development process involved in creating a book such as this. The support that I received from my current employers, Robert Venard and Tom Crayner at Bristol-Myers Squibb, was very encouraging and greatly appreciated.

I would also like to acknowledge the help of several individuals not directly connected with the production of this book. Special thanks to Jo Chamblee, James Garrett, and Steve McGuire for their encouragement and support while this was being written. Michael D. Parrot and Associates, in Raleigh, NC, have kept my finances in good condition so I can worry about meeting writing deadlines instead of paying bills. As always, my parents, Gordon C. Ogletree and Billie Jean Ogletree, have been supportive during the time it took to write this book.

Tell Us What You Think!

As the reader of this book, *you* are our most important critic and commentator. We value your opinion and want to know what we're doing right, what we could do better, what areas you'd like to see us publish in, and any other words of wisdom you're willing to pass our way.

As the associate publisher for this book, I welcome your comments. You can fax, email, or write me directly to let me know what you did or didn't like about this book—as well as what we can do to make our books stronger.

While I cannot help you with technical problems related to the topics covered in this book, Terry W. Ogletree welcomes your technical questions. The best way to reach him is by email at ogletree@bellsouth.net.

When you write, please be sure to include this book's title and author as well as your name and phone or fax number. I will carefully review your comments and share them with the author and editors who worked on the book.

Fax: 317-581-4666

Email: hardware@mcp.com

Mail: Macmillan USA
        201 West 103rd Street
        Indianapolis, IN 46290 USA

introduction

In just a few years, the Internet has started showing up in all facets of everyday life. During the next few years, connections to the Internet will become as common as a telephone for most of the population. With this growing technology comes a new territory called cyberspace. Traditional methods used for securing data and resources on a network will not be sufficient to provide protection in this new area.

To secure a network that is connected to the Internet properly, you need to use a firewall. The term *firewall* can be applied to a wide range of products that are designed to help protect your network from external threats by limiting the network traffic that can flow between your network and the Internet. The two basic technologies used to create firewalls are called *packet filtering* and *application proxy gateways*. If you understand how these work, you will be in a better position to construct or purchase a firewall for your network. In this book, you will learn about both of these, as well as other important features to look for in a firewall, such as logging, alerting, and authentication.

Although many vendors are now selling products they name *firewall appliances*, you should be careful to spend the time needed to understand how a firewall should be constructed and how it works before making a major purchasing decision. You might find it possible to create a more secure environment by constructing your own firewall, using software that is available for download from the Internet, such as the TIS Internet Firewall Toolkit or TCP Wrappers, instead of a commercial product.

There are only a few books available on the topic of firewalls, and of these, only a few have been issued in the past year or so. Some attempt to cover every possible topic, whereas others stick to a particular firewall product. In this book I have attempted to introduce the reader to all the important concepts used for creating firewalls and then to show how these are implemented, using specific products—both free and commercial products.

What Is in This Book?

This contents of this book are arranged to flow from a simple intro-duction to more complex topics from one chapter to another. If you are already familiar with a particular topic, you might want to skip that chapter. Cross-references within the text make it easy to find information should you find later that you need to go back to more fully understand a concept.

In Chapter 1, "Firewall Basics," the firewall is introduced. Here, you will find a good discussion of why you might need a firewall and information about the types of things a firewall can protect you from and the things it cannot protect you from.

Chapter 2, "Introduction to the TCP/IP Protocol Suite," is intended for users who might not yet have a good grasp of TCP/IP and the utilities that are associated with it to provide network services. If you've forgotten how address classes work or how to subnet an address space, this is the chapter to read.

Chapter 3, "Security and the Internet," discusses some of the differ-ences between how security is implemented in a simple network and how it should be implemented when connecting to a larger network such as the Internet. You will also find a discussion of some of the common methods that hackers use, such as denial-of-service attacks and IP address spoofing.

In Chapter 4, "Firewall Security Policy and Firewall Design Strategies," you will find information about the different architec-tures you can use to create a firewall. Here, you will learn what pur-pose a DMZ or a dual-homed host can serve, and you will get an introduction to packet filtering and application proxy techniques. This chapter will enable you to make important decisions about how to create a good security policy for your network and then how to implement that policy using a firewall.

Chapter 5, "Packet Filtering," discusses the earliest type of firewall. Here, you will learn about how techniques first used on screening routers have been developed to provide a mechanism that can keep unwanted IP traffic from crossing the firewall barrier and getting into your network.

Chapter 6, "Using a Bastion Host," covers important configuration issues you need to consider when selecting computers that will be used to provide firewall services. These computers are the most vulnerable hosts on the network because they are exposed to the Internet, and thus they need to be especially well-configured to keep out intruders.

In Chapter 7, "Application Gateways and Proxy Servers," a newer technique used in firewalls is examined. Whereas a packet filter can be used to permit or deny the flow of IP packets between your network and the external world, proxy servers can be used to provide network services without allowing a direct IP flow between the client and server.

Chapter 8, "Operating System Monitoring and Auditing Techniques," covers well-known methods for setting up auditing for both UNIX and Windows NT systems.

Chapter 9, "Encryption Technology," should be read if you do not yet understand basic cryptographic concepts. Here, you can learn the difference between private and public key techniques and the uses that each is best suited for.

Chapter 10, "Virtual Private Networks (VPNs) and Tunneling," continues along this same vein and shows how encryption techniques can be used to create secure tunneled connections over a public network such as the Internet.

Chapter 11, "Using Pretty Good Privacy (PGP) For Encryption," can show you how to quickly install and start using PGP for your own security needs, such as for sending encrypted email that has been signed with a digital signature. Installing PGP for both UNIX and Windows NT is covered here.

Chapter 12, "Firewall Tools Available on the Internet," gives you an overview of some of the more popular tools that you can download from the Internet and, in most cases, use for free to construct a firewall.

Chapter 13, "Using TCP Wrappers," goes into more detail about how to install and configure one of these free utilities. TCP Wrappers can be used on UNIX hosts to help secure access to and provide logging for important useful network services such as Telnet and FTP.

Chapter 14, "Using the TIS Firewall Toolkit (FWTK)," is another chapter that covers in more detail a product you can download for free. The FWTK can be difficult to configure if you are not already familiar with UNIX system management, but this chapter can get you started in the right direction by covering important concepts and showing you how the configuration files work.

Chapter 15, "SOCKS," covers the SOCKS security protocol. This protocol is widely implemented in commercial products, such as Internet Explorer, and is also available in libraries that can be used to "SOCKSify" existing applications.

Chapter 16, "SQUID," covers yet another freely available tool you can get from the Internet. SQUID is a caching proxy server that can be used to provide access control as well as to help manage network bandwidth by storing copies of frequently accessed Web objects in a local cache.

Chapter 17, "Using `ipfwadm` and `ipchains` on Linux," discusses the packet filtering capabilities that are built into the Linux kernel and how these two utilities can be used to manage these functions.

Chapter 18, "Microsoft Proxy Server," discusses how to install Microsoft's entry into the firewall marketplace. Here, you will also find a brief introduction into how services are configured using the server's graphical user interface.

Chapter 19, "The ELRON Commander Firewall," discusses another commercial product, this one for Windows NT Server. Installing the firewall and basic configuration issues are examined.

Chapter 20, "Firewall Appliances," looks at a newly emerging market for firewall products that try to be as close to plug-and-play as possible, hoping to make the firewall configuration process an easier one for the end user.

In Chapter 21, "Firewalls and Beyond," you will look at some possibilities for new security developments for the Internet, such as the next generation of the IP protocol, IPv6. You will also find here a discussion about protecting not just your business network, but also home computers that are used to access your network.

In Appendix A, "TCP and UDP Common Ports," you will find a brief discussion about TCP and UDP ports, along with a list of well-known ports and what they are used for.

Appendix B, "Other Security Tools You Can Use," contains a collection of security tools that you will find useful for making host computers on your network a little more secure. Included here, you will find where to download such utilities as SATAN and COPS.

Finally, in Appendix C, "Additional Resources," is a listing of valuable sources you can use to stay on top of Internet security issues and firewall technology. Because the threats on the Internet are changing rapidly, it is important to be knowledgeable about the current threats.

part

I

Understanding Firewalls and Internet Security

Firewall Basics 9

Introduction to the TCP/IP Protocol Suite 25

Security and the Internet 63

Firewall Security Policy and Firewall Design Strategies 85

Packet Filtering 109

Using a Bastion Host 131

Application Gateways and Proxy Servers 157

Operating System Monitoring and Auditing Techniques 177

chapter

1

Firewall Basics

Why You Need a Firewall ●

Using Your Site's Security Policy to
Design the Firewall ●

Firewall Technologies ●

Hardware or Software Firewalls?
Build or Buy? ●

What a Firewall Can Do ●

What a Firewall Cannot Protect
You From ●

Why You Need a Firewall

When it comes time to connect the company's network to the Internet, many things need to be considered, such as what kind of connection will be needed to provide sufficient bandwidth for the expected traffic and what ISP to use. Somewhere on your task list, you'll undoubtedly include an item that reads "Get a firewall." It is important to understand that this particular item of your plan should not be considered to be just a routine task, but it instead belongs at the very top of your list. Installing a firewall of some sort between your network and the rest of the modern networked world is one of the more important tasks you will have to perform when you connect to the Internet.

What Is a Firewall?

The term *firewall* is one you might not have heard of in relation to networking until about five years ago. Before its adoption by security experts to describe a way of keeping unwanted intruders from breaking into a network connected to a larger network, you most likely heard the term used in the building trades. For example, a firewall can be a fireproof barrier between multiple units in a condominium building. If a fire breaks out in one unit, the firewall can help keep the fire from spreading to the other units. In effect, the firewall helps to contain the problem.

When used in a network, a firewall works in much the same way: It helps to keep problems from other networks from getting into your LAN and compromising your systems or data. The firewall does this by allowing some traffic to flow between your network and the Internet while blocking other traffic. Whereas a firewall in a building is usually a simple composition of cement blocks or other sturdy fireproof materials, the construction of a network firewall is much more complex.

The mechanisms that are used to allow or block traffic can be simple *packet filters*, which make decisions based on the contents of the packet header, or more complex *application proxies*, which stand between the client and the outside world, acting as a middleman for some network services.

SEE ALSO

➤ *What is an application proxy? You can find out about this firewall technique in Chapter 7, "Application Gateways and Proxy Servers," page 157*

Because of its simple name, it is easy to think of a firewall as a single device or a single software product. In all but the simplest cases, however, it would probably be better to think of a firewall as a *system*. It is a system of components designed to control access to and from your network and an external network, based on the security policies in effect at your site. The term firewall has been adopted to refer to these components that generally sit between your network and the outside world because the firewall provides a barrier, much like a firewall in a building provides a barrier to help prevent the spread of fire.

As firewall vendors compete and try to make their product stand out from the others, new features are being developed for firewalls. Because a firewall stands at the perimeter of your network and acts as a sort of gateway to the outside world, it is an obvious place to do a lot of things, some not necessarily related to security. For example, some of the newer functions you might find on a modern firewall include the following:

- **Caching**   This is especially true for networks that have Web servers that provide a lot of content to users on the Internet. By storing frequently accessed data locally, a caching server can improve user response time and save on valuable Internet bandwidth that otherwise would be consumed from repeated fetches of the same data.

- **Address Translation**   A properly configured firewall can expose only its own network address to the outside world, enabling you to use any IP address space you want for your internal network.

- **Content Restriction**   A growing number of products enable you to restrict the kinds of information that users are allowed to access on the Internet, both by restricting access to known URLs that contain objectionable content and by examining incoming data packets for keywords.

- **Address Vectoring**   This feature enables the firewall to modify requests, such as HTTP requests, and send them to hosts using a different address than that found in the request packet. Thus, you can distribute a load over several servers while appearing to be a single host to users on the Internet.

These features do provide some security benefits, but mostly they are used to solve problems with performance. For example, address translation and vectoring help to hide your internal IP address space from potential hackers, which is definitely a security benefit. The less information a potential intruder has, the more difficult her job will be. However, these features also help an administrator to balance performance among multiple machines. Using address translation means that you do not have to obtain a large IP address subnet to cover every workstation and server on your network.

It's a Jungle Out There!

The Internet is a fascinating place. It is not, however, a very friendly place. Over time, as new standards and technologies evolve, this might change. However, as is always the case when new frontiers are being explored, there are going to be problems with technology and people while the Internet continues to grow at a rapid pace. Because not all the people you will find on the Internet will necessarily have the best intentions, you need to stay abreast of security issues after you connect your network to the Internet.

SEE ALSO

➤ *For details on the different kinds of threats that have recently caused problems on the Internet, see Chapter 3, "Security and the Internet," page 63*

Problems that you already might encounter, such as computer viruses, will be compounded when you connect to the Internet. Now, instead of having to worry about a virus being brought into work on a floppy disk, you have to worry about email attachments and down-loaded demo or shareware programs. Instead of having to worry about keeping employees from using the company email system to harass another worker, you have to worry about them using electronic mail that can go virtually anywhere in the world for the same purpose. If you have ever had problems policing company workstations or servers to keep out objectionable material such as humorous text files, pornography, or other similar material, just wait until you connect to the Internet!

Use Your Site's Security Policy to Design the Firewall

Before you design a firewall strategy, you should sit down and think about what you want to protect and how you are going to do it. If you are working at anything other than a very small business, you should have a company security policy. You can use this to start with. After talking with your users (or their managers), you can then make decisions on what kinds of services you will let go through the firewall.

SEE ALSO

➤ *You will find more information about how to go about creating a security policy if you do not already have one in Chapter 4, "Firewall Security Policy and Firewall Design Strategies," (page 85)*

➤ *For more information about the basic services that TCP/IP can be used for, see Chapter 2, "Introduction to the TCP/IP Protocol Suite," (page 25)*

After examining these services and their potential pitfalls, you can decide which ones are necessary in your environment.

New Security Threats to Consider

When you connect to the Internet, you open up a whole new world of security concerns that will most likely come back to haunt you if you do not take the appropriate precautions. Whereas you previously only had to be concerned about mistakes made by untrained employees or by security breaches perpetrated by a disgruntled employee, you now have, potentially, every hacker in the world to worry about!

Every few months you will hear a story on the nightly news about a new virus, Trojan horse, or possibly a worm program that has caused havoc on the Internet. You might think that the world is full of very clever programmers who spend months and years hacking away trying to develop a new malicious program or to break into a sensitive site. However, in actuality, it's not really such a difficult profession. Many of the horror stories you hear about come about not so much because of very clever programming skills as from exploiting known security holes or bugs in currently available operating systems or applications.

A few years ago, a paper was written by Dan Farmer and Wietse Venema, titled "Improving the Security of Your Site by Breaking Into It." In this paper, the authors walk you through examples of how a hacker can use ordinary system utilities and programs to gain information about your network and the computers on it. They show you some of the features of programs such as sendmail that have been exploited in the past. Although some of the abuses outlined in

Where can you find the paper?

The paper by Farmer and Venema, "Improving the Security of Your Site by Breaking Into It," is available for download from many different sites on the Internet. If you use the authors' names as input to a search engine, you will turn up many locations where you can probably find a copy. It is highly recommended that anyone who works in any kind of network security read this paper.

this paper have been fixed through the use of patches and updated programs, reading it will give you an idea of the kinds of things that can be done that you might never have thought about. Most of the major operating systems that are in use today were initially developed and used on standalone computer systems or in small networks. Networking functions were added and enhanced over the years, yet there still remain many features that just weren't designed for the interconnected environment that the Internet provides today.

Decide Which Services You Will Provide for Your Users

When it comes to creating a good security policy for the network, where should you start? First, decide what kinds of services you will need to make available to your user community. The very fact that you are establishing an Internet connection indicates that there is a need of some sort on the part of your clients. What is that need? What part of the business will this need provide a benefit to? What are the risks involved in trying to give your users what they want?

Some typical reasons a company might want to connect to the Internet include the following:

- **Email** To allow employees to interact with both suppliers and customers.
- **Remote Access** To allow mobile employees access to the local LAN resources.
- **Research** To give technical staff the ability to interact with colleagues at other companies or institutions.
- **Customer Support** To allow customers to review product documentation and other literature to reduce the load on your support staff.
- **Vendor Support** To allow you (the customer) to access support and documentation that your vendors have placed online.
- **Market Presence** To establish an e-commerce business and allow the company to market its products on the Internet.

Depending on which of the preceding apply to you, a combination of some or all of the following kinds of services might be used to give your users the access they require:

- **FTP**   The File Transfer Protocol could be used by your research staff to exchange data files with other sites. An *anonymous FTP* site might be used to allow your customers to access files or documentation.

- **Telnet**   Using this service to establish a remote login session might be helpful if your customer service support team needs to log into a customer's computer to diagnose a problem. You might want to use Telnet to check on the home network when you are away at a conference or at a remote site.

- **World Wide Web (WWW)**   A WWW server can give your company a marketing presence on the Internet. You can keep customers updated about new products or services by using a Web site. Online documentation and support can be easily presented using a Web site.

- **Email**   Using the Simple Mail Transport Protocol (SMTP), email can be delivered from your desktop to almost anywhere in the world. Email can be a great way to quickly communicate with customers and employees. When you consider the cost of postage today, it wouldn't be a surprise if most businesses started sending bills via email in the next few years as more consumers get connected.

SEE ALSO

➤ *You'll find a larger list of services in Chapter 2, "Introduction to the TCP/IP Protocol Suite," page 25*

These basic services are by no means an exhaustive list of services that are available on the Internet. Mentioning these here is done so that you can start thinking about how you want to use the Internet. When you have come up with a list of services that you think will benefit your company, you need to look at each service and ask a few questions. Is there a relatively secure form of the client or server application that is required for this service? Does the manner in which you want to use the service open up any possible security holes in your LAN?

SEE ALSO

➤ *Because most services based on TCP and UDP protocols use different port numbers for their sessions, when you are thinking about what kinds of services you want to provide to your users, see the list of well-known ports in Appendix A, "TCP and UDP Common Ports," page 395*

For example, your security policy might state that users are allowed to establish outgoing Telnet sessions that can pass through the firewall, but your policy might also state that under no circumstances can an *incoming* Telnet session be allowed. This allows your users to establish a remote session with a customer's system, but outsiders are not allowed onto your network. You can create similar policies for other important network services, such as FTP and SMTP, depending on your particular needs. As with almost any kind of policy, whether it pertains to security or not, there are bound to be exceptions.

SEE ALSO

➤ *For more information about how your security policy can help you design your firewall, see Chapter 4, "Firewall Security Policy and Firewall Design Strategies," page 85*

Firewall Policy

After you review the security issues involved, you can develop a firewall policy. There are two basic methods that the firewall can be used for to implement the policy:

- Permit any access unless it has specifically been denied by the rules.

- Deny any access unless it has specifically been allowed by the rules.

The second of these strategies is the one you should use. Why? From a logical point of view, it is much easier to specify a small list of what you will allow as opposed to a much larger list of what you will not allow. Also, because new protocols and services are being developed frequently as the Internet continues to grow, you won't have to be continually adding new rules to exclude new problems that come along. Instead you'll remain secure from new developments until you've had time to review the security issues and decide whether you will allow the protocol or service through the firewall.

SEE ALSO

➤ *For more information about creating a Firewall Policy, see Chapter 4, "Firewall Security Policy and Firewall Design Strategies," page 85*

Firewall Technologies

There are two basic methods used to create a network firewall: packet filtering and application proxies. Some administrators like to include other techniques, but these usually are found to be simply variations on the these two methods. Each technique has its advantages and disadvantages, so it is important to understand exactly how they work to protect your network.

The First Firewalls: Packet Filtering

Packet filters were the first kind of firewall developed to protect a network from the Internet. Routers were configured to allow or deny packets from passing through based on rules created by the administrator. Because routers only look at the header information in an IP packet, they are limited in what they can do. For example, a simple packet filter can be configured to allow or disallow the use of FTP, but it cannot be used to allow or disallow specific functions of FTP, such as using the GET and PUT commands.

SEE ALSO

➤ *To learn about packet filtering firewalls in detail, see Chapter 5, "Packet Filtering," page 109*

Using Application Gateways

Although a packet filter can only make decisions based on the information found in the packet header, an application proxy can be used to create a more complex firewall.

SEE ALSO

➤ *For more information about proxies and application gateways, see Chapter 7, "Application Gateways and Proxy Servers," page 157*

An *application gateway* or *application proxy* is a software program that runs on the firewall to intercept traffic for a specific kind of application. The proxy software intercepts user requests from the local network, for example, and then makes a connection to the server residing outside your local LAN for your user. The internal user never makes a connection directly to the outside service. Instead, the application proxy program acts as the middleman and talks to the client and the server, relaying application information between them. The advantage here is that the application proxy can be programmed to allow or deny traffic based on information contained in the payload section of the packet, not just the header information. That is, an application proxy understands the fundamental communication methods used by a specific service and can be programmed to allow or deny features of the service, not just block the communication based on the port as a packet filter would do.

Other Firewall Components

The packet filter and application proxy are the basic methods used to create a firewall. How they are configured and the devices used are a more complex topic. Bastion hosts, sacrificial hosts, and a demilitarized zone (DMZ) are terms you will commonly hear when talking about firewalls. Later in this book, you will look carefully at each of these so that you can decide which can be put to use in your firewall.

SEE ALSO

➤ *Strategies that use a bastion host are discussed more fully in Chapter 4, "Firewall Security Policy and Firewall Design Strategies," page 85*

➤ *An in-depth discussion of using a bastion host can be found in Chapter 6, "Using a Bastion Host," page 131*

Hardware or Software Firewalls? Build or Buy?

When firewalls were first being developed, they consisted basically of a router that was configured as a packet filter (accepting or rejecting packets based on header information) and a rule base constructed by the network administrator. As firewalls gained functionality, newer ones were implemented as software that ran on workstations or servers. Still newer firewalls are being created that are hardware and software configurations packaged together. These new hardware boxes, sometimes called *firewall appliances*, can consist of proprietary software applications installed on a standard operating system, such as UNIX, that has been stripped down to its bare essentials. Some vendors even design their own operating system as well, knowing that hackers will always have intimate knowledge of the weaknesses found in a commercial operating system.

SEE ALSO

➤ *To learn more about some of the firewall appliances you can find on the market and some tips for evaluating competing products, see Chapter 20, "Firewall Appliances," page 371*

Which kind of firewall should you use to protect your network? As with any purchasing decision, you should make your choice based on the security requirements of your network and the features offered by the firewall. Of course, you should also consider how a firewall purchase (and maintenance) will fit into your budget. It might be

PART I

Hardware or Software Firewalls? Build or Buy? **CHAPTER I**

that the requirements you draw up for a firewall will enable you to get additional funds from upper management when they become convinced of the importance of the matter.

If you have a highly technical networking support staff, you might find it a good idea to create your own firewall, using the routers and hosts you already have. If you are a small business that is just now connecting to the Internet and you have no in-house expertise, it might be better to use a vendor that can provide the hardware and/ or software, as well as perform installation and support duties.

Hardware or software? Build it or buy it? As you read through the rest of this book and begin to understand how different firewall products work, you will find yourself in a better position to ask questions and make intelligent decisions. Be sure to involve key users or managers who have day-to-day knowledge about your network operations in your decision-making process. Technical personnel might be aware of protocols or applications that might cause exceptions to arise to your firewall policy. By gathering as much information as you can up front, you will end up with a better firewall in the end.

Operating System Concerns

A firewall does not have to run on the same kind of system that you use on your desktop or your servers. For example, you might have deployed Windows NT throughout the network as the standard desktop for your users, and you might also use Windows NT for network servers. Does this mean that you will have to use Windows NT on the firewall if you want to use application proxies to allow your clients to access services on the Internet? Not necessarily.

You should choose a firewall based on the features it offers to enforce the security policy requirements of your network.

What is important, however, is that you have a detailed understanding of how the firewall works and know how to configure it accurately. This means that you will usually have to be familiar with the operating system that the firewall uses. If you do not understand the operating system, its security mechanisms, and the tools used to enforce security, you can never be sure that the firewall is not being compromised by someone exploiting a weakness (or *feature*) of the operating system.

For example, your firewall software might be running just fine on the UNIX box that you have placed at the perimeter of your LAN. You check the log files and feel secure that all is well and operating as it should. However, because you do not understand UNIX file protections, you didn't notice when that disgruntled employee made the password file readable by the whole world. You also didn't notice when that employee, who was later let go, was able to access your firewall from the Internet and make significant modifications to the firewall configuration.

If you really think about it, what could be worse than having a firewall you trust completely if you don't fully understand how it works? In the end, you would never really be sure that it is working as it should.

SEE ALSO

➤ *You will find a detailed study of security concerns for the UNIX, Linux, and Windows NT operating systems in Chapter 8, "Operating System Monitoring and Auditing Techniques," page 177*

You might be worried about using Windows NT, UNIX, Linux, or even some other operating system, based on the news you hear on a regular basis about a new bug or a new problem that is circulating on the Internet. Many critics have taken Windows NT to task for this in the past few years, saying that the platform is not stable enough to be used in a high-security environment. However, if you take the time to do the research, you will find that all operating systems have their flaws. New versions of Windows NT will most likely contain problems that will need to be fixed by the vendor. New versions of UNIX and Linux won't be perfect either. The more widely used an operating system is, the more likely that flaws will eventually be exposed.

What is important is that there is a responsible vendor standing behind the product that can monitor the discovery of these kinds of problems and remedy them in a timely manner. If you are confident that you have a good grasp of the operating system that is used on the firewall solution that you have chosen, it does not really matter if it is the same operating system used on desktops or servers in the rest of the network. In many cases today, a network is not a homogenous network anyway, but instead, it is a conglomeration of several kinds of computer systems and networking protocols.

What a Firewall Can Do

A firewall cannot do everything to protect your network and should not be considered a one-stop solution for all your security concerns. Understanding how a firewall actually protects your network is important. Understanding what the firewall cannot protect you from is equally as important. In general, the benefits you can expect to receive from a well-constructed firewall are the following:

- Protection from insecure protocols and services.

- Keeps information about users, systems, network addresses, and applications running on your network from prying eyes outside your network.

- Provides audit trails (via log files) containing security and statistical data that can be used to ensure that your network is safe and operating in an efficient manner. A good firewall also enables you to configure alerts so that you can be paged or otherwise notified of significant events, such as an attempted break-in.

- Provides centralized management of network security as it relates to the outside world. The firewall is the gateway to the Internet for your network. In a large network, you might have more than one connection to outside networks and, thus, more than one firewall. In that case, you should be sure to examine competing products carefully. Many newer products enable you to administer more than one firewall installation from the same command console.

What a Firewall Cannot Protect You From

A firewall cannot protect you from hacking from within. That is, if you have a user who is determined to cause harm to your network, you need to protect yourself by using the host-based security that you normally use. A very important thing to remember when you use a firewall is that it does not magically take care of all the security problems that can exist in your network. *A firewall is not a substitute for everyday system management and security measures*. It is just another layer of security.

What is network address translation?

Another feature of some firewalls that is becoming very useful as the Internet address pool becomes exhausted is NAT, which stands for *network address translation*. NAT provides some security benefits by hiding the actual network address of a computer host when that host makes requests from servers on the Internet. A firewall that uses NAT does this by using its own network address instead of the client's when it sends requests to servers out on the Internet. When replies come back in the NAT component, the firewall places the client's real address in the packet and forwards it to the client. By using NAT, it should become obvious that you only need to have one address to connect your LAN to the Internet.

No matter how secure you might think your firewall is, you should never ease up on host-based security. In fact, the opposite is true. When you connect to the Internet, no matter how secure your firewall might be, you should be more vigilant in monitoring the security mechanisms of individual workstations and servers in your local LAN so that you can ensure that no security breaches occur.

Some things that the firewall cannot protect you from include the following:

- **Viruses**   Though some firewall products do provide some support for detecting viruses in traffic that passes through the firewall, there are too many ways that a clever hacker can package virus software. If your firewall claims to scan for viruses, don't turn off the virus-detecting software you have running on individual computers in the network!

- **Trojan Horses**   Similar to the virus threat, Trojan horse programs are difficult to keep out of a network. It is easy to trick a user into downloading a program or opening an email attachment that can allow malicious code onto the local system.

- **Social engineering**   This term has come into vogue in the past few years to describe methods that hackers use to obtain information from "friendly" users. You would be surprised at how many people give out their password when someone calls up on the telephone and pretends to be a security officer "checking" something. A firewall cannot stop a loose-mouthed employee.

- **Physical Outages**   A firewall cannot protect you against a power outage or a break in a network or telephone cable. Precautions for these kinds of events should be the subject of your network disaster recovery plan.

- **Incompetence**   Poorly trained employees or a loose management style can lead to configuration problems, both in your local LAN and on the firewall itself. If employees do not understand how the firewall works and how to correctly configure it, you will have problems.

- **Insider Attacks**   A firewall cannot stop someone who is already on your network from performing misdeeds. This is one of the reasons why host security remains important after you have installed a firewall.

Maintaining a Firewall

A firewall is not a product that you can just purchase, configure, and forget. Because the nature of the threats that can potentially invade your network constantly changes as the Internet grows and new services and applications are developed, vigilance is necessary. Whether you build a firewall from scratch, build it from components you purchase from different vendors, or decide to purchase a complete firewall system from a single vendor, there are several things you should think about. These things relate to using and maintaining the firewall over time and include the following:

- **Documentation**   Good documentation is necessary if you are to become familiar with how the firewall components work. During troubleshooting efforts, a good set of documentation is an absolute necessity.

- **Good Customer Support**   If you purchase a firewall product from a vendor, be sure to ask a few questions about the company's background and their customer support policies. No matter how good the documentation is, there's bound to be a question or problem someday that you will need help with. Find out if support is available online or by telephone, what hours it is available, and more importantly, what the cost is.

- **Easy, Intuitive User Interface**   If the product is difficult to manage, it will be more prone to mismanagement. A good graphical user interface or a command-line interface that is well constructed can make day-to-day management chores easier.

- **Software Updates**   Does the vendor provide updates to the product at regular intervals? What is the cost? Are updates made available in a timely manner as new bugs are discovered in standard operating systems or applications?

- **Available Training**   Does the vendor provide training for the product? Is it available at your site, or is travel required? Is online or computer-based training available? Again, at what cost?

Any software application or computer hardware you purchase needs to be backed up with good support if it is to be used in a business environment. At home you might be able to live for a week while the computer is in the shop. At work a disabled computer or network can put many people out of work and cost the business money. A firewall is no different from any other critical business application from this perspective. If you support the firewall yourself, be sure that your staff has the technical skills to manage and update the firewall. If you purchase from a vendor, be sure that adequate support will be there when you need it.

Summary

A firewall is a necessity if you are going to connect your LAN to the Internet. Firewalls can examine the traffic coming into and going out of your LAN and make decisions on what kinds of traffic to permit or deny. Techniques such as packet filtering make decisions based on information found in a network packet header, such as the packet's address or the network protocol used. Application proxies act as middle-men and interact with servers on the Internet so that clients on your internal LAN are never exposed to direct communication, and, thus, potential abuse.

To decide on what kind of firewall you will build or buy, you first have to examine your current security policies and evaluate the services users expect to receive after connecting to the Internet. Using your security policy, you can design a firewall strategy, using routers, bastion hosts, and other techniques to secure your network.

In the next chapter, you will look at TCP/IP and some related protocols that are used to provide networks services on the Internet. After you gain an understanding of this technology, Chapter 3 will examine some of the security issues and pitfalls associated with an Internet connection.

chapter

2

Introduction to the TCP/IP Protocol Suite

What Is TCP/IP? ●

The OSI Networking Model ●

TCP/IP Protocols ●

IP Addressing ●

Examining the Contents of
an IP Datagram ●

What are TCP and UDP Ports? ●

Common TCP/IP Services ●

Other Network Services ●

What Is TCP/IP?

Protocol Stacks and Protocol Suites

When discussing protocols, the terms *protocol stack* and *protocol suite* are often used to mean the same thing. These terms are used to indicate that it is usually not a single protocol that is used for communicating, but instead there are several related protocols. Hence, when you talk about Internet communications, you are talking about the TCP/IP protocol suite (or stack) because the protocols used, which include TCP, IP, UDP, ARP, and SMTP, among many others, perform different functions but were designed to work together.

For example, both TCP and UDP make use of IP for addressing functions and getting data moved about the Internet. Yet, IP cannot do the whole job by itself. IP uses ICMP for management and error-reporting functions. Further down the protocol stack, you will find the Address Resolution Protocol (ARP), which is responsible for determining the actual hardware address of a computer that is associated with the IP address.

TCP/IP stands for Transmission Control Protocol/Internet Protocol. These are the main network protocols used on the Internet to transfer data from one place to another. In addition to these two important protocols, there are many other related protocols and utilities that are commonly grouped together and are called the TCP/IP Protocol Suite. This suite of protocols includes such things as the Address Resolution Protocol (ARP) and the User Datagram Protocol (UDP). End users might not recognize these terms, but they have probably heard of the Telnet and the File Transfer Protocol (FTP).

One of the tasks that you have to perform when configuring a firewall is deciding which protocols and services should be allowed to be used between your network and the Internet. Some are inherently more dangerous than others and need to be examined so that you can understand the risk associated with their usage. Remember the golden firewall rule: Deny everything and then allow only what you need.

The OSI Networking Model

If you have ever worked as a programmer, you will probably remember such terms as "structured programming" or "top-down programming," along with many other terms that are used to describe standard methods for designing and coding an application. Isolating specific functions of the program into modular components can make it easy to modify and maintain the program. In 1984, the International Standardization Organization (ISO) developed a model that was intended to help standardize how networking protocols were implemented so that specific functions could be isolated into components that could be easily maintained. The Open Systems Interconnect (OSI) networking model was the result. The ISO used this model to actually develop a set of open network protocols, but these were never widely adopted. However, the OSI networking model is still used today when discussing network protocols, and it is a good idea to become familiar with it if you will be working in this field. Figure 2.1 shows conceptually how the model is supposed to operate.

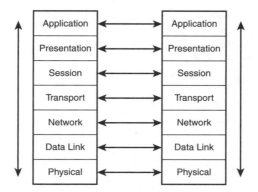

FIGURE 2.1
The OSI model is composed of layers that provide services to adjoining layers.

Each *layer* in the model provides services to layers that are adjacent to it. This means that the actual flow of information is from the topmost Application layer, which calls on services provided by the Presentation layer which makes use of services provided by the Session layer, and so on. At the very bottom lies the physical components of the network. How data is transmitted across the network, from the cabling to the network cards to the connectors used throughout the physical channel, are defined at this level.

When data arrives at another node at the Physical layer, the data then flows up through the other layers with software at each layer making use of functions of the layer above it until, finally, the information reaches the Application layer where it can be dealt with by the user.

This is the *physical* flow of information through the model. From a *logical* perspective, each layer in the model communicates with its corresponding layer on the remote node. The Application layer software is only concerned with how to communicate with the Application layer on the remote node. Software that is coded at this level does not have to understand how the data makes its way to its corresponding Application layer at the other end. It makes no difference whether the data travels over fiber-optic cable or 10Base-T connections—at least as far as the Application layer is concerned. Conversely, the components that operate at the Physical layer are not aware that the information being transmitted or received is ASCII text or binary-encoded data. The Physical layer is only concerned with working with the Physical layer on the remote node to get the data to and from its system.

Physical Layer

At this layer, the physical process of moving bits of data across a network medium is performed. Pieces of the network that are defined at this layer include the following:

- Cabling
- Connectors
- Signaling techniques (electrical and optical)

This layer is perhaps the easiest to classify. It is composed of all the physical parts of the network that are concerned with sending and receiving the actual raw bits of information. How many pins a certain connector has and how a signal is interpreted (such as Manchester and Differential Manchester Encoding) are examples of what gets defined at this level.

Data Link Layer

Functions performed at this layer are targeted at making sure that reliable data transmissions are made from one device to another on the network, such as basic error checking for the frames transmitted at the Physical layer.

At this layer, the individual bits of a message arrive at the Physical layer, and this layer organizes them into the proper frame format that can be understood by upper-level protocols.

The IEEE specifications divide this layer into two sublayers: the Media Access Control (MAC) layer and the Logical Link Control layer (LLC). Though not a part of the original OSI model, these sublayers play an important part in most Ethernet implementations. The upper layer (LLC) implements Service Access Points (SAPs), which other devices can refer to when sending information, whereas the MAC layer is concerned with sending or receiving error-free data between nodes on the network.

Network Layer

Network connections between nodes are controlled at this layer. A logical network connection between nodes is established and terminated at this layer. Functions that make up the services of the Network layer include the following:

How Can You Remember the OSI Network Model Layers?

If you are about to take a certification test and find that you are having a problem remembering the layers defined by the OSI networking model, use a time-tested method for memorizing a sequence of unrelated words. The following "nonsense" phrases are much easier to remember than the actual layers, and if you can remember one of these phrases, there's a good chance you'll be able to recall the layers, in order, when you take your test:

All People Seem To Need Data Processing.

Please Do Not Touch Steve's Pet Alligator.

Please Do Not Throw Sausage Pizza Away.

As you can see, the first phrase can be used to memorize the model from top down (Application layer, Presentation layer, Session layer, and so on), whereas the next two can be used to memorize the layers from bottom up (Physical layer, Data Link layer, Network layer, and so on). Good luck on the test!

- Logical and physical address translation
- Routing and switching
- Flow control and network congestion
- Packet fragmentation and reassembly (done until it is determined that a router or other device that the data will pass through cannot handle the packet at its current size)

This layer is the lowest layer in the reference model that has no knowledge of the underlying physical aspects of the network.

Transport Layer

This layer model, which provides user services to the layers above, is the lowest layer in the OSI model. At this layer, quality of service functions are also performed, such as the following:

- Error-free data transport. Data in large packets are divided up here to make transmission more efficient. They are reassembled at this layer when arriving from a remote system. The packet composition is dependent on the protocol the two nodes are using for data exchange.
- Sequencing to make sure packets are delivered to upper layers in the correct order.
- Acknowledgement of transfer or receipt of data packets.
- Flow control for the protocol in use.

Session Layer

Sessions between computers are established and managed at this level of the model. Applications must recognize their counterparts on a remote system and establish a common *session*, which is established to handle their data exchanges. At this layer, for example, the NetBIOS protocol operates to establish sessions based on names. To control a session, software at this layer referees between the two computers, telling each one when it can transmit and for how long. Sessions are created, maintained, and terminated at this level between application software.

Presentation Layer

How data is interpreted and presented to the application is determined at the Presentation layer of the model. Information must be presented to users in a way that it can be understood. Differences between nodes, such as how data is represented (EBCDIC versus ASCII, for example), is taken care of here. Data compression and protocol conversion are performed at this layer. Encryption is performed at this layer. The redirector works here to "direct" input/output operations to network resources instead of when they do not reside on the local computer.

Application Layer

Users' application communications are handled here. Functions at this layer directly support user applications that make use of the network. Services that allow a program to access a database that resides on a server do so by making calls to functions at this level. Other application services that are implemented at this level include the following:

- Directory services
- Email services
- File and print services
- Terminal sessions (for example, Telnet)
- Service advertisement
- Interprocess Communications

How Does TCP/IP Fit into the OSI Model?

Although the OSI model is widely used when discussing network protocol and network service issues, it can be difficult to strictly apply it to the protocols and services that make up TCP/IP. There is a very good reason for this: Development on TCP/IP started before the OSI model had been designed. However, TCP/IP was designed around a similar model, which is sometimes referred to as the DOD (Department of Defense) or DARPA model.

In Figure 2.2 you can see the four layers that make up the TCP/IP–DOD model and how each layer relates to the OSI model.

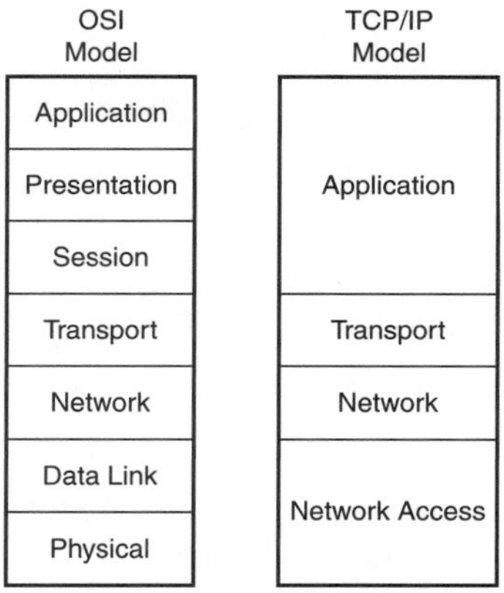

```
        OSI                    TCP/IP
       Model                    Model
  ┌──────────────┐        ┌──────────────┐
  │  Application  │        │              │
  ├──────────────┤        │              │
  │ Presentation  │        │  Application  │
  ├──────────────┤        │              │
  │   Session     │        │              │
  ├──────────────┤        ├──────────────┤
  │  Transport    │        │  Transport    │
  ├──────────────┤        ├──────────────┤
  │   Network     │        │   Network     │
  ├──────────────┤        ├──────────────┤
  │  Data Link    │        │              │
  ├──────────────┤        │ Network Access │
  │  Physical     │        │              │
  └──────────────┘        └──────────────┘
```

FIGURE 2.2
Comparison of the TCP/IP and OSI networking models.

So, although TCP/IP doesn't exactly fit into the OSI model, it is still possible to refer to the model when discussing certain aspects of the protocols and services that TCP/IP provides.

TCP/IP Protocols

As discussed at the beginning of this chapter, TCP/IP refers to a suite of protocols and applications, of which the Transmission Control Protocol and the Internet Protocol are the main ones. You will first look at the Internet Protocol because it is used by TCP and UDP and is the basis for the actual movement of data through the network.

The Internet Protocol (IP)

The Internet protocol is the second component of the TCP/IP acronym, but it is the first protocol in this discussion. This is because IP is the basic protocol in the suite that is used for getting packets from one place to another. IP provides a connectionless, unacknowledged network service. Some characteristics of IP include the following:

- Because IP is connectionless, each packet stands on its own. IP looks at the header information in a packet and uses that information to deliver the packet to its final destination. IP doesn't care whether packets arrive in the order in which they were sent.

What Does
***Encapsulation* Mean?**

TCP/IP provides for net-
works made up of different
underlying technologies to
interoperate. For example,
one network might use the
Ethernet 802 frame format,
whereas another might use
FDDI. Each of these lower-
level frames has its own
particular header that contains information needed
by that technology to send
frames through the physical
network. At this lower level
in the protocol stack, the IP
datagram rides in the data
portion of the frame. In
other words, after IP adds
its header information and
creates a datagram of the
appropriate size, it passes
the datagram to the
Network Access layer,
which wraps the IP data-
gram into, for example, an
Ethernet frame. At the
receiving end, the Ethernet
frame header information is
stripped off, and the IP
datagram is passed up the
stack to be handled by the
IP protocol.

When you configure a
packet-filtering router, it is
the IP header information
that is used to make determinations about passing or
dropping the packet.

- IP is unacknowledged. IP provides no mechanism to determine whether a packet ever arrives at its destination. It just sends the packet on its way and assumes it will either get there or, if not, some other protocol will be responsible for making that determination.

- IP is not concerned with the path a packet takes as it travels throughout the Internet. Routing decisions are usually left to other protocols. It is even quite possible for packets from the same host to take a different route to the same destination.

So, you might wonder, what exactly does IP actually do? IP takes the data from the host-to-host layer and fragments the data into packets (called *datagrams*) of a size that can be transferred through the network. On the receiving end, IP reassembles these datagrams and passes them up the protocol stack. To get each packet delivered, IP places the source and destination IP addresses into the packet header. It also performs a checksum calculation on the header information to ensure its validity, but IP does not perform this function on the data portion of the packet.

When you talk about a network address on the Internet, you are talking about an IP address. Later in this chapter, I will discuss how IP addressing works and why it is so well-suited to an Internet composed of many diverse networks.

The Transmission Control Protocol (TCP)

This protocol makes use of the IP protocol and provides a reliable connection service between two hosts on the Internet. Whereas IP simply sends packets on their way, TCP provides the mechanisms that make sure that the packets are actually received intact and that they can be put back into the correct order at the destination computer.

The TCP protocol provides checksums on the actual data that is transmitted. TCP also has mechanisms that regulate the flow of data to avoid problems associated with congestion. TCP uses sequence numbers in the TCP header so that IP datagrams can be reassembled in the correct order on the receiving end of the communication.

Other Related Protocols

TCP and IP are not the only protocols in this suite. Whereas the TCP/IP combination provides a channel of communication from one computer to another on the Internet, there are other protocols that are used to perform specific tasks.

The User Datagram Protocol (UDP)

The User Datagram Protocol (UDP) is similar to TCP in that it makes use of the IP protocol to actually move packets through the network. UDP does not provide an acknowledgement mechanism like TCP does, though, so it can be considered a *connectionless* service. For applications that do not require a guaranteed delivery service (and the overhead that comes with it), UDP can be used. An example of this is the Domain Name Service (DNS). DNS uses UDP packets so that it can efficiently exchange information with other computers.

The Address Resolution Protocol (ARP)

The nature of IP addressing makes it easy to route data through the Internet. When a packet is being sent to a network other than the one on which it originated, it is passed to a router. The router then makes decisions, based on the IP address and information it has in its routing table, to send the packet on its way to the correct network segment. Sometimes, the router doesn't have a direct connection to the destination network, so it instead sends the packet to another router that can perform this function. When the packet finally makes its way to the correct network segment, the local router or gateway needs to know the hardware address (MAC address) of the destination computer so that the packet can make the final leg of the journey.

IP addresses are used to form a hierarchical address space that can be understood by routing agents throughout the Internet so that they can determine how to get a packet from one network to another. When devices communicate directly on the local network segment (on the wire, so to speak), the actual address used to communicate between two devices, whether they are computers, routers, or whatever, is the built-in media access control (or MAC) address.

The Address Resolution Protocol (ARP) is used to translate between IP addresses and hardware addresses. When a computer wants to

Hostnames, such as www.microsoft.com, and IP addresses are used for the convenience of humans to make it easier to configure and manage a network in an orderly manner. At the lowest level, though, it is the hardware MAC address that network cards use when they talk to each other. Imagine what the Internet would be like if everyone had to memorize hardware addresses instead. Because the MAC address is simply a series of numbers that are "burned into" the network adapter when it is manufactured, it bears no relation to the actual location of a computer or other device in the network. Thus, to route messages throughout the Internet using only these hardcoded MAC addresses, it would be necessary for a router to keep an enormous table in memory that contained the MAC address for every other computer that exists on the Internet. An impossible task, of course!

send a packet to another device, it needs to know the MAC address of the device. To get this MAC address, it first sends out a broadcast message that every computer on the local segment can see. In this ARP message is the originating computer's own MAC address and also the IP address of the computer it wants to talk to. When a computer recognizes its IP address in this broadcast packet, it sends a packet that contains its own MAC address back to the computer that originated the ARP packet. After that, both computers know the MAC address of the other, and further transmissions take place using these.

To prevent a storm of broadcast messages that would result if this was done for each packet that needed to be delivered on the local network segment, each host keeps a table of MAC addresses in memory for some time. When it becomes necessary to communicate with another computer, this ARP table is checked first. If the destination address is not found in the ARP table, the ARP broadcast method is used.

The arp command, which is found in both UNIX and Windows NT operating systems, enables you to view the ARP table. It can also be used to add or delete entries in the table. Although the syntax varies between different systems, the following should work for most:

- arp -a Displays the current contents of the arp table.
- arp -d *IP_address* Deletes the entry for the specified host.
- arp -s *IP_address ether_address* Adds an entry to the table.

For example, to add an entry, use the following syntax:

```
arp -s 192.113.121.88    08-00-2b-34-c1-01
```

The Internet Control Message Protocol (ICMP)

Although IP provides no acknowledgment mechanism to let the originating computer know whether the datagram was received at its destination intact, it does provide for some error-reporting mechanisms, and it does this by using the Internet Control Message Protocol (ICMP). It is a required part of any TCP/IP implementation, and the functions it performs are very important to routers and other network devices that communicate via TCP/IP. Like TCP and UDP, this protocol uses the IP protocol to send its information through the network.

If you have ever used the PING or TRACEROUTE commands, you have used ICMP.

A field in each ICMP packet defines the message type. Message types are listed in Table 2.1. Each ICMP packet also contains a code field that is used to provide further details about the type of message.

Table 2.1 ICMP Message Types

Message Type	Description
0	Echo Reply
3	Destination Unreachable
4	Source Quench
5	Redirect Message
8	Echo Request
11	Time Exceeded
12	Parameter Problem
13	Timestamp Request
14	Timestamp Reply
15	Information Request (no longer used)
16	Information Reply (no longer used)
17	Address Mask Request
18	Address Mask Reply

The PING command uses the echo request and echo reply messages to determine whether a physical connection exists between systems. Another important function on the Internet is traffic control, and the source quench message can be sent to tell a sending host that the destination host cannot keep up with the speed at which it is sending packets. The destination computer can keep sending these quench messages until the sender cuts back its transmissions to an acceptable rate.

Routers make use of another valuable ICMP function to tell another router that they knows of a better path to a destination. This is done by using redirect messages. Routers can also use the time exceeded messages to report back to another device why a packet was discarded.

35

In addition to its use by routers and other intermediary devices, hosts can use ICMP. For example, when a computer boots and does not know what the network mask is for the local LAN, it can generate an address mask request message. Another device on the network can reply to assist the computer.

IP Addressing

In Table 2.1, the Information Request and Information Reply message types are shown only for completeness. Their functionality was originally developed to allow a host to obtain an IP address. This function is now supplied by the **bootp** protocol and by the Dynamic Host Configuration Protocol (DHCP).

IP addresses are used to provide a hierarchical address space for the Internet. Each network adapter has a hard-coded network address that is six bytes long. This address is burned in during the manufacturing process. When data packets are sent out on the wire of the local area network segment, it is this Media Access Control (MAC) address that is really used for the source and destination addresses that are embedded in the Ethernet frame, which encapsulates the actual IP datagram.

About the only meaningful part of the MAC address is the first three bytes, which identify the manufacturer of the card. The remaining three bytes are used simply to uniquely identify each device.

IP Address Classes

The terms MAC address, physical address, and hardware address are basically interchangeable. Each of these refers to the burned-in address that the manufacturer puts into each card they manufacture.

The MAC address assigned to each adapter is unique and is made up of a six-byte address, which is usually expressed in hexadecimal numbers to make it easier to write. For example, 00-80-C8-EA-AA-7E is much easier to write than trying to express the same address in binary (which is what the network sees), which would be a string of 0s and 1s 48 characters in length.

The Internet is a collection of individual networks that are connected together. The Internet Protocol, by its name, should make it obvious that it is used for exchanging data *between* networks. Remember that communications on the local network segment occur using MAC addresses. If there were no need to connect smaller networks into a larger structure, addressing could be quite simple. Either the MAC address or a simple numbering scheme (1, 2, 3...) could be used to uniquely identify each computer on the network. However, the IP protocol provides for computers on diverse types of networks to exchange data.

An IP address is 4 bytes long (32 bits). Although MAC addresses are usually expressed in hexadecimal notation, IP addresses are most often written using what is termed dotted-decimal notation. This is because each byte of the entire address can be converted to its decimal representation, and then the four bytes of the address are separated by periods to make it easier to remember. Table 2.2 shows how the decimal values relate to the binary value in the 32-bit address 10001100101100001101100110010100.

Table 2.2 IP Addresses Expressed in Decimal Notation

Decimal Value	Binary Value
140	10001100
176	10110000
217	11011001
148	10010100

As you can see, it is much easier to write the address in dotted-decimal notation (140.176.217.148) than to use the binary equivalent.

Because the IP address is used to route a packet through a collection of separate networks, a portion of the IP address is used to identify the network, while another part of the address identifies the computer. To complicate matters just a little, IP addresses are divided into three major classes (A, B and C) and two less familiar ones (D and E). Although each class uses a portion of the IP address bits to identify the network, the number of bits used is different for each class.

To identify the different classes, each class is identified by the first few bits of the address.

Because the total number of bits available for addressing is always the same 32 bits, using a different number of bits to identify the network portion of the address implies that some classes have the ability to identify more networks than others. Also, some have the capability of identifying more computers on each network.

To determine which class an address belongs to, examine the first four bits of the address. Table 2.3 lists the IP address classes and shows the bit values for the first four bits. The bit positions that are marked with an "x" indicate that this value does not matter in the determination of the IP address class.

Table 2.3 First Four Bits of IP Addresses' Class Relationships

Classes	First Four Bits
Class A	0xxx
Class B	10xx
Class C	110x
Class D	111x
Class E	1111

Any IP address that has a 0 in the first bit position is a Class A address. It does not matter what the values are of the remaining bits of the address. Any address that has 10 for the first two bits of the address is a Class B address, and so on. Remember that these are bit values and as such are expressed in binary. These are not the decimal values of the IP address when it is expressed in dotted-decimal notation.

Class A Addresses

The decimal value of a byte with all 1s (11111111) is 255. From this, you can see that it is not possible for an IP address to ever have a value for *any* of its four bytes that is greater than 255. Take the address 140.176.123.256, for example. This address is not valid because the last byte is greater than 255 decimal. When plotting out how to distribute IP addresses for your network, keep this in mind!

The range for Class A addresses is from a binary value of all 0s for all 32 bits up to a binary value of 0 in the first position with the remaining bits being 1s. If you convert each byte of the address into decimal, you can see that Class A addresses can range from 0.0.0.0 to 127.255.255.255, when expressed in dotted-decimal notation.

The first byte in Class A addresses is used for the network portion of the address. The remaining three bytes in a Class A address are used to identify each computer on that network. Because the first bit of the first byte of the address is always 0, there are only 7 bits left to create a network address with. Because only 7 bits are available, there can be only 127 network addresses (binary 01111111) in a Class A network. You cannot have 128 network addresses in this class because to express 128 in binary the value would be 10000000, which would indicate a Class B address.

This leaves 3 bytes in a Class A address that can be used for computer addresses on the network. The largest value you can express using 3 bytes is a string of 24 1s. In decimal, this would be 16,777,215. If you count zero as a possibility (0–16,777,215), this means that a total of 16,777,216 (2 to the 24th power) addresses can be expressed using 3 bytes.

That's a lot of computer addresses! This means that there can be a total of 127 Class A networks identified by the first byte of the Class A address, and each network can have up to 16,777,216 unique addresses for computers on the network. Thus, the range of addresses for Class A networks is from 0.0.0.0 to 127.255.255.255. When you see an address that falls in this range, you can be sure that it is a Class A address.

Class B Addresses

This address class can be identified when the first two bits of the address are set to "10." A Class B address can range from 1 followed by 31 0s to 10 followed by 30 1s. In dotted decimal notation, this is 128.0.0.0 to 191.255.255.255. The value of 128 decimal is 10000000 in binary. The value 191 decimal is 10111111 in binary.

In Class B network addresses, the first two bytes of the address are used to identify the network. That leaves the last two bytes to create addresses for computers on the network. Doing the math, there can be up to of 16,384 possible network addresses, from 128.0 to 191.255, in the first two bytes. There can be 65,536 (2 to the 16th power) individual computers on each Class B network.

Because the network portion and the host computer portion of the Class B network address are both two-bytes long, why is there a difference in the number of networks addressed and the number of host computers that can be addressed? It is because the Class B address always has 1 for the first bit position and 0 for the second bit position. In addition, other address classes are further defined by using the first three bits or the first four bits. This eliminates some of the possible values you can create using two bytes to create a network address.

All of that said, Class B addresses can range in value from 128.0.0.0 to 191.255.255.255.

Class C Addresses

A Class C address always begins with the value 110 in the first three bits. In decimal this means that a Class C network address can range from 192.0.0.0 to 223.255.255.255. The first three bytes of a Class C address represent the network part of the address, and only the last byte remains to create host addresses.

Again, doing the math, you can see that there can be up to 2,097,152 Class C networks. Each Class C network can have up to 256 host computers (0–255). This provides for a large number of Class C networks, each with only a small number of computers.

Addresses for Private Networks

It became apparent during the early 1990s that the IPV4 address space would become exhausted a lot sooner than had been previously thought. Request For Comments 1918, "Address Allocation for Private Internets," discusses using several IP address ranges for private networks that do not need to directly communicate on the Internet. These ranges are the following:

10.0.0.0 to 10.255.255. 255

172.16.0.0 to 172.31. 255.255

192.168.0.0 to 192.168. 255.255

Because these addresses are now not valid on the Internet, they can be used by more than one private network. To connect the private network to the Internet, you can use one or more proxy servers.

SEE ALSO

➤ *See Chapter 7, "Application Gateways and Proxy Servers," p. 157, for more about how this is done.*

Classes D and E

Classes D and E addresses function differently from Classes A, B, and C. Class D addresses are reserved for multicast group usage. Multicasting is the process of sending a network packet to more than one host computer. The range, in decimal, is from 224.0.0.0 to 239.255.255.255.

There are no specific bytes in a Class D address that are used to identify the network or host portion of the address. This means there can be a total of 268,435,456 possible unique Class D addresses that can be created.

Class E addresses can be identified by 1s in the first four bit positions. In decimal, this class ranges from 240.0.0.0 to 255.255.255.255, which is the maximum value you can specify in binary when using only 32 bits. Class E addresses are reserved for future use and are not normally seen on most networks that interconnect via the Internet.

Broadcast and Multicast Addresses

So far, I have identified the possible ranges that could be used to create IP addresses in the various classes. However, there are some exceptions that should be noted. When an address is used to uniquely identify a computer on the Internet, it is known as a *unicast* address.

The total number of unicast addresses in any of the classes will be less than you think because some addresses are typically reserved for a specific purpose. For example, any address that begins with 127 for the first byte is not a valid address outside of the local host computer. The address 127.0.0.1 (which is technically a Class A address) is commonly called a *loopback* address and can be used to test the TCP/IP stack on the computer. When you send a packet to this address (by using the PING command, for example), it never leaves the local network adapter to be delivered on the network. Instead, the packet merely travels down through the protocol stack and back up again to verify that the local computer is properly configured.

This address can be used with TCP/IP utilities other than PING. For example, you can telnet to your local computer using this address if you want to test the functionality of a local telnet server.

In general, do not use the value of 0 or 255 for any of the four bytes of an IP address. When used in the network portion of an address, 0s imply the current network.

The value of 255 is used in addresses to specify a broadcast message. This type of message is sent out only once but can be received by more than one host. Broadcasts can be used to send a packet to all computers on a particular network or subnet. For example, the address 10.11.255.255 would be received by all hosts in the network defined by 10.11.

Table 2.4 shows the actual number of addresses for Classes A–C that remain after the special case addresses have been subtracted.

Table 2.4   IP Addresses Available for Use

Class	Number of Networks	Number of Hosts
A	126	16,777,214
B	16,384	65,534
C	2,097,152	254

What Are Subnets?

IP address space is a valuable commodity. For a business entity (or an Internet service provider) to create more than one network, it would appear that more than one range of addresses would be needed. However, a method of addressing called subnetting can be used to take a single contiguous address space allocation and divide it into multiple networks called *subnets*. For example, a Class B address can have up to 65,534 host computers on one network segment. Not many people have a need for that many computers on a single network. To use such a range for only a small network would be a terrible waste.

Although IP address classes were established so that it would be easy to identify which portion of the IP address was being used to identify the network and host computer addresses, there needs to be a means to identify which part of the address is used to identify the subnet. This is accomplished by using a *subnet mask*. A subnet mask is a 32-bit binary value that is used for this purpose.

Class A, B, and C Subnet Masks

A subnet mask can be used to "borrow" a few bits from the host portion of the IP address so it can be used to identify the network or subnet. The subnet mask is expressed in dotted decimal format, just like an IP address, and its purpose is to "mask out" the portion of the IP address that specifies the network and subnet part of the address.

For example, the A, B, and C addressclasses that were just described all have a specific mask associated with them. The Class A address mask is 255.0.0.0. When expressed as a binary value, 255 is equal to a string of eight 1s. Thus, 255.0.0.0 would be 11111111000000000000000000000000. Using Boolean logic, this binary subnet mask can be used with the AND operator to mask out the network and subnet portion of the IP address. Using the AND operator, the TRUE result will be obtained only when both arguments are TRUE.

If TRUE is represented by the number 1 and FALSE is represented by the number 0, it is easy for a computer or a router to apply the mask to the IP address to obtain the network portion of the address. Table 2.5 shows how the final values are obtained.

Table 2.5 Boolean Logic for Subnet Masks

IP Address Value	Mask Value	Result
1	1	1
1	0	0
0	1	0
0	0	0

You can see that when you apply the subnet mask of 255.0.0.0 to a Class A address, the only portion of the IP address that is selected to be the network address is that portion contained in the first byte. It also follows that the subnet mask for a Class B address would be 255.255.0.0, and for a Class C address it would be 255.255.255.0. Each of these subnet masks only blocks out the portion of the IP address that the particular class has already set aside to be used as a network address. By modifying the subnet mask value, you can mask out additional bits that make up part of the host portion of the address, and thus, you can break a large address space into smaller components.

Subdividing an Address Using Subnet Masks

Subnetting becomes useful when you use it to take a particular network address space and further divide it into separate subnets.

The subnet mask 255.255.255.128, for example, can be used to divide a Class C address space into two distinct subnets. When you use this mask with a network address of 192.113.255, you end up with one subnet with host addresses ranging from 192.113.255.1 to 192.113.255.128 and a second subnet with host addresses ranging from 192.113.255.129 to 192.113.255.254. (In this example, addresses that end in all 0s or all 1s are not shown because those addresses are special cases and are generally not allowed as host addresses; 192.113.255.0, for example).

In another example, you can see that a subnet mask of 255.255.255.192 would divide a Class C network address space into 4 subnets, and each would have 62 host addresses available. To understand how this works, look at the binary representation of 192. It is 11000000. Because the first two bits are 1s, when this mask is applied to a byte, there are only 6 bits left that can be used for host addresses. The largest number you can store in 6 bits is 63. Because you cannot use a host address with all 1s or all 0s, this leaves only 1–62 for host addressing.

In Figure 2.3, you can see that the IP address now consists of three parts: the network address, the subnet address, and the host address.

I Don't Want to Calculate This Stuff!

If you don't want to go through the hassle of calculating subnet values yourself, there is a Request for Comments document that might help. Search the Internet for RFC 1878, "Variable Length Subnet Table for IPV4." This document lists potential values for subnet masks and shows you how they can be used. You can also search the Internet for shareware products called *subnet calculators* that you can use to do the math for you.

FIGURE 2.3
A subnet mask can be used to identify the network address, subnet address, and host portions of the IP address.

How to Calculate Subnet Addresses

To subnet an address space, you should first decide how many host addresses will be needed in each subnet. Take this number and convert it to binary. From this you can see how many bits you will need for the host portion of the address space. Subtract that from the amount of bits available (8 if you're subnetting the last byte of a Class C address). Then calculate what the decimal equivalent would be for a binary number that contains that number of left-most bits set to one.

For example, to create subnets that have 30 host addresses each, you will need to know what the binary value of 30 is. It is 11110. This takes 5 bits to write in binary, so when you subtract this from 8, you get only 3 bits that can be masked off to create the subnet mask part of the address (8–5=3). In binary the mask would be 11100000. Convert this value to decimal, and you get 224.

How many subnets can you create using this mask? Only 3 bits are used to identify the subnet, so the largest number that you can express here is 7 (111 binary = 7 decimal). If you include a 0, this gives you 8 possible subnet addresses you can create.

Putting this all together, a subnet mask of 255.255.255.224 when used to subnet a Class C IP address would result in 8 subnets, and each subnet would have 30 host addresses.

What would the actual host addresses be for each subnet? The first subnet address would be 000. Because the IP address is expressed in dotted decimal notation, calculate how many addresses you can store in an 8-bit binary value that always begins with 000, and then translate that to decimal:

`00000001 to 00011110 which is 1-30 in decimal.`

Using this mask, the second subnet address would be 001. The range of host addresses that could be created for this subnet would be the following:

`00100001 to 00111110, which is 33-62 in decimal.`

Using this subnet mask, the hosts on the second subnet would range from 192.113.255.33 to 192.113.255.62.

The third subnet address would be 010. The range of host addresses would be the following:

`01000001 to 01011110`

This is 65 to 94 in decimal. The range of hosts on this third subnet would be 192.113.255.65 to 192.113.255.94.

If you continue to do the math for the remaining subnets (011 to 111), you will find that you will have 8 subnets, each having 30 available host addresses.

You can continue to further subdivide the address space by using up to 6 bits for the subnet mask. This leaves only 2 host addresses available (because you can use all 0s or all 1s). However, using subnetting to create subnets with only 2 hosts is not really a practical idea.

The addresses of 00000000 and 00011111 are not valid because they result in a host address of all 0s or all 1s). If this mask were applied to a Class C network address of 192.113.255.0, hosts in the first subnet would range from 192.113.255.1 to 192.113.255.30.

Examining the Contents of an IP Datagram

After a frame is received by a network adapter at the Physical layer, the frame's header information, which is not relevant to the IP protocol, is stripped off and the IP packet is passed up the protocol stack. In Figure 2.4 you can see the layout of an IP packet.

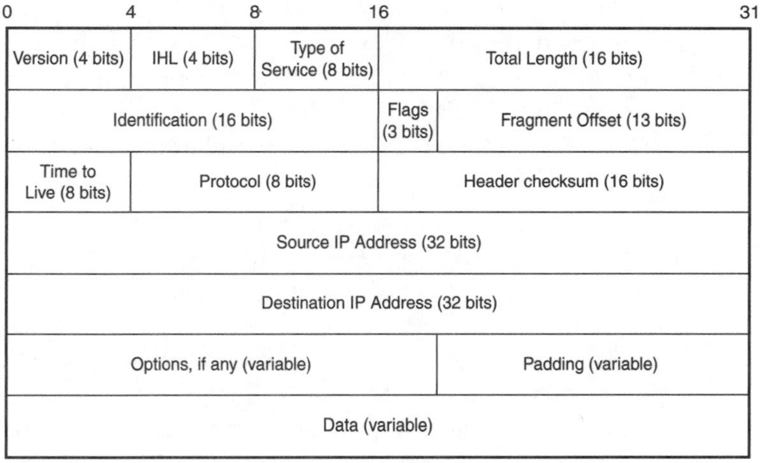

0 4 8 16 31
Version (4 bits) | IHL (4 bits) | Type of Service (8 bits) | Total Length (16 bits)

FIGURE 2.4
IP places header information into the datagram that can be used by a packet filter.

When the IP layer receives the datagram, it has no knowledge of the frame's header information and, instead, uses the IP header information for a variety of purposes. It is important to understand the contents of the IP header if you want to understand how a packet filter works because this is the information it bases its decisions on. The header fields of the IP packet are as follows:

- **Version**   This field indicates the version of IP that constructed the datagram. This field is 4 bits in length. Currently, IP version 4 is the most widely used version of IP. The "next generation" IP is called IPV6, which stands for version 6. Different versions of IP use different formats for header information. Because of this, if the IP layer on the receiving end is a lower version than that found in this field, it will reject the packet. Because most versions of IP at this time are version 4, this is a rare event.

- **Internet Header Length (IHL)**   This field contains the length of the header for the packet and can be used by the software to calculate where in the datagram the data actually starts. The length is expressed as a number of 32-bit words. This field is 4 bits in length.

- **Type of Service** This 8-bit field was created so that IP could make certain determinations about how to handle a particular datagram, such as giving a packet a higher or lower priority. However, no major implementation of IP version 4 uses the bits in this field, so they are all usually set to 0s.

- **Datagram Length** This field is used to specify the length of the entire datagram and is expressed in 8-bit octets (or *bytes*). Because this field is 16 bits in length, it can be used to specify a packet size of up to 65,535 bytes. By subtracting the IHL field from this value IP can determine the length of the data portion of the datagram.

- **Identification** When IP breaks a message into multiple datagrams so that they can be sent through the network (fragmentation), it needs to know on the receiving end which datagrams belong to the same message so that they can be reassembled. This field is used for that purpose. The sending computer will use a unique number for each message it sends, and each datagram for a particular message will have the same value in this 16-bit field.

- **Flags** This field contains several flag bits. Bit 0 is reserved and should always have a value of 0. Bit 1 is the *Don't Fragment* (DF) field (0=fragmentation is okay, 1=fragmentation is not okay). If a computer finds that it needs to fragment a datagram to send it through the next hop in the physical network and this DF field is set to 1, it discards the datagram. If this field is set to 0, it divides the datagram into multiple datagams so that they can be sent onward in their journey. Bit 2 is the *More Fragments* (MF) flag and is used to indicate the fragmentation status of the packet. If this bit is set to 1, there are more fragments to come. The last fragment of the original message that was fragmented has a value of 0 in this field. Together, these two fields control the fragmentation process.

- **Fragment Offset** When the MF flag is set to 1 (the message was fragmented), this field is used to indicate the position of this fragment in the original message so that it can be reassembled correctly. This field is 13 bits in length and expresses the offset value of this fragment in units of 8 bytes.

- **Time to Live (TTL)**   This field specifies the maximum amount of time (in seconds) that a datagram is allowed to exist on the network. This value is set at the start and is reduced by each machine that the datagram travels through. When this value reaches 0, the datagram is discarded. Note that although this field might be reduced by several seconds on a heavily loaded machine, it is always reduced by at least one second on each machine it passes through, even though less than one second was required to process the datagram.

- **Protocol**   This 8-bit field indicates the protocol type for the data contained in this datagram. The Network Information Center (NIC) designates the numbers used in this field to identify specific protocols. TCP, for example, is indicated by a value of 6 in this field.

- **Header Checksum**   A 16-bit computed value used to verify the integrity of the header information. When information in the header is changed this value is recalculated. For example, because the TTL value is decremented by each system the datagram passes through, this value also changes.

- **Source Address**   The IP address of the source of the datagram. This field is 32 bits in length.

- **Destination Address**   The IP address of the destination of the datagram. This field is 32 bits in length.

- **Options**   This is an optional variable length field that can contain a list of options. The option classes include control, reserved, debugging, and measurement. *Source routing* can be implemented using this field and is of particular importance when configuring a firewall.

- **Padding**   This field is used to pad the header so that it ends on a 32-bit boundary. The padding consists of 0s.

Important Packet Header Information

Packet filters operate on the information found in the IP header. Important fields include the source and destination addresses, protocol type, and fragmentation flags. For example, *IP spoofing* occurs when a hacker places a source address in a packet header that is not the real source of the packet. For this reason, you should be sure to configure a packet filter to reject any and all packets that arrive on the external network interface that have source addresses that indicate that the packet came *from* your internal network. Because the packet is arriving on the external interface, there is no way it can be a valid packet from within your network. Instead, it is an attempt by a hacker to get packets into your network that look as if they originated there.

The Options Field and Source Routing

Although the options field is an optional field, it can be put to some uses that you should be aware of when operating a firewall. It is here that *source routing* is defined for a datagram. When I first talked about the IP protocol earlier in this chapter, I told you that IP leaves routing decisions up to other protocols. In most cases, that is what happens. However, as you can see in Table 2.6, there are two options that can be used by IP for routing purposes. These are *loose source routing* (option 3) and *strict source routing* (option 9).

Table 2.6 Option Classes and Option Numbers

Option Class	Option Number	Usage
0	0	Indicates end of option list
0	1	No options
0	2	Security options for military use
0	3	Loose source routing
0	7	Activates routing records
0	9	Strict source routing
2	4	Timestamping active

Source routing can be used by hackers to force a packet to return to their computer using a particular route.

Both options provide a list of addresses that the datagram must pass through. With loose source routing, this list must be followed, but other routes can be used to get to each of the machines addressed in the list. With strict source routing, the list must be followed exactly, and if it cannot, the datagram is discarded.

SEE ALSO
➤ *In Chapter 3, "Security and the Internet" you can find more information about source routing and why you should disable it at your firewall.*

What Are TCP and UDP Ports?

If all applications that used the network only identified the destination for their data exchange as a single IP address, the information would arrive at the destination computer, but it would be almost impossible for the targeted system to figure out which process to give the data to.

Both the TCP and UDP protocols use port numbers to solve this problem. Each application that communicates on the network using TCP/IP also specifies a *port* number on the target computer. The port numbers are *endpoints* for the communications path so that two applications communicating across the network can identify each other. Think of a street address for a business. If all the mail arrived simply addressed with the street address, how would you determine who should get each letter? By using a person's name or the suite or room number, the endpoint of the communication becomes more fully defined. This is how ports work.

Well-Known Ports

The Internet Assigned Numbers Authority (IANA) is the organization that controls the first range of port numbers that are available (0–1023) and these are usually called *well-known ports*. The use for these ports has been defined in several RFCs (most recently RFC 1700), and change only occasionally.

SEE ALSO
➤ *You will find a list of these ports and a short description of their usage in Table A.1, in Appendix A, p. 397*

Well-known ports are usually accessible on a given system by a privileged process or privileged users.

For example, you can see that the Telnet utility uses port 23. In the table in Appendix A, note that in most cases the User Datagram Protocol (UDP) and Transmission Control Protocol (TCP) make the same use for a particular port. This is not required, however, so when you are using this table, be sure to check the protocol for each port when looking up its use.

One good use to which you can put this table is to help yourself in deciding which ports to block when building a firewall. Some of these applications will never be used by your system and because of that there exists no good reason to allow network traffic through the firewall that uses these ports.

Registered Ports

Ports numbered from 1024 to 65535 can also be used, but they are not reserved by IANA. These ports are called registered ports and can be used by most any user process on the system.

Common TCP/IP Services

A large number of services have been created to work with the TCP/IP protocol suite. Based on your security policy, you should decide which of these services you will allow to pass through the firewall, and in which direction.

Telnet

Telnet is an application that allows a user on one computer to log in remotely to another computer, using a character-cell interface. Telnet generally runs over the TCP protocol so that a connection can be established and maintained in a reliable manner. Whereas many modern computer applications that end-users make use of involve a graphical interface, Telnet is more suited for system management chores. Because Telnet has been implemented on many different operating systems, it is possible, for example, to log in to a UNIX computer from a Windows NT computer. However, when you use Telnet to log in to a UNIX system, you must use UNIX commands to accomplish your task on the UNIX system. Telnet simply gives you a window into the remote machine, and you must use the remote machine's command set to do any work.

Generally, a Telnet server is set up to provide protection for its host computer by using the normal authentication mechanisms of the operating system. That means that to log in to a remote computer, you need to know a valid username and password on that remote system.

It should become obvious that you should consider very carefully whether to allow Telnet to pass through the firewall. Although you might think that your system's authentication mechanisms are quite sufficient to protect you, that might not be the case when you connect your network to the Internet and, thus, make your system a potential target of attack from almost anywhere in the world. Hackers are quite good at using password cracking programs, and by using automated methods, they can usually quickly break a simple username/password authentication scheme.

If you are going to allow Telnet to be used, consider using a bastion host to provide the service and add an additional layer of security by using a proxy application that requires an additional layer of password protection.

SEE ALSO

➤ *Bastion hosts, and how they are configured, is discussed in greater detail in Chapter 6, "Using a Bastion Host," page 131*

The File Transfer Protocol (FTP)

Although Telnet can be very useful for executing commands on a remote system, another useful service is provided by the File Transfer Protocol (FTP). This utility allows you to move files between computers. Again, this might not be a good service to enable through the firewall. There are several reasons for this:

- Using FTP, a hacker can download malicious programs to your system. When a "Trojan Horse" application has been copied to your system, it can open up other security holes and even take steps to hide itself from your normal system utilities.

- If the hacker has already compromised your system by guessing a username and password, the files that are available using that identity can be stolen by the hacker. Your data is only as safe as the resource protections your operating system provides.

- A particularly bad hack that can be accomplished by FTP is to simply keep transferring large files to your computer until the disk storage is full. Some operating systems crash if this occurs on the system disk. Nevertheless, it can cause you a lot of headaches when you have to clean up the disk. Services such as anonymous FTP can be configured to use a disk other than the system disk. Although this prevents the system from crashing should the disk become full, it does not prevent the anonymous FTP service from stopping in this event.

Like Telnet, FTP usually requires you to use a username/password combination that is valid on the remote system. Unlike Telnet, which requires that the hacker understand the system he is logging in to, FTP does not make use of the underlying operating system's command set. Instead, the FTP commands, such as GET and PUT, are pretty much standard, and if you are able to get into a system using FTP, the chances are that you will be able to do pretty much whatever you want.

Anonymous FTP is often used to allow anyone to transfer files to and from a server specifically set up for that purpose. When logging in to such a server, you should use anonymous for the username. It is customary to use your email address as the password so that the host computer will keep a record of who has visited the site. This is only a custom, though, and should never be considered to accurately reflect the server's customer base.

The Trivial File Transfer Protocol (TFTP)

Similar to FTP, this service should always be stopped at the firewall. Trivial FTP is usually used by network devices such as routers to make it easy to download patches or other code to the device. Unlike FTP, TFTP does not require a username or password! Disable this service!

The Domain Name Service (DNS)

The Domain Name System (DNS) was created to centralize the task of making changes to the network name to address assignments and to automate the task of performing the translation functions. In the early days of the Internet, a central location (SRI NIC at Stanford Research Institute in Menlo Park, California) was responsible for maintaining a HOSTS file that contained the name of every host on the Internet along with its address. Administrators had to communicate changes to SRI NIC, and these changes were incorporated into the file periodically. Of course, this meant that the file then had to be distributed to every single host so that it could have the updated version.

DNS uses a hierarchical distributed architecture that is spread across many computers throughout the Internet. A root server holds information about top level domains (such as .COM, .EDU, and .GOV), and each domain throughout the Internet has a domain name server that is responsible for the computer names and addresses used in that domain. Client computers query DNS servers when they need to get the address for a hostname. If the local DNS knows the address, it returns it to the client computer. If it does not, it sends the query up the chain of DNS servers until a DNS server is found that can resolve the name, provided that it is indeed a valid name.

SEE ALSO

➤ *In Chapter 6, "Using a Bastion Host," p. 131, you will find some techniques that can be used for configuring a computer securely that will be used for a bastion host.*

The topmost entry in the DNS hierarchy is called the root domain and its represented by the period character (.). Underneath this root domain are the top-level directories that fall into two groups: geographical and organizational. Geographical domains are used to specify specific countries. For example, .au for Australia and .uk for the United Kingdom. Under each of the geographical domains, you can find organizational domains. Organizational domains you might be familiar with include the following:

- com   Used for commercial organizations.
- edu   Used for educational institutions.
- gov   Used for U.S. Government entities.
- mil   Used for U.S military organizations.
- int   International organizations.
- net   Used for Network organizations such as Internet service providers.
- org   Used for nonprofit organizations.
- arpa   Used for inverse address lookups.

The structure of the Domain Name System is similar to an inverted tree. In Figure 2.5 you can see that at the top is the root domain with the com through arpa domains underneath. Under the com domain are individual business organizations that each their own domain. Under any particular domain, there can be subdomains.

One of the first implementations of DNS was developed at Berkeley for their BSD UNIX (version 4.3) operating system. Thus, you will often hear the term BIND (Berkeley Internet Name Domain) used in place of DNS. There have been many security flaws discovered over the years in BIND. Make sure that you have the most recent version and that you follow security advisories to keep informed about new flaws so that DNS does not become a backdoor into your network. Better yet, you can implement DNS on a server so that it cannot be compromised by updates outside your network.

FIGURE 2.5
The Domain Name System is a distributed, hierarchical structure.

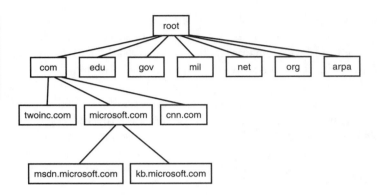

At each level, a fully-qualified domain name (FQDN) is created by concatenating the local name with the names of the entities above it in the hierarchy. Thus `msdn.microsoft.com` is used to name the `msdn` subdomain in the Microsoft domain that falls under the `com` domain. By using the FQDN, it is possible for a hostname to be used multiple times, so long as it is produces a unique FQDN. For example, `fileserver.twoinc.com` names a host called `fileserver`. This host cannot become confused with another host of the same name that resides in a different domain such as `fileserver.acme.com`.

There are a number of restrictions to the names you can use in the DNS system:

- The maximum length of a domain name or a host label is 63 characters.
- The maximum length for the FQDN is 255 characters.
- There can be up to 127 subdomains.
- All text is not case sensitive.

Primary, Secondary, and Caching-Only Name Servers

For each domain on the Internet there must be a primary server and a secondary server. The primary DNS server for the domain contains a collection of *resource records* that contain the address mappings for hostnames in the domain. The primary DNS server is the final authority for these mappings. The secondary DNS server contains a copy of the database maintained by the primary server and can continue to resolve the name when the primary server is offline. It is important to note that the primary DNS server is where changes are made to the database. Through the use of the *zone transfer* mechanism, the data is copied to secondary servers.

In many cases, a DNS server answers name queries for domains for which it is not the authority. In this case the DNS server contacts a DNS server further up the hierarchy until one is found that can resolve the name translation or that can point to another DNS server that is the authority for the name. The DNS server maintains a cache of names that have been resolved by this method so that it does not have to continually poll other servers for names that are frequently queried.

A third type of DNS server is a caching-only server. This type of server does not maintain a database for a particular zone. To put it in other terms, it is not authoritative for any zone or domain and does not use the zone transfer mechanism to keep a current copy of the entire database. Instead, a caching-only name server has to contact another DNS server to initially resolve a name, but like the other servers, it maintains a cache of names it has resolved so that it does not have to keep forwarding the query to another server. This type of server is usually used on a network segment that is connected to the rest of the network by a slower link or a more expensive one and is used to reduce network traffic.

Z1s

In many cases, it is not efficient to have a single server maintain the database for an entire domain. Instead, a primary DNS server can be authoritative for only a zone in the domain. A zone is a partition of the domain into subdomains. For example, one DNS server might be the authority for the zone `biz.twoinc.com`, whereas another could serve as the authority for the zone `research.twoinc.com`. Both subdomains exist within the same domain: `twoinc.com`. However, by dividing the domain into subdomains, it becomes easier to manage not only the DNS servers but also the individual business or organizational units that the domain services.

A *zone transfer* occurs when a secondary DNS server contacts a server that is primary for the zone and finds that it needs to obtain changes to the database. This is accomplished by using serial numbers contained in the database. If the secondary server has a lower serial number, a new copy of the database is copied to it.

DNS Database Files

There are four basic types of files used by DNS servers. In most DNS implementations, you need to use a text editor to make changes to these files. Some newer DNS servers, such as Microsoft's DNS server, provide a graphical interface that can be used for adding or changing information in the DNS files. The basic files are the following:

- **The database file** This is the file that stores the resource records for the zones that the DNS server is responsible for. The first record in this file is the Start of Authority (SOA) record.

- **The cache file** This file contains information for other name servers that can be used to resolve queries that are outside of the zone or domain that the server is responsible for.

- **The reverse lookup file** This file is used to provide a hostname when the client only knows the IP address. This can be useful for security purposes. For example, a Web server that receives a request from a client can query the DNS with the name of the client to find out whether the hostname associated with the IP address is correct.

Resource Records

DNS databases are usually composed of ASCII text files that contain records that can be used to translate a name to an IP address. There are several types of records that can be used in the database, each representing a specific type of resource, such as a computer hostname or a mailserver name.

When representing a domain name in DNS, a specific syntax is used. The term "label" is used in RFC 1035 ("Domain Names—Implementation and Specification") when describing this syntax. A label is a one-byte length field followed by a data field. The length field indicates the number of characters in the data field. A domain name is represented by a series of labels and the entire domain name string is terminated with a length field of zero. For example, Figure 2.6 shows the layout of a series of labels that would be used to define the domain name zira.twoinc.com.

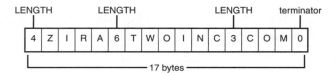

FIGURE 2.6
DNS uses a series of labels to represent a domain name.

Although this string is only 13 bytes long (excluding the periods), it takes 17 bytes to represent it in the database because of the length fields and the terminator field. To avoid repetition for domain names that are used a lot in the database, a pointer record can be used.

The general format used for a resource record contains the following fields:

- **Name** Owner name. This is the name of the domain to which this record belongs.
- **Type** A two-byte field that specifies the resource record type code.
- **Class** A two-byte field that specifies the resource record class code.
- **TTL** A 32-bit signed integer that specifies the time-to-live value. The TTL value specifies the amount of time a record can be cached before its value needs to be refreshed from the authoritative source. 0 indicates that the record cannot be cached.
- **RDLENGTH** An unsigned 16-bit integer that indicates the length of the data field that follows.
- **RDATA** The data field. This part of the record describes the resource. The contents depend on the values of the TYPE and CLASS fields.

The TYPE field indicates the type of resource record. Table 2.7 contains a list of the record types along with a description of their use.

Table 2.7 DNS Resource Records

Record Type	Description
A	Host IP Address
AAAA	Host IP Address (Ipv6)

continues...

Table 2.7 Continued

Record Type	Description
NS	Name Server Record
PTR	Pointer to another Domain Name Record
SOA	Start of a zone of Authority
WKS	Well-Known Service
HINFO	Host Information
MX	"Mail Exchanger" for the domain
MINFO	Mailbox or Mail list Information
TXT	Text entry for miscellaneous information
CNAME	Canonical Name for an Alias

In earlier implementations of DNS, other record types were also used. For instance, MD and MF were used to specify Mail Destination and Mail Forwarder records. RFC 1035 made obsolete three other RFCS: 882, 883, and 973. Four other types that are considered experimental are the following:

- **MB**   Mailbox domain name.
- **MG**   Mail group member.
- **MR**   Mail rename domain name.
- **NULL**   Null resource record.

The Start of Authority (SOA) record is used at the beginning of the database and is used to describe the database. It is used mostly by secondary DNS servers to get zone information. The fields in this record are the following:

- **Domain Name**   Name of the domain for which this database is the authority.
- **IN**   The class type of Internet.
- **SOA**   The Start of Authority record type indicator.
- **Primary Server**   The FQDN of the primary DNS server for this domain.
- **Email Address**   The email address of a person who is responsible for this domain.

- **Serial Number**   A 32-bit value that shows the revision number of the database file. It is incremented each time a change is made to the database so that secondary servers can detect the change.

- **Refresh Rate**   A 32-bit value used by secondary servers. After this interval has elapsed, the data for a record should be checked again in the primary server database.

- **Retry Rate**   A 32-bit value indicating the amount of time to wait before retrying to refresh data after a failed attempt.

- **Expire Rate**   A 32-bit value indicating the maximum amount of time a secondary server should try to refresh data before it stops processing DNS data for this zone.

- **Minimum TTL**   The minimum amount of time for a resource record's TTL. This value can be overridden by the TTL value specified in the record itself.

All time values in the SOA record are in seconds.

The NS record type can be used to indicate that another name server is authoritative for this subdomain. For example, the following record would indicate that the name server whose FQDN hostname is `zira.twoinc.com` is the authoritative name server to get information from about the subdomain `zork.twoinc.com`:

```
Zork.twoinc.com     IN     NS     zira.twoinc.com
```

To get the address of the name server `zira.twoinc.com`, an "A" type record would be needed:

```
Zira.twoinc.com     IN     A     216.65.33.219
```

The `CNAME` record is used to specify aliases or nicknames that can be used in addition to a hostname. For example:

```
ftp.zira.twoinc.com     IN     CNAME     zira.twoinc.com
```

Pointer records (PTR class) are used to get the name that is associated with an IP address—a reverse translation. For example, the following can be used to perform a query to get the name of this host when only the IP address is known:

```
219.33.65.216     IN     PTR     zira.twoinc.com
```

If you will notice, however, the IP address has been reversed. It is represented in a pointer record as 219.33.65.216 instead of

216.65.33.219. The reverse format is used to make a key-lookup in the database function properly. The special domain is called IN-ADDR.ARPA. This data is used when a server needs to look up the hostname for an address in the domain.

The Class field is generally IN, which stands for Internet. The numeric value for this code is 1. In addition to this class type, you might see references to CS, which stands for CSNET class, which is obsolete. The CH class stands for the CHAOS class, and the HS class code stands for the Hesiod class.

The Simple Mail Transport Protocol (SMTP)

This protocol is the basis for all email you send throughout the Internet. Of all the services that the Internet provides, this one has to be one of the most used and yet also one of the most abused. The original programs used for SMTP were quite large and complex and thus contained many security problems. One of the most obvious problems is the ability to forge the sender's address. If a hacker can get you to open an email attachment because you think you know and trust the sender, he can get a virus or other problematic program into your system.

SEE ALSO

➤ *In Chapter 6, "Using a Bastion Host," p. 131, you will find some methods that can be used to safely implement Internet email for your network with a minimum of risks.*

As far as computer viruses and other malicious programs go, you will not be able to solve these problems using a firewall. If you are going to have email on the network with access from the outside world, you have to take further precautions. Instead, you should be using a good program that is regularly updated by the vendor to seek out, identify, and destroy these kinds of programs.

The *r* Utilities

The Berkeley r services were designed to simplify some of the tasks that are commonly performed on the network. They are called r utilities because each of the utilities in this category are used for remote tasks, and each begins with the word "remote." The basic r utilities are the following:

- **rlogin**   Similar to Telnet, but less complex, this utility enables you to log in to a remote system and use its command set to perform tasks as if you were sitting at that remote computer.

- **rsh**   This utility enables you to execute commands on a remote system.

- **rcp**   This utility is similar to FTP in that it can be used to copy files between systems on the network.

- **rwho**   This utility runs a daemon on the remote system to gather information about users on the remote network.

- **ruptime**   This utility displays a list of computers on the remote network and information about them, such as the number of users and how long the system has been booted.

- **rexec**   This is an older utility that can be used to execute commands on a remote system.

These commands probably sound as if they might be useful, don't they? However, they can be quite dangerous not only when used through a firewall, but even when used on your local network. This is mainly due to the method used to authenticate the remote user who is using the r utility.

The user does not have to specify a username or password when using an r utility. Instead, there are two files that reside on the remote computer that can be used to allow access to the system. These are the hosts.equiv and .rhosts files.

The hosts.equiv file contains a list of remote systems that will be allowed into the computer. The system administrator is responsible for maintaining this file just as they do the password file. By placing only the hostnames of trusted systems in this file, you would think you were safe. However, you should consider what can really result from this. By placing a remote system's name in this file, you are opening yourself up to attack should any of those remote systems be compromised! If a hacker breaks into a particular computer, he will have access to all of the other systems in which this computer is trusted by the hosts.equiv file!

Unfortunately, it gets even worse. The file .rhosts is not under the control of the system administrator. This file is placed in a user's home directory and, like the hosts.equiv file, contains names of trusted remote systems. In this .rhosts file, the system name is then followed by usernames, and only those users will be allowed access—the same access that the user has on the local system.

As you can see, all it takes is one uneducated (or upset) user to create a security hole in your system.

Don't use the r utilities through the firewall. Disable them. If you do allow them to be used on the local network, you should regularly police the hosts.equiv and .rhosts files to make sure that they are not misused.

Other Network Services

This chapter has only covered the basic TCP/IP services that have been in existence for quite some time. Other protocols and services are being developed, and you will find new ones popping up every day. For example, the World Wide Web uses the HTTP protocol to transfer Web pages to your browser. RealAudio is a service that can allow your computer to function as a telephone or radio. It is beyond the scope of this book to detail the hundreds of services that are available. It should be emphasized again that when you design the firewall, you should disable all services and protocols and then enable only those you need. This will help to protect you from new protocols or services.

Summary

Before you can begin to understand how a firewall, whether packet filter or proxy server, protects your network, you need to have a good understanding of how TCP/IP and the services it can offer work. When users tell you that they need this or that service or that they must use a certain protocol, you should be able to discuss it with them in a rational manner and defend your firewall policy. If necessary, you can always use a standalone computer with its own Internet connection to provide really dangerous services. In the chapters that follow, you will look at some of the security problems that certain protocols and services can cause. You will also look at methods of implementing a firewall to make their use a little safer.

chapter

3

Security and the Internet

LANS and WANS •

Security in the Local Area Network •

Security in Wide Area Networks •

LANS and WANS

The greatest difference between security on a local area network and on a wide area network such as the Internet is control. On a LAN the network administrator, and possibly some system administrators, can exert a great degree of control over hosts on the network and on the operations and management of the network. When a local network is connected to the Internet, you become part of a much larger interconnection of networks over which you have little or no control at all. Because of this, the security problems you are likely to encounter on a typical LAN pale in comparison to those that can come from the Internet.

One reason is due to the sheer numbers of computers that are part of the Internet. It is no longer necessary for a criminal to break into your computer room and then into a computer. It is no longer necessary for a hacker to try over and over again to get into your network by trying to get past your modem security. The Internet means that an attacker can come from potentially almost any part of the globe to try his tricks.

Security in the Local Area Network

In the local network, you are in charge of which protocols are used and you can set up monitoring and auditing so that you can track abuse. Even in a large company network, tools based on the Simple Network Management Protocol (SNMP) or RMON provide centralized control and security tracking.

User Authentication

The most basic form of security used in a local area network is the user account and password. When implemented in a secure manner, each user who accesses the network has a unique account name (or username) that is assigned by the network administrator and a password that is usually under the control of the user himself. This form of authentication has its roots in early standalone (non-networked) computers that ran multiuser operating systems. The unique username allowed the operating system to keep track of which user was actually logged in to the computer, which made possible the ability

What Is RMON?

RMON stands for Remote Monitoring. RMON is a data gathering and analysis tool that provides for remote monitoring of network components, such as hosts, routers, switches, and other network devices. The functionality of RMON, which is described in RFCs 1513 and 1757, extends the monitoring capabilities that SNMP provides.

to grant differing rights and privileges to users depending on their needs. An initial password is created by the administrator who creates the user account. It is the responsibility of the user, however, to change that initial password to a value that is difficult to guess. It is also the responsibility of the user to safeguard the password so that it does not become known to anyone else.

When this sort of authentication is incorporated into local area networking technologies, it can become a little more complicated. When only one computer is involved, it is very easy to maintain a single secured database that stores usernames and passwords that the operating system can use to check against users. When multiple computers are linked together in a network, where does this security information reside?

In some operating systems, such as UNIX, each computer in the network has its own password database—the file /etc/passwd. This file stores usernames and passwords, along with other information pertinent to the user account. Although this file is a simple text file that can be printed out and examined, it is still relatively secure because the passwords stored in the file are encrypted. That is, it is secure if you trust the users on your network. Programs such as Crack can be used to discover what these encrypted passwords are, so as you can probably guess, this method of ensuring secure authentication leaves something to be desired when connecting to the Internet.

It should become obvious at the start that this method of using a different security database for each computer in the network has its drawbacks. For example, a good security policy dictates that the user must change her password after it has been in use for some time. If the user needs to access resources on multiple computers in the LAN, the user must change the password on more than one computer when it comes time to make a change.

Network operating systems can provide a solution by using a login database that contains accounts for all users on the network. In Windows NT, the concept of a domain is used to group users into a central Security Accounts Manager (SAM) database. When a user logs on to a Windows NT computer that participates in the domain, a dialog between that user's workstation and a server operating as a domain controller authenticates the user. Early version of Novell

---

Using a Shadow Password File

One way to enhance security of the passwords usually stored in the /etc/passwd file is to use a shadow password file that is not world-readable. Check the documentation for your UNIX distribution to see whether this feature is available.

Synchronizing Password Files

While UNIX has many built-in networking components, one thing that it lacks is a method for synchronizing password files between multiple systems on a network. In Windows NT domains, one or more servers act as domain controllers and process user logons for the domain. Under UNIX, each server has its own password file. If users are to log in to multiple systems on the network, they must have an account on each system. To fix this shortcoming, an application called Yellow Pages was developed by Sun to keep important system files synchronized. Because of a trademark dispute, Yellow Pages was renamed NIS, for Network Information Service.

NetWare enabled users to log on to each server they accessed. Novell Directory Services (NDS) now provides a centralized user database.

When a connection is made to the Internet, the problem of user authentication becomes more problematic. When mobile users are away from the office, should they use a modem to contact the home office, or can the Internet be used? If the Internet is used, how can you ensure a secure login session? There are many solutions to this problem, from Kerberos and public key encryption technology to virtual private networks (VPNs).

➤ *Encryption and secure communications on the Internet are important topics. For more information on these topics, see:*

➤ *Chapter 9, "Encryption Technology," page 199*

➤ *Chapter 10, "Virtual Private Networks," page 211*

➤ *Chapter 11, "Using Pretty Good Privacy (PGP) For Encryption.," page 227*

Resource Protections

User authentication is the first thing most of us think about when it comes to computer security. After a user has been authenticated to the computer or the network, the next mechanism that is used to control access is resource protections. UNIX, Windows NT, Novell NetWare, other operating systems, and network operating systems all provide some form of resource protections that enable you to specify which files, directories, printers, and so on, are accessible to users. Resource protections can be used to restrict which users can access objects, and auditing techniques can be used to track usage as well as abuse of privileges.

Like the user authentication databases, the systems and network administrators of the LAN are in control of resources on the systems connected to the network. This control, however, is based on the assumption that your user authentication methods are totally secure and that you have configured resource protections correctly.

I now know that simple authentication methods are easy to break, given enough time. Methods that were sufficient in a small LAN are not sufficient when you connect to a much larger network. If authentication methods fail, resource protections mean very little because an attacker can pretty much become whichever user he wants.

Resource protections do not provide complete security against intruders. With an Internet connection, you expose your network to many more potential intruders than you can imagine. To protect network resources, further measures must be taken. Firewalls, the topic of this book, are the next major step.

Physical Safeguards

When dealing with computers in a local area network, it is relatively easy to make sure that the physical site is secure. Using a computer room with a locked door for important servers can usually prevent them from being compromised. When the LAN spans multiple buildings, as in a college campus, physical security is still under control of someone locally.

When a network is connected to the Internet, it becomes part of a much larger network over which you have no physical control. You might have a little influence with your ISP and might be able to control how the router is configured for your service, but you have no control over the millions of other Internet host computers, routers, switches, and so on. The firewall is the method you use to create a strong front door that, hopefully, will keep out those who want to harm the network.

Security in Wide Area Networks

A connection to the Internet opens up the local network to an infinite number of security problems and potential attackers. The problems you have with users on the local network are small when compared to an attack by someone skilled in modern hacking techniques. When a network is connected to the Internet, there is all the more reason to further increase security on all local host computers. A good firewall, to serve as a single point of control for the Internet connection, is necessary to bolster your defenses. In the next few sections, you will examine some of the kinds of problems that can occur so that you will better understand why a firewall is necessary and why an Internet connection should not be taken for granted.

Network Protocol Backdoors and Holes

TCP/IP and many of its related protocols and utilities were developed years ago when the security threats to the Internet were minimal compared to the problems of today. Thus, most of these protocols and utilities were not written with security as a priority. Instead, they were designed for functionality and portability. That concept helped spread TCP/IP to many different computer platforms, and today it is the protocol suite that connects the Internet.

SEE ALSO

➤ *For more information about the TCP/IP suite and related protocols and services, see Chapter 2, "Introduction to the TCP/IP Protocol Suite," page 25*

Some of the utilities that were created turned out to have significant bugs that could be used to the advantage of someone with mischief in mind. The sendmail application, for example, has been abused many times over the years to cause headaches for network administrators. Sometimes a simple program design can cause an application to crash in a way that the designer had not anticipated. Memory buffers can overflow and if the program does not trap the unexpected error, the applications could then crash or behave in otherwise unexpected ways. It is when a hacker discovers a bug such as this and uses it to gain privileges or access that this kind of programming error becomes a security problem.

Unfortunately, it will be a long time before computers are designed that can catch all the mistakes that a human can make, so you can expect to see new programs come out and over the next few months watch as bugs are discovered. It is sometimes a good idea to lag behind leading-edge technology for a short time to see what does come about.

Keep up-to-date on patches and security advisories from vendors for the operating systems and applications that you use.

SEE ALSO

➤ *Keeping up-to-date on new security advisories is not as hard as it seems. There are several good Web sites that post documents describing new security problems as they are discovered, and many times procedures, patches, or other solutions that can help defend against the problem. Check out Appendix C, "Additional Resources," for a list of Web sites and mailing lists that relate to security issues.*

What Is Source Routing and Why Is It Not a Good Idea?

The IP protocol is an unreliable connectionless protocol. For the most part, the only information about a packet's destination that is available to the IP protocol is the source and destination addresses contained in the IP header. Other routing protocols implement the mechanisms for deciding which path a packet will take through the Internet to reach its final destination.

In Chapter 2, "Introduction to the TCP/IP Protocol Suite," the fields of the IP header were examined. You will remember that the Options field can be used to specify a route that the packet should take. This is called *source routing*, and it was developed for such uses as debugging network problems and other maintenance chores. This feature can be exploited by a hacker easily to get a packet inside your network that appears to have originated there. The packet contains a forged IP address that is valid on your network. The source routing options are used to specify a path that the packet should take to get to its destination.

Firewalls should be configured to drop all packets that have the source routing option turned on.

Denial-of-Service Attacks

Not all hackers are scheming to break into your network to steal information. Some simply want to aggravate you. A denial-of-service attack is a general term for the many methods that can be used to keep you from using part or all of the network. The goal of the attacker is usually one of the following:

- Overload a limited resource
- Crash a network device or host computer
- Reconfigure a resource to render it useless

Overloading a limited resource can manifest itself in many different ways. One simple way is to fill up a hard disk so that no one else can use it. This is why you should monitor closely any disk storage allocated to an anonymous FTP service that allows users to upload files. Obviously, you wouldn't place the root for an FTP service on the same disk as you would an operating system. Similarly, you should not place it on any disk that is used by another application or service that can suffer from such an attack.

Other valuable resources include memory, network bandwidth, and CPU time. Resources don't have to be physical components of the host computer. The SYN flooding attack works by filling up the queue that TCP uses to hold incoming connection requests for a particular port. Even if there is more memory available in the computer that can be used, it doesn't matter because the queue itself is limited by how the TCP/IP stack was implemented for the particular computer system.

Crashing a host computer obviously prevents it from servicing client requests. Some attacks that do this do so by exploiting bugs in the operating system or in network services. Sometimes, all that is necessary is to crash the application that provides the network service.

Reconfiguring a host can occur after an intruder has penetrated your network and has been able to modify operating system or application configuration files. This is why it is so important that the computers you use to provide network services be fully secured using the mechanisms provided by the operating system.

SEE ALSO

➤ *Chapter 6, "Using a Bastion Host," page 131 and Chapter 8, "Operating System Monitoring and Auditing Techniques," page 177, can assist you in constructing a secure host.*

It is also possible to reconfigure network information, such as routing tables, by using the ICMP protocol. This type of attack can make it appear that a host is unreachable when it is actually still on the network. If the router's routing table doesn't have accurate information about how to reach a given destination, it doesn't matter if the destination node is up or down because traffic won't reach it anyway.

The problem with trying to defend yourself against a denial-of-service attack is that you only have control over your network, not the entire Internet. Some attacks can be stopped at the firewall.

SYN Flooding

The TCP protocol is connection-oriented and uses a three-way handshake method to set up a connection before the actual data transfer can begin. The TCP header uses several fields to set up and manage the connection. The Sequence Number field is used to keep track of the order of packets exchanged. The SYN Flag field is used to start a connection request. The ACK Flag field is used to acknowledge a packet. The FIN Flag field is used to terminate a connection when the sender is finished.

The three-part handshake method used to set up a connection is a simple exchange of packets, as you can see in Figure 3.1.

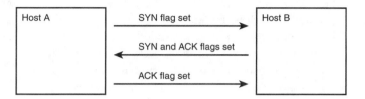

The sequence of events is as follows:

- Host A sends a packet to Host B with the SYN bit set to a value of 1. The Sequence Number field is set to the initial sequence number that Host A will use.

- Host B sets up several data structures in memory to be used in managing the connection and then responds to the connection request by sending a packet to Host A with the ACK field set to 1 to acknowledge Host A's packet. This second packet in the handshake also has the SYN bit set to 1, telling Host A that the Sequence Number field of this packet contains Host B's initial sequence number.

- Finally, when Host A receives an acknowledgement from Host B, Host A sends an acknowledgement back to Host B, acknowledging Host B's initial sequence number.

Under normal circumstances, a connection is set up, and the two hosts can then begin to exchange data. What happens if the sender of the initial connection request, Host A, uses a spoofed IP address in its first packet as the source address? When Host B tries to send an acknowledgement, it never gets back to Host A. Instead, the connection eventually times out, and Host B releases the memory used by the connection.

This is the method used to cause a SYN flood. The attacking host keeps sending connection request messages with a source IP address that is unreachable or does not exist. The receiving host keeps allocating in-memory data structures and starting timers for the connection attempts until it eventually runs out of resources and then begins to refuse further connection attempts. It is important that the spoofed IP address be one that cannot be reached by the attacked host. If not, the real host identified by the spoofed IP address might send a packet to the attacked host with the reset flag set, telling the attacked host to immediately terminate the connection. Because the purpose of the SYN flood is to keep resources tied up, this is not desirable.

An intelligent packet filter can be used to prevent this kind of attack by keeping track of incoming packets that have the SYN flag bit set and applying a little logic to compare IP addresses, port numbers, and other header information. When it appears that such an attack is being attempted, the other packets arriving on the external network interface can be dropped so that they don't get to the internal host that is being attacked.

ICMP Redirects and Other ICMP Problems

The Internet Control Message Protocol (ICMP) is responsible for providing status and control capabilities for the Internet Protocol. For example, a server can send an ICMP Source Quench message to another host to tell it that it is sending packets at a rate that is too fast for the server to handle at this time. Another useful function that is implemented using ICMP is the ability to PING a network node to determine if it is reachable. PING uses the Echo Request and Echo Reply message types to do this.

SEE ALSO

➤ *For a list of message types used by ICMP and a description of their function, see "The Internet Control Message Protocol (ICMP)," in Chapter 2, p. 34*

Unfortunately, there are some message types that can be exploited by hackers to cause you problems. One in particular is the Redirect message type. It was created to allow one router to tell another that a better route exists for a particular destination.

Consider this example. Router B receives an IP packet from Router A that is destined for Router X. Router B does have the capability of sending the packet to another hop in its journey to Router X but, on consulting its routing table, finds that there is a quicker route that Router A can use to get the packet delivered. In this case, Router B can send an ICMP Redirect packet back to Router A to tell it of this new route. If Router A is responding to Redirect messages, it updates its own routing table, and from then on when it wants to send an IP packet to Router X, it uses the new route and does not route the packet to Router B.

The problem with ICMP Redirect (and all other ICMP message types) is that the simple ICMP protocol has no method for authenticating the source of the message. It can be used to cause a denial-of-service attack on your network. It isn't difficult to forge ICMP packets. By sending Redirect messages to your routers, an outsider can reconfigure your network routing tables. In addition to this denial attack, the Redirect message can be used to cause your network traffic to be routed through one or more hosts that the attacker has control of, thereby making it easier for him to perform further malicious acts against you.

Similarly, the Destination Unreachable message is used to tell a router that the destination of an IP packet is unreachable. By forging Destination Unreachable packets, an outsider can make it appear to your clients that other important hosts cannot be reached. For these reasons, blocking incoming ICMP Redirect and Destination Unreachable messages is a good idea.

In addition to being very useful when troubleshooting network problems, the PING utility is very useful when trying to gather information about a network. One of the functions of a good firewall is to prevent anyone outside your network from gathering any information about the hosts on your network. Every little bit of information a hacker can obtain leads him closer to finding a way to break in to your network or to cause you trouble. At the firewall you might want to consider blocking at least the incoming ICMP Echo Request messages. You are still able to PING hosts outside your network because outgoing Echo Request messages and incoming Echo Reply messages are not blocked.

Ping of Death

This attack showed up a few years ago and involves sending an ICMP packet that is grossly oversized when compared to a normal Echo Request packet, which is usually 64 bytes. Instead, sending a packet that is larger than the maximum size allowable, or greater than 65,536 bytes, crashes some operating systems. The IP layer would have to break up such a packet into fragments, of course, but when they get to the destination host they are reassembled and the attack succeeds. This was not limited to just different variants of UNIX or Linux. The Ping of Death proved harmful to a large number of operating systems.

Fortunately, all major vendors have patches that can be used to prevent this attack from succeeding. If you are installing a new system using source CDs that are more than a year or two old, you might not be protected. Read the documentation and, as always, check with the vendor's Web site to look for updates and patches to all operating system software that you use.

Distributed Denial-of-Service Attacks

When a server is subjected to a denial-of-service attack from a single host somewhere on the Internet, it can be very disruptive. Just a few years ago, several new sets of tools designed for the hacker's toolkit were developed that allow the attacker to use multiple computers to mount an overwhelming attack on an unsuspecting victim. The first of these tools was called Trin00, which was followed by Tribe Flood Network (TFN). A newer version called TFN2K (for Tribe Flood Network 2000) has recently been found. A tool that goes by the name of Stacheldraht (German for barbed wire) is the newest of the crop.

What makes these tools different from those used in earlier forms of denial-of-service attacks is the distributed nature of the attack, which is coordinated by a single host managed by the attacker. In Figure 3.2 you can see a simple overview of the method of attack and start to see why it can be such a problem.

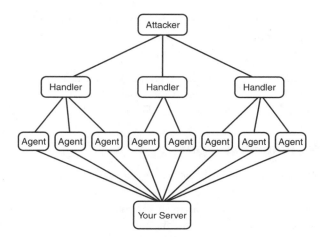

FIGURE 3.2
A single attacking computer coordinates attacks by multiple systems all concentrating on a single target.

This is not an easy attack to mount. The attacker must first infiltrate other vulnerable systems—those with only weak security measures in force—so that he can build up a roster of systems to use as handlers and agents. The systems that are designated to be agents carry out the actual attack on the target system. They are controlled by the systems designated by the attacker to be handlers. At the top of this control structure is the attacker's computer.

Trin00 uses TCP/IP for communications and is capable of sending a flood of UDP packets to the targeted victim. The newer tools are more sophisticated, using encryption for their communications and allowing the attacker to choose several different types of attack. These include UDP, SYN, and ICMP floods, or a combination of them.

The distributed nature of the attack allows the agents to overwhelm the network connection of the target host. Any legitimate traffic trying to compete with this flood of packets is either shut out completely or works at a very slow pace. The encryption in later versions of these tools and the use of forged addressing information can make it difficult to track down the original computer used by the attacker to begin the onslaught. The target of this flood is not the only victim in the attack, however. The agents that were infiltrated by the attacker when he was planning the attack are also victims. These agents don't have to be high-speed servers on a business network. They can be home PCs hooked up to the Internet using DSL or

Read More About Distributed Attack Tools

At the Computer Incident Advisory Capability Web site of Lawrence Livermore National Laboratory, you can find the latest advisory bulletins about recent discoveries as well as an archive of bulletins from the past few years. Bulletin CIAC-2319, "Distributed Denial of Service," covers distributed attack tools in detail and offers recommendations for defending your site against them. You can get to the CIAC Web site by using the URL:

```
http://ciac.llnl.
gov/
```

some other high-speed access that stays online as long as your computer is booted up.

This gives the attacker literally millions of systems that can be commandeered into the attack forces because most home computer users don't know a great deal about how to secure their computers to protect them from the initial break-in.

Packet Fragmentation

Not all network links use the same size for frames of data transmitted through them. Because the Internet is a wide collection of interconnected networks, this means that it is possible for an IP packet, which is being routed through a particular link, to be larger than the size that the link allows. The IP protocol is capable of breaking a packet into several smaller packets and reassembling them when they get to their final destination.

SEE ALSO

➤ *To review the header fields of an IP packet, see "Examining the Contents of an IP Datagram" in Chapter 2, page 45*

There are several header fields of an IP datagram that are used to control the fragmentation process. The Fragment Offset field indicates where in the original packet this fragment fits. Because fragments can arrive out of the order that they were sent and because fragments from different messages can be arriving at a host intermixed, the Identification field is used to identify fragments that belong to the same original message. The Flags field is used to indicate which fragment is the final part of the message. When all fragments have arrived at a host, they are reassembled and sent up the protocol stack.

Remember that the TCP protocol places its own header on messages and then passes the result down the stack to the IP protocol, which then attaches its own header to the packet. At this point as far as IP is concerned, the TCP header is part of the IP packet's payload, just like the actual data contained inside the packet. Thus, when IP needs to fragment the message, the TCP header, which is at the beginning of the payload, is placed into the first fragment (see Figure 3.3). The remaining fragments contain the rest of the TCP packet, but no TCP header information.

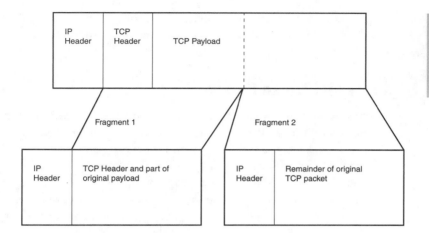

FIGURE 3.3
The TCP header is found only in the first IP fragment.

As long as the packet is reassembled correctly, there is no problem. However, this means that when fragments pass through a packet filter in the firewall, only the first fragment can be filtered based on TCP header information—such as the port number. Remember that the port number for TCP and UDP is used to indicate the network service that the packet is used for. This means that although the packet filter can block the first fragment if it violates some access rule you have set up, the remaining fragments cannot be examined based on TCP information and can pass through.

An old trick for getting a packet past the packet filter is to simply set the fragment sequence number field in the IP packet to a value of 1 so that it looks as if it is a fragment of a larger packet. This value would be 0 if it were the first fragment containing the TCP header information. Because the router assumes that the fragment is not the first in the sequence, there is no TCP header information to be checked, so the packet does not get evaluated against rules that the router might have to block certain ports.

Older TCP/IP stacks would sometimes reassemble multiple fragments that get through even if fragment 0 never arrives, just so long as the fragments make up a valid packet when reassembled—that is, the packet passes checks for checksum values. Another method is to simply send a packet that is already complete, with the sequence number set to 1 and the FIN Flag bit set to 1, indicating that it is the last fragment.

To be sure that your host computer is protected from this kind of attack, review the documentation that comes with it and any updates or service packs that are available.

Viruses and Trojan Horses

A firewall cannot protect you from everything. Sometimes, no matter how good the security precautions and user training, a malicious program, such as a virus or Trojan Horse program, gets into your network. Viruses can hide inside other programs or even in the boot sector of a disk. Trojan Horse programs appear to be something that they are not. Both can cause significant damage if not detected in time. This can happen when a user brings in software on a floppy disk or downloads a program from the Internet. Email exchanges can also provide an easy route into the network.

The problem of these destructive programs existed before the Internet became popular. However, the Internet now gives these kinds of programs a whole new breeding ground and distribution network. There are sites that post information on how to write these kinds of programs, along with sample code and instructions for defeating security devices.

Some firewalls can provide limited protection in that they can look for indications, or fingerprints, for known virus programs or Trojan Horse programs. For this kind of software to function correctly, though, you need to be sure that the vendor responds to new discoveries in a timely manner and makes the updates for your detection software available to you.

Don't depend on the screening capabilities of just the firewall to protect you from these kinds of programs. Continue to be vigilant about individual host security and use virus scanning software on all hosts on the network.

Forged Email

Forging email is not a difficult thing to do. The Simple Mail Transport Protocol (SMTP) is not a terribly secure protocol, mainly because it lacks good authentication procedures. If someone on the Internet can connect to your mail server, usually through port 25, she can issue the necessary commands to send email that appears to come from that server, and she can use any user as the source of the forged email.

For those who do not have the time to fool around with the SMTP protocol, it is often easy to configure a mail client so that it sends messages with a forged username. As it stands today, when you receive an ordinary email message, you cannot really be 100% sure that you know where it comes from. Because of this, spoofing email can be very dangerous to the network. Try sending an email to users on your network asking them to email a copy of their password to you. If you receive any replies, you can see how dangerous spoofed email can be. It can be a tool that enables an outsider to gather information about your network. It can be a tool that allows an outsider to get files into your network.

To help eliminate the problem of identifying the creator of an email message, you can use *digital signatures*. There are two benefits of using a digital signature. The signature provides for the following:

- Authentication of the originator of the message.
- Assurance of the integrity of the contents of the message.

Digital signatures involve using a private key to encrypt a message that can only be read using the matching public key.

SEE ALSO

➤ *For more information about how digital signatures work, see Chapter 9, "Encryption Technology," page 199*

Break-Ins

When the local network is under your control from a physical point of view, you can usually control how and when the network is accessed. Even if modems are used to allow users to dial in to the network, you can still configure their use for certain hours and use features such as call-back to help keep out potential hackers. The Internet connection, however, means that there are millions of potential hackers over whom you have no control. Any trust that you extend to other hosts on the Internet presents a possible security issue because the hacker then only has to compromise that trusted system to begin to learn more about yours.

Password Theft

Using a valid user account and valid password is the easiest method for breaking into a network. After all, when using a valid account and password, the intruder is not likely to get caught until someone suspects that the user is performing actions inconsistent with his job. Passwords can be guessed by the intruder, or they can be cracked by using a tool such as Crack to decipher the encrypted passwords in a supposedly secure password file.

A good password policy makes users choose passwords that are difficult to guess—more than 6 characters in length, using a combination of numeric and alphabetic characters and symbols and uppercase and lowercase letters. You shouldn't make the password policy too restrictive, however. Often, when passwords are difficult to remember, users simply write them down. This, of course, defeats the whole purpose of using a password for authentication.

Tools available to modern hackers allow the entire processing power of a fast computer to be brought to bear when trying to crack an encrypted password file. Other programs automate the process of attempting login after login to try to guess a password using common words.

Depending on user accounts, to be secure based on password security alone is not feasible when you connect to a larger network. There are simply too many tools that make it an easy defense to break. Instead, a firewall can be used as the first barrier to outsiders, and stronger authentication techniques, using one-time passwords or external physical tokens, should be considered for networks with high security requirements.

SEE ALSO

➤ *For more information about stronger authentication techniques, see Chapter 9, "Encryption Technology," page 199*

Friendly Customer Service (Social Engineering)

An area often overlooked that makes all the difference for security implementation is user education. Too often, users are funneled through a process by the human resources department, where they sign papers indicating that they understand and will abide by the site's security policies. In fact, many do not understand everything they read in these documents, much less how important security can be. An easy tactic for getting information about a network is to simply ask someone who is already on the network.

In an earlier section, I discussed how easily an email message can be forged. Trusting users usually respond with information when they are asked by someone in authority. In fact, users should be trained to not give out information, such as a password, even to a superior. Passwords can be changed by the administrator if access to an account is required. Accounts can be created for temporary users. There is rarely ever a need to allow more than one user to share an account or resource password.

Be sure to train users also to verify any requests they receive through insecure channels, such as email, before responding. Train users that information about their workstation, network servers, and security matters, should never be discussed on the telephone with those from outside the business.

Backdoors

When an intruder has gained even a small kind of access into your network, her next step is usually to create some sort of entry point that makes her job easier in the future. Creating a *backdoor* into a network can be as simple as creating a new user account with all privileges on an important computer. Backdoors can be created using Trojan Horse programs or by exploiting a bug in an application or operating system. A backdoor into the network can even be created by altering the configuration of the firewall or hosts that reside in the DMZ. Again, this is why individual host security should not be ignored or made second-place when a firewall is used.

Snooping: Monitoring Network Traffic

Intercepting network communications in a LAN can be as simple as connecting a host computer to the network and using a network adapter set to promiscuous mode. You can protect yourself from this by monitoring the network and placing controls on which kinds of devices can be attached to the network. On the Internet, packets can be intercepted on any link through which they travel. For this reason, insecure versions of network utilities, such as basic FTP and Telnet client software, should not be used. These applications send usernames and passwords as clear text across the network.

The Internet also offers no protection for other payloads that might be traveling in IP packets to or from your network. The only way you can ensure that you have a secure connection on the Internet is to use encryption technology, either on individual files that are transmitted or by using a virtual private network (VPN) that tunnels your network's regular protocols through an encrypted stream of data.

SEE ALSO

➤ *In Chapter 10, "Virtual Private Networks," page 211, you can learn more about encryption technology.*

Because a secure communications channel is so important and because the firewall is positioned at the border of your network, you will find many firewall products that provide for VPN connections between firewalls.

IP Spoofing and Impersonation

In an IP packet, the Source Address field in the header is used to indicate the host from which the packet originated. This is one of the fields you can configure a packet filter to examine when deciding which network packets can pass through the firewall. There are some hosts you trust and some you do not. Filtering rules can be set to forward or block packets based on a host address or a network address.

How can you be sure that the source address is real? There are a number of tools freely available on the Internet that enable a malicious user to send out packets with a source address of the user's choosing. This spoofing means that your firewall might receive packets that it thinks come from a trusted host computer or network but that in fact are being generated by someone who wants to get data inside your local network.

The trusted host can be a host on the Internet that you interact with or one that is on your local network. If the spoofed IP address is an address that appears to come from inside your network, it is easy to configure the packet filter to protect you by having it simply drop all packets arriving on the external interface that have source addresses from the inside local network. This should be done on all routers connecting you to an external network because the bonds of trust between hosts on the local network are usually configured more loosely than those with hosts on the Internet.

Of course, if such a packet does get through and the target host responds, the response is sent to the host identified in the source address field, so the attacker is not be able to see the response. In many cases, this does not matter. The point is that by spoofing an IP address, the attacker can get a packet into your network. For example, if the attacker had previously been able to inject a Trojan Horse program into your network that is listening on a high port number, this method could be used to send in a packet that could instruct the dangerous program to perform some action.

If the hacker already has some knowledge about your network and is willing to take the time to do so, an even more serious attack can result from IP spoofing. This kind of attack involves disabling a host on the Internet that is known to be trusted by your network and then impersonating that trusted host. The trusted host is one that has some special kind of access to your network, so that if the attacker can get a packet into your network that appears to be coming from an existing connection that the real trusted host had set up, damage can be done. The attacker disables the trusted host using some kind of denial-of-service attack and then sends a packet to your host that appears to come from the original trusted host.

This kind of attack can be complicated and involves guessing what the next sequence number will be for the interrupted connection. This isn't too difficult if the attacker is knowledgeable about TCP and how it is implemented on your host.

Summary

The security problems that you can encounter on a simple local area network are many. When the network is connected to the Internet, the possible avenues of attack are greatly multiplied. In this chapter, you looked at only a few of the potential threats that you can be subject to from the Internet. In the next chapter, you will examine some of the strategies that can be used to construct a firewall and how this can help to protect your network from these new security problems.

Firewall Security Policy and Firewall Design Strategies

The Design Comes Before the Firewall ●

Firewall Strategies ●

Incident Reporting and Response ●

Keeping Up-to-date on Security
Advisories ●

The Design Comes Before the Firewall

In Chapter 1, "Firewall Basics," a firewall was defined to be a system of components that are designed to protect the resources on your LAN from those on the Internet that would want to do them harm. Which components you decide to use and how you configure them is not a decision you should make lightly. Instead, you should sit down and review carefully the security requirements of your site and proceed to design a firewall that can be used to rigidly enforce this security policy.

Although it might be tempting to listen to a vendor's sales force and simply buy the latest and greatest (so they say) firewall, this is not the wisest course of action to take. It might be easy to rely on the sales literature and promises made by a vendor with whom you frequently do business. Long-term relationships of this sort usually imply that the vendor is not going to try to sell you something just to make the sale. However, with new software companies springing up all over the place, you might find that you have purchased a firewall solution from a company that has inadequate resources to support it. If your vendor cannot back you up, you might find yourself totally unprepared when a major security event occurs.

Based on your company's security policy. you can then create a security policy for the firewall. Although the overall security policy for the company might consist of more than one document and can cover a wide variety of topics, the security policy for the firewall provides details about how to implement the firewall so that it can be used to enforce your security requirements as they relate to connections made through the firewall.

Your Company's Security Policy

What is a security policy? Put simply, it is a statement of what can and cannot be done on a computer or the network. Although that might sound pretty simple, a good security policy encompasses many different topics and spells out in detail allowable actions that users can take as well as penalties that are imposed if inappropriate behavior occurs. One caveat to a detailed security policy is that the user might not understand all of it or might not even read it if it is quite lengthy. Still, it is better to let your users know up front what is allowed and what is not tolerated than it is to argue about the details later down the road. If you don't believe that, just consult your legal department if you have one!

A security policy should be formulated as one or more written documents. Before allowing an employee to make use of any computing resource, you should have her review the security documentation and acknowledge that it has been read. In most large businesses, this function is done by the human resources department and usually consists of several documents, such as a network connection policy and an acceptable use statement that must be signed by the employee. In addition, you might draft a document that describes actions to be taken when a security problem is discovered.

The Network Connection Policy

A network connection policy should describe the kinds of devices that you allow to be connected to the network. For example, although you most certainly want to allow network servers and user workstations on the network, you might not want to allow a terminal server equipped with a modem bank. Similarly, the network connection policy should detail how systems must be configured that are allowed on the network. The policy might include things such as the following:

- How the operating system is to be installed, which features are to be used, and details about how the operating system and applications are to be configured.

- Where in the network (physical subnet) certain types of systems can be installed and how network addressing issues are to be handled.

- Virus protection software must be installed and regularly updated as needed.

- User rights and resource protections provided by the operating system must be configured in a specified manner.

- Procedures to be followed to obtain a new user account, and on a similar topic, procedures to be followed when deactivating a user account.

- Installation of additional hardware or software components not approved by the network administrator (or other responsible authority) is prohibited.

This is not an exhaustive list, of course. You should base the contents of your specific network connection policy on the requirements of your site. For example, if you have users with laptop computers, do you allow them to connect to the network or do you force them to exchange data with their desktop via other methods such as a floppy disk or other removable storage device? If you allow laptop computers to be connected to the network, is each laptop configured with a specific network address, or do you use DHCP for network configuration? To carry this even further, do you allow them to connect the laptop to other networks, such as the network of a customer when the user is on the road?

The network connection policy should also take into consideration the functions that particular computers are used for. Although you might allow a department to set up a Web server or FTP server, the policy might specifically state *where* in the network this kind of server is to be connected. For example, later in this chapter you will learn how to create a *demilitarized zone* that can be used to allow these kinds of servers to be accessed by your customers via the Internet, without allowing that kind of network traffic to flow through the entire LAN.

The Acceptable Usage Statement

A desktop computer is probably the most abused business machine in use today. That is, in addition to its important business functions, such as word processing and database applications, the computer can also be used to play games and run other programs that have nothing to do with the user's job functions. Other business machines, such as the photocopier and telephone, are also often misused, but probably not to the extent that the desktop computer is. When you throw in an Internet connection, the potential for misuse is magnified tremendously!

You probably don't care that a co-worker makes an occasional telephone call to check on a doctor's appointment or uses the photocopier to make a copy of a tax return form. Such trivial actions do not amount to a great dollar loss to the business. Indeed, in some ways this overlooked "misuse" can be considered an employee benefit. When you look at the kinds of things that the computer can be used for, however, the costs involved can quickly become anything but trivial. All it takes is for one user to load a program from floppy disk onto the computer to start a virus spreading throughout your network. All it takes to get your company sued is for a single employee to write a slanderous email message to another employee or, possibly, one of your important customers.

Because of the greater potential for misuse and abuse, it is important that you spell out just what kinds of things the computer can be used for and what kinds of actions are to be unacceptable. An acceptable use statement is a good way to do this.

Some of the things you might want to consider including in an acceptable use statement are the following:

- No applications not approved by and supplied the company are allowed to be installed on the computer. This includes "illegal" copies of programs brought in from a home computer as well as shareware programs that can be easily downloaded from the Internet.

- No applications supplied by the company can be copied for use elsewhere, such as on the user's home computer.

- A workstation should not be left logged in to a user account when the user is away from the workstation. Alternatively, a screen saver program that uses password protection should be used to secure the workstation when it is unattended.

- Any suspicious activity should be reported to the appropriate authority.

- The computer and its applications cannot be used in any way to harass or threaten another person.

- Email cannot be used for personal purposes.

- Attempting to access data that is not relevant to the user's job, sometimes called *probing the network*, is not permitted.

If any of these items sounds too harsh to you, think about the possibilities that can result from them. For example, there are thousands upon thousands of shareware and freeware programs available for downloading on the Internet. Allowing an employee to download a file containing graphics for use in company memos, for example, might not seem like a dangerous thing to do. However, suppose the

Harsh Security Policies

Above all, it should be noted that a security policy should also be reasonable and not too harsh. Although you need to include prohibitions against actions that can potentially become a security problem, you want to make sure that you leave enough room for users to get their jobs done. Confronted with an absolute policy and a security administrator who does not listen or compromise, a user might find other means to get the job done that cause more problems than their original intention. If users request new software applications or perhaps permission to use a shareware product, a good administrator evaluates the request fairly. If the application is useful, it can be tested in a laboratory environment before it is deployed on the network.

file that is downloaded contains a computer virus? Suppose the freeware file is really a copy of material that is protected by copyright? Do all your users have the ability to make decisions about which files are dangerous and which are not?

Again, the preceding list is not a complete list of all the things you should put into an acceptable use policy statement. Evaluate the environment in which your business operates to come up with your list. Discuss the usage policy with managers in all departments so that you can understand what they expect from the network and try to come up with a policy that allows users to get their job done without compromising the network or getting the company involved in messy legal issues.

Employees, Contractors, and Outside Service Providers

A good security policy goes a long way toward protecting your network resources from misuse and abuse. However, you will probably find that it is difficult to anticipate every situation that can occur. For this reason, it is a good idea to discuss not just the specifics of the policy with the user, but also to give them an idea of the reasoning involved in formulating the policy.

Prohibiting network probing is a good example of a topic you can discuss. Many users might operate under the idea that "if it's not locked up then there is nothing wrong with my looking at it." You should make them understand that although it is possible to use rights and permissions to prevent data from being accessed by those who should not do so, there is always the possibility that something will be overlooked. Make the users understand that if it doesn't pertain to their work function then they should not be looking at it. This goes for hardcopy also. Just as you would not be justified in looking over someone's shoulder and reading their email, you should also not be reading reports that come off the printer while you are waiting for your print job.

To put this very concisely, make sure the users understand that in a work environment, it is expected that they will exhibit only the best of ethical behaviors!

Although it might seem very obvious that you will have a written security policy document that an employee will have to read and acknowledge before he is allowed to make use of the network, don't leave a hole in your security procedures by forgetting others that might have a need to use the network.

Outside contractors are a very popular method for staffing short-term projects, and in some cases, it is cost-justified to fund positions for the long term with users who are not actual employees of the company. These users should not be overlooked when creating a security policy. Third-party vendors who supply assistance when you have problems with software or hardware should also not be forgotten. If you create a user account that is to be used by such a person, it might be appropriate for the vendor to understand and acknowledge your security policy.

The Firewall Policy

Often confused with the security policy is the *firewall policy*. After you have designed your security policy and have decided on which services and protocols you will allow to pass through the firewall, and in which direction, you need to decide how to implement this policy on the firewall itself. By design, a firewall uses rules to decide which packets (in the case of a packet filter) or services (in the case of a proxy service or an application gateway) are allowed through. The policy can be either of the following:

- Permit any access unless it has specifically been denied by the rules.

- Deny any access unless it has specifically been allowed by the rules.

Although these might seem pretty straightforward and you might think that there is not much difference between the two, that is not the case. If you use the first policy, you need to create rules on the firewall that can take into consideration every single instance when a denial should be used. Not only can that result in a lot of rules being designed, but it also leaves you open anytime some new protocol or service comes along that is not covered by your rules.

The second policy is more straightforward and secure. If you explicitly deny all network traffic passing through the firewall and supply only the rules needed to grant access through the firewall for the

Software Piracy

Making illegal copies of computer software is a widespread problem. Many users don't think that they are really committing a crime when they make a copy of a program and run it on their own computer at home. It is important that you take steps to make all your users understand that the consequences of pirating software can be quite enormous. If you need help in deciding how to enforce a good antipiracy program at your business, you can visit the Software & Information Industry Association Web site at `www.siia.net`. This organization is the result of a merger between the Software Publishers Association (SPA) and the Information Industry Association (IIA) that occurred on January 1, 1999.

specific instances you require, you have a much more secure grasp on controlling the firewall. In this kind of situation, the potential intruder must find some means to take advantage of the limited conditions you have set to provide access.

Next, specify which services you will allow to pass through the firewall, and in which direction. You can decide this by looking at your overall security policy. For example, if you do not allow downloading files from the Internet, you want to have an item in the firewall policy that prohibits the use of incoming FTP. If you are worried about users using FTP to send confidential data or program files to computers outside the company, you want to have an item that prohibits outgoing FTP. Similarly, you might want to restrict other services, such as Telnet or HTTP.

It is important that you work closely with users, or at least their managers, to determine which network services are really necessary. Indeed, although you might decide to specifically prohibit both incoming and outgoing FTP services, how will you obtain new releases of software, updates, or patches? You might specify that all FTP access is denied and then provide an exception for a highly secured host computer that allows only certain users to log on. Another solution is to use a computer that is not connected to your LAN but that has instead its own dial-up Internet access that can be used for this kind of function.

The items that you decide to implement using the firewall might include such things as the following:

- Email is allowed for clients to and from the Internet, but it must pass through a secure SMTP server.

- No service is allowed that involves a direct network connection between an internal client and an external service. Any service that is allowed makes use of a proxy server.

- Outgoing Telnet access is allowed for users in the Research & Development department, but it is denied to all other users. No incoming Telnet access is allowed. Users who are authorized to log in to the network from an external source use a modem installed in a secured server that that is placed in a screened subnet.

- Incoming and outgoing FTP access is prohibited.
- DNS servers on a secured subnet allow resolution of names of firewall and application proxy computers, but they are not allowed to resolve names for clients on the internal LAN.

This is a short list. It is easy to create a short list if you follow the principle that everything is denied except for that which is explicitly allowed.

In addition to specifying the types of services that will be allowed and how they will be implemented (that is, proxy or packet filter, for all users or for selected hosts), you should also include in the firewall policy items that specify how often log files are reviewed, how alarms are configured, and so on.

Finally, be flexible when dealing with user requests to make exceptions, but don't go overboard and create so many exceptions that the firewall becomes, for all practical purposes, worthless!

Firewall Strategies

After you have determined what the security requirements should be for your site and have formulated a good written policy, you can begin the process of designing the firewall. Which components you use depends on what kinds of services you want to make available to the users on your LAN. Which services to choose depends on how the services relate to the actions your security policy allows.

The two basic components that you can use to construct a firewall are the following:

- A packet filter
- An application proxy server

You might want to use just one of these or both of them. These components can be implemented in various ways to provide differing levels of security. The way you configure the components of your firewall can be thought of as the *architecture* of the firewall. The architectures that you will consider here are the following:

- A packet-filtering router or host computer
- A dual-homed gateway

- A screened host
- A screened subnet

Using a Packet Filter

Today, firewalls can consist of one or more routers or hosts running firewall software that use various methods to grant or deny access to and from your local LAN. The first type of firewall that was put into general use, however, was a simple *screening router*, which today is commonly called a *packet filter*.

SEE ALSO

➤ *For a more in-depth discussion about packet filtering used in firewalls, see Chapter 5, "Packet Filtering."*

A *router* is a networking device that is configured with multiple interfaces and is attached to two or more networks. When a computer on the network needs to send a packet to a computer that sits on a different network, it sends the packet to the router's address and lets the router determine the best method for delivering the information to its final destination. The router makes these decisions depending on addressing information it finds in the packet's header.

If the router can determine that the packet is destined for a host that resides on a subnet that is directly connected to one of the router's network interfaces, the packet is quickly retransmitted on that interface so that it can finish the trip. If the router determines that the packet is not destined for any of the networks it is directly attached to, it sends the packet to another router (the next "hop" on its journey) that might know how to get the packet to its final destination. Of course, if the router doesn't know of another hop that might get the packet delivered, it can simply drop the packet and return an ICMP message to the source to tell it that "you can't get there from here."

A *screening router* is a router than has been configured with a set of rules that specify which kinds of network traffic are allowed to come in through, or go out through, the network interfaces attached to the router. In other words, after the router has decided that it can deliver the packet (either to the next hop or to its final destination), it then consults a set of rules that tell it whether it *should* route the packet.

For example, suppose the router receives a packet from a host some-where out on the Internet that makes a request to establish a Telnet session with a host on your internal LAN. Of course, the router decides at once that it knows how to route the packet—just retransmit it on the same interface that the destination host is attached to, after first placing the destination host's MAC address into the packet so that it will be recognized by the host. However, because this is a screening router, the rules must next be examined. Here, you find that all incoming Telnet requests are to be rejected. Thus, as you can see in Figure 4.1, the hosts on your internal LAN are protected from possible compromise by an intruder using Telnet as a method of getting in.

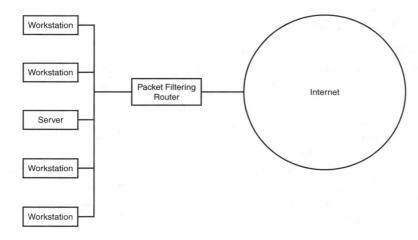

FIGURE 4.1
A packet filter decides which packets can travel between your LAN and the Internet.

This basic method of filtering is called *stateless packet filtering* because each packet is judged on its own merits—by the data contained in its header. A newer method of packet filtering, called *stateful packet filtering* or *stateful inspection*, takes the process a step further by keeping information in memory that records the state of current sessions. When a packet is received that claims to be a response to a packet that was sent out from your local network, the stateful packet filter checks its tables to see that the packet is indeed a response to a request that was previously sent out. Thus, when using stateful inspection techniques in a packet filter, it becomes much more difficult for a potential intruder to get a packet through that contains forged addressing information.

What Information Can a Packet Filter Use?

A packet filter operates on information found in the header of the network packet, and different products are able to filter based on some or all of the following:

- IP source address and destination address

- Protocol (such as TCP, UDP, or ICMP)

- Source and destination TCP or UDP ports

- Message type, if ICMP

In addition, another important piece of information that the packet filter has, which is unrelated to the packet header information, is the interface that the packet arrives on. This is an important piece of information! For example, if the filter receives a packet on the interface that connects to the external network, yet finds that the packet has a source address that appears to come from within your LAN, it is a simple matter for it to reject this spoofed packet because it could not possibly have arrived on the external interface using that address.

Although this discussion so far has used a router as a packet filter, you can also find packet-filtering capabilities in most commercial firewall products. In many cases, packet-filtering software running on a host computer is preferred over a router because of ease of use and also because of logging capabilities. Routers can be difficult to configure, especially when your needs require a large number of rules. Making a change to a rule set that is large can involve a lot of time because you have to check each rule to be sure that it does not block or allow that which you are trying to do with a new rule! Routers are also not known for having extensive logging capabilities. A good firewall product provides detailed logging and alarm capabilities and, hopefully, software that can be used to analyze log files.

Using an Application Proxy Gateway

A packet filter can only make decisions based on the information found in the packet header. Unfortunately, this information is mostly just addressing data and other information about the packet that the protocol needs to move the packet through a maze of networks to get it delivered. The packet header data does not tell the packet filter specific details that can be used to make a better decision on whether the packet should be allowed to transverse the firewall. For example, a router can determine that a particular protocol, such as FTP, is the purpose of the packet. It cannot tell, however, whether the FTP request is a "put" or a "get" request. Although you might not mind "get" requests that are destined for a specific host, you most likely do not want to have "put" requests allowed through for this particular host.

SEE ALSO

➤ *For more information about proxies and application gateways, see Chapter 7, "Application Gateways and Proxy Servers."*

An *application gateway* or *application proxy* is a software program that runs on the firewall to intercept traffic for a specific kind of application. The proxy software intercepts user requests from the local LAN, for example, and then makes a connection to the server residing outside your local LAN for your user. The internal user never makes a connection directly to the outside service. Instead, the application proxy program acts as a man-in-the-middle and talks to the client and to the server, relaying application information between them. The advantage here is that the application proxy can be pro-grammed to allow or deny traffic based on information contained in the payload section of the packet, not just the header information.

One disadvantage to proxies, however, is that they are application-specific. For each service or application you want to support on the firewall, a separate proxy application must be developed. Another disadvantage is that client software must be able to work with the proxy server application. Most newer software packages are designed with this in mind, so it is no problem. For example, Netscape's Navigator browser and Microsoft's Internet Explorer browser both allow you to specify proxy servers if they are used on your network.

SEE ALSO

➤ *For more information about network address translation, see "Network Address Translators (NATs) in Chapter 7, "Application Gateways and Proxy Servers."*

Older programs that do not understand proxy servers might still be made to work. For example, using Telnet a user can first log in to a proxy server and be validated by the proxy server before being allowed to then create a Telnet session with an external host. This two-step method is not as preferable as the transparent method pro-vided by client applications that were coded to work with proxy servers.

Another avenue to explore if you want to adapt applications so that they will work with proxy servers is to use the Trusted Information Systems Internet Firewall Toolkit (FWTK) or a package such as SOCKS. SOCKS provides a programming library that can be used to create or modify clients so that they will interact with a SOCKS proxy server application. The TIS Firewall Toolkit can be used to create proxy services for many common services, such as Telnet, FTP, and HTTP.

SEE ALSO

➤ *For more information about SOCKS, see Chapter 15, "SOCKS."*

➤ *For more information about the TIS Firewall Toolkit, see Chapter 14, "Using the TIS Firewall Toolkit (FWTK)."*

Combinations

As you can see, both packet filters and proxy servers can be used to create a firewall, and each method has its strengths and weaknesses.

What Is Network Address Translation (NAT)?

One form of proxy server that is very popular at this time is the Network Address Translator, or NAT. This type of server helps to improve your network secu-rity by hiding information about the actual network addresses that are used on your internal LAN. It accomplishes this by using its own valid IP address when it makes proxy requests to outside ser-vices for clients on your internal LAN. Another ben-efit that makes NATs popu-lar is that, because only the actual proxy server needs to use an address that is valid on the Internet, you are free to use almost any range of IP addresses on your internal LAN clients. Because the IP address space on the Internet is diminishing at a rapid rate, this technique can be used to expand your internal LAN without having to first obtain a large range of addresses from your Internet provider.

You can probably also guess that the next step is to combine the two to come up with a more secure firewall solution. When using both a packet filter and one or more application proxies, you can start to understand why a firewall is more a system than it is a single entity.

There are many ways you can combine these two technologies. However, no matter how you configure your packet filter or how hard you work at designing an application proxy, it is always possible that you will need another solution. When designing your firewall, you should examine the strengths and weaknesses of each strategy to decide which applies best to your situation. Again, review your security policy and choose a firewall architecture that can provide the best enforcement of that policy.

When reviewing these strategies, you will come across terms such as *bastion host* and *DMZ*. These terms describe important firewall components that can, when put to their proper use, go a long way toward providing for a secure firewall. These terms are covered in greater detail throughout the remainder of the chapter.

Using a Dual-Homed Host

A router that connects the network to the Internet must have at least two network interfaces. One is used to connect to your LAN, whereas the other makes the connection to the outside world. Each network interface has its own unique IP address. Based on rules that you configure, the router makes decisions on which packets to forward from one interface to the other.

A *dual-homed host* functions in a similar manner. A computer is configured with two network interfaces and, like the router, one adapter connects to the internal LAN, whereas the other connects to the Internet (see Figure 4.2). However, unlike a router, many operating systems recognize that two adapters have been installed and automatically forward packets from one interface to the other if that is what it takes to get the packet delivered to its destination. In other words, the dual-homed host operates as a router. This routing function is usually called *IP forwarding*, and it must be disabled if you are to use the computer as a component of the firewall.

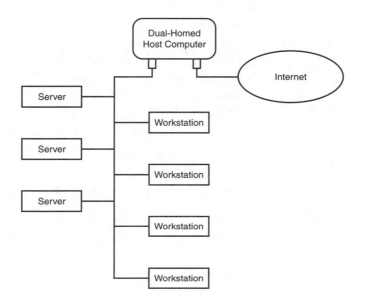

FIGURE 4.2
A dual-homed host can be used to mediate network traffic between your LAN and the Internet.

When you place a dual-homed host between your LAN and the Internet, the client computers on the LAN are no longer directly reachable from the Internet. The network packets that come in from clients on the LAN through one interface are controlled by the application proxy software running on the dual-homed computer. The proxy software determines whether the client's request is allowed and then proceeds to make a request for the client by sending out packets on the external interface. If your site has high security requirements, you might not want to use a dual-homed host computer as your only protection from the Internet. Computer operating systems are very complex animals and it is very difficult to absolutely guarantee that no security-related holes exist. Windows NT, for example, is composed of literally millions of lines of code. Every now and then someone discovers a new bug that can be exploited to compromise your security. You need to keep up-to-date on security advisories issued by your vendors and obtain new patches or updates to fix any new problems as they are discovered.

Another difference between using a dual-homed host and a packet-filtering router is that the dual-homed host usually operates as an application proxy server, not as a packet filter. Instead of using a rule base to make decisions on which packets to forward between interfaces, the dual-homed host runs one or more proxy applications.

Using a Screened Host

The screened host firewall architecture takes advantage of the protective capabilities of both a packet filter and an application proxy gateway. In this setup, shown in Figure 4.3, a packet filter is used to connect to the Internet, and a proxy server is used to provide services to clients on the Internal LAN.

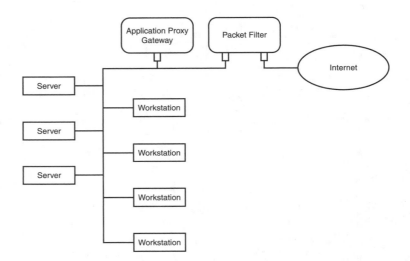

FIGURE 4.3
A screened host firewall provides the protection of both a packet filter and an application proxy gateway.

Notice that the proxy server in this figure does not make use of two network interfaces. The packet filter is configured so that traffic arriving from the Internet side is allowed to pass only if it is destined for the proxy server that sits on the protected side. The same goes for clients on the internal LAN. Although the proxy server and its clients are connected to the same subnet and it is possible for a client workstation to send packets directly to the packet filter, they are rejected. The packet filter only allows communications coming into the LAN that are targeted at the proxy server and only accepts outbound packets that come from the proxy server.

Of course, this all depends on the proper configuration of the packet filter. Although it is impossible for packets to travel between the Internet and the LAN with a proxy service when using a dual-homed host, that limitation does not apply here. For example, there might be services you need to use, but for which there is no proxy application. In that case, it is a simple matter to configure the packet filter to allow certain kinds of packets to be routed between clients on the internal LAN and the Internet while forcing all other services to use the proxy gateway. The decision to allow clients to communicate directly with the router and bypass the proxy server should be based on your security policy.

Using a Screened Subnet to Create a Demilitarized Zone (DMZ)

Carrying the screened host concept a little further, you can probably guess what the screened subnet architecture is. Again, a packet filter is used to provide the initial security between the LAN and the Internet. In Figure 4.4, however, you can see that another router has been added to the configuration.

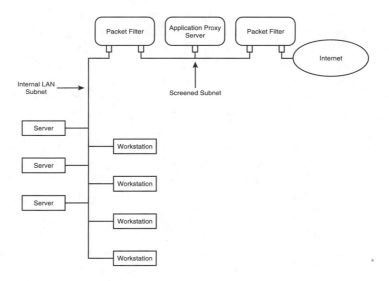

FIGURE 4.4
A screened subnet architecture uses two packet filters to isolate the LAN from the Internet.

This combination of routers creates an additional network segment between the Internet and your LAN. The router that connects to the Internet operates in a manner similar to the way a router in a screened host architecture does. It allows communications from the outside world to be made with specific hosts that run application proxies. Clients on the internal LAN still communicate with the application proxy servers, which are still responsible for acting on the client's behalf with servers residing on the Internet. The second router, which connects the LAN to this screened network segment, provides additional security because all traffic that flows between the LAN clients and the proxy servers must first go through it. To

101

operate properly, the external router is configured to allow traffic between a proxy server on the screened subnet and the external network. The internal router allows traffic to flow only between the internal client computer and a proxy server in the screened subnet.

The term demilitarized zone (or DMZ) is sometimes used to refer to this screened subnet that stands between the LAN and the Internet. In Figure 4.4, there is only one proxy server in the DMZ. Notice also that it is not dual-homed. The routers that bound the DMZ make sure that no network traffic from the Internet can travel directly to computers on the LAN, so the proxy server does not have to provide this functionality. The proxy server only needs one network adapter to communicate with either internal LAN clients or the external router.

There is another advantage to be gained by using a DMZ in your firewall configuration. When using a dual-homed host computer as a proxy server, you inevitably experience some slowdown in network traffic between the internal LAN and the Internet. This is because a computer and the operating system that it runs are not designed with optimizing network communications in mind. A computer must perform multiple tasks, such as running user applications and managing peripheral devices such as the keyboard or a printer. A router, however, *is* designed with speed in mind. A router doesn't have to worry about queuing up disk access requests, running programs, or displaying high-resolution graphics on a monitor. Instead, it monitors the network interfaces that are attached to it and does the best it can to decide on how to get packets to their destination.

In Figure 4.5, you can see that the DMZ can be a place to connect multiple proxy servers. By using more than one computer for this purpose, possibly a separate computer for each service to be proxied, you will find that management tasks are made much less complicated. If your network users make heavy use of services that must flow through proxy servers, using multiple servers will also most likely provide a faster, more efficient service as opposed to using a single computer to run all the services.

There are other types of hosts that should be considered as candidates for placement in the DMZ. If you manage your own Web server, for example, you could connect it directly to the Internet and rely only on the computer's security mechanisms to protect it from possible attack. If you place the Web server in the DMZ, however, you can greatly enhance its security. The packet-filtering router that stands between the DMZ and the Internet could be configured to allow HTTP Web traffic with the Web server, but at the same time it could deny FTP access. Instead, the inner router, which connects the DMZ to your LAN, can be configured so that Web development staff can use FTP to transfer files to the Web server.

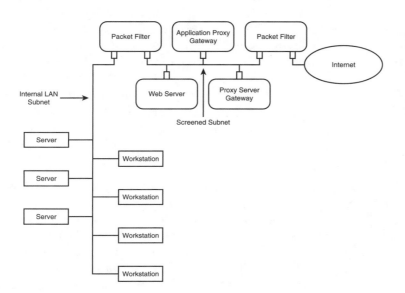

FIGURE 4.5
You can locate multiple proxy servers, along with other types of servers, in the DMZ.

Another excellent candidate for DMZ placement is a modem pool. If you go to the expense of establishing and managing a firewall, wouldn't it be foolish to install modems on computers located on the LAN? A modem on one of your user's desktop systems provides a backdoor into the LAN and creates a single point of failure for all your security. *The security of your network is only as good as the weakest link in the network!* Although you might enforce a rigid password protection policy at your site and although you might think that there is no chance that a user account will ever be compromised, is it really worth taking the chance? If you have ever had to dismiss an employee under less than ideal circumstances, I'm sure you will understand this point. Although you can easily deactivate the employee's user account so that he cannot successfully dial back into the network through the desktop machine, you will probably not be able to prove beyond a doubt that this former employee hasn't discovered the password to other accounts.

Using Bastion Hosts and Sacrificial Hosts

Multiple Screened Subnets

You can extend the concept of the screened subnet even further by creating multiple screened subnets that are placed between your LAN and the Internet. For example, instead of using just two routers to create a single screened subnet, you can use three to create two subnets. The outer screened subnet is the most vulnerable subnet and can used for hosts that run services that are not as easy to trust or that do not work as securely as you would like them to. On the inner screened subnet, you can place hosts running services that require additional protection.

To make this concept work, it is important to note that you do not configure all the routers with the same packet-filtering rules. If you did, getting past the second router would be no more difficult than getting past the first one, and so on.

Also, it is a common practice to use different firewall products (packet filter or application proxy) on different screened subnets. Why? If the hacker has already been able to compromise one component of the firewall, his job becomes more difficult if he has to start over when trying to get through the next component.

When you use a screened subnet architecture and place multiple proxy servers in the DMZ that is created, it should be obvious that the computers running the proxy applications need to be highly secured. Whereas client computers on the internal LAN are protected from direct connections from the Internet, the proxy servers are specifically designed to accept this kind of traffic. Although a packet filter does provide some protection for the proxy servers, it cannot guarantee that nothing can harm them. Thus, it is important to concentrate on the security mechanisms provided by the computer's operating system to ensure that you have done all you can to make them capable of withstanding attack from malicious sources on the Internet.

SEE ALSO

➤ *For more information about security programs, see Appendix B, "Other Security Tools You Can Use."*

The term *bastion host* is used to identify a computer host system that has been especially prepared for this kind of work. The bastion host has been hardened by removing unnecessary applications and services and by carefully using security tools provided by the underlying operating system. The very fact that the bastion host computer is more exposed to the Internet than clients on the internal LAN means that it needs to use every trick in the book to enforce its own host-based security.

Unlike workstations or servers on the internal LAN, the bastion host is exposed to attack from would-be evildoers on the Internet.

Because the bastion host resides in the DMZ, the security mechanisms of the operating system are critical to its success.

SEE ALSO

➤ *An in-depth discussion of using a bastion host can be found in Chapter 6, "Using a Bastion Host."*

Another kind of system that you might want to place in the DMZ is, in a manner of speaking, the opposite of the bastion host. A *sacrificial host* is a computer that is used to lure prospective hackers. Instead of trying to keep out a potential evildoer, the sacrificial host computer allows them in and, in most cases, tracks their steps, recording information that might later be helpful in tracking them down or in better securing your network. Another handy feature of using this kind of host is that it can keep hackers busy so that they don't try harder and end up locating more important hosts on your network and trying to break into them.

Creating a sacrificial host need not be an expensive proposition. Because the computer won't be used in production mode, you don't have to select a system with the fastest CPU or with other superior equipment, such as a high-resolution monitor or extensive disk storage capacity. Instead, you can simply recycle an older computer that you no longer have any use for. What is important is that you configure the computer so that it is not too difficult for it to be compromised, yet is difficult enough to keep the hacker busy so that you can begin to track him down.

Incident Reporting and Response

A good site security policy is only going to protect your network if you enforce the policy. Simply creating a written document and filing it away does nothing to protect you. To make the policy work, you need to develop methods of monitoring computer and network usage and come up with specific actions that will be taken when the policy is violated.

Many firewall products can be configured to sound alarms when suspicious actions take place. Most also produce log files that can be reviewed periodically. Decide ahead of time just how you will react to specific alarms and create escalation procedures that can be used to document the problem and repair the damage. It is an almost impossible task to anticipate every kind of security breach that might occur on your network. Thus, escalation procedures should be something that you can modify and add to as new problems arise.

For example, when reviewing a log file that shows user accounts that have been used to Telnet into a server, you find that a user account you thought had been deleted still exists and is being used to infiltrate your network. What should you do? Some possible immediate steps might be the following:

- Change the password for the suspected user account.
- Disconnect the compromised server or workstation from the network.

Monitor All Hosts that Live in the DMZ

Because a bastion host usually resides in the DMZ, it is the computer that is most susceptible to attack. Although you can take extreme measures to protect the bastion host by removing unnecessary services and user accounts and by using all the operating system's security mechanisms, you should never assume that this computer is totally safe. Thus, be sure to regularly review all log files produced by the operating system or the proxy software so that you can detect an unwanted intrusion before it becomes a major problem. For UNIX systems, you can also use a product such as Tripwire. This program uses cryptographic hashes of important system files to detect whether changes have been made. If an intruder has gained entry to the bastion host and has planted a Trojan horse or has modified an important file, this program usually detects it.

You can download an open-source version of Tripwire from `ftp://coast.cs.purdue.edu/pub/COAST/Tripwire`. A commercial version of Tripwire can be purchased from Tripwire Security Systems, Inc., and they can be reached at `www.tripwiresecurity.com`.

- Disconnect the network from the outside world by unplugging the router if you find that many computers have been compromised.

Instead of changing the password for the user account, you might want to delete the user account so that there is not chance it will be used to get into the system again. However, because this account is a common point of reference between you and the malicious person who has broken into your network, it might be a better idea to change the password and then actively monitor the situation so that you can gather further information that can be used to identify and track down this person.

After you have responded to a hole in your security and have effectively plugged it up, consider what other steps have to be taken to determine the extent of damage, if any, that was done and what you have to do to repair it. If a database has been manipulated, do you want to restore the files from a backup? If so, how far back do you go in your sequence of backups to be sure you have files that have not been tampered with? How do you re-create records for good information that has been added by your users between the time of the backup and the security breach? Depending on the type of information, are there any legal issues you have to consider?

If you think about these things ahead of time and create written incident reporting and response procedures, you will find your job to be a lot easier when something does happen.

Keeping Up-to-date on Security Advisories

Managing most ordinary computer applications, such as a word processor or an Internet browser, usually involves reading the documentation and performing routine tasks. Managing a firewall is not so simple. In addition to installing and configuring the firewall, you should make use of all available logging, alarm, and notification mechanisms that are provided. Checking log files on a weekly basis would be a foolish idea. Checking log files on a daily basis would be more appropriate. When you configure alarms or other notification mechanisms, be sure that they are configured so that the report gets to someone who is actually in a position to respond to it within a short amount of time.

Maintaining security is not a static business. It is an ongoing process of evaluating and responding to new software bugs and problems as they are discovered. If you have purchased a commercial firewall product, be sure to read any security advisories issued by the vendor as soon as you get them. New software patches should be evaluated and installed on a timely basis if they are pertinent to your network and its software or firewall.

In addition, there are many resources on the Internet that can be used to help you keep yourself up-to-date on new situations that can cause a compromise to your network security. In Appendix C, "Additional Resources," you will find a listing of many good sites, such as FIRST (Forum of Incident Response and Security Teams) and CERT (Computer Emergency Response Team). These organizations, along with others listed in the appendix, also have mailing lists that you can subscribe to so that you can help yourself stay informed.

Configuring a firewall is not something that you do and forget. It is an ongoing process of monitoring, evaluating, and updating.

Summary

Before you begin to build (or buy) a firewall, you need understand fully the security policies that are enforced at your site. If you do not already have written security policies, you really should develop them before you even begin to think about a firewall. The security policy needs to be flexible enough to allow your users to accomplish their jobs, yet restrictive enough to reasonably prevent your network from being compromised. Remember that an overly-harsh security policy might result in two undesirable consequences: users not getting work done and users finding other methods to subvert the policies you establish. The security policy you develop should be fair and should be developed with input from the departments and users it will affect.

The way you design your firewall depends on several factors, including the degree of security necessary for your site as well as your budget. Although a simple packet-filtering router is cheap—it's free if you already have router connecting you to the Internet—it provides only a minimal amount of protection. A more complex design, using

Keep Log Files for at Least a Year!

Log files, whether produced by the operating system, application software, or the firewall, can be a very useful weapon for tracking down hackers and determining how the network or computer system was compromised. Because a computer virus, or other malicious program such as a Trojan Horse, can hide in your network for many months before becoming activated, it is a good idea to keep log files for a long time. It is a simple matter to write a script file (or command procedure, depending on your operating system) that can regularly archive log files to another system or to a backup device. Keep these log files for at least a year before recycling the backup media.

multiple screened subnets, can quickly become an expensive proposition, both in its creation and in its maintenance.

Finally, the security you enjoy for your network is only as good as it is up-to-date. New bugs are being found every day in software applications and operating systems. If you don't know about the latest security advisories, you might not be protected from them.

chapter

5

Packet Filtering

The First Line of Defense •

IP Header Information That Can
Be Used to Filter Packets •

TCP and UDP Header Information •

ICMP Packets •

Stateless Operation Verses
Stateful Inspection •

Hardware and Software Packet Filters •

Advantages and Disadvantages
of Packet Filters •

The First Line of Defense

Screening routers were the first firewalls. You usually think of a router as a network device that's job is to make decisions on how to forward a packet so that it can eventually be delivered. The addition of access control lists allows a router to also screen which packets are allowed to flow through its network interfaces. This simple method of forwarding or dropping a packet based on rules that the network administrator supplies is the basis of a packet filter. The screening router performs a filtering function so that only packets that meet certain criteria are allowed to pass through them.

In previous chapters, you learned a little about packet filters. The most important thing to remember is that a packet filter should never be the only method you use to build a firewall. It should be considered the first device you use, and it should be backed up by one or more proxy servers and, in some architectures, another router.

Where to Use Packet Filters

In Figure 5.1, you can see three different scenarios that employ a router to filter packets before they are delivered to your LAN. In each of these cases the screening router is positioned closest to the Internet connection. That is, it lies at the perimeter of the network and acts as a *gatekeeper*.

In the first instance, the router screens packets before they are delivered to a dual-homed host computer. The router is acting as a packet filter. The dual-homed host computer has been configured in a very secure manner as a bastion host. Unnecessary services and user accounts have been removed from this computer and the operating system has been modified so that no packets are automatically forwarded from one interface to the other. The result of this is that no IP packet is allowed to travel directly from the local network to the Internet. Instead, software on the dual-homed host (application proxies) is responsible for talking to clients on the internal network and interacting with servers on the Internet on behalf of those clients.

SEE ALSO

➤ *For more information on configuring a bastion host, see Chapter 6, "Using a Bastion Host."*

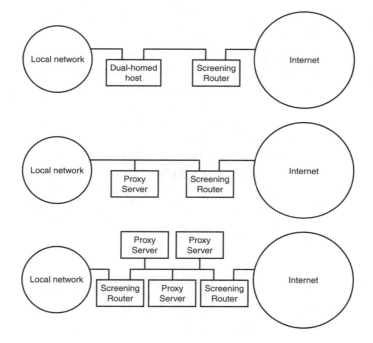

In the second case, you can see that it is not absolutely necessary to use a dual-homed computer to host the proxy services. One connection suffices. However, in this type of setup, it is important that the router be configured so that it allows packets to travel between the Internet and the proxy server and does not allow any traffic to pass directly from the Internet to the internal LAN. This design is usually called a *screened-host configuration*. It is considered less secure than using a dual-homed host for proxy applications. This is because clients on the internal network need to be configured correctly so that they send packets to the proxy server and do not attempt to directly communicate with servers on the Internet.

From a security standpoint, it is easier for you to control the security configuration on the dual-host computer than it is to control the security configuration on every client in your network. Although you might have policies and procedures in effect that control how clients are configured, a malicious employee can always reconfigure his workstation to bypass the proxy server. A Trojan Horse program planted by an intruder can also do the same. Forcing all IP traffic to flow through the dual-host computer gives you a single choke point to control Internet access.

The third configuration, which employs two routers, creates a subnet between the Internet and the internal LAN and is referred to as a *screened subnet*. Host computers that reside on the screened subnet are protected by the router connected to the Internet. To further protect clients on the internal LAN, another router is used. When using a screened subnet, you can place one host or many hosts on the screened subnet. Because you have an extra router in place to screen traffic before it gets to the internal LAN, it is okay to place some computers on the screened subnet that aren't necessarily configured as securely as a hardened bastion host. For example, in addition to proxy servers, the subnet can also hold Web servers, modem pools, and other servers.

SEE ALSO
➤ *For more information about using a dual-homed host, as well as a screened host and screened subnet, see Chapter 4, "Firewall Security Policy and Firewall Design Strategies".*

The point of reviewing this is to understand that how you configure a packet filter does, in the end, depend on the use to which it is put. If you use a setup similar to the first case, the screening router can be configured to filter out a lot of unwanted traffic, but the dual-homed host is responsible for any interaction that clients on the internal LAN have with servers outside the network. In this case, you might not have to use a lot of complicated rules to configure the router.

In the second case, the router has to be configured securely to prevent any packet not addressed to the proxy server from getting through. In the last case, the router closest to the Internet can be configured in a more lax manner, but the router closest to the internal LAN needs to be configured very securely, allowing only communication between the proxy servers (or other hosts) and clients on the internal LAN. This situation could make for some complex rules. For example, most of your clients might need to communicate with a proxy server so that you can provide Web access or other popular services. If you have a Web server sitting on the screened subnet, you might want to configure the router so that only a very few select clients are able to communicate with it. These would be the workstations for users who are responsible for producing the Web content you provide to the Internet.

Another consideration for packet filters involves using multiple firewalls in a large network to separate a company's network into functional components. For example, the security requirements of a company's research division might have different security and Internet connectivity requirements than those of the accounting and manufacturing departments. Thus, it might be useful to use a firewall between the LANs that make up these departments. In this situation, your rules are probably easier to configure because you already have a firewall at the perimeter of the network to take care of the outside world.

In any case, remember that the packet filter, whether it is a router or a host computer with packet filtering software, needs to be configured according to how you set up your firewall. To make a packet filter, there is no easy answer to the question of "what rules do I need to configure?" It depends on what services you want to provide, to whom you want to provide them, and how you want to go about doing so.

Creating Packet Filtering Rules

To decide how you will configure the rules on a packet filter, first make decisions about the following:

- What services do you want to offer on the network, and in which direction (internal to external, or external to internal) do you want them to work?

- Do you want to limit any of your internal host computers' ability to connect to Internet services?

- Are there any trusted hosts on the Internet that will need some form of access to your internal network?

The kinds of information that you can use to create rules varies a little from one product to the other, but in general, you will find the following items to be the most useful:

- **Interface and direction** Whether the packet is arriving or leaving your network, and which interface it is passing through to do this.

- **Source and destination IP addresses** You need to be able to check both where a packet says it is coming from (source IP address) and where it wants to go (destination IP address).

- **IP options**   You need to be able to check this field, especially to prevent source routing.

- **Higher level protocol**   The type of protocol that is making use of the IP packet. For example, TCP or UDP.

- **For TCP packets, the ACK bit**   Checking this field can help determine if a connection attempt is being made, and in which direction.

- **If ICMP (Internet Control Message Protocol), the message type**   You can prevent some attempts to probe for information about your network.

- **Source and destination ports for TCP and UDP packets**   This information can help you figure out which services are being used.

When creating rules on a packet filter, there are several important conventions to follow.

First, for rules that are used to permit or deny access by a host or a network, use the IP address, not the host or domain name. Although it is not terribly difficult to spoof an IP address or a hostname, for many kinds of attacks, a spoofed IP address doesn't work simply because if the hacker expects a response and uses a spoofed IP address, he likely will not get the response back without a lot of work. Spoofing a host or domain name is a simple matter if the hacker has access to the DNS database. In this case, the name might look familiar to you, but the address it translates to might not be the one you would expect.

SEE ALSO

➤ *For more information about IP spoofing, see Chapter 3, "Security and the Internet."*

Don't return all ICMP codes via the external interface. They can reveal information to an attacker, specifically which packets get in and which do not. Returning ICMP codes for only some packets can tell the attacker that there indeed is a packet filtering mechanism in place. In this situation, any information about your network is better than none to the hacker. One of the primary functions of a firewall is to hide information about your internal network. By the process of elimination, a hacker can find out what doesn't work and eventually find out what does. If you don't return ICMP codes, you help to limit the information available to an informed hacker.

Reject all packets entering through the external network adapter that have source addresses that can only originate from inside the protected network. These packets are probably from someone trying to use address spoofing to get through your security. I've discussed this before, but it bears repeating here. There is always the chance that someone on your internal network has created another connection to the Internet, perhaps by mistake if another router has been misconfigured or if a dial-up line has been installed without your knowledge. You should always be aware that a firewall can't protect you from attack (or stupidity) from within. Remember that regular monitoring and vigilance must be maintained for normal security measures, such as understanding what is on your network and how it is supposed to be configured.

Dangerous Services

Some services are more dangerous than others. TCP/IP was created in a time before the Internet allowed commercial and home use. It was an internetwork of networks from military and academic sites and a few large companies that did business with both. Some of the security issues that are so important today were not even thought of when TCP/IP was developed or when some of the more popular network services were created. Some "dangerous" services you should definitely not allow to pass through the firewall include the following:

- **Network File System (NFS)**   If you allow this kind of traffic to pass through the firewall, it is possible that someone outside your network will be able to mount a file system from your network and access files and directories just as if they were connected to the local LAN.

- **Network Information Services (NIS)**   This service, which was once known as "Yellow Pages," can give out valuable information to hackers, such as the names of hosts and users on your network.

- **X Windows**   There are many security problems caused by using X clients and servers. In addition to the problems associated with how applications are run and privileges used, allowing an X Window session can be as damaging as a Telnet session.

Remember to deny all services with a rule at the end of your rule list. Only open up services that you specifically know will be used by your clients and only in the direction that is safe for the service. If you use services such as Telnet or FTP through the firewall, be sure to use a version that provides for some form of strong authentication or the use of a proxy service, as is explained in the chapter that follows this one.

IP Header Information That Can Be Used to Filter Packets

In general, packet filters usually operate only on the header information found in the packet. Because there are several different protocol headers in each packet, you will look at the ones that are important to packet filtering. Header information found at the Ethernet frame level is not used by most packet filters. The source address and other similar information is of little use because it is either a local MAC hardware address for a system on the local LAN or the same for a router responsible for the last leg of a packet's journey through the Internet.

Next up in the protocol stack would be the IP packet header information. In Figure 5.2 you can see that this information is very limited in the header of an IP packet.

FIGURE 5.2
Fields in the IP header can be used to select packets for filtering.

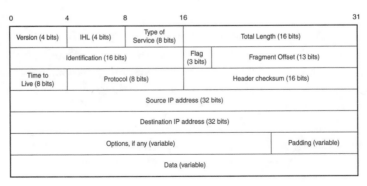

What useful information can the packet filter use from this header? There are three important pieces of information here:

- **IP Address**   Both source and destination address
- **Protocols**   Such as TCP, UDP and ICMP
- **IP Options**   Such as source routing

The most obvious piece of information that can be used is the source and destination address fields. If you have only a limited number of host computers on the Internet that you want to allow through the firewall, you can filter incoming packets based on their source address. The same thing works in reverse: You can filter packets coming from inside your network so that only certain destination addresses are allowed to get through the firewall and onto the Internet.

The next IP header field that can be useful is the Protocol field. This field defines the protocol that the packet payload will be used for. This can be, for example, TCP or UDP, the two principal transport protocols used on the Internet. It can also be something such as ICMP. As a rule, drop packets for any protocol that is not used on your network or that can allow someone outside of your network to reconfigure how your network operates. For example, some of the uses to which ICMP can be put include telling your routers that a destination is not reachable or telling your router to reconfigure its tables to change the route to a particular network. If you want to look at the list, use a search engine to find Request For Comments 1700.

TCP and UDP Header Information

Every layer in the protocol stack adds header information to the data it receives from a layer above it. Because IP is used by other protocols, such as TCP and UDP, you can expect that inside the data portion of the IP packet there will be header information placed by those protocols. Some of this information is very useful for filtering packets. In Figure 5.3, you can see the layout of the TCP header. This header information is sometimes referred to as the *TCP Protocol Data Unit*.

Remember that TCP is responsible for establishing a reliable connection-oriented session between two applications across a network. TCP receives data (called *messages*) from layers above it in the protocol stack, adds its own header information, and then passes it to the IP layer, which then adds its own header information. The message sent to TCP from applications up the stack is usually called a *stream* of data because the amount of data can vary and is not limited to a set number of bytes. TCP takes these messages and, if they are too large to fit into a packet, breaks them into smaller segments and sends each segment in a separate packet. The TCP layer at the receiving end reassembles these messages before passing them up to an application.

FIGURE 5.3
The TCP protocol header fields can also be used for filtering packets.

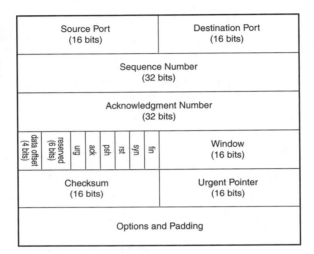

Most of the header information you looked at in the IP header was used for routing the packet through the Internet—the source and destination addresses, for example. The information in the TCP header is concerned with other issues, such as reliability of the connection and ordering of the messages that are being sent. Quickly review the fields that TCP uses:

- **Source port** This is a 16-bit field used to identify the port being used by the application sending the data.
- **Destination port** This is a 16-bit field used to identify the port where the packet will be delivered on the receiving end of the connection.
- **Sequence number** This is a 32-bit field that is used to identify where a segment fits in the larger message when a message is broken into fragments for transmission.
- **Acknowledgement number** This is a 32-bit field that is used to indicate what the next sequence number should be.
- **Data offset** This is a 4-bit field that is used to specify the number of 32-bit words that make up the header. This field is used to calculate the start of the data portion of the packet.

- **Reserved**   These 6 bits were reserved for future use and, because they were never used, are to be set to zeros.

- **URG flag**   When this bit is set to 1, the field titled Urgent Pointer points to a section of the data portion of the packet that is flagged as "urgent."

- **ACK flag**   This is the acknowledgement bit. If set to 1, the packet is an acknowledgment. If set to 0, the packet is not an acknowledgement.

- **PSH flag**   This bit, if set to 1, indicates a push function; otherwise, it is set to 0.

- **RST flag**   This bit, if set to 1, is a signal that the connection is to be reset; otherwise, it is set to 0.

- **SYN flag**   This bit, if set to 1, indicates that the sequence numbers are to be synchronized. If set to 0, the sequence numbers are not to be synchronized.

- **FIN flag**   This bit, if set to 1, specifies that the sender is finished sending information. Otherwise, it is set to 0.

- **Window**   This 16-bit field is used to specify how many blocks of data the receiving computer is able to accept at this time.

- **Checksum**   This 16-bit field is a calculated value used to verify the integrity of both the header and data portions of the packet.

- **Urgent Pointer**   If the URG flag is set, this 16-bit field points to the offset from the sequence number field in the data portion of the packet where urgent data is stored. TCP does not use this field itself, but applications above TCP in the stack do.

- **Options**   This field can be of variable length and is similar to the options field in the IP header. One function this field is used for is to specify the maximum segment size.

Because the options field can vary, the header is padded with extra bits so that it will be a multiple of 32.

With all this information available to TCP, you can see that it would be possible for TCP to exert a great deal of control over the connection. By manipulating some of these fields, hackers can also exert a great degree of control over a connection. For example, by manipulating the ACK and SYN flag bits, hackers are able to use denial-of-service attacks called SYN flooding. By manipulating TCP header information, especially the sequence and acknowledgement numbers, it is possible to "hijack" a TCP connection.

The UDP header is much smaller than the TCP header. In Figure 5.4, you can see that it only has four fields, and of these only two, the source and destination ports, are useful for packet filtering.

FIGURE 5.4
The UDP protocol uses a smaller header.

Source Port (16 bits)	Destination Port (16 bits)
Length (16 bits)	Checksum (16 bits)

UDP is a connectionless protocol that does not guarantee delivery or do much of anything else except to send the data out onto the network.

Ports and Sockets

The two important fields in both of these headers that are used by packet filters are the source and destination ports. If you haven't read the introduction to TCP in Chapter 2, you might wonder what a port is used for. After all, the source and destination addresses in the IP header are used to identify the two machines in the network sending packets to each other. So why are ports necessary?

Ports are used to identify the application end-points of the connection. Because a particular computer can have more than one application using the TCP stack at the same time, there must be a way to differentiate which packets go to which applications. For example, suppose you've established a Telnet session with a remote computer and decide you want to download a file to that computer. Telnet doesn't transfer files, so you would have to open an FTP connection. Because the source and destination addresses would be the same in the IP packet for both of these sessions, port numbers are used to indicate the application.

When you combine an address with a port number, you have an identifier that can uniquely identify both of the endpoints of a communication. The name used for this combination of numbers is a *socket*. This is illustrated in Figure 5.5, where two computers have established two communication sessions, one for Telnet (port 23) and one for FTP (port 20). FTP actually uses two ports—port 20 for sending data and port 21 for exchanging command information.

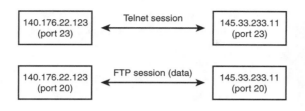

It should become quickly apparent to you why a packet filter would find these port numbers useful. Instead of having to permit or deny packets based only on their source or destination address—and thereby allow or disallow *all* communications—it is possible to selectively allow or disallow individual *services*. Although you might not want your users to Telnet to a remote host computer (or vice versa), you might not care if they exchange files via anonymous FTP sessions. By using port numbers in packet filtering rules, you can enable or disable network services one at a time.

In the original BSD implementation of TCP/IP, port numbers from 0–1023 were called *privileged* ports. That is, they were to be used by programs that run as root on the UNIX machine, and these programs are usually the server program for a particular service. Following this convention, client programs would choose a port number that was greater than 1023. Although this is not something that has been standardized in an RFC, it is still commonplace to find other TCP/IP stacks that adhere to this.

This information can be put to good use when creating packet filtering rules. A good packet filter allows you to specify *both* the source and destination ports in the rules you create. Some older routers did not allow specifying the source port, and this can lead to some very large holes in your firewall security.

For example, look at a few sample rules that you might create to allow incoming and outgoing SMTP connections so that email can be delivered. In this first example, only the destination port is allowed in the rule:

Rule	Direction	Protocol	Source Address	Dest. Address	Dest. Port	Action
1	inbound	TCP	external	internal	25	allow
2	outbound	TCP	internal	external	>= 1024	allow
3	outbound	TCP	internal	external	25	allow
4	inbound	TCP	external	internal	>= 1024	allow
5	*	*	*	*	*	disallow

In this example, you can see that rules 1 and 3 allow for inbound or outbound connections to port 25, which is the port usually used by SMTP. Rule 1 allows an external host to send a request to port 25 on a server inside your network. Rule 2 would allow that server on your network to reply to the SMTP server, assuming it had used a source port number greater than 1023 because the rule allows connections to ports greater than or equal to 1024.

Rules 3 and 4 allow an SMTP connect in the reverse direction, where the SMTP server on your internal LAN wants to make a connection to port 25 on an SMTP server residing on the external network. The last rule, number 5, disallows any other connections. So, it looks like we've written a few good rules that will keep the internal LAN safe while allowing SMTP connections in both directions. Right?

Wrong. Remember that when creating a set of rules for a packet filter you have to look at all of the rules together and not just at one or two at a time. In the example you just looked at, rules 2 and 5 allow a connection, either inbound or outbound, for any service that uses ports that are greater than 1023. This hole can be used by hackers to do all sorts of things, including communicating with a Trojan horse program.

To fix this set of rules, you need to be able to specify the source port in addition to the destination port. Look at the next example:

Rule	Direction	Protocol	Source Address	Dest. Address	Source Port	Dest. Port	Action
1	inbound	TCP	external	internal	>= 1024	25	allow
2	outbound	TCP	internal	external	25	>= 1024	allow
3	outbound	TCP	internal	external	>= 1024	25	allow
4	inbound	TCP	external	internal	25	>= 1024	allow
5	*	*	*	*	*	*	disallow

From this, you can see that rules 2 and 5 no longer allow a connection between two ports that are greater than 1023. Instead, those connections must be tied, at one end of the connection, to the SMTP port number of 25.

The *SYN* Bit

In Figure 5.3, one of the bit fields is named SYN. This synchronization bit is set when a request is sent during the initial connection attempt indicating that sequence numbers should be synchronized. Setting up a connection is much more time-consuming than managing one already being used to exchange data. The overhead involves many CPU cycles as the TCP layer creates entries in its state table for the new connection.

Why is this of concern when configuring a firewall? One of the more common methods of attack is the denial of service. A SYN *flood* is nothing more than a hacker continuously sending packets with the SYN bit set so that the targeted computer spends its valuable CPU time trying to set up a new connection and allocating memory for it. Although you can't filter out all packets that have the SYN bit set, you can monitor log files to find hosts that repeatedly try to send these kinds of packets so that those particular hosts don't get past the firewall.

The *ACK* Bit

Another bit field you can see in Figure 5.3 is the ACK, or acknowledgement bit. This field is set only after a connection has been established. The first packet sent to request a connection has this bit cleared. At the other end of the connection this bit is set and a reply is sent back. By examining this bit and looking at the direction of the communication, it is possible to create rules in the packet filter only allowing a connection in the direction you want—inbound or outbound.

For example, suppose you want to allow your clients to establish a Telnet session from their workstation to a server on the Internet, but you don't want the same thing to work in reverse. You could use rules that are similar to the following:

Rule	Direction	Protocol	Source Address	Dest. Address	Source Port	Dest. Port	ACK	Action
1	outbound	TCP	internal	external	>= 1024	23	both	allow
2	inbound	TCP	external	internal	23	>=1024	SET	allow
3	*	*	*	*	*	*	*	disallow

Here, you can see that rule 1 allows a host on your internal LAN to send out a packet to a Telnet server on the Internet. This is because the port number for the destination port is the Telnet server port of 23 and because you allow the packet to pass through the filter if the ACK bit is cleared or if it is set. The first packet the internal host will send to port 23 will have this bit cleared, whereas subsequent packets will have it set. That's why you have to allow for both situations for this outbound rule.

The second rule allows the Telnet server on the Internet to send packets back to your internal host. The server will not be able to start a Telnet session because you have indicated in this rule that the ACK bit must be set or the packet will be dropped. Because the ACK bit is cleared for an initial connection request, this should be enough to keep an external computer from starting a Telnet session with a server on your internal LAN. Of course, this all depends on you having a secure server that has not had some hacked version of a Telnet server placed on it. Once again, remember that the firewall, especially the packet filter, is only the first line of defense. You still need to maintain tight control over security on hosts in your network.

ICMP Packets

The Internet Control Message Protocol is used by TCP/IP stacks to send control and management information to each other. For example, one type of ICMP message is called a *source quench* message. This message type is sent by a computer to tell the sending side of the connection to stop sending packets. This is used for flow control so the receiving end of the connection does not become overwhelmed and discard packets. This message type is one you would probably not want to block using a packet filter because flow control management is important. The *redirect* message can be used to tell a host or router that a different route should be used to get to a particular destination. Using this message type, a hacker can send inaccurate data to your routers and screw up your routing tables.

SEE ALSO

➤ *"The Internet Control Message Protocol (ICMP)", Page 34*

➤ *Page xx, Table 2.1, "ICMP Message Types," Page 35*

ICMP packets can be quite useful, but they can also be used to get information about your network. One important function of a firewall is to keep outsiders from gaining any information about hosts on your network. Because of this, you might want to block several message types, such as the following:

- **Inbound *echo request* and outbound *echo reply* messages** Allow your users to use PING to test connectivity to outside hosts, but not the other way around.

- **Inbound *redirect* messages** These can be used to reconfigure routing tables on your network.

- **Outbound *destination unreachable* and *outbound service unavailable* messages** Don't allow someone to probe your network. By finding out what is not reachable or what services are not offered, the hacker's job is narrowed down.

Stateless Operation Versus Stateful Inspection

Using source and destination ports for making rules about TCP connections is quite useful. This is because TCP is a connection-oriented protocol. UDP, however, is not a connection-oriented protocol. Each UDP packet stands on its own. When used to perform request/reply functions, it can be impossible to determine from each packet's header information whether an incoming packet is something sent in response to an earlier UDP packet. A simple packet filter can't be used to control services that use UDP packets like this. A simple packet filter, called a *stateless* packet filter, makes decisions on a packet-by-packet basis and you cannot create rules that can filter packets based on a relationship between one packet and another.

The technique of *dynamic packet filtering*, also known as *stateful inspection*, takes the concept of packet filtering to a higher level by keeping a table in memory that tries to match up outgoing and incoming packets. The information retained will usually include the source and destination addresses and source and destination ports. A timer is used so that an entry in this table can't be exploited easily. If a response is not forthcoming for a sent packet, the entry in the table will time out so it cannot leave open hole in your security.

Although an older router doesn't provide this kind of functionality, most modern firewalls allow you to perform this type of filtering.

Hardware and Software Packet Filters

If you already have a router connecting your LAN to the Internet, you probably have packet filtering capabilities that could be used as the first part of a firewall. If you think that performance might be a problem, use a dedicated router to do packet filtering and another dedicated router to connect to the Internet. Most routers today would not encounter a performance problem from performing both chores. However, using one router for both purposes can make configuring the rules a little more complex and, thus, a security risk. If you have one person responsible for configuring the router to maintain routing tables, for example, and another who is responsible for the rules used to filter packets, it would be easy for them to step on each other's toes.

In a small network, a single router should pose little risk because you have only a few hosts to worry about and probably fewer services to configure. In a larger network, using dedicated devices is a better choice.

You don't have to actually use a router for the packet-filtering functions of the firewall. A dual-homed host with appropriately configured software could serve as well. Some firewall vendors package packet filters and proxy servers as a system to run on a single host.

A third alternative is a *firewall appliance*. These boxes are being marketed as easy-to-install, fully functional firewalls. Some use a standard UNIX operating system as their underlying platform, whereas others use a proprietary solution. When looking at these kinds of devices, you should weigh their ease of use with the features offered and the flexibility of the command interface and logging options. More about firewall appliances can be found in Chapter 20, "Firewall Appliances."

Using a Router to Restrict Access

Routers differ in the syntax used to create access control lists, or *rules*. Some allow you to create a set of rules that apply to all interfaces equally, both inbound and outbound. Others allow you to specify one set of rules for one interface and another set of rules for another interface. Other products, such as CISCO, allow you to create sets of rules and group them by names, then assign one or more named groups to interfaces individually. When you are looking at buying a router, you might want to keep in mind that a more flexible syntax might make the job of configuration a little more difficult, yet also might make the router easier to adapt to future situations as network connections become more important to your business.

Another consideration for choosing a router is the method you use for entering the rules. Routers usually have an interface to which you can connect a character-cell terminal or a PC to establish a command session. Most routers also allow you to edit configuration files on another system and use a program to download the file to the router. Another common method for exchanging configuration files with a router is to use the Trivial File Transfer Protocol (TFTP). Keeping configuration files offline on another system can also make recovering from a hardware failure or other disaster a much quicker and simpler process.

The rate at which a router can filter packets will probably be greater than your Internet connection. So, for most practical applications, you shouldn't be too concerned about this.

Important features for a packet filtering router include the following:

- Good logging capabilities. Routers usually have limited disk storage, so the ability of routing log information to a `syslogd` daemon on another secure system is a good idea. You should be able to log both packets dropped as well as those permitted through the firewall.

- Uncomplicated command syntax that allows rules to be created based on fields that included the source port for TCP and UDP packets. This is so you can create a tighter set of rules.

- Rules should be evaluated in order. If the router performs some type of "optimization" of the rule set, it can be difficult to diagnose problems when you are testing the firewall.

Using a Dual-Homed Host to Restrict Access

A dual-homed host can serve as both a packet filter and as a proxy server. If you already have a router connecting to the Internet, a

---

Use Caution When Enabling TFTP!

The Trivial File Transfer Protocol was created for purposes such as updating a router or other network device. It allows for a simple file transfer process that doesn't require a lot of overhead. It also does away with a username or password. For this reason, use caution when you use TFTP with a router. Be sure that the service is enabled only when you are using it and not as general practice.

dual-homed host sitting between the inside secured LAN and the router can be an inexpensive method for creating a packet filter. There are literally hundreds of different competing software products that can be used for this purpose. You only have to search the Internet using the text "firewall" to see how many choices there are. Many can even be downloaded for evaluation.

Advantages and Disadvantages of Packet Filters

The packet filter is the first step toward creating a firewall. Compared to proxy servers, packet filters have their advantages and disadvantages. Some of the advantages to be gained by using a packet filter are the following:

- Packet filtering is "free." If you already have a router, it probably supports packet filtering. On a small LAN a single router can be sufficient for use as a packet filter.

- Theoretically, you only need one, at the point where your LAN connects to the Internet or an external network. This provides a "choke point" for the network.

- You don't have to train users or use any special client or server programs to implement packet filters. The screening router or packet filtering host transparently does all the work to the clients in your network.

Some of the more obvious disadvantages posed by packet filters are the following:

- Routers can be difficult to configure, especially if you try using a complex configuration with a large number of rules. In this situation they can also be difficult to test thoroughly.

- When a packet filter fails, or is not configured correctly, the damage that might be done to your network could be much worse than when a proxy server fails. Although a router might allow forwarding of IP packets due to a bug or a misconfigured rule set, when a proxy application breaks, there is no direct forwarding of IP packets. The breakdown of the proxy severs the connection.

- Packet filters work on a small set of data—the header information in the IP packet. Because this is all the information that can be used to decide whether a packet should be allowed to pass through the firewall, a packet filter is limited in the decisions it can make. Stateful inspection techniques improve on this, but you should still consider using proxy servers (in addition to a packet filter) for a complete firewall solution.

- Many packet-filtering routers lack robust logging capabilities, so it is difficult to get a lot of helpful information when a system has been infiltrated or attacked.

Configure the rules for a packet filter carefully so that you can understand exactly why you are trying to protect yourself. Test the rules to make sure they work. Use a packet filter at the perimeter of the network as the first component of the firewall.

Summary

A firewall should be comprised of both a packet filter and application proxies. In this chapter I discussed some of the things you can do with a packet filter and the importance of creating a good set of rules. In the next chapter, you will look at the other important component of a firewall: the application proxy server.

chapter

6

Using a Bastion Host

Configuring a Bastion Host •

Installing a Secure Operating
System from Scratch •

Eliminating Unnecessary Services
and Applications •

Removing Unnecessary
Applications and Files •

Resource Protections
and Access Control •

Configuring Auditing and Logging •

Running Proxy Software
on the Bastion Host •

When the Bastion Host Is
Compromised •

Configuring a Bastion Host

Most large networking shops have standardized configuration procedures that are used when configuring servers or workstations to be placed on the network. Chapter 4, "Firewall Security Policy and Firewall Design Strategies," emphasized the importance of establishing policies that governed how hosts on the network should be configured. In this chapter, you will examine some of the issues that are involved when setting up a particular kind of server on your network—a bastion host. This system should not be bound to the policies you establish for a workstation or ordinary server on the network. Instead, a bastion host configuration requires careful consideration of many issues involving security and functionality.

The term *bastion host* is used to refer to a computer system that has been hardened by increasing security to a degree that would not be practical on an ordinary workstation. A hardened computer makes use of the underlying operating system's resource protections, auditing, and authentication mechanisms to the *fullest* extent. Applications and services that are not needed for the job the bastion host performs are removed from the computer so they cannot become targets for compromise. User accounts are removed from the computer so that only those necessary for the operation of the software that runs on the computer, or those used for the host's administration, remain.

This stripped-down computer is called a bastion host because of the function it serves. A good firewall is composed of more than one device. Usually a router is used to connect the LAN to the Internet, and this router can be configured to perform packet-filtering duties. The packet filter stands as the first line of defense between the LAN and the Internet. Standing behind that packet filter, depending on the architecture you choose for the firewall, is usually one or more bastion host computers providing proxy services for the users on the internal network.

A screened host or screened subnet architecture provides a host or a subnet of several hosts that can be used to provide proxy services behind a packet filter. The computers used for this job are bastion hosts. In a small network, there might be only one server here to provide for company email and a little browsing on the Web. In a large network, it might be necessary to create specialized hosts, each running a proxy for a specific application.

Make a Backup First!

In this chapter, I discuss making edits to configuration files and removing files that are not needed for the operation of the bastion host. After you have installed the operating system and are getting prepared to begin the secure configuration process, make a backup of the system. If you divide the configuration chores up into several major tasks, do a backup between each task. This enables you to backtrack more quickly should you find that something you have done was incorrect or unnecessary.

How you configure the bastion host, however, doesn't have a lot to do with the size of the network. You should configure it in the most secure manner that you can while still allowing it to perform its job. Security is always a balance between user needs and the potential threats to a network. Never forget that there are new threats arising every day on the Internet. Don't take lightly the process of configuring a bastion host. If you have a commercial firewall product, review the vendor's documentation carefully. The documentation for configuring the product should mention any operating system–dependent configuration issues that should be attended to.

Some of the things you will consider in this chapter than can aid you in hardening a computer for bastion host use are the following:

- Installing a secure version of the operating system from scratch.
- Getting rid of unnecessary services.
- Removing end-user applications and applications not related to the bastion host's firewall functions.
- Using the operating system's resource protection mechanisms to tightly control access to all files and directories.
- Configuring detailed auditing and logging securely.

Installing a Secure Operating System from Scratch

If at all possible, you should install the operating system for a bastion host from scratch. If you are recycling an older system that already has an operating system and applications installed, it is better to zap the disk and start over than it is to attempt to examine and try to validate that no vulnerabilities exist. Be sure to check with the vendor to make sure you have the latest information about patches or updates and only apply those that have been around long enough so that any major bugs or security problems have already been exposed.

Although not practical for some operating systems, you will find that some, such as OpenVMS, can be booted and run from a CD-ROM. Having the operating system CD-ROM or a read-only disk partition takes away the operating system files as a potential target of an intruder. You can't replace or tamper with important system files if

Windows NT Service Packs and Hotfixes

You can access the latest Windows NT Service Packs by visiting www.microsoft.com and using the download button to locate the packs. When important security problems are discovered, they are usually fixed quickly, and you shouldn't wait around to get the next service pack, which might be months away, to incorporate the fix into your system. Instead, periodically visit the following FTP site to check for new hotfixes as they are issued:

ftp://ftp.microsoft.com/bussys/winnt/winnt-public/fixes/

they are on a read-only partition. Some popular firewall products make use of this technique to secure the operating system and important application files. Files that need to be opened for write or update access can be stored on another partition. It is possible, on some systems, to place important data on another system entirely. For example, many UNIX systems can be configured so that the syslogd daemon sends important logging information to another system.

It is also a good idea to install only one operating system on the bastion host. Do not use this kind of platform as a dual-boot host. Any files that are found on the hard disk are targets that a hacker might use against you when he gets a foot in the door. Just as you do not leave behind application files that are not needed, there should be no other operating system files on the bastion host except for those that are necessary.

For UNIX systems, take advantage of a shadow password file if that function is part of your installation package. This extra security measure helps to prevent an intruder from downloading your regular /etc/passwd file and using his spare time to crack your passwords. Although the regular password file is usually world-readable, the shadow password file is not.

You should also consider using strong authentication methods, such as SecureID or Skey. By using mechanisms that provide for one-time use passwords, security can be greatly enhanced. Using an external physical device, such as a SecureID card that has been synchronized with the host, can be very difficult to defeat on a bastion host.

Eliminating Unnecessary Services and Applications

On UNIX systems, background processes that provide services are called *daemons*. These daemon processes can be designed to perform a variety of tasks, and not all of these are needed on a computer being hardened for use as a bastion host. Windows NT Servers also have background service processes running that might present a problem on a bastion host. You will look at these two separately because they use different methods for managing background services.

UNIX

On UNIX systems, daemon processes are usually started in one of three ways:

- By the `inetd` daemon
- By startup files at boot time
- As part of the kernel

For many common network services, the `inetd` daemon responds to network requests and uses information in its configuration file, `/etc/inetd.conf`, to start up a background server process to satisfy each request. You can edit this file to prevent some unwanted services from starting. If this firewall bastion host is only accessed by the local console, you might want to do away with services such as FTP and Telnet, for example.

SEE ALSO

➤ *For more information about the* `inetd.conf` *configuration file, how it is configured, and how services are started, see "Configuring the* `inetd.conf` *File," in Chapter 13, page 257*

Services that you might want to consider commenting out—or removing entirely—from the `inetd.conf` configuration file might include the following:

- **The r services**   These convenient utilities, such as `rlogin`, `rcp`, and `rexec`, are convenient for hackers also. If they are able to alter a `hosts.equiv` or `.rhosts` file on the target system, they will be able to wreak havoc on your system. Consider replacing the `r` services, if you absolutely need them, with the Secure Shell (`ssh`) services that perform essentially the same functions but that add encryption and strong authentication to the utilities.

- **FTP**   Use a proxy for this service. Standard UNIX services such as FTP and Telnet send passwords as plain text across the network, which can be intercepted easily by a sniffer program. You can use the TIS Internet Firewall Toolkit (FWTK), for example, to provide a more secure FTP service to and from the firewall.

SEE ALSO

➤ *For more information about the FWTK, see Chapter 14, "Using the TIS Firewwall Toolkit," page 263*

- **Telnet**   Like FTP, use a proxy, such as the one available in the FWTK, as well.

- uucp   Although not as widely used as it once was, the Unix to Unix Copy Program (uucp) is still around in some UNIX distributions and can be found running here and there. This utility was written in the early days of the Internet and TCP/IP, and it is not a secure method for distributing information among computers on the modern Internet. The functionality provided by uucp has been replaced by other utilities that are easier to use and that operate more securely.

- finger   This standard UNIX utility gives out information about users on the network. Remember that on a firewall host, you want to make available as little information as possible. If you absolutely need to use finger, consider replacing the standard executable with one of the "safe" finger utilities that are available on the Internet.

SEE ALSO

➤ See Appendix B, "Other Security Tools You Can Use" p.445

- inetd   It might be possible to remove the inetd daemon server itself because many commercial products provide this functionality in their product. To provide substitutes for the r services, check out the SSH Secure Shell, which can be used in place of these problematic services.

If you need to make use of one of the standard network services, such as Telnet or FTP, to access the bastion host remotely, you can also use TCP Wrappers, or an equivalent package, on the bastion host. TCP Wrappers enable you to create a relatively secure Telnet session in the bastion host for management purpose by using a Telnet gateway. TCP Wrappers can be configured to use strong authentication techniques and log all successful and failed attempts via syslogd.

SEE ALSO

➤ For more information about TCP Wrappers and how they are configured, see Chapter 13, "Using TCP Wrappers," page 253

Look through your inetd.conf file to locate any other trivial services or services that you aren't sure about. For example, if you use a talkd daemon to allow users to engage in keyboard conversations, this service is hard to justify on the bastion host. Some sites use one or more

---

What Is Secure Shell?

Secure Shell is a set of utilities using the SSH protocol that allow services similar to the Berkeley r services to work in a manner that doesn't present glaring security risks. End-to-end encryption and strong authentication techniques are used to make the utilities secure. The newest version of the protocol is SSH2, which includes support for the Secure File Transfer Protocol (SFTP) and for multiple public key algorithms.

To find out more about Secure Shell, you can visit the URLs www.ssh.org or www.ssh.com/products/ssh/.

"standardized" copies of an inetd.conf file that was created as a policy measure to ensure that identical copies are on certain kinds of systems, such as workstations or servers. If that is the case at your site, dump the file and start over, listing only the services that absolutely have to run for the bastion host to perform its firewall functions. Convenient or fun services should be relegated to other systems that are in a more protected environment. The bastion host is up there on the front lines of your defense and should not be used for anything other than that.

Some services are started when the system boots, generally from the /etc/rc.* files. Check your documentation for the appropriate startup file directory structure and to determine which files start up which processes. This is typically how services such as NFS (Network File System) are started. NFS is a complex creature built on routines that use remote procedure calls (RPC). The Mount protocol is used to make the initial connection to a remote file system.

RPC itself is a simple client/server protocol application that defines how clients and servers interact. It was originally developed for use in constructing NFS, but it is now widely used for many other services. Both the client and server hosts using RPC run the rpcbind daemon.

NFS is a stateless protocol. This means that the server maintains no information to keep track of one client request to the next. NFS does not even handle functions such as file opening or closing, which you might expect would be necessary in a networked distributed file system. Instead, another protocol, the Mount protocol, performs this function for NFS. This means another background service, the mountd daemon, runs on both the client and server computer.

As you can see from this short discussion, if you are running NFS on a host, you are really running several background processes. Perhaps the most problematic of these is the RPC daemon because so many other services have been implemented using it. The point here is that you should carefully examine the startup files for your UNIX (or Linux) system and eliminate any and all services that are not absolutely necessary! Default installations performed by set programs can leave behind all sorts of things that you are unaware of. Hackers know to look for these things and how to find ways to turn them on or otherwise abuse the files left around. Check the documentation

Why Would You Not Want to Use NFS on a Host That Sits Close to the Internet?

NFS is a networked distributed file system. Although it might be very convenient to use it in the local network to allow many users to share files across the network, do you want to make these files and directories available for mounting by someone outside your network—someone on the Internet? The security provisions that you will find with different implementations of NFS are not sufficient to allow this kind of service across untrusted links.

More Information about NFS

Since Sun Microsystems first developed the Network File System protocols, the technology has been improved and ported to many different UNIX variants and other operating systems. To learn more about the internals of how the NFS protocols work, see Request for Comments (RFC) 1094, which defines the most widely used version of NFS (version 2). RFC 1813 documents version 3, which adds better support for wide area networking.

for your UNIX (or Linux) distribution and find out what components of the kernel can be safely removed. Recompile the kernel (and don't leave the old version lying around on the box!) and test to make sure that your changes worked as expected.

Other UNIX Network Files to Review

After you finish editing files that are used to configure or start up network services, there are a few other files you should examine. If you still use the /etc/hosts file, for whatever reason, check to see that it's not a copy of one from another system full of host information that is not needed on the bastion host server. If the bastion host is compromised, any information a hacker can find that describes your network or the hosts on it can only serve to make further intrusion into the network easier.

A few other standard UNIX network configuration files to check out include the following:

- /etc/networks   This file is similar to the /etc/hosts file, which maps friendly names to IP addresses. This file does the same thing for network addresses. Although it is convenient to refer to remote hosts by name, this functionality is not really needed by many end-users for a network name. Most end-users have no idea of the networks to which they are connected. This file is not used for much other than to define the local network's name to address translation, but it should be examined to be sure it does not contain records that are not needed or that look peculiar.

- /etc/protocols   This file is used to associate a number with a protocol name. For example, the IP packet header contains a field that defines whether the packet is for the TCP or the UDP protocol. In the IP packet, the protocol is identified by a number. This number can be cross-referenced in the /etc/protocols file to get the name of the protocol. Check to be sure than an application installation or other configuration procedure did not add new protocols that you are not using to this file.

- /etc/services   This file matches up network service names with the port number typically used by the service and the transport protocol (UDP or TCP) used by the service. You might find yourself editing this file if you want to add more than one kind of server for a particular proxy. For example, you could create two versions of the Telnet daemon using the TIS Internet Firewall Toolkit, with each daemon using a different port number.

Windows NT

To check which services are running on a Windows NT 4.0 Server, use the Services applet found in the Control Panel. This brings up a dialog box (as shown in Figure 6.1) that lists the services in a scrollable area. You can scroll up and down to locate all services that are currently configured on the system.

You can start, stop, or pause services using this utility. Although stopping a service is a good idea, it is also a good idea to remove the service from the system entirely if it is not needed. For example, in Figure 6.1, the TCP/IP NetBIOS Helper service is running. Because the server is only using TCP/IP to communicate with either clients or the Internet, you do not need to even have the NetBIOS protocol installed at all. Make a list of services shown in this utility, disable them, and then begin to remove them.

To disable a network service, first stop it by clicking the service and using the Stop button. Then use the Startup button to change the way in which the service is started. In Figure 6.2, you can see the Service dialog box that pops up.

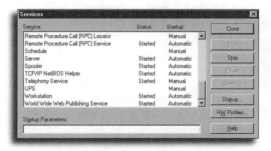

To remove a network protocol or service from the system, use the Network applet in the Control Panel. In Figure 6.3, you can see the Network applet with the Services tab selected. If NetBIOS is not to be used on the system, you can remove this service here by clicking it and then clicking the Remove button.

What Services Are Running?

To see which services are currently running on the system, use the `ps` command. This command gives you a quick snapshot of what is running on the system. The output depends on the UNIX variant, but it generally consists of a single line for each process, showing the command being executed along with other information such as the process ID and the UID it is running under. After you have removed unnecessary services from a system, reboot it and use this command to check for those that you might have missed in the startup files or kernel configuration. Use this command when monitoring the system to be sure that no unauthorized services are being started by the `inetd` daemon.

FIGURE 6.1
The Services applet enables you to manage services running on a Windows NT Server.

FIGURE 6.2
Set a service to be disabled on startup using this dialog box.

FIGURE 6.3
To remove a service, highlight it and click the Remove button.

To take things a little further, you can remove the NetBEUI protocol also. Figure 6.4 shows the Network applet with the Protocols tab selected. Here, you can click on the NetBEUI protocol and then use the Remove button to remove the protocol from the server.

Before you start to remove services or protocols, check the documentation for any proxy applications or other firewall software that will run on the server. It is likely that you will find specific suggestions for which protocols and services to remove, as well as how to configure those that will remain.

FIGURE 6.4
Use the Protocols tab to remove network protocols from the server.

Removing Unnecessary Applications and Files

When you have removed services that are not needed on the bastion host, be sure to clean up after yourself and remove the executable programs that these services use as well. Anything you leave behind that falls under the eye of an intruder might be useful for further compromising the system.

When a computer is stripped down to make it into a bastion host, only necessary software should be left behind. In addition to removing user accounts and services that are not needed, don't forget to check other applications that the host might have access to. For example, there is probably no real need for a compiler of any sort on a bastion host. Why do you need to compile a program on that system? Can't you perform development and compilation on another, perhaps dedicated, system instead? Other development tools, including libraries and script files, should be removed from the file system of a bastion host.

A bastion host should concentrate only on the functions it performs for the firewall. You don't need a first-class word processor or spreadsheet on the bastion host because you shouldn't be performing those kinds of tasks on this kind of machine. If you have performed a clean install of the operating system, check the documentation (and the running system) to determine whether, by default, you have also installed any applications that are not needed.

A standard installation of Windows NT, for example, is heavily laden with accessories that are rarely justified on a firewall bastion host. Use the Add/Remove Programs applet in the control panel to remove items that are not needed, such as games, Microsoft Photo Editor, Calculator, and so on. You might want to keep around WordPad or NotePad for use when editing files on the system, but most of the other accessories can be removed.

Although you might need an editor on the host for performing management duties, you do not need several editors. UNIX has many popular editors, and you usually get more than one on any given UNIX distribution. Make a hacker's job more difficult by giving him less of a choice. Figure out which editor is the easiest for you to use and remove any others.

When you need to test a new product or component for a firewall, try to do so first in a lab setting before deploying the product on a bastion host. After you have deployed software on a bastion host, be sure to remove it when it is no longer needed. It can be tempting to leave demos or other trial products installed past their expiration date. Although the application might seem to pose no problem, you shouldn't leave something around that a hacker might know how to exploit, be it the actual executable software or perhaps something such as the directory structure created by the application.

Resource Protections and Access Control

To secure the operating system, as well as the applications that you will run on the bastion host, become very familiar with the mechanics of resource permissions that the operating system employs. UNIX and Windows NT use similar terms, such as the standard read, write, and execute, to describe access controls. What they mean and how you can manage them is vastly different between the two systems. Windows NT uses a GUI environment where you point and click, whereas UNIX uses a command-line interface.

UNIX Resource Permissions

The UNIX operating system enables you to assign permissions to files and directories based on three basic categories. The first group of permissions applies to the owner of the file or directory.

The second applies to the user group that the file belongs to. The third specifies permissions for others who try to access the file. The types of basic permissions you can apply to a file or directory are the following:

- **Read (r)**   This permission allows the user to list the files stored in a directory (including their attributes) and allows the contents of a file to be read.

- **Write (w)**   This permission allows the user to add or delete files in a directory and to change the contents of a file.

- **Execute (x)**   This permission allows a user the right to access a directory and to execute (run) a program file.

Viewing Permission Values

To see what permission values are assigned to a file or directory, you can use the ls command, as in the following example:

```
ls -l /usr/bin/fwadm
dr-xr-xr-x   1 fwadm   bca              0 Jan 1   2000 html
dr-xr-xr-x   1 fwadm   bca              0 Feb 3   2000 documents
-r-xr-xr-x   1 fwadm   bca           1624 Feb 6   2000 sources.txt
-r-xr-xr-x   1 fwadm   bca           1624 Feb 22  2000 misc.dat
```

The first string of characters, called the *permissions array*, in each line of this listing is used to determine the type of entry (directory or file) and the permissions associated with the entry. The first two lines of this listing show directory files, which is indicated by the d character that starts this string for those entries. The next two entries are ordinary files, indicated by the hyphen character (-) that starts this string. It might appear that the remaining three fields can be determined by the remaining hyphens in the string. This is not true, however. Each position in the string after the directory bit can be a permission that is granted or denied. The hyphen character is used to show that the permission is not granted.

For example, for the html directory the permissions array is dr-xr-xr-x. This can be broken up into four parts:

- **Position 1**   Indicates directory or file.

- **Positions 2–4**   Permission values for the Owner.

- **Positions 5–7**   Permission values for the Group.

- **Positions 8–10**   Permission values for all others.

143

Thus, the permissions array is a 10-character string, and all positions are meaningful. In the `html` directory example, the permissions can be interpreted then as the following:

- **Owner**   read and execute permission
- **Group**   read and execute permission
- **All others**   read and execute permission

With this setting, no one would have write access to this directory.

SUID and SGID

In addition to these basic permissions, there are two other important permissions that need to be discussed: SUID and SGID. When a program is run on a UNIX system, it runs using the permissions that apply to the user running the program. If the user is the owner of the file, the owner permissions are used. If the user is a member of the same group as the program, the group permissions apply.

However, if the SUID (Set User ID) permission is applied to a program, when it is executed it takes on the permissions that are the same as those of the owner of the file, even if the user running the program is not the owner. Similarly, the SGID (Set Group ID) permission allows the program to acquire the permissions that would be granted to the group. These powerful permissions allow a program to be run to perform functions that would be denied to the user if he tried to do them directly. This is necessary for some procedures. For example, when a user changes his password, the password application accesses the `/etc/passwd` file with write access to make the change. The user does not have write access to the `/etc/passwd` file, so the password application must be able to obtain the permission itself. The problem with these permissions comes not from their legitimate usage, but from bad programming practices and bugs.

When a program makes use of these permissions and a known bug exists, it might be possible for a hacker to employ that bug to break the program and then, with the elevated permissions, perform functions you had not intended. One good programming practice to use is to check the return status of all routines and to trap any and all errors that can be determined in this manner.

To determine whether a file or directory has had the SUID permission set, you can again use the `ls` command and look for the letter `s` in the owner's permission field in the permissions array. This indicates the SUID permission. If this letter appears in uppercase, the execute permission is not allowed for the owner. If it is there in lowercase, the execute permission is allowed for the owner.

When set for a group (SGID), you will find the s character in the position used for the group's execute access.

Changing Owner and Permission Values

There are two simple commands you can use to change resource ownership and permissions. These are the chown (change owner) and chmod (change permission mode) commands. To change the owner of a file or directory, use the following syntax:

```
chown [ -fhR ] owner [ : group ] file ...
```

In this syntax, owner (or group) should be the new user or group ID you want to own the file or directory (file...). The parameters you can use will do the following:

- -f   Suppresses error reporting.
- -h   Changes the ownership on a symbolic link to a file, not the actual file itself.
- -R   Causes the ownership change to be applied to files and subdirectories under the current directory, as well.

To change access permissions for a file or directory, use the chmod command. The syntax for this command enables you to use two different methods for specifying permissions. The first uses a numeric value, whereas the second method uses a text string. To make this a little clearer, first examine the numeric values you can use to specify permissions:

- 0   No access
- 1   Execute file (or search a directory)
- 2   Write
- 4   Read

To change the access permission on a file using these values, you specify one digit each for the owner, group, and all others fields. For each of these, you can add together the values for multiple permissions to come up with the value between 0 and 7.

For example:

```
chmod 660 /etc/bca/sw2dd.asc
```

The permissions here are being set to read and write (4 + 2 = 6) for the owner and the group. All others are denied access to the file (0).

The second method you can use to change the permission values on a file or directory uses characters instead of numeric values.

To specify who the permission value is being set for, the following letters are used:

- u   Owner
- g   Group
- o   Others
- a   All

To specify the permission being granted, use the following characters:

- r   Read
- w   Write
- x   Execute
- s   SUID or SGID

To use the chmod command, you need to specify whom the permission change applies to, what the permission being added or taken away is, and what file or directory the change is set on. The syntax for this is the following:

```
chmod who function permission
```

For *who* and *permission*, use the characters that you just reviewed. For *function*, you can use any of the following:

- =   To set a permission
- +   To add a permission
- -   To remove a permission

For example:

```
chmod a=rw /etc/bca/sw2dd.asc
```

This gives everybody (a for *all*) the read (r) and write (w) access permissions to the file. In the following example, I remove write (w) access for the other group:

```
chmod o-w /etc/bca/sw2dd.asc
```

Windows NT

When you install Windows NT (or Windows 2000) on a partition that is formatted using NTFS, you enable the capability for setting resource protections down to the single file level. This applies to every disk on the system that is formatted using NTFS, not just the partition on which you install NT. Using a FAT partition, which does not enable you to set resource protections for individual files or directories with a Windows OS, is unacceptable on a host that runs Windows NT and works as part of a firewall.

To begin an examination of the kinds of permissions that can be used to control resources on a Windows NT platform, you need to first look at the two methods that are used. You can either use the *special permissions*, which are very basic in nature, or assign permissions using groups that combine several of these more granular permissions into a unit for the purposes of assignment.

Special permissions give you the most complete control over resource access:

- **R**   Read permission
- **W**   Write permission
- **X**   Execute permission
- **D**   Delete permission
- **P**   Change permission
- **O**   Take ownership permission

Most of the standard permissions that can be used with files combine several of these more precise special permissions into units that can be more convenient to use when assigning permissions:

- **Read**   RX
- **Change**   RWXD
- **Full Control**   RWXDPO
- **No Access**

If you look at the standard permission Read, you can see that it includes the special permission Read as well as the special permission Execute. When you grant a user the right to read a file, in most cases you also want her to be able to execute the file. If that is the case, using the standard permission Read is easier than using the special permissions and making two permissions assignments, one for read access and one for execute access. One standard permission that you can use that is not made up of several of the special permissions is the No Access permission. This permission is a convenient way of denying any access to a resource.

For directories, there is a different list of standard permissions. When you define this type of permission, there are two sets of permissions that are listed: those that apply to the directory itself and those that apply to files in the directory. The standard permissions for directories are the following:

- **List**   (RX) (unspecified)
- **Read**   (RX) (RX)
- **Add**   (WX) (unspecified)
- **Add & Read**   (RWX) (RX)
- **Change**   (RWXD) (RWXD)
- **Full Control**   (RWXDPO) (RWXDPO)
- **No Access**

Here, you can see that the Read permission works for directories just as it does for files; both read and execute access are granted on the directory. In addition, files that are created in the directory are also granted the read and execute permissions. Files created in a directory inherit permissions from the directory. Note that not all the directory standard permissions operate to grant the same permissions to the directory and its files. For example, the Add & Read right grants read, write, and execute access to the directory file. Files created in the directory, however, inherit only the read and execute rights.

Viewing Ownership and Permissions on Files and Directories

To view the permissions on any file or directory, you can use Windows Explorer.

Viewing Permissions with Windows Explorer

1. Click Start, Programs, Windows NT Explorer. In Figure 6.5, you can see that the IIS fw folder has been selected.

FIGURE 6.5
The Windows NT Explorer can be used to view files and directories and to manage permissions.

2. Right-click a folder or a file and select Properties from the menu. In Figure 6.6, you can see the Properties sheet for the `fw` folder, with the Security property sheet selected.

FIGURE 6.6
The Security Properties sheet for the folder can be used to modify permissions.

3. Click the Permissions button to modify the resource permissions for the folder.

4. Use the Directory Permissions dialog box that appears (Figure 6.7) to view existing permissions on the folder. Currently, there are several user groups that have access permissions granted for this folder.

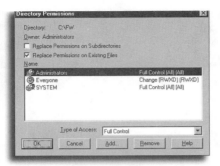

FIGURE 6.7
The Directory
Permissions dialog box
can be used to display
existing permissions.

Modifying Permissions

In the previous example, there is a folder where the Administrators
group and the System account both have full control access over the
directory. The Everyone group has the Change permission. Suppose
that you just created a new user account called `fwadmin1` and you
want to grant full control access to this new account and remove it
for the Administrators and Everyone groups. You can also make
these changes using the Windows NT Explorer. First, locate the
folder or the file you want to change using Explorer and bring up the
Directory Permissions dialog box as you did in the previous example.

Modifying Permissions with Windows Explorer

1. In the Directory Permissions dialog box, check the Replace
   Permissions on Subdirectories and the Replace Permissions on
   Existing Files check boxes.

2. Click the Add button. Figure 6.8 shows the Add Users and
   Groups dialog box that appears.

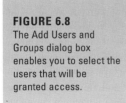

FIGURE 6.8
The Add Users and
Groups dialog box
enables you to select the
users that will be
granted access.

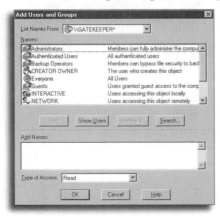

3. At the bottom of the dialog box, use the Type of Access menu to select Full Control. Click the Show Users button and scroll to find the fwadmin1 user account (see Figure 6.9). Click the Add button and the account GATEKEEPER\fwadmin1 is displayed in the Add Names field.

FIGURE 6.9
Select the access type and a user account (or user group).

4. Click the OK button to return to the Directory Permissions dialog box. The fwadmin1 user account now displays showing the Full Control access permission.

5. Back in the Directory Permissions dialog box, select the Administrators group by clicking it and then clicking Remove. Do the same for the Everyone group. The Directory Permissions dialog box now shows that only the fwadmin1 user and the special SYSTEM account are allowed access to this folder. Because the Replace Permissions on Subdirectories and Replace Permissions on Existing Files check boxes were selected, all files and subdirectories found under the fw folder have also had permissions changed.

This example showed how to add or remove the standard permissions for selected users or groups. If you look back at Figure 6.7, you can see that where permissions are listed for users or groups, you first see the standard permission Full Control, and then in parentheses you see two other permissions: (All) and (All). Remember that there are two sets of permissions for directories (or folders). These last two permission strings indicate the special permissions for the directory

When you use the Directory Permissions dialog box to change permissions on an existing directory, the new permissions are in effect for new files created in the directory. If files exist there already, be sure to use the Replace Permissions check boxes that you used in the example, if you want to propagate the permission changes to the existing files and/or subdirectories.

FIGURE 6.10
Select the special permissions you want to apply to the directory using this dialog box.

and the special permissions to be applied to the files created in the directory.

If you want to modify the permissions for a user or group that already has access, you can do so from the Directory Permissions dialog box. Just select the user by clicking once and then use the Type of Access menu to select the new permission value for that user or group. You will note that in addition to the standard permissions you were able to select with the Add Users and Groups dialog box, the Type of Access menu on the Directory Permissions dialog box allows you to select also Special Directory Access. This is how you can use the Explorer to modify permissions for an object using the granular special permissions instead of the standard permissions.

In Figure 6.10 you can see Special Directory Access dialog box, used to specify the special permissions you want to apply to the directory.

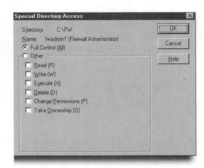

After you select one or more of the special permissions you want to apply, click OK. When you return to the Directory Permissions dialog box, you will see that Special Access has replaced the text Full Control, and the first special permissions value, for directory access, has changed. To make changes for the second special permissions field or those that will be applied to files created in the directory, use the Type of Access menu to select Special File Access. From a dialog box similar to the one shown in Figure 6.10, you can select the special permissions to be applied to files created in the directory.

Configuring Auditing and Logging

After you have set resource permissions on resources that will be needed by the bastion host, you should next make sure that the facilities provided by the operating system for logging and auditing are configured correctly. This is such an important topic that an entire chapter is devoted to it: Chapter 8, "Operating System Monitoring and Auditing Techniques."

No matter what protections you set up by using permissions to restrict file and directory access, you will never be certain that your methods are working unless you take the appropriate steps to monitor the situation. Log files and monitoring techniques, such as the `syslogd` daemon for UNIX systems and the Windows NT Event Viewer, need to be understood and implemented properly. Additionally, you need to set up procedures for reviewing the data collected on a frequent basis so that you can quickly catch any suspicious activity. Although this is true for security on all systems on your network, it is even more so important for a bastion host.

Running Proxy Software on the Bastion Host

The typical use of a bastion host is to provide some kind of proxy service to the Internet for users on the inside protected network. Proxy applications might include standard TCP/IP utilities like FTP, Telnet, newer Internet protocols like HTTP, or for important business functions such as email (SMTP).

SEE ALSO

➤ *For more information about proxy services and application gateways, see Chapter 7, "Application Gateways and Proxy Servers," page 157*

In this chapter we discussed the need to make the bastion host as secure as possible, leaving on the host only the components necessary for it to serve its function in the firewall. This functionality will be determined by the proxy software applications that you choose to run. When the budget permits, it is a better idea to use several proxy servers to provide multiple services rather than to make one host responsible for many services. By using one bastion host for each important service you can help spread the load around and probably improve response time for users.

Using more than one host to provide the same service, you can also load balance between servers. For example, both Microsoft Proxy

Server and the SQUID proxy server provide support for communicating between proxy servers so that requests can be satisfied using a distributed, hierarchical network of servers. In a large network a hierarchy of proxy servers can be more efficient at responding to user requests than a single server.

Using multiple servers means that your system management tasks will increase. However each system should be simpler to maintain given that it will be used for only one proxy. Another advantage of using multiple systems is that if one server goes down, other Internet services aren't affected. If you are using multiple servers for the same service, the loss of one means you can still keep providing a connection for clients until the failed server is returned to working order.

When the Bastion Host Is Compromised

Because a bastion host sits closer to the Internet than most systems on your network, it makes sense to say that this host stands a better chance of being infiltrated by outsiders. That is why we have taken a whole chapter to talk about creating a very secure system. Although you can make the hacker's job a difficult one, there is no 100% foolproof method for preventing all forms of attack. This is especially true because new attacks are being developed all the time.

By using good auditing measures you should be able to quickly detect when an intrusion has occurred. However, no matter how quickly you realize that something is wrong, it might not be time enough to prevent further damage. The intruder might have altered system files or planted other applications such as Trojan horses. The intruder might have changed files associated with an application proxy. For these reasons you cannot simply change a password and set the host back into service. Instead you need to start from scratch again and evaluate the bastion host to make sure it is what you think that it is.

Although it might be tempting to simply restore the bastion host using a recent backup tape, this method is not as secure as starting from scratch, using known good application setup programs. If the bastion host has been compromised, you cannot be 100% sure of when the attack was first begun. For example, if the host has just crashed, is it because of a program downloaded to it recently, or might it be a Trojan horse program that has been waiting around for several months for a trigger?

There are several good utilities that can aid you in this examination, such as TripWire. For more information about programs like this see Appendix B, "Other Security Tools You Can Use."

When the bastion host is compromised, all other hosts residing in the DMZ must also be examined. If one system has been penetrated it is likely that information gained from that break-in can be used to further penetrate the network. When a bastion host is compromised you should examine all other hosts that interact with the bastion host, such as routers or other gateways, to make sure you have determined the real extent of any damage.

Summary

Configuring a system for use as a bastion host means that you must take all the necessary steps to ensure that the host is well protected from almost anything you expect could happen (and a lot of things you don't expect). This means using the built-in resource protections that the underlying operating system provides and by making sure that the operating system itself was correctly installed. In the next chapter we will examine how proxy services, which you will use the bastion host for, work.

Application Gateways and Proxy Servers

Using Proxy Servers ●

Classical and Transparent Proxies ●

Network Address Translators (NATs) ●

Content Screening and Blocking ●

Logging and Alerting Facilities ●

Client Considerations ●

Using Proxy Servers

Whereas packet filters work at the network transport layer by inspecting IP and other protocol header information, proxy servers work at the application layer and can be used to provide a variety of services to the network. A proxy server, through which all network packets must travel for a particular connection, provides a gateway between the client and the server. Another term commonly used for proxy server is *application gateway*. Whereas packet filters pass actual IP packets between the internal and external networks, a proxy server does not. Instead, a proxy server receives a request from a client and makes the actual request to the server on the client's behalf. No actual IP packets get passed between client and server. The proxy server sits in the middle of the connection and talks to both sides to mediate the connection.

One of the main differences between a packet filter and a proxy server is that the proxy server must understand the application. A packet server can be programmed to pass or drop network packets based on a limited amount of information found in the packet header. The proxy server is application-specific and can be programmed to allow or deny access to a service based on the functions the user wants to perform.

In Figure 7.1 you can see how a proxy server works to block actual IP traffic from flowing between your network and the Internet. The user browsing the Web from his workstation requests a Web page from the Internet. Because the user's browser has been configured to send HTTP requests to a proxy server, the request never gets to the actual Web server directly.

Instead, the proxy server receives the request on its network adapter connected to the local network. The proxy server does not route (or forward) the IP packet containing the request to the actual target server on the Internet. Instead, the proxy application that runs on the proxy server consults a set of rules, configured by the administrator, to decide if the request is allowed. If so, the proxy server formulates a request for the page, using its other network adapter's address (which is connected to the Internet) as the source of the request. When the Web server on the Internet receives the request, it can only assume that the proxy server is the client requesting the page, and it sends the data on its way back to the proxy server.

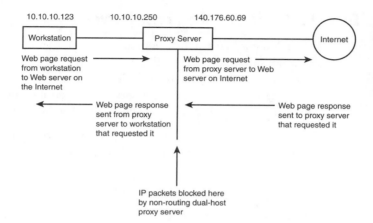

10.10.10.123   10.10.10.250   140.176.60.69

FIGURE 7.1
A proxy server presents a boundary through which IP packets cannot travel.

When the proxy server receives the requested Web page it does not pass the IP packets back to the original requesting client. Instead, the proxy server performs some checks on the data returned, as configured by the administrator. If all is well, the proxy server creates new IP packets with the address of its local network adapter and returns the Web page data to the client.

As you can see, blocking IP traffic is not the only benefit you receive by using a proxy server. You can also use it to perform certain checks based on the type of request and on the content of the data returned. Plus, based on a set of rules you configure, you can program the proxy server to allow or deny the data.

You will need a separate proxy server application for each kind of network service you'll allow your clients to access through the firewall. Standard proxy applications are abundant for typical TCP/IP utilities such as FTP and Telnet, and for popular services such as HTTP. You might not be able to find proxy software for newer services or for those that are rarely used. Although generic proxy solutions exist, they do not offer the same degree of security that an application-specific proxy does.

Proxy servers can work in both directions. Just as you can use a proxy server to control which users on your network are allowed to make Internet requests, you can also use a proxy server to decide which external users or hosts you will allow to send requests to servers inside your network. Either way, no IP packets get passed between the two networks, and you can allow or deny requests by configuring a set of rules.

159

Disable Routing on the Proxy Server

When you configure a dual-homed host computer for use as a proxy server, be sure to disable routing between the two network adapters. This feature is usually enabled by default. By disabling IP forwarding or routing by the host, all client/server connections will be forced to flow through available proxy applications or be blocked.

Windows NT and many versions of UNIX do route between adapters by default. For Windows NT 4.0, you can disable this feature quite simply:

1. Click Start, Programs, Control Panel.

2. Double-click the Network applet.

3. Select the Protocols property sheet.

4. Double-click the TCP/IP Protocol (or highlight TCP/IP with one click and click the Properties button).

5. In the dialog box (Figure 7.2), deselect (clear) the check box labeled Enable IP Forwarding.

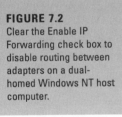

FIGURE 7.2
Clear the Enable IP Forwarding check box to disable routing between adapters on a dual-homed Windows NT host computer.

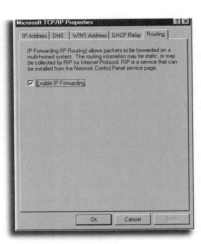

6. Reboot the computer for this setting to take effect.

If you are using a UNIX system, the method will vary from one UNIX variant to another and might even be different between different releases of the same UNIX. For example, in Solaris 2.4 and previous versions, add the following line to the end of the file /etc/init.d/inetinit:

`-set /dev/ip ip_forwarding 0`

For Solaris 2.5, however, all you need to do is touch the file
etc/notrouter.

SEE ALSO

➤ *For more information on configuring a dual-homed host for use by proxy applications, see
Chapter 6, "Using a Bastion Host," page 131*

Advantages and Disadvantages of Proxy Servers

Proxy servers are only a single component of a good firewall. Just as
packet filters have their good and bad sides, so do proxy servers. By
combining the two, you can cover more security matters and better
protect your network. Some advantages you can achieve from using a
proxy server include the following:

- Hiding network information about clients or servers on the protected network.

- A single point in the network where you can control access to
  network services between the protected network and the
  Internet. Even if the proxy application crashes or fails, there is
  no mechanism left on a properly configured bastion host to
  allow traffic to pass through.

- Proxy servers can be configured to log information about provided services and to alert you to suspicious activity and attempts
  at unauthorized access.

- Some proxies can screen the content of data returned and block
  access to certain sites. They can also block content containing
  known viruses or other questionable objects.

Some of the disadvantages include the following:

- Although a proxy server provides a single place to control access,
  it also becomes a single point of failure.

- Each network service will require its own proxy server application. Generic solutions exist, but do not offer the same level of
  security.

- Clients might need to be modified or reconfigured to use a
  proxy server.

> **IP Forwarding in
> Windows 2000**
>
> By default, IP forwarding is
> disabled in Windows 2000.
> To enable IP forwarding you
> need to edit the Registry.

> **What Is touch?**
>
> This UNIX command is
> used to set the access and
> modification times of a file.
> If the file you touch does
> not exist, it will be created.

Classical and Transparent Proxies

In Request for Comments 1919 (RFC 1919), the RFC's author describes and contrasts two basic kinds of proxies and names them *classical proxies* and *transparent proxies*.

Classical Proxies

As the name implies, a classical proxy refers to the first kind of proxy that was developed. In a sense, this kind of proxy is basically a program that sits between the client and server. It makes the client end of the connection authenticate itself to the proxy before the proxy begins relaying data back and forth. For example, a user making use of a classical proxy for FTP would use it as the target of the FTP command, authenticate to the proxy server and then inform the proxy server of the actual target of the connection.

The problem with this kind of proxy is that it involves extra work by the client. For example, when using FTP directly, with no proxy, the steps are quite simple:

1. The user executes the FTP client command, such as `ftp www.twoinc.com`.
2. The server prompts for a username, the user responds.
3. The server prompts for a password, the user responds.
4. The user executes commands to send or receive files, and so on.
5. The server responds to commands by receiving files from the user's client application, or by sending files to the client's application.

Using a classical proxy, the situation becomes a little more involved:

1. The user executes the FTP client command, such as `ftp proxyserver.twoinc.com`.
2. The proxy server prompts for a username, the user responds.
3. The proxy server prompts for a password, the user responds.
4. The user indicates to the proxy server the actual target of the FTP connection, usually in a format similar to *username@target.com*. Here *username* is a valid username on the target system and *target.com* is the final target of the FTP session.

5. The proxy server relays the login information to the intended target and, if authentication is successful, informs the client application that the user can now begin executing FTP commands.

6. The proxy server receives the FTP commands from the user's client software. The proxy server relays the commands to the target server.

7. The target server responds to commands from the proxy server as if it were the actual client and returns data to the proxy server, depending on the commands issued by the user.

8. The proxy server relays data it receives from the target server back to the user's client application.

From this example, you can see that to the actual end target server, the proxy server looks just like another FTP client. To the end-user's FTP client, the proxy server looks just like the actual end target server. Because the proxy server sits in the middle, it requires the additional steps of having the user authenticate to the proxy server and then giving a command telling the proxy server what the actual intended target is. Because authentication is performed at the proxy server and at the target server, the user is burdened with additional commands.

This might not seem like such a big deal to most users. However, using a proxy of this sort does require that the user be educated in its use. Not all proxy server applications work exactly in the same way, so using a Telnet proxy might not be exactly the same as using an FTP proxy, and so on. The extra steps and user education required make this sort of proxy an acceptable, but not perfect, solution.

SEE ALSO

➤ *The TIS Internet Firewall Toolkit (FWTK) contains several proxies that work in the manner of a classical proxy. For more information on FWTK and the proxies that come with it, see Chapter 14, "Using the TIS Firewall Toolkit (FWTK)," page 263*

Transparent Proxies

To make the deployment of proxy applications easier to manage and to make them easier to use for the end user, what is needed is a proxy application that is transparent to the user. That is, no additional commands should be needed, and the user should not even be aware

---

The Proxy Server Blocks Direct IP Traffic

Note also in this example that the real client software never actually communicates directly with the actual target host providing the service. To be more precise, an IP packet sent out by the client's host *never* reaches the target server. This packet's final destination is the *proxy server*. The proxy server interprets the information in the packet and then sets up a connection between itself and the target server. Thus, there are really two connections established here: one between the client and the proxy server and one between the proxy server and the target server. This situation prevents an ill-formed packet from being sent into the network. Remember that not all attack methods require that information be relayed back to the attacker. Sometimes it is enough just to get a packet inside the network to cause an action that can be exploited by the attacker through another avenue.

---

that they are using a proxy server at all. A transparent proxy works, from the user's point of view, just like a direct connection. This kind of proxy would be much easier to implement because the user would not have to be trained in its use. The user would not even have to know the proxy server existed.

Instead of using the proxy server as the target of the FTP command, the user executes the command with the actual end target server as its command line parameter. Because the proxy server lies in the path between the user and the target server and has been programmed to intercept certain kinds of network traffic, the proxy server can evaluate the request and make a determination as to whether or not to allow it. This means that the client issuing the FTP request believes it is communicating directly with the target server. The proxy server's TCP/IP stack has been modified to pick up network packets that are destined for its own IP address, as well as IP packets being sent to target servers protected by that proxy server.

Because the transparent proxy server is intercepting what would otherwise be a direct connection, it can determine the address of the target server by evaluating the intercepted packet. There is no need for the user to enter the name of the target server as is done with a classical proxy.

The user has to authenticate himself to the target server, just as in a direct connection. However, the proxy server sits in the middle of this connection and can allow deny certain actions. For example, the proxy server might allow the user to retrieve files from the target server (the GET command), but not allow the user to send files to the target server (the PUT command). The proxy server can provide access controls by deciding who and what actions are allowed and can provide logging and alerting capabilities just like a classical proxy server. However, to the user, the process is transparent acting just like a direct connection.

The transparent proxy, however, does not hide IP information from both sides of the connection being proxied. The client needs to know the IP address of the target server. If you are using a proxy to allow external hosts to make a connection to a server inside your network, the server on your internal network still thinks its client is the proxy server. The external client, however, knows the IP address of the server. A solution for this is to place the servers on a separate subnet on the internal network, such as a DMZ. In this manner, any attacker who tries to harm those servers still will not have any information about the rest of the network that resides on the other side of the DMZ. Remember that the hosts you place on a DMZ to provide services are usually called bastion hosts and need to be secured especially tight because they are the most vulnerable hosts on your network.

SEE ALSO

➤ *For more information about the Demilitarized Zone (DMZ) and how it fits into a firewall architecture, see Chapter 4, "Firewall Security Policy and Firewall Design Strategies," page 85*

Whichever method is used, the important thing to remember is that unless proxy applications have been configured to allow the user (or host) to establish a connection through the firewall, the connection will be denied. Although the packet filter works by examining the packet header information (such as address and port numbers) the proxy server application has been written to understand the actual actions that the network service performs. It can be programmed to allow or deny communication on the connection by specific actions.

Classical Proxies Can Hide DNS Information About Your Network

One important fact should quickly become apparent to those using classical proxy applications: The client only needs to know the name of the proxy server and the name of the target system with which it wants to establish a connection. From the client's point of view, it will be necessary to translate the proxy server's DNS style name into an actual IP address before the actual connection can be attempted. It is *not* necessary, however, for the client application to translate the target server's name to an IP address. Because clients will only need to know the name of the target system, there is no need to publish DNS information about your internal network. The proxy helps to hide information about your internal network from the outside world.

A common method for deploying DNS in this kind of situation is to use an internal DNS server that can resolve names for clients on the internal network for clients on the internal network. This internal DNS server does not provide name resolution for hosts outside the internal network. Another DNS server is configured to resolve names for hosts outside the network.

SEE ALSO

➤ *For more information about the Domain Name Service (DNS) and how it is configured, see Chapter 2, "Introduction to the TCP/IP Protocol Suite," page 25*

A transparent proxy does not provide this separation. In a transparent proxy the client system must know the actual IP address of the target server. Thus, it needs to be able to resolve the target server's hostname to an IP address, hence, some information about the internal network needs to be made public by a DNS server.

Creating a Custom Proxy Application

Some proxy servers allow you to create a custom proxy for services. For example, in the TIS Firewall Toolkit (covered in Chapter 14), which includes the standard proxy applications, you can use the plug-gw gateway to create proxied connections for known, trusted outside servers. However, this plug-through method does not allow you to perform any analysis on the actual data transferred, so it is not a true proxy. Instead, it acts more to allow you to make exceptions to the firewall security policy and plug together two servers/ports so that they can talk through the firewall. This kind of proxy enables you to specify which users or hosts can make use of services on the other side of the firewall. It can perform logging and alerting duties, just like any other good proxy. However, it's an all or nothing gateway, and in many cases it is not desirable from a security point of view.

➤ *If you want to know more about plug-gw, see Chapter 14, "Using the TIS Internet Firewall Toolkit," page 263*

Network Address Translators (NATs)

Network Address Translation (NAT) is a very popular proxy service. One of the important security functions performed by a firewall is to hide information about the internal network from outsiders. This information includes TCP/IP addressing and configuration data for workstations and servers on the network. To hide information about your hosts, a NAT application uses its own IP address (or range of IP addresses) when making requests on the Internet on behalf of clients on the internal network. On your protected network, your clients communicate using their actual assigned IP address. When a request is sent through the firewall, the NAT application substitutes its own

---

Using a hosts File

There is another method you can use to allow clients on the Internet to resolve server names on your internal network: the /etc/hosts file. This file, which contains lines that map IP addresses to hostnames, was a common method for name resolution in the early days of TCP/IP. The major drawback to this solution is that if you change an IP address or a hostname, you need to go to each client and make a change in the hosts file. For a large number of hosts, this can be very time-consuming. Using a DNS server, you only need to make the change once. If you are using a transparent proxy and there are few clients outside your network, using a hosts file might be an acceptable solution. It is not a practical solution, however, if you are offering a service to the public (such as an anonymous FTP site).

address for the source address field. When a reply comes back to the NAT application, it replaces its own address in the destination field with that of the original client making the request.

An important thing to note here is that there are many methods used to implement NAT. Some NATs use *static address assignments*, in which a client address on the internal network is bound to a fixed IP address used by NAT on the outside world. NATs that use *dynamic address assignment* can assign an IP address for use on the outside network when a client makes a request that passes through the proxy server. When the client session ends, or after a certain timeout period, the address which is valid on the outside network is returned to a pool of addresses and awaits its next assignment.

NAT can work in either a uni-directional manner, where clients on the internal network are assigned an address by NAT when outbound sessions are initiated. It can also be bi-directional, so that incoming destination IP addresses can be modified to send a packet to a server on the internal network using a different address.

Basic NAT

The concept of network address translation I have discussed so far is usually referred to as basic NAT. This implementation requires that one or more valid Internet addresses be assigned to the NAT server so that it can use them to establish connections for a number of clients on the internal network. This means that the number of valid IP addresses you need to set aside for NAT use will need to be equal to the number of active outgoing sessions, at any point in time. If you assign 10 IP addresses for NAT to use, only 10 clients on the internal network will be able to establish outside connections at the same time.

Figure 7.3 shows an example of this. Here, Workstation A has the address 10.10.10.1 assigned to its network adapter. When it makes an Internet connection request, the NAT server uses the address 140.176.123.1 from its pool of addresses to make the actual connection.

When Workstations B and C make connection requests, the NAT server uses the next two addresses in the pool. However, when Workstation D attempts an Internet connection, no more addresses are available, and the request will fail. If static NAT is used, Workstation D will never be able to successfully make an Internet

Application-Level and Circuit-Level Gateways

Proxies are generally designed to work at the application level, whereas packet filters work at the network level. In the literature you can find two other terms used to refer to proxies. An application-level gateway is a proxy server that understands the inner workings of the protocol or service (the application) being used. A circuit-level gateway, such as `plug-gw`, is generic and does not understand the service or protocol for which it is providing a proxy service. Circuit-level gateways are configured by the administrator to patch a particular connection through the firewall. Although the circuit-level gateway does not enable you to control which features can be used, it does provide for logging and alerting capabilities.

request. If dynamic NAT is used, Workstation D can try again later, after another workstation has returned an address to the pool.

If your usage of outbound connections is limited, basic NAT might be ideal for your network. If you have a large number of clients that need to establish connections simultaneously and you do not have a sufficient number of valid IP address for NAT use, this method will not work.

FIGURE 7.3
Basic NAT uses a one-to-one address translation when letting clients make use of its address pool.

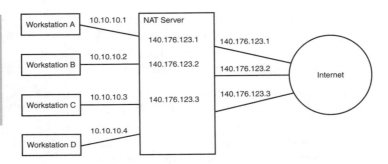

Network Address Port Translation (NAPT)

In Chapter 2, I discussed the concept of *sockets*, the combination of an IP address and a port number used to uniquely identify an endpoint in a TCP or UDP communication. The usual standard (which is not always followed) is that ports 0–1023 are reserved for usage by servers, and those above 1024 are available for clients or other uses. Taking a TCP connection, for example, the client will send a request to a server and include a destination IP address and a port number in the header information. The client will also include its own source IP address and a port number. The port numbers do not have to match each other. They only need to uniquely identify the connection so that the host computer can keep track of which application is communicating with which application on the other host.

The port number that the client uses for the destination of the packet is usually interpreted by the target server to indicate the service to be used. For example, Telnet servers generally listen on port 23. The source port that the client sends to the server, however, can vary. All that is necessary is that the Telnet server knows what this port number is and uses it when sending replies back to the client.

You can probably see where this discussion is going. To further expand the allowable outside connections, without having to increase the number of IP addresses that are allocated exclusively for NAT usage, a newer form of NAT, called network address port translation (NAPT), can replace the client's IP address and the client's source port number. By using this method, a single IP address that is valid on the Internet can be distributed to multiple clients on the internal LAN, by simply varying the source port number. The NAT server keeps track of clients by maintaining a table that translates the client's connection to an outside IP address and a port number that is unique for that IP address.

In some implementations of NAPT the terms Port Address Translation (PAT) and NAT Overloading are used.

The result is that a single IP address can be used on the Internet to represent a large number of clients on the internal network.

Using NAT to Hide Information About the LAN

As you can see, NAT can be used to hide information about the internal network. Because the client's actual IP address is never used on the Internet, it becomes difficult, if not impossible, for someone on the outside network to find out what it is.

There is, however, an exception to this. Some applications embed source or destination addresses into the payload of the packet. A good example is the Internet Control Message Protocol (ICMP). Most ICMP packets, such as destination unreachable and parameter problem packets, include, as part of their payload, the original IP packet for which they are reporting an error. If the NAT server is to work properly, it must be designed with this in mind so that it can modify these kinds of packets. First, it needs to be able to change the IP information in the header of the IP packet that carries the ICMP message. Second it will need to modify the IP information that is stored in the original IP packet that is now encapsulated by the ICMP packet.

When you are evaluating products that use NAT technology, be sure to closely review the documentation to be sure that it supports the services you need for your network.

Other Data That NAT Changes

In addition to changing the source IP address and possibly the source port number, don't forget that there are other fields that also need to be modified. These are the checksum fields found in packet headers. Changing an IP address will require that the checksum for the header also be changed. Failure to do so will result in the packet being dropped at the other end of the connection. The TCP/IP stack there will determine that it must have been modified or corrupted in some manner during transmission. NAT servers do make these modifications.

Using NAT to Increase the LAN Address Space

Another advantage of NAT is that it can allow you to dramatically increase your internal network address space. Before NAT was developed, it was necessary that every host connected to the Internet have its own unique IP address. If two networks, using identical address spaces, were connected to the Internet, there would be no way to decide how to route packets. Think what would happen if several houses on your street all had the same address. How would the postman determine where to deliver a letter?

By using NAT you can take advantage of the address ranges that have been set aside by the Internet Assigned Number Authority (IANA). Instead of having to be stuck with a small Class C address, with only 256 possible addresses, you can use one of the reserved address ranges. Of course, anyone else can use the same address range that you choose. The point is that NAT will translate your private internal addresses into valid ones on the Internet. If you are using basic NAT, you will need to set aside a valid range of addresses to use. If you are using NATP, you can set aside fewer addresses because varying the port number can be used.

One of the major factors behind the next version of the Internet protocol, IPv6, was the belief that the IPv4 address pool was becoming quickly exhausted. NAT reduces this urgency because each network does not need to have a unique IP address for every host in the network. In the last year or so, several educational organizations that have been connected to the Internet since the early days (and which were issued huge Class A address ranges) have been reconfiguring their networks to use a private address range. That way, Class A network addresses could be returned for reuse by other organizations. Although IPv6 is undoubtedly the future of the Internet, in the short term, NAT relieves the address-shortage urgency.

SEE ALSO

➤ *IPv6 is in your future. For more information about this next-generation IP protocol, see Chapter 21, "Firewalls and Beyond," page 381*

What Is Address Vectoring?

The function called *address vectoring* is very similar to NAT.

Suppose you have a popular Web site that receives a huge number of hits every day. To satisfy these requests you could employ a huge server that uses multiple CPUs and RAID disk subsystems to satisfy the load. There will eventually come a point, however, when the server, no matter how large, begins to get bogged down and response time will suffer. For a large Internet site, using a single server is simply not feasible. One solution would be to use more than one server and assign each server a different IP address and a different DNS name. This is not very practical, however. Using this method, clients would have to be aware of several hostnames to access your site. They would have to try one after another until they received a satisfactory response.

Instead, address vectoring allows you to distribute the load across several servers, all acting as if they were the same server being addressed by the client. Only one DNS name and IP address are needed. NAT allows several internal client addresses to be translated into one valid, external IP address. Address vectoring works similarly, allowing a single incoming IP address to be translated to more than one IP address on your internal LAN. Thus, you can add servers to balance the load as you see fit. Use a proxy application that supports address vectoring to decide which server (usually the least busy) will satisfy the request.

SEE ALSO

➤ *To learn how to install and configure Microsoft Proxy Server, see Chapter 18, "Microsoft Proxy Server," page 333*

Content Screening and Blocking

The topic of screening Internet access has become a hot topic in recent years. This capability allows the administrator to designate certain sites that will be blocked to users on the internal network. Some products allow you to specify specific sites to be blocked, whereas others screen the content of network traffic and can be configured to block certain words or other data. After all, if you are operating a business network, you might want your employees to spend their time producing something for the company, not surfing the Web, looking at "interesting" sites.

The reasons you might employ screening and blocking techniques are not limited to keeping employees working on company business. It can also be employed to reduce legal liability. For example, if one of your employees downloads objectionable material (such as pornography or information from a "hate" oriented site) could your company be held liable if that employee shows this material to someone who finds it offensive? Prevention is much easier than trying to pick up the pieces afterward. As a result, screening and blocking techniques are becoming quite popular today.

Because a proxy server sits between the client and server for a network service, several methods can be used at the proxy server to screen or block access:

- **URL blocking**   You can specify specific URLs that will be blocked (or logged). The disadvantage to this method is that URLs change quite frequently on the Internet. Thousands of pages are added every day, and it would be impossible for a busy administrator to evaluate every new site.

- **Category blocking**   This method allows you to specify a specific category of information content that will be blocked. For example, sites with sexual content or hate content.

- **Embedded content**   Some proxy software applications can be configured to block Java, ActiveX Controls, and other objects that might be embedded in a response to a Web request. These kinds of objects can be used to run applications on the local computer and, hence, can be used by hackers to gain access.

Content blocking software is not perfect. It should not be relied on as your only means to keep certain kinds of data from traveling into your network. Although you might be able to specify a long list of specific URLs that you want to block, a knowledgeable user could bypass this by using the site's IP address in the HTTP request. As if that weren't bad enough, IP addresses don't have to be written only in dotted-decimal notation. An IP address is actually a 32-bit number, and dotted-decimal notation is a convenient method for writing it down. Most browsers will gladly accept a decimal representation of the 32-bit address (for example, a whole number value for the 32-bit value). For example, take the address 216.65.33.219. In binary, this would be the following:

```
216 = 11011000
```

```
65 = 01000001
```

```
33 = 00100001
```

```
219 = 11011011
```

If you string these bits all together you get, in binary, 110110000100 00010010000111011011. Take that number, convert it to decimal, and you get 3628147163. So, to access the Web site that uses the address 216.65.33.219, you can use either of the following in most browsers:

```
http://216.65.33.219
```

```
http://3628147163
```

Don't rely on blocking software as your only defense against Trojan horse programs and computer viruses. Programs that filter these kinds of applications do so by looking for a known "fingerprint." They cannot guarantee protection against new virus threats until the filtering software can be updated by the vendor. It is also easy to disguise virus programs inside an email message. For these reasons, deploy a good virus screening (and cleaning) program on all computers in your network, and be sure your site's security policy prohibits users from bringing in software (especially on floppy disks) from home.

Logging and Alerting Facilities

An important security function that proxy servers provide that should not be overlooked or taken lightly is the ability to log information about their activities. Some can be configured to trigger an alert (for example, an email to the administrator, a pop-up message on the console) based on predetermined conditions.

Application-level proxies are usually able to provide more information for logging purposes than generic or circuit-level proxies. This is because the circuit level proxy only knows about and makes decisions based on addressing information (IP address, port number) much like a packet filter. Application-level proxies are written for specific services or protocols and, thus, are able to extract a greater amount of information for logging purposes because they "understand" the service or protocol.

Logging is an important component of auditing any system, proxy server, file server, or even a plain old user workstation. In Chapter 8, "Operating System Monitoring and Auditing Techniques," this topic is covered in more detail for Windows NT and UNIX operating systems. In addition, be sure to read all the documentation that comes with any proxy software that you purchase. Experiment with logging options, reviewing the captured data, until you become familiar with the information that you can trap in this manner. Configuring a system or application for logging should not be considered a static function. Although you might initially configure the server to log only a small amount of information during normal operations, when you suspect that your network is under attack, you should understand how the logging mechanisms work, so that you can enable more detailed logging.

Client Considerations

If you want to provide transparent access to network services using proxy servers, you will need to do one of the following:

- Modify existing client software so that it will work with the proxy server.
- Obtain new client software that can be configured to use a proxy server.

If neither of these is feasible, you might consider using a classical proxy approach, such as the proxies found in the TIS Internet Firewall Toolkit. This will require user education.

Most new applications have the ability to use built-in proxy servers. For example, Microsoft Internet Explorer can be configured to use a proxy server for some or all network service requests.

1. In Internet Explorer, click Tools and then Internet Options. When the Internet Options property sheets appear, click Connections and then click the LAN Settings button.
2. In the Local Area Network (LAN) Settings dialog box select the check box labeled Use a Proxy Server.
3. Enter the IP address of the proxy server and the port to use.
4. Use the Bypass proxy server for local addresses check box if this client is directly allowed to contact servers on the local network.
5. Alternatively, to specify a different proxy server and/or port, click the Advanced button. In Figure 7.4 you can see the Proxy Settings dialog box which allows you to enter proxy server configuration information separately for HTTP, Secure server, FTP, Gopher, and Socks.

FIGURE 7.4
Use the Proxy Settings dialog box to configure proxy servers for different services.

If you select the check box labeled Use the Same Proxy Server for All Protocols, only the first field will be available for you to enter a proxy server address and port.

6. In the Exceptions box, list any servers you want the client to contact directly, bypassing the proxy server. Separate hosts using a semicolon.

7. Click OK when finished.

In the Local Area Network (LAN) Settings dialog box you can also select to have the proxy server automatically configure itself using a script provided by the administrator. For large networks, this convenience can save time.

Summary

Proxy servers are an important component of a firewall. Working at the application level, proxy servers can be configured to selectively allow or disallow features that a network service or protocol provides. Their ability to perform extensive logging and alerting is more robust than that provided by packet filters because many proxy applications have a good understanding of the service or protocol. In later chapters you will look at a few proxy solutions, including the TIS Internet Firewall Toolkit, SQUID, and Microsoft Proxy Server.

chapter

8

Operating System Monitoring and Auditing Techniques

Auditing and Log Files •

UNIX •

Windows NT •

Application-Specific Log Files •

Other Considerations •

Auditing and Log Files

The safety assurance that a well-configured firewall architecture provides should not be an excuse for you to become lax when it comes to ordinary security procedures. Although you might trust the users on your local network—which in itself is not necessarily a good idea—you should not implicitly trust the firewall to protect you from *all* the possible evils that can be visited on your network from the outside world. The Internet allows a malicious hacker to perpetrate an attack on your LAN from almost any location on the globe. There are programs on the Internet that automate the process of seeking out and penetrating system and network vulnerabilities. After a firewall has been configured and is in place, you should think of it only as a first line of defense—not a complete solution.

What Is Auditing?

When you talk about *auditing*, which is the process of recording certain events that occur on a computer or the network, it is important to understand that is only through this technique that you will ever be able to begin to track down the source of a network compromise. Oh, if an infiltrator is able to destroy important data or crash an important server, you will find out about it soon enough! However, will you be able to determine the cause? For example, when a server crash does happen, how can you be sure it was not a bug in the operating system that caused the event? Could it possibly be some new application that you have just installed? Worse yet, does the person who caused the problem reside inside or outside your network?

Both UNIX and Windows NT have extensive auditing capabilities. However, you cannot take for granted that the default installation of the operating system will generate the audited events that will be most useful to you. In this chapter, I will go over these and discuss the kinds of information they can reveal and how to configure the auditing features that these systems provide.

Reviewing Those Log Files!

It does no good to employ extensive auditing techniques if you are not going to also set up a schedule to regularly review log files. The time that can be expended on plowing through voluminous files that are used to log events can be very time-consuming, and it is easy to put the review off when you are having a busy day. However, there are programs on the market that you can use to help streamline the process. You might not have to read every single event in the Windows NT event log or in the large files that can be created by using the UNIX `syslog` facility.

There are several important things to remember about log files:

- If it is possible to hack into your system, how can you be sure that the log files themselves have not been compromised? That is, can you really trust the information in your log files? If the intruder manages to break into the system using a highly privileged account (such as root), the intruder has the ability to edit log files to cover his tracks.

- It is easy to become complacent when performing a routine procedure over and over. If you have the daily job of reviewing multiple log files (containing very boring information), how alert are you going to be? Is it possible after several months—or years—of reviewing files with no important discoveries that you might just miss that one important record that shows a security breach?

- Log files can become quite large. It is tempting to delete them or even to restrict the kinds of logged events so that you do not have to worry about disk space.

Trusting that the information recorded in a log file is accurate can be a tricky proposition. However, in many cases, it is all the data you have to go on when you try to discover the source of an intrusion. If your budget allows it, you can solve most of this problem by locating log files on a drive that uses write-once media. The price of writable CD-ROMs and other write-once devices has dropped dramatically in the past few years, so it shouldn't be difficult to cost-justify this measure to upper management. This technique does not protect you from fraudulent data created by programs that have been hacked. That is, if the intruder has managed to replace important system files that write to log files, you still have a big problem. This technique does, however, prevent the intruder from editing a log file to remove all tracks of his penetration into your network.

Security is an important job. You shouldn't leave it to a single person. To overcome the boredom problem that can occur when reviewing log files, you can do several things. First, automate the process by using tools that are designed to consolidate or search through log file information. Second, make the job of reviewing this data the responsibility of more than one person. Let them swap this duty back and forth every few days so that the boredom factor is less likely to kick in. Of course, you, the administrator, should frequently check up on the auditing and reviewing process yourself. Having one person responsible for reviewing important security information presents a potential security problem in itself. It is better to place trust in two or more persons than in a single person.

It is better to produce large log files that contain a wide variety of events than it is to select only the few events that you think might really be a problem. For example, in Windows NT you can choose to audit successful logins or unsuccessful logins. Choose to log both! Although auditing login failures might not produce the large number of records that successful logins might and it thereby might keep the event log to a smaller size, the successful login records can be a more valuable tool for tracking down how, when, and why your network security was breached. Frequent or large numbers of login failures might be a sign of someone trying to infiltrate the network by guessing passwords and should be cause for alarm. Successful logins, however, can show you when a user account is used to get into the system during off-hours or from a computer that should not be used by that account.

Consider log file data to be just as valuable as the most valuable data that you store on your network. Don't regularly delete log files to save disk space. Instead, if you are not using write-once media, which can be safely stored away for future reference, back up log files to offline media and keep them for an indefinite period of time. When a security breach occurs, you might find that it was because of a Trojan Horse program that was planted in your system many months, possibly even a year or so, ago. Keeping log files around so that they can be further scrutinized at a later time is a very good idea.

If you have been at your job for a number of years without any major security problems, you might just dismiss these arguments about log files as a waste of energy that could be put to better use elsewhere in your business. However, when you connect your network to the Internet, it is not going to be "business as usual" anymore. This is just the beginning of a revolution in computers and communications, and past experience will pale in comparison to the kinds of problems that are on the horizon.

The Front End of Auditing: Resource Protections

Auditing is one side of system security. The other side is resource protection. Whereas this chapter focuses on the auditing end of the security process, Chapter 6, "Using a Bastion Host," gives you a good introduction into how to protect valuable system resources and data by using the resource protection mechanisms of the UNIX and Windows operating systems. If you set up user rights and privileges and file protections in a secure manner, you might not find yourself sifting through log file data in the middle of the night trying to find out what went wrong.

UNIX

UNIX was once heralded as *the* portable operating system. It was a solution to the many proprietary operating systems that proliferated when there were only a few large companies making computers— minicomputers and mainframes, that is. However, today there are many varieties, or flavors, of UNIX on the market, and it is probably the most used operating system for computers connected to the Internet for business purposes. Its baby cousin, Linux, is making great strides into the market at this time and, because of its similarity to UNIX, some of the discussion here of UNIX also applies to Linux. Because there are different distributions of UNIX out there, you should be sure to check the specific syntax for commands shown here as examples. As the old expression goes, your mileage may vary.

Using the *syslog* Utility

One important auditing facility provided by UNIX is the `syslog` utility. It takes input from a variety of other programs and utilities and stores them in a central location. Because it is so flexible, it can be a valuable auditing tool only if you are educated in how it is configured and understand the events that are logged.

The syslog daemon (syslogd) should be started when the system boots. This is done in one of the rc files. The syntax for starting the daemon is as follows:

```
/etc/syslog [-mN] [-ffilename] [-d]
```

The default configuration file name for syslog is /etc/syslog.conf. You can specify another file by using the -f option with the name of the configuration file you want to use. This can be useful for two reasons. First, by specifying a nonstandard filename, you make it a little more difficult for a hacker to find it and possibly make changes. Second, when you are testing different logging configurations, you can use multiple files so that if you need to go back to a specific configuration, you just have to restart the utility with the correct filename.

The -m option can be used to place timestamps into the file. The -d option turns on debugging mode.

To configure the operation of syslogd, you should consult the documentation that comes with your firewall product. Many firewall applications will use syslogd for logging purposes, and the vendor should suggest the appropriate manner for its configuration.

The *syslog* Configuration File: *syslog.conf*

The syslog configuration file is an ASCII text file that you can modify using any standard text editor. You can use the default /etc/syslog.conf file, or as explained in the previous section, you can use a different file so long as you start the utility specifying that as an option. This file contains a record for each type of message that you want to the facility to log. Each record is composed of two parts:

- A selector defines the kind of event to be logged—the source and severity of the event.
- An action defines what the syslog daemon should do when the event occurs.

The selector portion of the record is itself made up of two pieces of information, which are separated by a period. The first part of the selector is the name of the system facility that generates the event message. The second part indicates the severity level of the message. Multiple selectors can be placed on the same line, but they need to be separated by a semicolon.

Where Does syslog **Get Messages From?**

The syslog daemon runs as a background process listening for messages and deciding on which ones to act on based on its configuration file. Where do these messages come from? They come from three sources. First, a socket named /dev/log receives messages from processes that run only on the local computer. Second, a device named /dev/klog gets its messages from the UNIX kernel. Third, the UDP port 514 receives messages from other computers in the network.

Table 8.1 lists the different facilities of UNIX that can be used in the selector. Table 8.2 lists the severity levels that you can specify.

Table 8.1   Facility Names Used in the *syslog* Configuration File

Facilities	Description
user	Generated by user applications
kern	Kernel messages
mail	Mail system messages
daemon	System daemons
auth	Authorization file (for example, login)
lpr	Line printer spooler system
news	USENET
uucp	UUCP (not currently implemented)
cron	cron and at utilities
local0-7	Reserved for local use
mark	Timestamp messages
*	All of the preceding except for mark

Table 8.2   Severity Levels Used in the *syslog.conf* File

Severity Levels	Description
emerg	Panic condition. Something usually broadcast to all users.
alert	A condition that needs immediate attention.
crit	Warnings about critical situations.
err	Other errors not warranting emerg, alert, or crit.
warning	Warning messages.
notice	Situations that require attention, but not as important as a warning or other error. Not necessarily an error condition.
info	Informational messages.
debug	Messages generated by programs running a debug mode.
none	Suppresses messages for this entry.

Creating the selector portion of the record is an easy task. All you need to do is to combine one of the facilities listed in Table 8.1 with one of the severity levels listed in Table 8.2. To separate them, use a period:

```
kernel.alert
auth.warning
mail.notice
lpr.crit
```

This action portion of the record tells the daemon what to do when it receives a message that matches criteria set by the selector portion of the record. To complete the record, you need to specify an action to take. One or more space characters are used to separate the selector portion from the action portion of the record. The kinds of actions that syslog can take include the following:

- Write the event message to a log file (/var/adm/messages, on many systems).
- Send the event message to another computer (via UPD port 514).
- Send the event message to the console device (/dev/console).
- Send the event message to a user logged in to the system.

You can direct syslog to take more than one action for a particular event. For example:

```
*.err;auth.notice              /dev/console
*.err;auth.notice;daemon.info  /var/adm/messages
```

In the first line of this example, all events of the severity level of err are written to the console device. The same goes for significant events relating to user authorization. In the next line, both of these kinds of events are also sent to the messages file. By sending the message to the console device (or possibly a user who is logged in to the system), it is likely to get immediate attention. By recording the event in the messages log file, it is available for review at a later time.

When using a UNIX host computer as part of a firewall, you should consider using the ability of syslog to send messages to another computer. Why? This is because it is always possible that the firewall host has been compromised by an intruder. If a hacker has managed to get into the system, he just might be able to edit, otherwise

Notice also in this example that multiple spaces are used to separate the selector from the action portion of the record. This makes it easier to read and maintain the file because you can clearly see both portions of the records. Why is readability so important? It is because in addition to reviewing log files, you should also review the syslog configuration file on a periodic basis to be sure that it has not been modified by an intruder! You can also place comments into the file by beginning the line with the # character. If you use good formatting techniques and comments to help you understand why certain records were placed in the file, it makes the job of reviewing it a lot easier. Appendix B, "Other Security Tools You Can Use," contains information about security programs, such as Tripwire, you can use to help check the integrity of system files.

modify, or even delete the message log file that you use. By sending the messages to another system, the level of security is raised a little because the hacker also has to manage an entry into that system to attack the log file.

Depending on how important you consider security to be at your site, you might want to dedicate a single computer to use as a link for `syslog` messages from other systems. By hardening this system—removing most user accounts, disabling unnecessary services, and employing good file protections—you can make it very difficult indeed for anyone to disturb this audit trail. When configuring security solutions such as this, remember that you are protecting yourself from attack from both inside and outside your network.

The format for sending messages to another computer is as follows:

```
kern.*;ath.*  @yoko.karma.com
```

Using a log file for messages is a good idea no matter what other actions you take. Remember that large log files can be moved to offline storage on a regular basis so they don't have to take up a lot of space on the running system. In the preceding examples, the standard file `/var/adm/messages` was used. You can use this, or any file, to hold all messages, or you can use separate log files for different kinds of events. By using multiple log files, you can make it easier to divide the chore of reviewing the files among several people who might be best able to understand the messages that are logged. For example, the mail administrator might be the most logical person to review messages about the email system. The system administrator might want to personally review messages related to the UNIX kernel. Using multiple log files also makes it easier to write script files that can be used to help in the review process.

> While creating multiple log files to help categorize messages that are logged, note that some versions of UNIX limit the number of log files that the `syslog` daemon can open. In some cases, this can be as few as 16 files. Check your documentation!

Miscellaneous UNIX Log Files

The `syslog` daemon is not the only method used to produce log files on the UNIX system. Because UNIX has an evolutionary past in which different authors or vendors have, over time, contributed new components, you will find that there are many log files generated by different utilities that can be useful for review.

usr/adm/wtmp, /etc/utmp, and *lastlog*

These three binary files keep track of users on the system. The file /etc/utmp only shows users that are currently logged into the system, whereas the file /usr/adm/wtmp is a historical file that records logins, logouts, and other information such as when the system is shut down.

The /etc/utmp file is mentioned here not because of its usefulness in security matters, *but for just the opposite reason.* The contents of this file continually change as users log on and off the system. The major flaw in this file is that it is generally world-writable on many UNIX implementations. That means, of course, that an intruder into the system can edit the file to remove the entry for her current login. The contents of this file are used as input for the who command (and also the rwho and finger commands), so you might want to remember that this command isn't necessarily a great way to accurately determine who is logged in to the system.

The /usr/adm/wtmp file does not remove records when a user logs off the system. Instead, it keeps an audit trail of logins and logouts. Because the file is continually written to and records don't get removed, it is an excellent candidate to put to write-only media. By doing so, you can prevent it from being edited (or replaced) by a hacker. Several commands can be used to get information from this file. The last command can be used to display the information, in reverse order as it is found in the file, so that you can see the most recent information.

When you log in to a UNIX system, the login program uses a file called lastlog to determine the last time this username was used to log in. In most versions of UNIX, this information is displayed when you log in. On some versions, the login program also displays successful or unsuccessful login attempts. Although this doesn't give you a lot of information to go on, it can be useful in triggering an alarm in your head if it doesn't look right. For example, if you are the only person who should be using a particular account and you notice that a previous login was accomplished on a weekend and you know you weren't there to do it, it's time to start looking through other log files to determine whether someone has been using your account!

/var/adm/sulog

The su command enables a user to switch users. That is, while logged in to her own account, a user can use this command to log in again, using another username and password. Usage of the su command is recorded in the /var/adm/sulog file, so you can review it. The sudo command is used for a similar purpose, but a password is not required with it.

These commands have valid usage. You might have an administrative user who needs to temporarily use a different username to gain access to a particular system file, for example. However, a hacker who has managed to get into the system might also use this command. In either case, review the file periodically to determine whether either of these commands is being misused.

/var/adm/aculog

This file is used to track users who dial out through modems to other systems. It is also used by UUCP commands to record their activities, though UUCP is not used much anymore and has been replaced by better utilities. The file records the user who made the call, the telephone number dialed, and whether the call was actually completed.

Dial-in and dial-out capabilities are best done from a secure host that resides in the DMZ or perhaps on a system that is not connected to the network. Remember that allowing network computers to have internal modems means that you pretty much don't care about access into the network, so why would you bother with a firewall in the first place?

/var/log/cron

To automate tasks on a UNIX system, the cron daemon is used. This daemon enables you to create script files that can be run at a specified time without user intervention. Although most modern implementations of the daemon make use of the syslog facility, there is also a log file for this daemon, and it is /var/log/cron. Hackers who are able to manipulate the cron daemon configuration file might be able to schedule a job to run that they can use later to gain entry to the system or to get elevated privileges. Review both the cron configuration file and the log file regularly. Better yet, configure syslog to track its usage.

The *ps* Command

Although it doesn't use a log file, the ps command can still be as helpful as a log file when you are investigating a possible security breach. Instead of log file data, the ps command uses the UNIX kernel's process table and displays information about current processes. If an intruder has managed to get into your system and start a background process, you can use this command to search for it. Because the information comes from the kernel and not a log file, there is less of a chance that it is inaccurate. The ps command, depending on the UNIX variant, gives you the following information:

- Process ID
- Username
- TTY (or terminal the process uses)
- Execution time
- The command currently being executed
- CPU usage
- Memory usage
- When the process was started

When I talked about the /etc/utmp command, I noted that it could be modified by a knowledgeable hacker. So, by using this command and comparing it to the contents of that file, you might be able to identify suspicious processes that warrant further investigation. Also, look for processes that have been running for longer than they should, at a time other than when they should, or by a user who should not be executing certain commands.

Windows NT

The Windows NT operating systems enable you to audit a large number of events. Just as you must first configure the UNIX syslog daemon to define the events that will be trapped, you must first set up the events that Windows audits.

Unlike UNIX, however, you only have to use one utility—the Event Viewer—to view the event messages that are produced. One caveat is that this applies only to the operating system. Some applications, such as the Internet Information Server, also maintain log files in addition to writing to the Event Log files. Third-party applications can do one or the other or both, depending on how the vendor has coded them.

Setting Up Auditing Events

Whereas the Event Viewer administrative tool is used to examine the events that are audited by Windows NT Server, there are utilities that are used to set up the events that will be audited. The three utilities you use are the following:

- The User Manager (or User Manager for Domains in a domain environment)
- The Windows NT Explorer utility
- The Properties Sheet for a printer

The first utility you will examine is the User Manager. This system management tool, found under the Administrative Tools folder, is used to define the auditing policy for the server and for managing user accounts and domain trust relationships.

Selecting Events to Audit Using the User Manager Administrative Tool

1. Click Start, Programs, Administrative Tools, and then User Manager.
2. From the Policies menu, click Audit. The Audit Policy dialog box is displayed (see Figure 8.1).
3. Click the Audit These Events radio button.
4. For each event that you want to be audited, select the Success or Failure check box, or both.
5. When you are finished selecting events, click OK.

For each event type listed in the Audit Policy dialog box (see Figure 8.1), you can select to audit success events and failure events. A success event is one in which the access, such as a user logon, was successful. A failure event is the opposite. For example, if you only want to know when users attempt to log in but fail to do so due to an incorrect password or some other reason, you select the check box under Failure for that event. You can also select to audit both success and failure events.

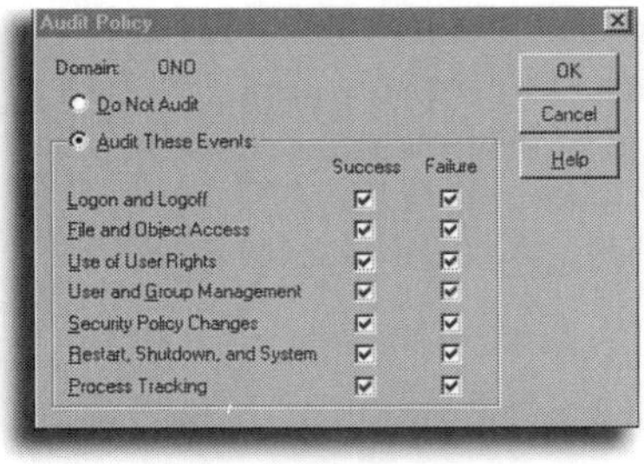

FIGURE 8.1
The Audit Policy dialog box in the User Manager for Domains is used to configure events to audit.

Disabling Auditing Events

In Figure 8.1, you can disable auditing all events that can be set up using the User Manager by clicking the Do Not Audit radio button. If you want to disable auditing for only a short period of time, use this button. By using this button, the events you have already selected by using the Success and/or Failure check boxes remain selected. When you later decide to re-enable auditing, you do not have to remember which events you had previously selected. You only need to click the Audit These Events button again.

Table 8.3 provides a brief explanation of each of the events you can audit.

Table 8.3 Auditable Events You Can Set Up Using the User Manager Tool

Event	Description
Logon and Logoff	Tracks users logging in to the system. This also tracks network logins from remote systems.
File and Object Access	Includes file and directory access and sending jobs to printers. This category requires you to further define the events for the file, directory, or printer that will be audited.
Use of User Rights	Records when a user makes use of rights you grant to them when you set up his account with the User Manager for Domains.
User and Group Management	Tracks changes to group accounts. Creating, deleting, and renaming user groups is done in this category, as are changes to passwords.
Security Policy Changes	Keeps track of changes to user rights and audit or trust relationships.
Restart, Shutdown, and System	Tracks when the system is shut down or restarted and other events that relate to system security. This category also includes changes to the security event `log on the system`.
Process Tracking	Records voluminous information about user processes, including when programs are executed, object accesses, and program exits.

Of the events listed in Table 8.3, the last one, Process Tracking, produces the largest number of event records. Although you might want to enable all event types on a server that has been "hardened" to survive in the DMZ, you need a huge amount of disk space for log files if you select this event type. Instead, enable Process Tracking only when you are investigating a specific security threat and need to have this amount of detailed information to conduct your investigation.

After you have selected the events to audit, the operating system begins to create records in the Event Log Files for all the events listed in Table 8.3, except for the event type File and Object Access. If you have selected to audit this event type, you need to further define the kinds of events that will be audited by using the Windows NT Explorer (for file and directory objects) and the Print Manager (for printers).

First, you should decide on which directories or files you want access to be audited. Second, you need to decide on the kind of access to be audited. Next, use Windows NT Explorer to locate and enable auditing.

Enabling Auditing for a File or Directory

1. Click Start, Programs, and then Windows NT Explorer.

2. Right-click the file or directory. Alternatively, click the file or directory name to highlight it and select Properties from the File menu. The Properties Sheet for the object is displayed. Select the Security tab at the top of the object's Property Sheet.

3. Click the Auditing button. The Directory (or File) Auditing dialog box is displayed (see Figure 8.2).

4. Under Events to Audit, select the Success or Failure check boxes, or both.

5. Select the Replace Auditing on Subdirectories check box if you want to propagate these auditing changes to all subdirectories under the current directory.

6. Select the Replace Auditing on Existing Files check box if you want to propagate these auditing changes to all files that currently exist under this directory (and subdirectories if you have chosen that option).

7. Click the Add button to bring up the Add Users and Groups dialog box (see Figure 8.3).

8. To select a group of users, click the group name and then click Add. The group shows up under Add Names at the bottom of the dialog box.

In Figure 8.1, the Audit policy dialog box enabled you to set up the auditing policy for the entire domain. Note that Windows NT Server can be installed as a standalone server or as a domain controller. When using a standalone server, the audit policy you define applies only to that server. When you define an audit policy on an NT Server that is operating as a domain controller, you are setting the policy for the entire domain.

For this reason (among many others), it would be unwise to use a Windows NT domain controller as a bastion host and then select to audit a large number of events. Instead, if you are using Windows NT Server as a bastion host, install the operating system to make it a standalone server and not a domain controller.

191

9. To select individual users, click a group and then click the Show Users button. Click the username and then the Add button. The user shows up under Add Names at the bottom of the dialog box.

10. Alternatively, use the Search button to search for a user or group.

11. When you have finished selecting users and/or groups that will be audited for the events you have selected for this file or directory, click the OK button to return to the Directory Auditing dialog box.

12. Click the OK button to finish. The access events you have selected for this file or directory are now logged in the Event Log files.

FIGURE 8.2
Select the events that will be audited for this file or directory.

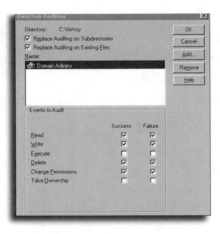

In Figure 8.2, there are six kinds of events that can be selected for auditing for file and directory objects. These are the following:

- Read
- Write
- Execute
- Delete
- Change Permission
- Take Ownership

To audit printer usage, you use pretty much the same method. Instead of using Windows NT Explorer, though, you can bring up the Properties Sheet for a printer by right-clicking the printer icon under My Computer or in the Printers Folder.

The events you can audit for printers, however, are different than those for files and directories:

- Print
- Full Control
- Delete
- Change Permissions
- Take Ownership

Using the Event Viewer to Review Log Files

The Event Viewer is also found in the Administrative Tools folder and is used to examine all events that are audited by the Windows NT operating system. Three different log files are used to hold event records, and you can select which file to examine by using this utility. The three log files are described in Table 8.4.

Table 8.4 Using the Event Viewer to Examine Events in Log Files

Log File	Description
System	Events relating to system operation, such as startup and shutdown and device failures.
Application	Events logged by applications.
Security	Events relating to security issues that have been selected for auditing.

193

Whereas the System and Application log files can be useful for troubleshooting purposes, it is the Security log file that contains events that you have selected for auditing.

Using the Event Viewer to Examine Audited Events

1. Click Start, Programs, Administrative Tools, and then Event Viewer.

2. From the Log menu, select Security to open the Security event log file (see Figure 8.4).

3. Use the scrollbar to move up or down through the file. The most recent events are displayed at the top of the file by default.

4. To see the details associated with a particular event, double-click the event in the listing or highlight the event.

FIGURE 8.4
The Event Viewer displays a list of records that resulted from auditing.

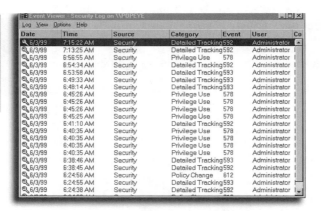

In Figure 8.4, you can see that the first line of each event record begins with an icon. These each have a special meaning that makes it easy for you to scan through the file looking for serious events:

- **Red stop sign**   This one stands out and is easy to see. It indicates an error.

- **Exclamation point inside a yellow circle**   This is a warning message.

- **Letter "I" inside a blue circle**   This is an informational message.

- **Grey padlock**   Of particular interest for security matters, this icon indicates an invalid authorization event.

- **Gold key**   Also of interest for security matters, this icon indicates a successful authorization event.

Managing Event Log Files

Using the Event Viewer, you can configure how events are stored in the files, and you can export the data to a file so that it can be further manipulated using a spreadsheet or other program. To save the event records in a comma-delimited ASCII text file, select Save As from the Log menu. Select Comma Delimited Text from the Type field. When a log file begins to grow too large, you can use this method to save it and then empty the file by using the Clear All Events selection from the Log menu.

To manage the size of the log file, use the Settings selection from the File Menu.

Managing Event Log Files

1. Click Log and then Settings. The Event Log Settings dialog box appears (Figure 8.5).

2. Use the Change Settings field to select the Security log file.

3. Use the Maximum Log Size field to set the maximum size that the log file can grow to.

4. Use the Event Log Wrapping radio buttons to control whether older events are overwritten.

5. Click OK to finish.

FIGURE 8.5
You can control the size of the each log file using the Event Log Settings dialog box.

Application-Specific Log Files

A vendor that creates an application can choose whether to implement logging for their product. If security is important, you should take this into consideration when evaluating competing products. If logging is desired, delve into the documentation to find out how it is implemented. For example, for an application that runs under UNIX, does the program create and manage its own log file? Does it use UDP port 514 to send messages to syslog? If it creates a log file, can you specify the location of the log file? The same goes for an application that is written to run under Windows NT: Does the product create its own log file, or does it make use of the Event Logging facility? The ability to control the location of an application-specific log file is important, especially so when you are installing the application on a host that will be vulnerable. Directing the log file output to a write-once device can help protect it from changes made by an intruder.

Other Considerations

When I first talked about auditing at the start of this chapter, I also discussed the fact that auditing is the back-end of security. Log files only tell you what has happened and do nothing to provide a secure system by themselves. It is important that you also make use of the resource protection features of the operating system to limit access to important resources so that in the event someone does make it into your system without permission, he has to then use all his skills to get at your data or system. Chapter 6, "Using a Bastion Host," contains a lengthy discussion of resource protections as implemented by UNIX and Windows NT.

Summary

Auditing is a valuable tool that can be used to enhance security for every system on your network. When a security breach or network intrusion is suspected, the trail of event records that you can find in various log files can help to track down what was compromised and possibly who the person was. Auditing should not be considered a "set and forget it" operation. Regularly reviewing log files to look for unusual events should be the norm. In this way, you are more likely to discover a minor intrusion before the hacker has had time to perpetrate more damage to your network.

part

II

Encryption and Secure Communications on the Internet

Encryption Technology   199

Virtual Provate Networks (VPNs)   211
and Tunneling

Using Pretty Good Privacy (PGP)   227
for Encryption

# chapter 9

Encryption Technology

Protecting Sensitive Information •

What is Encryption? •

Practical Applications for
Cryptography on the Internet •

Protecting Sensitive Information

Using the Information Superhighway, as many like to refer to the Internet now, for the transfer of valuable or sensitive information can be risky. Because most of the systems that your data will travel through on its way to its destination are not under your control, there are many points in the link where your data can be intercepted. To make this communications channel safe for businesses to use, encryption techniques are used to render ordinary data into *ciphertext*. That is, a mathematical algorithm, in conjunction with a key, is used to perform an action on ordinary data that produces a result that appears to be nonsense. Those who possess the key can reverse the process. Those who do not possess the key cannot understand the encrypted data, unless, of course, they are skilled cryptographers who excel in breaking cryptographic codes and have lots of computer power and time on their hands.

This isn't the only use for which cryptography can be used on the Internet. For the total picture, there are three basic functions for which cryptography is being used for on the Internet:

- Privacy
- Data integrity
- Authentication

It's easy to see that the purpose for encrypting data is to make it private. Only the sender and the intended recipient will be able to understand the data, so it is a private communication. However, if you are unsure of exactly who originated the data, how can you trust it? Once you are sure of the sender, how can you be sure that the data was not intercepted by a man-in-the-middle and modified? By using cryptographic techniques to solve these last two problems—authentication and data integrity—you form a basis for secure communications on the Internet.

In the next chapter I will discuss a very practical application of cryptography which can be used to solve all three of these problems—virtual private networks (VPNs). But first you will use this chapter to quickly review some basic encryption techniques.

What Is Encryption?

Encryption is any method that can be used to hide the contents of a message from those who should not understand it. In practice, most modern cryptographic techniques are based on mathematical formulas that are used to manipulate data so as to render it very difficult to understand by anyone who does not have the *key*. The key is a numeric or alphabetic string of characters that is used for encrypting or deciphering the message. Obviously, the larger the key, the more difficult it will be to decipher a message if you do not know the key.

There are two basic kinds of encryption that have good applications when applied to the Internet. These are single key (symmetric) encryption and public key (asymmetric) encryption.

Single Key Encryption

The most basic form of encryption is called single key encryption. This method uses a mathematical algorithm and a single key to encrypt the data. The same key that is used to encrypt is also used to decrypt the ciphertext. This means that both parties that are involved in the communication need to have possession of the same key and must keep it secret. Revealing the key would allow anyone to read the text.

This form of encryption is also known as *symmetric encryption* because only one key is used to encrypt or decipher the data. Symmetric encryption can be very fast, and that is one of the benefits of using it. Although a single key makes it easy to construct a very fast encryption algorithm, it is also the main problem with the technique. Before communication can begin, one party must be able to securely send a copy of the key to the other party. For governments, spies, and large businesses, this is not really a problem. A courier can be dispatched to safely deliver a secret key to those who will later need it for encrypted communications. Obviously this technique will not work for a business that wants to conduct secure communications with many thousands (or more) of clients on the Internet. It is simply too costly to send a courier around to all those clients.

So although symmetric encryption techniques can be used to create cryptographic programs that are extremely fast and efficient, the lack of a secure method for key exchange at first seems to limit the usefulness of this type of encryption on the Internet.

Examples of symmetric encryption include the following:

- **DES**   The Data Encryption Standard encryption method was developed by IBM and the National Security Agency. DES uses a key of 56 bits and operates on 64-bit blocks of plain text. A newer version, called 3DES, uses three different keys to encrypt the data three different times.

- **IDEA**   The International Data Encryption Algorithm uses a 128-bit key and is therefore much more resistant to brute-force attacks which attempt to decipher the text by trying every possible key.

- **Slipjack**   This new algorithm, which is classified as secret, was developed by the National Security Agency and uses an 80-bit key.

- **Blowfish**   This is a symmetric encryption algorithm that can be used as a "drop in" replacement for DES and IDEA. It can use a key size from 32 bits up to 448 bits.

<aside>
Free Encryption?

Because it is unpatented and the source code is freely available on the Internet, usage of the Blowfish algorithm (developed by Bruce Schneier) is spreading rapidly. For more information about Blowfish, including a list of products that currently use it, or to download the source code, visit the following Web site:

`www.counterpane.com/blowfish.html`
</aside>

Public Key Encryption

The problem of key distribution is solved by using public key cryptography. This method uses not one key, but two keys, hence it is called asymmetric. One key is used to encrypt the data, and the other key is used for decryption. The two keys are mathematically related and together are known as a key pair. The user keeps one key a secret (the private key) and publishes the other key (the public key) so that anyone who needs to can use it. When you want to send an encrypted message to someone who has generated a key pair, you simply encrypt your data with the public key that the person has published. Once the message has been encrypted, only that person's private key, which is his or her secret, can be used to decipher the message and read it.

As you can see, the public key encryption method solves the problem of making data unreadable and the problem of key distribution. There is no need to keep the public key a secret. Indeed, it really doesn't matter who knows the public key because it can only be used to encrypt data, not to decipher it. This method also lends itself to widespread use. If everyone on the Internet can be assigned a key pair and if the public keys can be published, much like phone numbers are distributed in a phone book, it would be possible for almost anyone to communicate securely with anyone else.

The drawback to using this method of encryption is that it is usually not as fast as single-key encryption. For small, simple text files the speed would make little difference. For much larger files, the difference can be important. For a business wanting to establish a secure channel, such as a virtual private network (VPN) to another site, speed becomes a necessity.

Hybrids

Symmetric cryptographic techniques are fast. Public key cryptographic techniques are slow. By combining the two into a hybrid system it is possible to make the most of the advantages offered by each system.

For example, the Pretty Good Privacy (PGP) encryption software uses both symmetric and public key encryption. A message is first encrypted using a special randomly generated key that is valid only for that particular use—a session key. After the message is encrypted using a symmetric technique (fast), the session key itself is then encrypted using the public key half of the key pair. Because the session key is much shorter than the message it was used to encrypt, the time needed to encrypt this session key with a user's public key is minimal in comparison.

SEE ALSO

➤ *Installing and configuring Pretty Good Privacy (PGP) is covered more fully in Chapter 11, "Using Pretty Good Privacy (PGP) for Encryption," page 227*

When the recipient of the message wants to decode the message, he uses his private key to decrypt the session key. The message can then be deciphered quickly using a symmetric algorithm and the session key.

The Secure Sockets Layer protocol (SSL), developed by Netscape, is also a hybrid that uses symmetric and asymmetric encryption and is covered in more detail later in this chapter.

Can the Private Key Be Computed from the Public Key?

It is always possible to break any cryptographic technique, given enough computer power and enough time. However, for all practical purposes, if you use a fairly large key size it would be very difficult for anyone to determine what your private key is given only the public key to go on. Because computing power is multiplying every year, it might be that the key sizes and algorithms used in the future will change to accommodate these advances. But for the time being, if you use a good encryption application from a reliable vendor, you shouldn't worry too much about someone discovering your "secret."

Practical Applications for Cryptography on the Internet

Earlier in this chapter, I mentioned using PGP to encrypt email messages. However, to make efficient use of encryption on the Internet, it will be necessary to establish standards and services based on these standards that can be incorporated into diverse applications, many more complex than simple email systems. If each application vendor were to use a proprietary algorithm to produce secure applications, you would end up with a lot of secure applications that could not talk to each other. Several important steps that have been taken toward standard methods include using digital signatures and digital certificates for authentication purposes, and the Secure Sockets Layer (SSL) protocol to enable secure Web traffic exchanges.

What Are Digital Signatures?

The use of public key cryptography solves the problem of securely rendering a message unreadable except by the intended recipient who possesses the private key needed to unlock the message. It solves the problem of key distribution because knowledge of the public key does not enable one to crack the message. One thing it does not solve is the problem of guaranteeing to the recipient that the sender is who he says he is. For example, if you received an email from Bill Gates, you would most likely assume it to be a joke someone has created by spoofing an email address. How would you ever be able to prove that 1) Bill actually sent the message and 2) that the message is exactly as Bill sent it?

A digital signature is the solution to this problem. Consider, for example, what would happen if you used your private key to encrypt a message instead of the recipient's public key. Because only you possess your private key, a recipient who is able to unlock the text by using your public key would know it had to come from you. Of course, as you can see, this means that anyone else who also has access to your public key will also be able to decipher the message. Remember that public/private key pairs work in both directions. Data that is encrypted with one key can only be decrypted with the other key.

To overcome this, a digital signature usually operates not by encrypting the entire message, but instead by encrypting data produced by using a hash function of the message. A hash function will produce a string of data that is typically much smaller in size than the original message, such as 160 bits. As shown in Figure 9.1, the output from this hash function, sometimes called a *message digest*, is then encrypted using your private key and sent along with the message. If the recipient can decrypt the hash text, he can perform the same hash function on the rest of the message. If the hash value that the recipient computes on the message matches the hash text that was encrypted by using the sender's private key, the message can be assumed to have come from that person, and the message has remained intact and unchanged. The *data integrity* remains intact. Any change to the message will cause the recalculation by the hash function to produce a different hash text than that produced by the original message.

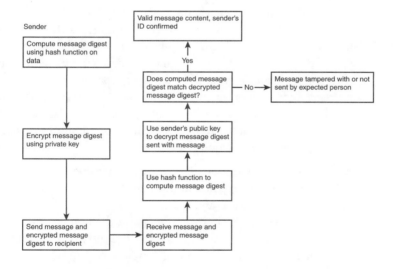

FIGURE 9.1
Digital signatures can be used to guarantee the integrity of data and the identification of the sender.

As you can see, this method means that the sender will find it very difficult to deny a message sent using their digital signature. This is called *nonrepudiation* because the digital signature can only be applied by the original sender of the message, provided the private key is kept secret.

Another thing that should become obvious is that when you use a digital signature, you don't have to encrypt the actual message text. You can if you want to, but that is not a concern of the digital signature computations. It might be that the contents of the message are not sensitive data, but that you simply want to guarantee the authenticity of the sender and the integrity of the message. The hash value can be computed on the message whether it is encrypted or not. The point is that because the same hash function is employed at both ends of the communication, and because the sender is the only person who holds the private key used to create the signature, the source of the communication can be verified.

Digital Certificates

Digital certificates work in a similar manner to digital signatures. A certificate is a document that basically says you can "trust" a certain piece of information. Suppose you wanted to send someone a message using public key encryption. You first obtain their public key so you can encrypt the message. However, and here's the sticky part, how do you confirm that the published public key really is the public key of the recipient? If you haven't already securely communicated with someone and you receive a copy of their public key in an email message or from a provider of such things on the Internet, how can you be sure it is a valid key? It might be someone else, sending you their public key, hoping to trick you into communicating with them thinking they are someone else!

A digital certificate can be used to verify that the public key really belongs to the person who you think it does. A digital certificate relies on using a known and trusted third party. The certificate will contain the public key, information about the holder of the key, and finally a digital signature that verifies the contents of the certificate. The third-party responsible for issuing the certificate —called the Certificate Authority (CA)—must be someone who is known and who you can trust to issue the certificate. The Verisign company is an example of this kind of third-party certificate issuer. Because you trust the certificate authority and can verify their signature, you can trust the information on the certificate.

It is not necessary to rely on an outside third-party for CA services. If your needs are all internal, your business can easily set up its own certificate server, using software available for UNIX systems as an add-on, or by using the certificate server that comes with Windows 2000 Advanced Server. Using your own CA will require that you create procedures for issuing and managing certificates, but will be much less expensive than using the services of an outside party.

If your needs for digital certificates include exchanging data with other businesses or with users outside the company, using a third party, such as Verisign, for this purpose, is the solution.

The Secure Sockets Layer (SSL) Protocol

The growing market for e-commerce on the Internet would never have been possible without a technology to ensure secure communications. To meet that need, the Secure Sockets Layer (SSL) protocol was developed by Netscape. SSL employs cryptographic techniques to encrypt the data stream, to provide for authentication, and to guarantee the integrity of the data transmitted.

SSL is a layered protocol that is made up of two other protocols: the SSL record protocol and the SSL handshake protocol. The handshake procedures that the client and server use to authenticate to one another and exchange key information are performed by the SSL handshake protocol. The SSL record protocol is responsible for formatting the data.

The handshake process (as shown in Figure 9.2) is as follows:

1. A browser connects to a page that is enabled to use SSL. The server sends a request to begin an SSL session to the client browser.

2. The browser, if it supports SSL, sends a response back to the server, which contains a session ID that will be used to identify the session, and a list of the encryption algorithms and compression methods supported by the client browser. This initial message also includes the current time and date and some randomly generated data.

Get Your Own Digital Certificate

There are several certificate issuing authorities on the Internet that can be used to obtain a digital certificate, or to look up the public key for someone who possesses one. You can visit Verisign at the following URL to learn more about their service, which includes a 60-day free trial:

`www.verisign.com`

SSL 2.0 and SSL 3.0

The newest version of SSL is version 3.0. This version adds to version 2.0 by allowing the authentication of a client to the server.

Which Web Pages Should Use SSL?

Because of the overhead involved with encryption, it makes sense that you would only want to use SSL for Web pages that do indeed contain or solicit sensitive or confidential data. Enabling SSL for every page at your site might make it seem slow to respond and discourage users from visiting you. By using SSL only on Web pages that actually need it, such as an order form, your Web site will produce a faster user response than if you use it for all pages.

3. The server selects an encryption and compression method and sends a message back to the browser, along with the session ID and some randomly generated data. To authenticate itself to the client, the server also sends its digital certificate.

4. Optionally, the server might also send a request to the client to ask the client to send its digital certificate to the server.

5. Depending on the type of cipher that has been chosen for the session, the client creates a message called the *premaster secret*. It encrypts this data using the server's public key and sends it to the server.

6. The server decrypts the premaster secret data by using its private key. The server and client then use the same sequence of steps to manipulate the data that was used to create the secret. This produces data that is called the *master secret*.

7. Both the client and server use the master secret to generate keys that will be used for the session, the process depending on the kind of cipher chosen for the session.

8. Data transfer begins. Data exchanged is encrypted using a symmetric algorithm and the session keys.

FIGURE 9.2
The SSL protocol uses a handshake process to determine encryption methods and keys to use for each session.

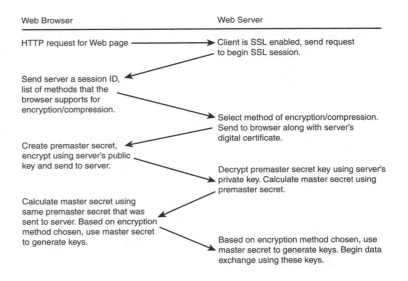

SSL can be used with a number of different types of cryptographic techniques, including DES, DSA, MD5, RC2, RC4, and several others. This flexibility means the most clients and servers will be able to select a common cipher and use it for secure communications.

Is That Web Page Using Encryption?

Before you give out your credit card number, or other sensitive information, to a solicitation from a Web page, you might want to check to see if the Web page is enabled for and using some form of encryption. To find out for Internet Explorer, look for a padlock at the bottom of the browser window. To find out what type of encryption is being used, right-click somewhere on the Web page and select Properties. In Figure 9.3, you can see the Properties page shows you several things about the Web page, but most important, the type of encryption used is shown in the Connection field.

What Is TLS?

TLS stands for the Transport Layer Security protocol. TLS version 1.0 is described in RFC 2246, "The TLS Protocol Version 1.0." This protocol is based on SSL 3.0 and is intended to be the successor to SSL. The differences between SSL 3.0 and TLS 1.0 are minor, but significant enough to prevent their interoperability. For more information about the emerging TLS, refer to the RFC and the Web site for the IETF committee working on TLS:

www.ietf.org/
html.charters/
tls-charter.html

FIGURE 9.3
The Properties page for a Web site can be used to determine the encryption being used.

If you want more information about the server's certificate used for this session, click the Certificates button. In Figure 9.4, the Certificate dialog box shows general information about the certificate.

By clicking the Details tab at the top of the Certificates dialog box you can examine the certificate in more detail, such as the issuer of the certificate and the algorithms used. The Certificate Path tab can be used to see more information about the server that issued the certificate.

FIGURE 9.4
Using the Certificates button on the Properties page, you can view information about the certificate.

Summary

Using encryption will solve three problems associated with using the Internet for the exchange of important data. Cryptographic methods can be employed to authenticate the parties to a communication, verify the integrity of the data exchanged, and also to make the communication private by rendering any intercepted message unreadable.

Symmetric encryption techniques, which use a single key, are generally faster than asymmetric techniques, such as public/private key-pairs which use two keys that are mathematically related. In practice, both of these techniques are often used together to further increase security. Examples of technology which use both methods include the Secure Sockets Layer (SSL) protocol and the popular Pretty Good Privacy (PGP) encryption product discussed in Chapter 11.

In the next chapter, you will look at a practical application of cryptography: creating virtual private networks (VPNs) to create secure channels of communication on the Internet. In this chapter, you will also look at two important protocols that can be used for to create VPNs: IPSec and PPTP.

chapter

10

Virtual Private Networks (VPNs) and Tunneling

Secure Communications
on the Internet •

The IPSec Protocol Suite •

The Point-to-Point Tunneling Protocol •

Secure Communications on the Internet

If you want to create a secure channel that can be used to communicate with a remote office, the first thing that probably comes to mind is to use a dedicated leased line (or possibly a dial-up line if the traffic is light and infrequent). However, with the Internet already providing a quick path between most points on the globe for an insignificant charge compared to leased lines or toll charges, doesn't it make sense to consider using the Internet? A dial-up connection or leased line can provide more security, you might say, because the data travels along a dedicated path that cannot be easily intercepted by a third party. On the Internet, you have no control over which direction packets take to get routed to their destination. You have no control over the links between points A and B.

Products such as Pretty Good Privacy (PGP) can be used to send email and attachments over the Internet with protection that is extremely difficult to defeat. For Web pages, as you saw in the previous chapter, the Secure Sockets Layer (SSL) protocol can be used for exchanging confidential information.

SEE ALSO

➤ *For more information about using PGP to secure your email transactions, see page 227*

For a general purpose connection that can allow two networks to securely exchange multiple kinds of data that uses the IP protocol for transmission, another solution is needed. The solution is a Virtual Private Network (VPN), through which you can tunnel network traffic from one point to another in an encrypted format to protect it from prying eyes.

What Is a Virtual Private Network (VPN)?

A virtual private network is a tunnel over a shared network infrastructure such as the Internet. It is a *tunnel* because the data being transferred is encrypted and then encapsulated in IP packets, preventing any intercepted packets from being understood and protecting the sender and recipient's identity. There are three basic methods used to create VPNs with the current level of technology:

- **Network to network**   This is usually with a firewall or high-end router on each end used to create the VPN.

The Virtual Private Network Consortium (VPNC)

This trade association for vendors of VPN products has a Web site that can be useful for those who want to pursue VPN technology in more detail than can be presented in this chapter. At the following URL, you will find the home page for VPNC:

`www.vpnc.org`

This Web site includes links to documents about VPNs, such as white papers and the pertinent IETF Drafts and RFCs. You can also subscribe to their mailing list on the site to be kept informed of future developments about the consortium or VPN technology.

- **Host to network**   A remote computer equipped with VPN client software can connect to the home office.

- **Dial-up ISP to network**   Some ISPs provide VPN service for dial-up clients.

As you can see, although VPNs are typically created between firewalls or routers, VPNs can also be used to connect a remote host to a network across the Internet, provided the client host is suitably configured. In Figure 10.1, you can see an example using a VPN connection to join two networks together using Internet connections.

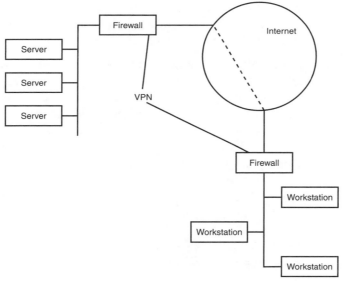

FIGURE 10.1
A typical VPN is created between two firewalls.

The firewall on each network in this example is responsible for encrypting and encapsulating IP traffic that is then routed to the other network. When a workstation on one network needs to access a server on the other network, the firewall takes the client workstation's IP packets and wraps its own IP packet around the clients. The packets that are then transmitted through the Internet contain source and destination addresses that identify the firewalls, not the client or server on either network. This VPN feature helps to hide the identity of your network hosts. The original IP packet travels in a compressed, encrypted format, so if it is intercepted by the wrong party, the contents are useless.

Another important feature that the VPN provides for is authentication. The two firewalls in the example use strong authentication techniques to ensure that every packet that is exchanged does truly come from the other side of the connection.

Most firewalls that support VPNs also provide you with client software that can allow an individual host computer to dial in to the Internet and create a secure connection with the firewall. Microsoft Windows clients include VPN software based on the Point-to-Point Tunneling protocol (PPTP), which is discussed later in this chapter. Using PPTP, a client can dial in to the Internet using an ordinary ISP. The client can then use the PPTP client software to connect to a remote access server (RAS) on the home network to establish a secure VPN channel.

Some ISPs provide another method that might be useful for mobile users. The remote user can dial in to the ISP and, after proper authentication, the ISP can create a VPN with the remote site for the user. This method has the advantage that the user does not have to configure any client software to create the VPN. The disadvantages are that the ISP needs to have dial-up lines for all locations where you will need access, and using the ISP means that you are placing part of your security management into a third party's hands.

What Can a VPN Do?

VPNs enable secure communications over a wide geographic area. The major areas that a VPN can impact in a business are the following:

- Connect branch offices or remote company sites to the home office.
- Allow telecommuters to work from home or mobile users to work from on the road.
- Create a secure connection with a business partner.
- Reduce your telecommunications budget.

Connecting remote company sites can be expensive when using dedicated leased lines. You can use your existing Internet connection, in conjunction with a good firewall VPN product, to create your own private communications channels with remote branch offices for a lot less money than a leased line. If you have users who regularly work from home or employees who travel, VPNs can be used to secure their connections to the office network. Because VPNs can be implemented using dial-up Internet accounts through an ISP, you can throw out most of your expensive modem bank and equip your off-site users with VPN client software instead. Instead of paying for large numbers of phone lines to dedicate to the modem bank, you can use a single high-bandwidth Internet connection to service these employees.

SEE ALSO

➤ *Windows NT and Windows 2000 include client VPN capabilities that can be used with Remote Access Services to create virtual private networks. For more information about using Windows VPN client software, see Chapter 21, "Firewalls and Beyond," page 381*

Fax machines and overnight delivery services work day and night to help businesses exchange data. When it absolutely has to be there—right now—you can use the network instead. Business partners might find that VPN technology can make it easy to establish a secure connection between their two networks. Because you are using a firewall for this kind of VPN, you can ensure that your network remains secure. Creating a VPN for a business partner for only short-term usage might also be cheaper than using a VPN. Installing and terminating a dedicated link would be far more costly for a short-term connection of this sort.

Disadvantages of VPNs

Although a VPN has many advantages over using leased lines for wide area communications, there are a few things that should be considered when weighing the pros and cons of this technology. First, because of the nature of the Internet, where an IP packet can be routed through a number of fast or slow intermediate links, the speed of the VPN is limited by the slowest link its traffic is routed through.

Second, when you use the Internet, you are not in control of the hardware that gets your network packets from one place to another. A major hardware failure at any point along the link can result in delays or even network down time. If you are using a leased line solution, your contract can specify high levels of service and a quick response time for problems. You can't get this guarantee from using the Internet.

If your remote or mobile users are using local ISPs for dial-up access to use VPN client software for the home connection, you should be sure to check out the quality of the service the ISP provides. If the user cannot get through during important business hours because the ISP's lines are busy, the user has to resort to the old dial-up to a modem method. Although VPNs can be an efficient, cost-effective method for allowing a few remote users to connect to the network, compared to the price of maintaining a modem bank, this might not always be the case. If you have a large number of remote users, it might be cheaper to provide the modem bank than it is to pay the fees necessary to establish a dial-up ISP account for each user.

In the rest of this chapter, you will look at two important protocols that are being used to create VPNs based on standards.

The IPSec Protocol Suite

Request For Comments (RFCs) about IPSec

To learn more about the intricate details of IPSec, you can look up the RFCs on the Internet. RFC 1825, "Security Architecture for the Internet Protocol," gives a good overview. Others include the following:

RFC 1826, "The Authentication Header"

RFC 1827, "IP Encapsulating Security Payload (ESP)"

RFC 1828, "IP Authentication using Keyed MD5"

RFC 1829, "The ESP DES-CBC Transform"

These documents will give you some insight into how the different components that make up IPSec work.

Several times throughout this book, I have discussed the fact that the TCP/IP protocol suite was not designed with a lot of security concerns in mind. The next generation of IP, called IPv6, will have security mechanisms built into it. The current IPv4 that you use on the Internet does not. Because of this, a new standard called IPSec has been developed to satisfy this security need. IPSec will be mandatory in IPv6, but it can also be implemented transparently on the current IPv4-based Internet.

SEE ALSO

➤ *For more information about the next generation IP protocol—IPv6— see Chapter 21, "Firewalls and Beyond", page 381*

IPSec is being adopted more and more by firewall vendors to replace proprietary methods used in the past for encryption. There are several good reasons that can lead you to expect that IPSec will be heavily implemented on the Internet in the near future:

- IPSec is a standard. In addition to the RFC documents that define the architecture and major components of IPSec, there are many other Internet drafts and RFCs that have been written to standardize the cryptographic methods that can be used and other protocols relating to IPSec.

- IPSec is transparent to the user and to the current generation of routing equipment that ties the Internet together. IPSec works at the network layer, so there is no need to modify applications or the underlying physical structure of the network.

- IPSec is flexible. It can be used with a wide variety of cryptographic methods.

IPSec is not a single protocol. It is, like TCP/IP, more of a suite of related protocols. The three main components that make up the foundation of IPSec are the following:

- **Internet Key Exchange (IKE)** This protocol is used during the initial negotiation stage to agree upon the encryption methods, keys, and other data that will be used to set up a secure session.

- **Authentication Header (AH)** A security header is inserted into each IP packet that can be used to determine whether the packet has been altered in transit, and to authenticate the sender of the data. AH does not encrypt the payload of the IP packet; it merely guarantees its contents to be valid.

- **Encapsulating Security Payload (ESP)** To ensure private communications, ESP encrypts the payload of the IP packet, along with other header information.

Internet Key Exchange (IKE)

As they say in the SSL protocols, a method for negotiating what encryption methods will be used and a way to exchange keys is necessary before encrypted communications can begin. For IPSec, the Internet Key Exchange (IKE) is used to exchange data during the initial setup phase for a secure connection. IKE is used to decide what encryption methods will be used and what keys will be used with them. IKE keeps track of all secure connections, using a concept called a *security association*. In RFC 2048, "Internet Security Association and Key Management Protocol (ISAKMP)," a security association is defined broadly as "a relationship between two or more entities that describes how the entities will utilize security services to communicate securely."

IKE is a combination of ISAKMP and parts of the Oakley key exchange method. ISAKMP defines the format of packets that are used to create and manage security associations. One of the important

The Oakley Key Exchange Method

To learn more about the Oakley key exchange method that is used with IPSec, check out RFC 2412, "The Oakley Key Determination Protocol."

features about IKE is that it is independent of the particular encryption method you want to use for authentication or data encryption. IKE defines a procedure for exchanging information, in a secure manner, that can be used with many different cryptographic methods. For the purposes of IPSec, IKE is the component that sets up a security association and manages all the security associations on a particular host.

Each security association is unidirectional. For two hosts to communicate securely, two security associations are required, one for each direction. The security association describes attributes pertinent to each connection, such as the following:

- **Cryptographic algorithms**   Each association negotiates specific encryption methods that will be used for the session.
- **Key data**   These are the keys that are negotiated or generated by the parties to the association.
- **Frequency at which new keys will be exchanged**   Using session keys for only a limited amount of time improves security.
- **The length of time the SA will be valid**   The SA should not "hang around" after the need for a secure session has finished.
- **The source address of the SA**   Because security associations are unidirectional, the source address of the party initiating the SA is used to identify the SA.
- **Security Parameter Index (SPI)**   This is a 32-bit number that is used to uniquely identify the security association.
- **Other information**   This includes whatever is pertinent to the association and cryptographic methods chosen for use with it.

IKE works in several modes to accomplish the setup of an association. In *main mode*, IKE creates a secure channel with a remote host that will be used for further negotiations. To create the secure connection, the node that initiates the connection sends a list of parameters it proposes for the association, including encryption and hashing algorithms, a method to be used for authentication, whether the security sought will use Authentication Header or Encapsulation Security Payload techniques, and other necessary data. Using public key methods, the two sides of the session are authenticated to each other. For purposes of authentication, digital certificates are used.

The recipient of the certificate can check first that the certificate matches the host at the other end of the connection and then that the certificate itself is valid, having been issued by a known certificate authority (CA).

A second method to begin the setup of a security association is called *aggressive mode*. The main difference between the main and aggressive modes is that the aggressive mode works with fewer exchanges between the parties, with more information passed during each exchange. Because of this, aggressive mode is not as careful as main mode and does not protect the identity of the parties on the network. Whichever mode is used, they both result in what is called an *IKE SA*, or a security association to be used for IKE. After this has been accomplished, IKE can be used to set up the actual security association that the hosts need to use for a secure communications channel.

After the initial main mode or aggressive mode phase, another mode called *quick mode* is entered for the purposes of negotiating the services that will be used and for generating session keys. Because a secure communications channel has already been established between the parties during the initial setup, packets used for quick mode can travel encrypted. One quick mode message is sent to request that an SA be set up. In response, two SAs are set up, one for each direction between the hosts negotiating the channel. The party at the receiving end of each unidirectional SA is responsible for choosing a unique number to use for the SPI for the association and communicating it to the initiator of the SA.

When IKE has been used to create the necessary security associations, there are two techniques that IPSec supplies that can be used to protect or render private communications between the two hosts.

The Authentication Header (AH)

This method does not provide for encryption of the actual payload of the IP packet, so using an Authentication Header (AH) by itself will not give you privacy and confidentiality. However, what it does provide is a method for determining whether the contents of the packet or pertinent header information have been changed during transit and authentication of the sender.

Learn More about IKE and ISAKMP

It would take several chapters to fully cover the details that make up IKE and ISAKMP. If you want to pursue it further, the recommended reading is the RFCs that describe the individual components is the following:

RFC 2408, "Internet Security Association and Key Management Protocol (ISAKMP)"

RFC 2409, "The Internet Key Exchange (IKE)"

RFC 2412 "The OAKLEY Key Determination Protocol"

For IPv4, the AH inserts its own header directly after the IP header in the packet (Figure 10.2). Because the IP header is unchanged, routers that are not familiar with IPSec can continue to route packets as they usually would.

IP Version 4 Header	AH Header	Upper-level protocol, such as TCP or UDP

FIGURE 10.2
The Authentication Header is placed directly after the IP packet header for IPv4.

The AH is composed of five fields of a fixed length, followed by authentication data, which varies in length due to the variable amount of information that might need to be included for the authentication or cryptographic methods chosen (Figure 10.3)

FIGURE 10.3
The Authentication Header fields.

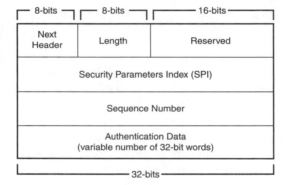

The information fields in the AH include the following:

- **Next Header**   This 8-bit field identifies the protocol that follows the AH. This is a valid IP protocol number as defined by IANA. For example, TCP is identified here if a TCP packet follows the AH. If ESP is being used in combination with the AH, ESP is the protocol identified here.

- **Length**   This 8-bit field specifies the length of the AH as a number of 32-bit words.

- **Reserved**   This field is not currently used, but according to the standard, it should be filled with zeros.

- **Security Parameters Index (SPI)**   This 32-bit number is chosen by the receiving end of a security association to uniquely identify the security association. Zero indicates no security association exists. Numbers 1–255 are reserved by IANA.

- **Sequence Number**   This is a counter that increases for each packet sent for a particular SPI.

- **Authentication Data**   This is the actual data, such as a digital signature, for the packet. This field is padded to make the length equal to a number of 32-bit words.

Although the AH can be used for authentication purposes and to guarantee the integrity of the data transmitted between the two cooperating parties, it cannot be used to encrypt the actual data of the IP packet. For this, another technique is used.

Encapsulation Security Payload (ESP)

The Encapsulating Security Payload (ESP) method provides for authentication and integrity of the datagram and also encryption of the data in the datagram. In *transport mode*, ESP provides for protection of the data and headers created by upper level protocols (such as TCP). It does not provide protection for the actual IP header. This mode is usually used for host-to-host implementations (or host-to-gateway connections) and is compatible with routers that do not understand IPSec protocols.

In *tunnel mode*, ESP is used between two gateways, such as firewalls, and does protect the IP header information. In this mode the entire IP datagram is encapsulated by the ESP protocol, and the new header information that is applied specifies the security gateways that the packet is being sent between. The actual end-point addresses of the communication are contained in the encrypted header information now carried as part of the payload of the packet. When the packet reaches the destination gateway, it is unpacked and sent to the actual destination host.

AH and ESP

For a tight, secure communications channel, both the AH and ESP can be used together. In this manner authentication, integrity, and confidentiality are ensured. When used together, the AH follows the IP header. Following the AH is the ESP-encapsulated IP packet.

> **What IP Header Fields Does the AH Protect?**
>
> The Authentication Header method uses cryptographic calculations performed on the IP datagram, excluding fields that change during transport, such as the time to live (TTL) field. The datagram can be evaluated at the receiving end to determine whether any part of the datagram has been modified. Information that does not change, such as the source and destination address, is protected by the AH.

The Point-to-Point Tunneling Protocol (PPTP)

Most people who have an Internet connection at home have some idea of what PPP is: the Point-to-Point protocol. PPP is a protocol that encapsulates other protocols (such as TCP/IP, IPX, or NetBEUI) and relays them between your ISP and your home computer. The Point-to-Point Tunneling protocol (PPTP) builds on PPP by adding encryption to the data that is encapsulated. This means that PPTP can be used by remote or mobile clients who need to create a virtual private connection, across the untrusted Internet, back to the home office network.

Benefits of using PPTP include the following:

- Encrypted communications channel over the Internet.
- Support for encapsulating multiple network protocols, such as TCP/IP, SPX, and NetBEUI.
- Software for PPTP is built into recent Windows operating systems.
- Allows the use of private IP addresses because the PPP connection uses the IP address assigned by the ISP; the client can tunnel packets using a network address that is valid on the home network.

PPTP was initially developed by Microsoft and several other companies. The PPTP forum submitted an Internet Draft document to the Internet Engineering Task Force (IETF) in 1996, and Request For Comments (RFC) document 2637, "Point-to-Point Tunneling Protocol (PPTP)," defines the current standard for the protocol.

In a typical scenario, a remote client first makes a connection to a local ISP using PPP (Figure 10.4). When this connection has been established, a second connection is created for PPTP over this PPP connection. The end points of the PPTP connection are the remote user and a Remote Access Service (RAS) server on the user's targeted network. The connection between the remote user and the RAS server is called a *tunnel*, and all data passing between the two end points is encrypted and protected by PPTP. At the RAS server, PPTP packets are unpacked, and the original IP datagram (or other network protocol datagram) is evaluated and sent on to its destination in the local network that the RAS server serves.

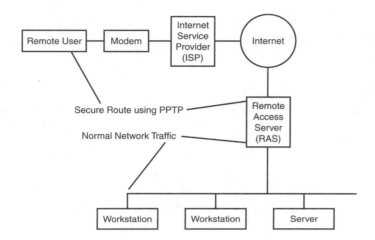

FIGURE 10.4
A remote client uses a PPTP tunnel between the workstation and the RAS server on the home network.

To establish a secure PPTP connection, a control connection is established, and data transmission can then begin.

The PPTP Control Connection

Control messages are sent between the PPTP client and the PPTP server to create and manage the PPTP tunnel. Although PPTP can be used with PPP to tunnel multiple network protocols, PPTP uses a TCP datagram for messages sent for control purposes. A TCP connection is established between the client and the PPTP server, and PPTP control messages are exchanged. The messages that can be used on this control connection are the following:

- Start-Control-Connection-Request
- Start-Control-Connection-Reply
- Stop-Control-Connection-Request
- Stop-Control-Connection-Reply
- Echo-Request
- Echo-Reply
- Outgoing-Call-Request
- Outgoing-Call-Reply
- Incoming-Call-Request
- Incoming-Call-Reply
- Incoming-Call-Connected

223

- Call-Clear-Request
- Call-Disconnect-Notify
- WAN-Error-Notify
- Set-Link-Info

The start session request and its associated reply message are used to begin a connection and to exchange data about the capabilities of the client and server. This includes information such as the PPTP version, the maximum number of individual sessions that can be supported, and the DNS hostname of the requestor. The stop connection messages are used to end a PPTP connection. When a control connection is stopped, all sessions associated with the tunnel provided by the control connection are also terminated.

The echo messages are used to maintain the control connection so that a failure on either end can be detected after a time and the connection can be torn down. A connection is terminated if a reply is not received within 60 seconds of an echo request.

After a control session has been established between the client and server, the various call message types are used to establish sessions between the two.

The WAN error notification message can also be used to exchange information about the connection.

Data Transmission Using PPTP Tunnel

When a connection has been established, a virtual tunnel exists that can be used to exchange data between the client and PPTP server. The PPP packet that the client sends out is first encrypted and then encapsulated inside an IP packet that can be routed to the PPTP server. Because the original PPP packet is encrypted, it can be sent safely across the Internet. If the IP packet that encapsulates the PPP packet is intercepted, only the IP header information would be meaningful. The data contained in the PPP packet is protected by the encryption used.

One difference between the tunneling method used by PPTP and that used by IPSec is that whereas IPSec uses a different security association for each session between a client and server, PPTP uses only one tunnel and multiplexes multiple sessions between the client and server on the same tunnel.

Layer Two Tunneling Protocol (L2TP)

An emerging new standard for VPN technology is being created by combining the best parts of PPTP with L2F from Cisco: the Layer Two Tunneling Protocol (L2TP). This protocol was only recently described in an Internet standards track protocol document, RFC 2661, "Layer Two Tunneling Protocol (L2TP)." As this technology is further developed, you can expect to see its deployment in client and server VPN software. If you are interested in following the further developments of this protocol, visit the IETF working group home page that has been established to further extensions to the protocol:

```
http://www.ietf.org/html.charters/l2tpext-charter.html
```

Summary

Virtual Private Networks allow businesses to create secure, private communication channels over insecure networks such as the Internet. Using VPN connections can be cost-effective for joining offices together that are geographically distanced and for those who have a large need to connect remote or mobile users. The IPSec and PPTP protocols are being widely used at this time to create VPNs that are based on standards, rather than the proprietary solutions that have been used in the past. The development of standards will eventually mean that VPNs can be created using software and hardware from multiple vendors. In the near future, this will make VPNs a commonplace feature of the Internet.

chapter

11

Using Pretty Good Privacy (PGP) for Encryption

Security Information Transfers
on the Internet

Installing PGP

Securing Information Transfers on the Internet

In the previous two chapters, I discussed the topics of encryption and virtual private networks (VPNs). Before the Internet can ever be trusted by ordinary people to transmit confidential information—such as a credit card number—it will be necessary to convince people that such information can be encrypted in a manner that makes it incredibly difficult to intercept. Although you might be able to use VPNs and other techniques to connect your network to a remote site, this might not be practical when you deal with customers or vendors. For this kind of situation, you might consider using one of the popular encryption tools, such as the Pretty Good Privacy (PGP) utility.

PGP, which was initially developed by Phillip Zimmerman, is a public key encryption system. The most current version is based on patented technology called *RSA* public key encryption. The name RSA is taken from the initials of the developers of the technology: Rivest, Shamir, and Adelmen. Because of the patent, commercial usage is allowed only if you purchase PGP. If you want to use it for noncommercial uses, however, you can obtain a free copy for non-profit personal use from Network Associates at the following URL:

`http://www.nai.com/default_pgp.asp`

RSA patent

At the time this book was published, the RSA patent is still in effect. However, in late 2000 the patent is due to expire, and the encryption techniques protected by the patent will become public domain.

At this download site, you will find that PGP is available both as source code (for UNIX systems) and as executable programs for several different operating system platforms, including Windows, DOS, and Macintosh. Depending on your preference, you can use PGP's command-line interface or the graphical interface it provides.

The freeware versions available from Network Associates come in versions for the following platforms:

- Windows NT, Windows 95/98 (executable, GUI, or command-line form)
- Macintosh (executable and source code, GUI)
- Linux (executable, command-line form)
- Solaris (executable, command-line form)
- DOS or UNIX (source code, command-line form)

Installing PGP

The method you use to install PGP depends on the operating system you use. In this chapter, I will go over installation techniques for UNIX and Windows NT.

Installing PGP on UNIX Systems

To install PGP on a UNIX system, you must first compile the source code and place it in the appropriate directory. After that, you can configure it for use by creating a public/private key pair.

When you unpack the `.tar` file, you should first read the `setup.doc` text file, which contains the instructions for compiling PGP on different UNIX and Linux variants. After you have compiled the source code, you should then create a directory to use exclusively for PGP and define an environment variable `PGPPATH` to point to this directory. For example:

```
#mkdir .pgp
#setenv PGPPATH /user/ogletree/.pgp
```

You might also want to add this definition to your `~/.csh_env` file so that you do not have to enter it again.

The next step is to generate the public/private key pair that you will use. The `-k` option of the PGP command is used for this purpose:

```
# pgp -kg
```

PGP issues several prompts to get the information it needs to perform this function:

- **Key size**   The larger the key size you specify here, the more safe your data will be. You can enter 1 (512 bits), 2 (768 bits), 3 (1,024 bits), or any number other than 1 through 3 to specify a key size.

- **Key User ID**   This is the name you will use to reference the key. The common method of naming keys is to use your name followed by your email address enclosed in angle brackets. For example, `Terry W. Ogletree <ogletree@bellsouth.net>`.

- **Pass Phrase**   A pass phrase is used by PGP to help generate the key pair. The term *phrase* is used because it is not a single word, like a password, but instead is a longer phrase to make the

Defining an environment variable

Different versions of UNIX use different methods to define environment variables and different startup files to store them in. For example, when using the bash shell, you would add the following to the file `~/.sh_env`:

```
PGPPATH=/user/
ogletree/.pgp;
export PGPPATH
```

key more secure. The text you enter is not echoed to the screen, so PGP prompts you to re-enter it to confirm that you have indeed typed what you think you have. Remember that as in all UNIX utilities, text is case sensitive. Remember not only your pass phrase, but also how you enter it.

- **Random typing** PGP asks you to simply start typing randomly. You can type any characters you want, as the text you enter is not important. PGP is using the timing of your keystrokes to generate a series of random numbers that will be used to help create the key pair. PGP beeps when it is finished with this timing exercise.

SEE ALSO

➤ *For more information on keys, check out Chapter 9, "Encryption Technology," page 199*

After these prompts, PGP generates the public/private key pair. This might take some time and depends on the size of the key you have requested. A series of dots are generated on the screen so that you know the program is still working.

Key Rings

To store keys, PGP uses a file called a *key ring*. This file, which is named `keys.asc`, stores not only your public/private keys, but also keys that you receive from others you want to communicate with. To ensure the security of this file, you should consider placing it on a floppy disk and keeping this disk locked away until you need to use it. If you store the file on your local hard disk or on a network drive, it is more susceptible to compromise.

In addition to using the key ring file, there are many public key servers on the Internet that you can use to get or store keys. This makes it easy for others to obtain your public key when they want to send you an email, for example. There is actually a network of key servers on the Internet to which you can publish your key. This is done by extracting your key to a file and sending it to one of the servers. Servers, which are part of the key server network, regularly update each other, so you don't have to send it to all the servers, just to one of them.

For more information about PGP public key servers and the commands used to access them, send an email with the text `help` in the subject line to `pgp-public-keys@keys.pgp.net`.

Remember your pass-phrase!

The pass phrase is used when you want to access your secret key, just like a password is used to gain access to your user account on the network. Thus, when deciding on a phrase to use, it should be something that is not hard for you to remember. Of course, it should also not be something that is easy for others to guess.

PGP Commands

First look at the command that you use to extract your public key so that you can give it to others:

```
#pgp -kx userid keyfile [key ring]
```

In this example, `userid` is the name that you gave the key, and `keyfile` is the name of the file you want PGP to place it into. This output file contains a copy of your public key. This is the file you give to others who want to send you messages. The `key ring` argument in the command is optional and is used if you have more than one key ring file.

To add a public key to your key ring file, use the following command:

```
#pgp -ka filename
```

Here, `filename` is the name of the file that contains the person's public key.

To view the contents of your key ring, use the following command:

```
#pgp -kvv
```

This displays information about the keys that are in the key ring file. Use the following command to remove keys from the file:

```
# pgp -kr
```

So far, you have looked at "maintenance" or "housekeeping" commands provided by PGP. But the real function of PGP is to encrypt files, so look at how that is done next.

First, create the message you want to encrypt and store it in a file. You can use any UNIX text editor or a word processor. Of course, you can also encrypt binary files, such as executable program files or graphics files. When you have the file you want to encrypt, use the following command:

```
#pgp -e messagefile userid
```

The `-e` argument tells PGP to encrypt the file you specify (`messagefile`) using the public key for the person represented by `userid`. The output file produced by the encryption command is a binary file. Because some email programs or other programs do not like using binary files, you might have to use another command to produce a file using a format called *ASCII Armor*, which is the same binary file encoded in ASCII characters. This is done by attaching a to the -e argument:

```
#pgp -ea messagefile userid
```

The file that results consists of nothing but standard ASCII text, which most email programs can work with.

Using PGP to Create a Digital Signature

Encrypting a file only solves part of the problem of secure communication. Although encryption protects the text from being read by anyone except for its intended recipient, it doesn't offer any guarantee to the recipient as to its origins. That is, when you receive a file, how can you be sure that it really comes from the person who it says it is from? It is a simple matter to spoof an email address, as you have probably seen in some of the junk email that clutters up the Internet.

This problem is solved by attaching a digital signature to the file that you just encrypted before it is sent on to its destination. You do this also by using your secret key:

```
#pgp -sea messagefile userid
```

Remember that pass phrase you had to enter when PGP was generating your key pair? Here's where you need to use it. You didn't need it to encrypt the file because that was done using the recipient's own public key. However, when you want to access your private key, PGP needs to be sure it's really you, so it asks for your pass phrase. Protect that pass phrase!

Using PGP to Access Encrypted Files

To read a message that was encrypted by PGP using your public key, use the following command:

```
#pgp filename
```

filename is the name of the file you want to read. Because PGP needs to use your private key to unlock the file that was encrypted by using your public key, it asks you for that pass phrase again. After the file is decrypted, PGP attempts to verify the digital signature (if one was attached to the file). To do this, PGP searches your key ring for the public key of the sender and uses it to verify the signature.

Installing PGP on Windows NT

To install PGP on a Windows NT computer (or Windows 95/98), a setup program is provided, making the process a simple one. The freeware version is a compiled application, so you don't need a C compiler. After you start the setup program, you are presented with the standard license and disclaimer text, to which you should agree in order to continue.

The next dialog box solicits your name and company name. After that, another dialog box enables you to choose the directory that will be used for the installation. In Figure 11.1, the Select Components dialog box is shown. This dialog box is used to decide which features you want to install.

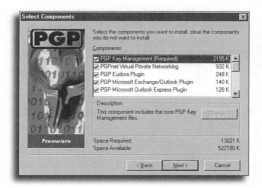

FIGURE 11.1
Select the components of PGP you want to install.

The components you can install include the following:

- **PGP Key Management**   This component is required. It is used for the same purpose as the ring file I talked about in the UNIX version of PGP.

- **PGPnet Virtual Private Networking**   You can use PGP to create a VPN for secure communications on your network.

- **PGP Eudora Plugin**   Select this component if the Eudora mail program is your emailer.

- **PGP Microsoft Exchange/Outlook Plugin**   Select this component if the Microsoft Exchange mail client or Microsoft's Outlook is your emailer.

- **PGP Microsoft Outlook Express Plugin**   Select this component if Microsoft's Outlook Express, a version of Microsoft Outlook with fewer features, is your emailer.

- **PGP Command Line**   Select this component if you want to use PGP at the Command Prompt (usually referred to as the MS-DOS box by us older folks) in a command-line mode similar to the UNIX version.

- **PGP User's Guide**   Select this component! It's exactly what it says it is!

When you select one of the plug-in components from the preceding list, PGP adds security-related items to the menus of the particular client the plug-in refers to. This means that you won't have to exit your email program to encrypt (or decrypt) a file; you'll be able to do it from within the client as a menu option instead.

When you have finished selecting components, click the Next button, and the setup procedure copies the necessary files for the components you selected to their target directories. If you elected to use the PGPnet Virtual Private Network component, you are prompted to indicate which network adapter to use, as is shown in Figure 11.2.

FIGURE 11.2
PGP prompts for the network adapter to use for the VPN component.

If you have a previous version of PGP installed or if you have a key ring file from another workstation, you can use it with the PGP version you have just installed. The setup program prompts you for a filename if you want to use this option. After that, the setup program tells you to reboot the computer before you begin to use the newly installed PGP version or application plug-ins.

Configuring PGP for Windows NT

After the reboot is finished, you must next configure PGP before you can use it. Just like the UNIX version, you need to create your public/private key pair first.

Configuring PGP

1. Select Start, Programs, PGP and then PGPkeys.

2. From the main PGP window (see Figure 11.3), click the Keys menu and then select New Key. The Key Generation Wizard is launched.

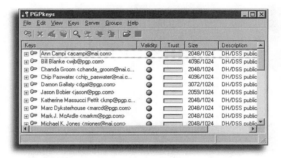

FIGURE 11.3
Select New Key from the Keys menu to create your public/private key pair.

3. When the Key Generation Wizard dialog box appears, click Next to continue.

4. Enter your full name and email address in the dialog box that appears next (see Figure 11.4).

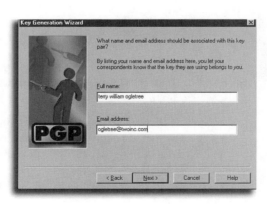

FIGURE 11.4
Enter your name and email address when prompted.

5. In the next dialog box, select the type of encryption to use, either RSA or Diffie-Hellman/DSS (see Figure 11.5).

FIGURE 11.5
Select RSA only if you correspond with others who use an older version of PGP.

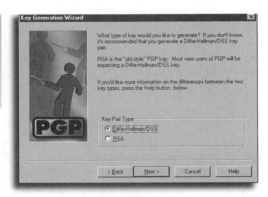

6. In the next dialog box (see Figure 11.6), select the key size you want to use.

FIGURE 11.6
Select the size of the key to be generated.

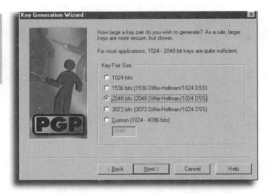

7. In the next dialog box (see Figure 11.7) either enter an expiration date or click Key Pair Never Expires.

8. Finally, PGP prompts you to enter a pass phrase (see Figure 11.8) that is used to protect your secret key. Enter a phrase that you can remember but that is not easy for others to guess.

FIGURE 11.7
Select how long the key
will be usable.

FIGURE 11.8
The pass phrase is used
to access your secret
key.

**Should you use RSA or
Diffie-Hellman/DSS
encryption?**

Older versions of PGP used
a method known as RSA.
The newer PGP versions
(from 5.0 and higher) use
Diffie-Hellman/DSS.
Choose the encryption
method you want to use
based on the version used
by others you will exchange
messages with. In general,
you should probably select
the newer method unless
you have a lot of contacts
that use an older version of
PGP. If you have a need for
both versions, you can generate two different key
pairs, each one using a different form of encryption.

It might take a few minutes for the Key Generation Wizard to create
your key pair. This depends on the speed of your computer and on
the size of the key you have selected. When the wizard has finished,
it asks if you want to automatically send the public key to a key
server on the Internet. You can do this now or at a later time. The
wizard also asks if you want to make a backup. If so, put the backup
copy to a floppy disk and store it away in a safe location.

Using PGP With Windows NT

You can use PGP to encrypt files after you have created your pub-
lic/private key pair. Based on the plug-in you selected during the
installation setup process, you should see new menu items when you
launch the email client. For example, Microsoft Outlook now has an
entry for PGP under the Tools menu.

**What is your name and
address used for?**

When the Key Generation
Wizard prompts for your
name and email address,
you do not have to use your
real name or address. This
information is used to make
your public key recognizable
by others you will give it to.
This information is also used
when a plug-in needs to
look up your email address
to find a key. If you are producing a key that will be
used by a business for multiple users, you should enter
text here that will make the
key easy to identify if it does
not match an email address.

**How long should a key
pair be valid?**

When you create a key
pair, you can tell PGP to
create a key pair that will
never expire. This can be a
good choice if you are making a single key pair for
yourself that you intend to
use for a while. However, if
you are working on a spe-
cial project that will only
run for a limited amount of
time, you might want to
give a key an expiration
date. When the key
expires, it will not be
usable to encrypt files after
the expiration date.

You can also use PGP at the command prompt. The commands are similar to those used in the UNIX command-line version:

- `pgp -kg`   This command generates a new key pair. See the section "Installing PGP" for help on using this command.

- `pgp -e filename userid`   This command encrypts the file specified by `filename`, using the key referenced by `userid`.

- `pgp -s filename [-u your_userid]`   This command signs a file using your secret key.

- `pgp -es filename userid [-u your_userid]`   This can be used to encrypt the file and then sign it using your secret key, both in one operation.

- `pgp encrypted_file [outputfile]`   This command decrypts an encrypted file.

Just as in the UNIX version, you can create an encrypted file that is based on ASCII text instead of a binary file (ASCII Armor) by adding the `-a` parameter to the `-e` parameter (`-ea`). This is useful when you have an email client that does not reliably transfer binary files.

Summary

PGP is a useful tool, especially so for email purposes. It enables you to encrypt text or other files before sending them out on the network (or the Internet). PGP can also use digital signatures to help provide a guarantee to recipients that the file was actually generated by you.

part

III

Firewall Installation and Configuration

Firewall Tools Available on the Internet	241
Using TCP Wrappers	253
Using the TIS Firewall Toolkit (FWTK)	263
SOCKS	291
SQUID	301
Using ipfwadm and ipchains on Linux	313
Microsoft Proxy Server	333
The Elron CommandView Firewall	357
Firewall Appliances	371
Firewalls and Beyond	381

chapter

12

Firewall Tools Available on the Internet

Using Freeware and Shareware
Products ●

TCP Wrappers ●

The TIS Firewall Toolkit ●

SOCKS ●

SQUID ●

Drawbridge ●

SATAN ●

Other Handy Security Software ●

Using Freeware and Shareware Products

There are new firewall vendors springing up almost daily. If I wanted to make a list of all the current vendors who are jumping into this market, it would fill up half the book. Unfortunately, by the time this book gets printed and distributed to retail outlets, some of those vendors will be gone and others will have joined the fray.

When you begin to think about how you want to implement a firewall, one of the things you have to do is to evaluate the available products and determine how they can fit into the architecture you design for the firewall. Some vendors offer a one-stop service and can provide you with everything, including packet filtering, application proxies, other security software, and even training and full-time support around the clock. If you do not have the skilled in-house resources to maintain a firewall, you might want to choose this route.

Before you decide on any specific solutions, though, you should read through this chapter to learn about some of the firewall-related products available for download from the Internet. Most of these are either free or available for a small charge. Some, such as the TIS Firewall Toolkit, can be downloaded for free, yet have a "cousin"—a commercial version containing more features than the free version—that you can purchase.

Even though you might not decide to use any of these products in your firewall, simply understanding how they work can make you a better purchaser when it comes to evaluating the products you do have to pay for. In this chapter, you will examine a few of the more popular products. In the chapters that follow, you will look at some of them in more detail.

TCP Wrappers

This set of programs was created by Wietse Venema to help protect the network at the Eindhoven University of Technology, where he was employed at the time. The purpose of the wrapper program is to insert a layer of access control and logging into the client/server-based TCP/IP network services model.

TCP Wrappers uses a daemon process named `tcpd` that is started in place of the actual network services defined in the `inted.conf` file. In the usual configuration, the Internet Daemon (`inetd`) listens for incoming network service requests. It determines which service is needed by matching the request's port number with the service as defined in the file `/etc/services`. Using the service name, `inetd` then uses the configuration information found in `inetd.conf` to determine which protocol to use and how to start the needed daemon process.

SEE ALSO

➤ *For more information about how ports are used by TCP and UDP, see page 49*

➤ *For a list of well-known TCP and UPD ports, go to page 395*

The problem with this scenario is that it provides no access control. Some of the services that it starts, such as FTP and Telnet, implement their own access control by requiring a username and password. However, this method is not sufficient to fully protect the system or the network it is on. Why? Because these utilities, along with others, transmit the username and password as clear text that even a hacker with only moderate skill set can intercept. There is no control based on the host that the username and password are coming from. There is no method in place that can be used to deny access unless it comes from network hosts or addresses that are known to you and that you can extend some amount of trust to.

TCP Wrappers provides that capability. In addition, it makes up for another deficiency of the `inetd` daemon: TCP Wrappers provides logging of the service request and of the host that makes the request. This information can be invaluable when trying to determine whether your network has been infiltrated.

To use TCP Wrappers, you first download the source code and compile it on your system. Instructions for compiling the code for the most popular UNIX variants are included in the documentation that accompanies the source code. After you have compiled the program, you can edit several files to configure its use:

- `inetd.conf` In this file you substitute the `tcpd` daemon program for the service program that `inetd` usually calls to handle the service request. The actual service program is passed as an argument to `tcpd`, which is then responsible for determining whether

access is allowed, logging the request, and starting the real
service daemon.

- `hosts.allow` This file is not a regular UNIX configuration file.
It is specific to the TCP Wrappers program. In it, you create a
list of rules that are used to determine which hosts are allowed
to access which services. In this file you can use hostnames,
domain names, or IP addresses for access control. You can also
execute shell commands based on the service and host.

- `hosts.deny` This is a companion file to `hosts.allow` and is used
for the opposite purpose. Here, you create rules that deny access
to specific hosts, domains, or IP addresses.

The TCP Wrapper daemon uses the `syslogd` daemon for logging
purposes and sends its log data to the same place as the sendmail
daemon. You can configure how `syslogd` operates by editing the
`syslogd.conf` file.

SEE ALSO

➤ *To learn more about* `syslogd` *and the* `syslogd.conf` *configuration file, see page 181*

TCP Wrappers is a very popular utility. It is even included in some
UNIX and many Linux implementations. Although not a complete
firewall solution by itself, it can provide an extra measure of security
for any host that offers services in your network.

TCP Wrappers is available for download from the following site:

`ftp://ftp.porcupine.org/pub/security/`

In Chapter 13, "Using TCP Wrappers," this product is covered in
greater detail, showing how to make edits to `inetd.conf` and how to
create rules for the `hosts.allow` and `hosts.deny` files.

The TIS Firewall Toolkit

The Trusted Information Systems Internet Firewall Toolkit—
usually just called FWTK or The Toolkit—has been around for
quite some time. When Trusted Information Systems (TIS) merged
with Network Associates, this new company was also the vendor
responsible for the Gauntlet firewall. Although Gauntlet was originally developed as a commercial version of The Toolkit, it has since
been developed and enhanced and for the most part does not share

the same code as The Toolkit.

Since FWTK was developed for the Defense Advanced Research Projects Agency (DARPA), the code was placed into public domain. You can download it from the Internet, but you must first agree to the license. This is done by sending an email request to TIS. In response, you receive an automated email message, usually a few minutes later, that tells you the name of a temporary directory (available for only 12 hours) from which you can FTP the software.

Like TCP Wrappers, The Toolkit is provided in source code format, using the C programming language. You need to compile it on your particular system before you can use it. Whereas TCP Wrappers merely adds logging and access control to services that already exist on the server, the components provided by The Toolkit are actual proxy applications. That is, when configured correctly on a hardened bastion host, the proxies allow use of network services through the firewall without ever allowing IP packets to pass directly between inside and outside your protected LAN.

SEE ALSO

➤ *"Using Bastion Hosts and Sacrificial Hosts," Chapter 4, page 104*

➤ *"Using a Bastion Host," page 131*

➤ *"Using an Application Proxy Gateway," page 96*

➤ *"Application Gateways and Proxy Servers" page 157*

Major components of The Toolkit are proxies that are used for the most popular TCP/IP utilities. The software tools that are included are the following:

- `netacl` To provide for Telnet, Finger, and network access control lists.

- `smap` and `smapd` To provide for a secure SMTP service.

- `ftp-gw` To provide a proxy server for FTP.

- `tn-gw` To provide a proxy server for Telnet.

- `rlogin-gw` To provide a proxy server for Rlogin.

- `plug-gw` To provide a general-purpose proxy service.

- `authd`   To provide an authentication service to enhance "strong authentication" practices.

- `telnetd`   A Telnet server that can be used to manage the firewall.

- `login-sh`   An enhanced login program that provides support for secure logins using token authenticators, such as a smart card.

- `syslogd`   A replacement of the traditional UNIX logging daemon.

The `netacl` component is usually configured to provide service access to the firewall itself, whereas the other proxies—such as `tn-gw` and `ftp-gw`—are used to provide pass-through proxies. They enable external users to access services that reside on hosts in the internal LAN, and vice versa.

SEE ALSO

➤ *In Chapter 14, "Using the TIS Firewall Toolkit (FWTK)," I will go into more detail about how the toolkit works and configuring proxy services to run on a UNIX system.*

SOCKS

SOCKS is a protocol designed to work in a client/server environment. A SOCKS server runs on the firewall host and provides a proxy service. When a client outside the protected LAN wants to connect to a particular service, it does so directly if a direct connection is available. If not, it then tries to contact the SOCKS proxy server and, by exchanging messages defined by the SOCKS protocol, negotiates a proxy connection. When a connection is established, the client communicates with the SOCKS server using the SOCKS protocol. The application server communicates with the SOCKS server as if it were the actual client.

There are two versions of the SOCKS protocol at this time. Version 4 is in wide distribution and supports TCP-based applications. Version 5, which is described in several Request For Comments documents, adds support for UDP applications and authentication.

SEE ALSO

➤ *"The Transmission Control Protocol (TCP)," page 32*

❱ *"The User Datagram Protocol (UDP)," page 33*

Unlike the proxy services provided by the TIS Firewall Toolkit, clients that use the SOCKS proxy protocol must first be

"SOCKSified." This means that they usually need to be recompiled to add the SOCKS client functions to the code. There are some exceptions to this. Vendors have developed libraries for Windows clients that can SOCKS-enable existing client software. The SOCKS protocol has also been adopted by a large number of software manufacturers who have enabled their clients with SOCKS functions. In addition, the SOCKS Version 4 implementation, available from NEC, includes clients for Telnet, FTP, Finger, and WHOIS. Their SOCKS Version 5 package adds clients for Archie, PING, and traceroute.

SEE ALSO

➤ *Because it is such a popular proxy server solution, a chapter is devoted to covering SOCKS. See Chapter 15, "SOCKS" for more information about how the protocol works and for sources of client applications and SOCKS libraries.*

SQUID

SQUID, as the FAQ for this application states, is usually available at sushi bars. It is also the name of a proxy caching server available on the Internet. Like the TIS Firewall toolkit and several other products I have discussed in this chapter, SQUID comes in source-code format and compiles on many of the popular UNIX variants.

A proxy server, as I have discussed, works by intercepting the flow of IP traffic between and client and server. The proxy server communicates with each of these systems and acts as a man-in-the-middle so that no actual IP packets are ever exchanged between the client and server. Proxy servers can hide the identity of clients sitting behind the firewall. A caching server, however, performs a different function. Caching is the process of holding copies of "hot objects"—those that are frequently requested—so that when another object request is received, it can be retrieved quickly from the cache. By servicing requests from the cache, the response to the client is usually faster than actually querying the source of the object directly.

Objects that the caching server buffers in memory (or in disk files) include data that comes in response to requests by FTP, HTTP, and

SQUID Supports the Lightweight Internet Cache Protocol

A cache server stores objects it has retrieved for a client for a period of time so that it can make the same data available more quickly should another request be made for the data. Cache servers use the HTTP protocol, for example, to get Web pages that are then passed on to clients of the server. However, cache servers can also exchange information among themselves. The protocol used for this is called the Lightweight Internet Cache Protocol, or ICP.

Two RFC documents describe the ICP protocol: RFC 2186, "Internet Cache Protocol (ICP), Version 2," and RFC 2187, "Application of Internet Cache Protocol (ICP), version 2."

other network clients. In addition to caching these objects, SQUID also supports caching DNS lookups. SQUID is composed of several programs, including the proxy caching server (called `squid`), a DNS lookup program called `dnsserver`, and other optional applications.

SEE ALSO

➤ *Chapter 7, "Application Gateways and Proxy Servers," page 157*

➤ *Chapter 18, "Microsoft Proxy Server," page 333*

➤ *Chapter 16, "SQUID," page 301*

SQUID servers can be configured in a hierarchical fashion with parent servers located closest to the Internet backbone and child servers located closer to users in the internal network. When a child server cannot service a request for an object by using data in its cache, it sends a query to a parent server. The parent server satisfies the request from its cache or by making a request of a server further up the line in the hierarchy. Using this hierarchical organization can help save valuable bandwidth at the Internet connection because requests can sometimes be satisfied locally without resorting to a single server that must satisfy the request from its store or make a request to the Internet. SQUID uses the Lightweight Internet Cache Protocol (ICP) to communicate between child and parent servers.

One advantage that SQUID has over some of the other freely available products I have discussed is that support can be obtained not only from Web pages, mailing lists, and other Internet resources, but also from vendors who can help implement the product and provide support for a fee.

To configure SQUID, you need to edit a file called `squid.conf`. SQUID also produces several log files that include information access information and cache performance information.

SEE ALSO

➤ *Again, because this software is so widely used, a separate chapter is devoted to its installation and configuration. For more information, see Chapter 16, "SQUID."*

Drawbridge

So far in this chapter, I have covered products that work basically as proxy servers. Remember, however, that for a proxy server to work optimally, you should place it behind a packet filter instead of connecting the proxy server host directly to the Internet. You can use a screening router as a packet filter, or you can use a software solution that also runs on a host computer.

Drawbridge is a free, high-speed packet filter that, although it originally ran on a DOS platform, now runs on the FreeBSD UNIX platform. Like Drawbridge, FreeBSD is also available at no charge—hence its name! This packet-filtering application was developed at Texas A&M and was designed specifically with the academic environment in mind.

SEE ALSO

➤ *"Using a Packet Filter," Chapter 4, page 94*

➤ *"Packet Filtering," page 109*

To install Drawbridge, you should use a fresh install of FreeBSD because Drawbridge changes some of the files in the /etc directory. It is also a good idea, as with any bastion host computer, to use the system only for the packet filter and not place a lot of user accounts or other applications on the computer.

Drawbridge is made up of three basic components:

- **Drawbridge Filter Engine**   This component does the actual packet-filtering work and is compiled into the kernel of the operating system.

- **Drawbridge Filter Compiler**   This is a user-level application used to compile rules you place in the configuration file so they can be used by the engine. This program is called dbfc.

- **Drawbridge Manager**   Obviously, this is the management application that you use to control Drawbridge. This program is called dbmgr.

Configuring the filter is a simple matter of creating a text file of rules based on the commands supported by Drawbridge and then compiling and loading the filter. The configuration file is created using any text editor and is compiled using the dbfc command:

```
dbfc input-file [output-file]
```

After you produce the compiled output file, you can then use the dbmgr command to load the filter.

The filters that you create can be used to allow or block access based on the network service (as defined in the /etc/services file), a numeric port value, or a numeric ICMP type. You can also filter based on the source or destination port or the protocol used (TCP, UDP, or ICMP). Like most good packet filters, you can also design the filter rules based on whether traffic is inbound or outbound and also based on IP address or hostname information.

Because this is not a commercial product, support is not available on the Internet. You need to be well-acquainted with UNIX system management (preferably FreeBSD) and TCP/IP networking.

To find out more about Drawbridge or download the documentation or the package itself, visit the Drawbridge Web site:

drawbridge.tamu.edu/

SATAN

With such an infamous name, you might think that the SATAN utility is a hacker's tool designed to destroy your network. Actually, the term is an acronym, standing for System Administrator's Tool for Analyzing Networks. If the name offends you, there is an option in the utility you can use to change its display name to SANTA. Regardless, this tool uses passive probing techniques to search out possible security problems in your network. SATAN is not really a proxy server or a packet filter or a firewall component at all. It is mentioned in this chapter because it is one of the more important tools that, if used correctly, can be valuable in helping you determine whether your firewall will do what you expect.

SATAN is, like other applications described in this chapter, provided in source code and compiles on many UNIX systems. It is primarily used to probe UNIX hosts.

When you use SATAN, you can choose to have it perform a light scan or a heavy scan. A variety of checks are performed on the target systems, particularly for ports used by many popular network services, such as FTP, HTTP, NFS, NIS, Remote Shell Access, sendmail, and so on.

After you download the SATAN code and uncompress the file, you are left with several subdirectories that fall under a directory called `/rules`. These subdirectories are used as follows:

- `/facts`   These rules are used to deduce new facts based on the data SATAN gathers.

- `Hosttype`   These rules are used by SATAN to determine the type of host. This is done by examining "banners" displayed by the operating system or utilities, such as FTP and sendmail.

- `/services`   These rules are used by SATAN to determine what kind of host is probing based on the services it finds—client or server.

- `/todo`   These rules are used to decide what SATAN will do next, based on scans already run against specific hosts.

- `/trust`   Satan decides what type of hosts the probed system trusts.

- `/drop`   These are rules that tell SATAN what facts to ignore. Currently, this only includes a rule telling SATAN to ignore NFS exported CD-ROM directories.

There are also other directories that hold PERL routines, executables, documentation, and executable programs.

If you are going to use this tool to look for security problems in your network, you need to spend some time reading the documentation and configuring the rules. This tool is not for an inexperienced novice, but it instead is meant to be used by someone who has a good understanding of the UNIX operating system and TCP/IP. Although it might be time-consuming to set up SATAN, using it on a regular basis and keeping up to date with new versions can help improve the security of your network. The tool automates many processes that you would otherwise have to perform manually, and it produces reports that summarize its findings.

If you would like a better understanding of this tool without going through the trouble of downloading and installing the entire package, visit the following Web site:

```
http://www.am.qub.ac.uk/world/documentation/satan_doc/html/docs/
satan_reference.html
```

"Improving the Security of your Site by Breaking Into It"

This is the title of a paper written by Dan Farmer & Wietse Venema, the authors of the SATAN utility. This paper discusses some of the more common methods used to break into networks. It makes for a very good read if you are just starting out in the field of network security. This paper can be found on many locations on the Internet, including the following:

```
http://www.alw.nih.
gov/Security/Docs/
admin-guide-to-
cracking.101.html
```

SATAN Is an Extensible Utility

Because security issues are changing rapidly on the Internet, some tools become quickly dated as new vulnerabilities are discovered. SATAN is an extensible utility, however, and can be adapted to new events in this changing environment. You can add your own probes to SATAN and configure rules that govern their operation. If you become well-acquainted with SATAN documentation and possess a little skill at C programming, this utility can go a long way.

This URL points to a reference file for SATAN and describes in some detail the entire product, including configuration files, rules, and so on.

Other Handy Security Software

This chapter briefly covered some of the tools you can download from the Internet and use to construct a firewall. You also took a quick look at the SATAN security reporting tool. Although the main topic of this book is firewalls, it is important for you to also be able to monitor your network so that you can be sure that the firewall is really protecting you against known methods of attack.

In Appendix B, "Other Security Tools You Can Use," you will find a reference that describes a lot of good tools—some which are new and others which are tried and true and have been around for years. Most of the tools listed in the Appendix are also freely downloadable from Internet sites. Remember that the hacker you are trying to stop knows about these tools too and might be using them to gather information about your LAN. It is highly recommended that you read through the appendix and, at your leisure, further investigate some of the utilities that are described there.

Summary

Firewalls can be purchased, some for a small sum of money and others for an astronomical amount. In many cases, you do get what you pay for. However, with so many firewall components downloadable from the Internet for free, you should consider looking at them so you can become better acquainted with what to expect from a commercial product. If you have the requisite skills in UNIX system administration and TCP/IP, you might find that the free tools are all that you need.

In the next few chapters, you will look at some of these tools in greater detail.

chapter

13

Using TCP Wrappers

Introduction to TCP Wrappers •

Obtaining TCP Wrappers •

Configuring TCP Wrappers •

Limitations of TCP Wrappers •

Introduction to TCP Wrappers

The basic TCP/IP protocols were developed many years ago to help join together a variety of diverse networks. Most of the systems that first implemented TCP/IP were academic and government sites, and at that time the security needs of this community of users was nothing like it is today. Indeed, neither the Transmission Control Protocol, the Internet Protocol, nor the User Datagram Protocol were developed with security in mind as an important goal. It was enough that these protocols could allow different proprietary computer systems to exchange data. The utilities that followed, such as Telnet and FTP, bear this same heritage. Telnet and FTP, for example, enforce security by requiring a username and password that is valid on the target system. This security mechanism falls apart when you realize that both the username and the password are transmitted on the network as clear text that anyone with a little knowledge can intercept.

When personal computers started making inroads into the business environment in the early 1980s, many different network protocols were developed by vendors trying to cash in on a new market. Novell Netware was there in an early form and quickly caught on. As the UNIX operating system began to be widely adopted, however, TCP/IP became more and more popular. When the Internet boom started, TCP/IP became, for all practical purposes, the default network protocol suite and has since been adopted by all major computer and software vendors that produce network products.

There are many different products that can be used to enhance your network's security, such as firewalls—which are the subject of this book. A firewall is composed of multiple components, and TCP Wrappers can be one of those components. Although the packet filter might provide a good start for a firewall, it isn't able to catch everything.

TCP Wrappers was developed by Wietse Venema at Eindhoven University of Technology to help protect the university's computers from attack. TCP Wrappers restricts which network services can be used and which hosts are allowed to use them. TCP Wrappers can be configured to handle most of the basic network services that you typically find on a UNIX system, such as the following:

- Telnet
- Finger
- FTP
- Exec
- RSH
- Rlogin
- TFTP

The main thing that these services have in common is that there is a one-to-one mapping between the service name and an executable program that provides the service.

How TCP Wrappers Works

When the inetd daemon receives a network request, it determines which service to start based on the port number. The file /etc/services contains a mapping of port numbers to service names. After inetd has determined which service to start, it reads its configuration file (inetd.conf) to find what program it should run to satisfy a network request.

SEE ALSO

➤ *For more information about how ports are used by TCP and UDP, see Chapter 2, "Introduction to the TCP/IP Protocol Suite," page 49*

➤ *For a list of well-known TCP and UPD ports, see Appendix A, "TCP and UDP Common Ports," page 395*

For the TCP Wrappers daemon (tcpd) to make access control decisions and to perform its logging duties, you have to edit the inetd.conf file to specify that the tcpd daemon run instead of the executable that normally satisfies the service request. The tcpd daemon performs its chores and, if the host making the request is allowed to use the service, tcpd starts the executable for that service. Thus, TCP Wrappers works by inserting itself between the inetd daemon and the network service.

Logging via *syslogd*

TCP Wrappers not only provides access control for network services it is used with, but it also provides logging so that you know who is using the services. Logging information is sent to the UNIX `syslogd` daemon, which also provides a central logging facility for many components of the UNIX operating system. By default, TCP Wrappers sends its logging information to the same place as the transaction logs of the `sendmail` daemon. In general, `syslogd` can log information to one or more files, the system console, a user console, or a user via an email message. How `syslogd` determines what to do with logging data is controlled by entries made into its configuration file, usually named `/etc/syslog.conf`.

SEE ALSO

➤ *To learn more about* `syslogd` *and the* `syslogd.conf` *configuration file, see Chapter 8, "Operating System Monitoring and Auditing Techniques," page 181*

Obtaining TCP Wrappers

Where do you find TCP Wrappers?

Many tutorials or other documents you will find on the Web have references to locations you can go to in order to download TCP Wrappers. However, note that many of these locations no longer have the code. Instead, the URL given in this section (at `porcupine.org`) is now the official location of Wietse Venema's utilities.

You might already have TCP Wrappers. It is such a popular set of programs that it comes with some of the UNIX and Linux implementations as part of the package. If it is not on your system, you will find that it is available at many places on the Internet. You can use the following URL to get TCP Wrappers using FTP, as well as other useful tools developed by Wietse Venema, such as the SATAN utility:

`ftp://ftp.porcupine.org/pub/security/`

TCP Wrappers is usually available as source code, which is what you will find at this site. After downloading the files, be sure to check the `readme` file first for any updates and information on how to compile the source code on your system.

Configuring TCP Wrappers

To use TCP Wrappers on your UNIX system, first compile the source code (as described in the documentation for your particular flavor of UNIX). When you have the `tcpd` daemon executable, you can then edit the configuration files that control how it is used. These are the following:

- `inetd.conf` Edit this file to place references to the `tcpd` daemon executable in the entries for services you want wrapped.

- `hosts.allow` This file contains rules that define who is allowed to use each service that `tcpd` starts.

- `hosts.deny` This file contains rules that define who is explicitly denied access to each service that `tcpd` starts. This file is read last, so if a rule is found in `hosts.allow` that grants access, a rule in this file is not able to deny access.

An important thing to remember when configuring these files is that if no matching rule is found in either file, access is granted by default. Later in this chapter, you will learn how the ALL keyword can be used at the end of the `hosts.deny` file to deny access to hosts not listed in the `hosts.allow` file specifically.

Configuring the *inetd.conf* File

The first file to be edited is the configuration file that the `inetd` daemon uses. Each record consists of one line and is used for a single service. Table 13.1 describes the fields that make up a record in this file.

Table 13.1 Fields in the */etc/inetd* Configuration File

Field Name	Description
Name	The name of the service, such as `ftp` or `telnet`. This name is used as a cross-reference into the `/etc/services` file, which contains the port number for each service.
Data type	`stream`, `datagram`, or `dgram`, to indicate a connection-oriented (stream) or connectionless protocol for the service.
Protocol	The network transport protocol used by the service, such as `tcp` or `udp`. Protocols are defined in the `/etc/protocols` file.
Wait-state	`wait` or `nowait`. If `wait`, the `inetd` daemon starts a process for a request and then waits until it finishes before servicing another request. If `nowait`, the daemon starts a process for a request and continues to listen on the socket for other requests and services them.
UID	The userID (UID) under which the service process runs.
Server	The name of the server program that the `inetd` daemon starts to service the request.
Process arguments	Command-line arguments passed to the service program. The name of the service task is always specified as the first argument.

Where does the `tcpd` daemon reside?

Although UNIX was once touted as the universal portable operating system, it would be a mistake to call it that today. There are many different implementations of the operating system, and the location of files doesn't stay the same from one vendor's version to the next vendor's version. Do not copy the examples in this chapter word-for-word. Check the documentation and configuration files for your system to determine where daemon process executables reside and where the `tcpd` daemon should be placed.

Restart the `inetd` daemon after you make edits.

After the `inetd.conf` file has been edited, you need to restart the `inetd` daemon so that it will reread the file and pick up the changes you have made. Until the daemon is restarted (or the system is rebooted), the changes will not take effect. The command used to restart the daemon depends on the UNIX variant you are using. Under Solaris 7, for example, you can use the following:

```
# pkill -HUP
  inetd
```

As you can see in Table 13.1, there is no provision made for who is allowed to run a network service. The `inetd.conf` file simply matches up a service name with the executable program that will satisfy the request, along with the protocol to use and the userID that the executable program will run under.

TCP Wrappers can be used to provide that access control. Take the following `inetd.conf` file entry used to start the FTP service, for example:

```
ftp         stream   tcp      nowait    root     /usr/etc/in.ftpd
in.ftpd
```

Based on this entry, `inetd` would start the executable defined by the path `/usr/etc/in.ftpd`. For the TCP Wrapper program to become involved, this line needs to be changed so that the wrapper daemon is started instead:

```
ftp         stream   tcp      nowait    root     /usr/etc/tcpd
in.ftpd
```

You need to make this sort of change to each line in `inetd.conf` that starts a service that you want to use with TCP Wrappers. When making edits to this file, it is a good idea to first make a backup copy so that you will have it available later in case you make a mistake.

The *hosts.allow* and *hosts.deny* Files

After you have configured the `tcpd` daemon to manage network services by editing the `inetd.conf` file, the next thing you need to do is to edit two other files that are used to store information about who is allowed (and who is not allowed) to use each service. These two files are the `hosts.allow` and `hosts.deny` files. Their names should tell you what they are used for. When the `tcpd` daemon accesses these files, it does so by first checking the `allow` file and then the `deny` file.

The basic syntax for both of these files is as follows:

```
daemon-list : client-list [: shell-command]
```

For *daemon-list*, you supply the name of the service to which the rule applies. When placing more than one service on the same line, separate them by commas. For *client-list*, you use a host name, domain name, or IP address. Again, you can place multiple hosts in the *client-list* portion of the rule by separating them with commas.

The last component you can include in the rule is an optional shell command. This optional command can be quite useful, as you will see shortly in the examples.

One very important thing to remember is that the first matching rule that tcpd finds when making its search is the one it will use. It stops looking when it finds a match. More importantly, *if no match is found in either file, access is granted by default!* For this reason, you should always explicitly deny access to everyone and then selectively grant access only to those who need it!

There are a few keywords you can use for these parameters that make configuration easier:

- ALL   This keyword can be used to match all services or all hosts.
- LOCAL   This keyword matches any host whose name does not contain a dot character.
- UNKNOWN   This keyword matches any user whose name is not known and any host whose name or address is not known.
- KNOWN   This matches any user whose name is known and any host whose name and address are known.
- PARANOID   This keyword matches any host whose hostname does not match its address. You must build the tcpd daemon using the -DPARANOID option to use this.

There is also an operator keyword that can be used to modify the behavior of a rule: EXCEPT. The syntax for using this operator is as follows:

list1 EXCEPT *list2*

Now look at the following simple examples:

Here is the hosts.allow file:

```
ALL : localhost
in.telnetd : twoinc.com
inet.ftpd  : zira.twoinc.com
```

Here is the hosts.deny file:

```
inet.telnetd : ritchie.twoinc.com
```

In the allow file, you can see that all hosts in the twoinc.com domain are allowed to use the Telnet daemon. Only one host, zira, is allowed to use the FTP daemon. Suppose that there was one host in the `twoinc.com` domain that did not do a good job of enforcing security—`ritchie`—so you want to deny that host access. The last line in the `hosts.deny` file appears to do this, but it doesn't work. The TCP Wrapper daemon will never get to that line because it will match `ritchie.twoinc.com` with the record for `twoinc.com` that is found in the `hosts.allow` file. Because it finds this match, it can stop checking the rest of the file and won't even get to the deny file to read the record that you might think would deny access to host `ritchie`.

To enforce the security policy that all which is not explicitly allowed is denied, you can configure the `hosts.deny` file with the following line:

```
ALL:ALL
```

Then configure the `hosts.allow` file to contain only those hosts that you will allow to make use of network services. In this kind of configuration, any host that is not found when `tcpd` scans the `hosts.allow` file is denied.

The `EXCEPT` operator can also be useful. For example:

```
ALL : .twoinc.com EXCEPT zira.twoincom
```

If this line is used in the `hosts.allow` file, all hosts in the `twoinc.com` domain are allowed access (to all services) except for the host named `zira.twoinc.com`.

You can also use the optional shell command feature within a rule. The command you place here is started as a child process with its standard input, output, and error pointing to `/dev/null`. When using shell commands, you should always use the full pathname for the command. Some variables that you can use with substitution in the command are listed in Table 13.2.

Table 13.2 Variables You Can Use with Shell Commands

Variable	Description
%a (or %A)	Returns the client (server) host address.
%c	Returns information about the client. It can be `user@host`, `user@address`, just a host name, or just an address. The value returned depends on what information is available in your implementation.

Variable	Description
%d	Returns the name of the daemon process (obtained by `argv[0]`).
%h (or %H)	Returns the client (server) hostname. If unavailable, returns the address.
%n (or %N)	Returns the client (server) hostname or the values `unknown` or `paranoid`.
%p	Returns the daemon process ID.
%s	Returns server information. This can be `daemon@host`, `daemon@address`, or just the daemon name. The value returned depends on what information is available in your implementation.
%u	Returns the client username or the value `unknown`.
%%	Expands to a single % character.

An example of using a shell command follows:

```
in.ftpd : .twoinc.com : (/usr/bin/safe_finger -l @%h |
/usr/ucb/mail -s %d-%h root) &
```

If this rule were used in the `hosts.deny` file, the root user would receive an email when this rule denies access to hosts residing in the `twoinc.com` domain. Note that the `%h` variable is substituted with the client's hostname and the `-%d` variable is substituted with the name of the service.

Limitations of TCP Wrappers

Table 13.2 discussed the variable substitutions that can be performed when using shell commands. One of these, `%u`, is dependant on being able to query the host from which the user's request originates, as defined in RFC 931.

Remember also that TCP Wrappers should not be the only line of defense for your system. IP addresses and hostnames can be spoofed. TCP Wrappers cannot always be expected to determine whether this is the case. Because the wrapper program is only used to initially start up the correct daemon that will satisfy the service request, it should not be used with services such as NFS, which works by servicing requests from multiple clients when started. Only services that are started on a per-connection basis by the `inetd` daemon can make use of TCP Wrappers. Background daemons that are started in boot time startup files do not work in this manner.

What is safe_finger?

To prevent problems that can occur because of what remote hackers might do in response to a `finger` probe, do not use the `finger` program that comes with your UNIX version. As with any UNIX program written many years ago, there are glitches with this program that can be exploited by a knowledgeable hacker. Instead, use the `safe_finger` program that is included with TCP Wrappers. Safe versions (and there are several) are better coded and can be restricted from giving out too much information to those who are not supposed to see it. Like other components of the package, it is a C program that you can compile to run on your system.

What is RFC 931?

RFC 931 defines the Authentication Server Protocol. This protocol allows retrieval of a username based on the TCP ports used for a connection between two hosts. The server for this protocol listens on TCP port 113. When a connection is made to this port on the server, it reads a line of data that describes the connection. If the connection exists on the server, the username that owns the connection is returned to the requestor. This service is not implemented on all UNIX or TCP/IP products, so you should not depend on it to any great degree. In addition, since RFC 931 was written, others, such as RFC 1413, have come about, changing the name of this service to the Identification Protocol (or Ident Protocol).

There are several utilities provided in the package that can be used to help troubleshoot the configuration. The `tcpdchk` program can examine the rules in the `hosts.allow` and `hosts.deny` files and report back to you any problems it locates. The `tcpdmatch` program can be used to help simulate how access control will work for the rules you have created. The syntax for this program is as follows:

```
tcpdmatch process-name hostname
```

or

```
tcpdmatch process-name address
```

The process name is the name of the service as it appears in the rules files. The hostname and address are an actual name or address of a host that you want to evaluate against the rules.

Summary

TCP Wrappers can be used to add access control to common TCP and UDP services that run on a host in the network or on a firewall host. Although not a complete solution to all your security needs, the wrapper daemon can be quite useful, especially due to the logging functions it provides. Just don't depend on the wrappers as your sole means of security. Remember that a firewall is composed of many components, and those that you choose will depend on your security policy and the architecture of your network and firewall.

chapter

14

Using the TIS Firewall Toolkit (FWTK)

Building a Firewall Using the Toolkit   •

FWTK Components   •

Configuring Proxy Services   •

Installing the Toolkit on a Bastion Host   •

Building a Firewall Using the Toolkit

The TIS Internet Firewall Toolkit (FWTK) is not an off-the-shelf firewall solution. Instead, as the name says, it is a kit composed of many different tools which, along with good system administration practices, can be used to construct a firewall. FWTK is a UNIX-only solution and works with TCP/IP implementations that use the Berkeley type of socket interface. However, if you have a network of Windows NT or Windows 98 computers you still might want to become acquainted with FWTK. You might find that the flexibility of being able to build a firewall solution from scratch so that it exactly matches the security policies of your network can justify the expense of placing a UNIX box at your network perimeter.

A Short History of the Toolkit

FWTK has a long history. It was originally developed by a company called Trusted Information Systems, Inc., for the Defense Advanced Research Projects Agency, or DARPA. When FWTK was created, the only kind of firewall protection that was available was the basic packet filter. Although a packet filter does have its place in a firewall strategy, something more was needed to assist in enforcing a firewall security policy, and FWTK was developed to meet this need.

FWTK is not a packet filter. Instead, it is a collection of different programs that you can use to create proxies for the most popular TCP/IP services. Remember that a good firewall usually is constructed using both packet filtering and proxy servers. Although FWTK does not provide the packet filter capability, it can function quite well on bastion hosts that are protected by a packet filtering router.

Obtaining FWTK

The toolkit is freely available on the Web. First, use your Web browser to go to the site www.fwtk.org. From there, choose a mirrored site nearest you. Click the "download" link and read the software license. If you agree with the software license, you must then send an email to TIS indicating your acceptance before you will be allowed to download the code. Send the email message to fwtk-request@tislabs. com. For the body of the message, simply use the word "accepted" (without the quotes). This word must appear as the body of the email, not the subject line, if you want to get a response back from TIS.

Within a very short time you should get an automated response back from TIS. The email message that you receive will have the name of a temporary directory at `ftp.tislabs.com` that you can then use to download the software and documentation. This temporary directory will only exist for 12 hours, so it would be a good idea to start your download shortly after you get the message. If you are unable to do this download before the time limit expires, simply send another request email, and you will receive another directory name.

After you have downloaded the software, be sure to read any readme files to get any last minute notices about compiling or using components of the toolkit, which is provided in source-code format. That means that you will have to compile it to use it on your system. It does not come as a prepackaged application with a "setup" program to automate the process. To make good use of the toolkit, you need to have a good understanding of TCP/IP and the UNIX operating system. This is not a product for a beginner. If you do not understand how the individual components work or how your operating system is configured, it will be next to impossible for you to use the toolkit with the assurance that you have done all you can to secure the network. Because the toolkit is written using the C programming language, you should be well versed in that language as well.

> **Reverse Name Lookup**
>
> The host computer that you use to download the toolkit must support reverse name lookup. Although the usual function of a DNS server is to resolve a name into an IP address, reverse name lookup is used to resolve an IP address into a name. This is done for security reasons to make sure that you really are who you say you are!

How Does Gauntlet Firewall Differ from FWTK?

After TIS developed the toolkit, the company went on to create the Gauntlet firewall. In 1998, TIS merged with another company, Network Associates, and this company still sells the Gauntlet firewall. At first glance there are many similarities between the two, and many think that the toolkit is simply a stripped-down version of Gauntlet. However, since version 1.0 the two products have not used the same code base. The source code for Gauntlet is available—to buying customers—so you can make the comparison if you want to.

FWTK does not support the entire set of services that Gauntlet does. What the toolkit does provide is the following:

- Source code
- Proxies for FTP, TELNET, Rlogin, HTTP, Gopher, SMTP, NNTP

- X11 Gateway
- Authentication Server
- Miscellaneous tools to help test the firewall

Gauntlet adds to this additional proxies, support for SSL, SHTTP, POP3, a DNS server, and many other features. Of course, because Gauntlet is a commercial product, you also can obtain training and support from TIS. FWTK is end-user supported and about the only help you will get is through the Web site devoted to it and kind souls you might find in an Internet newsgroup or mailing list. Still, if you have the necessary expertise in TCP/IP and UNIX system administration, the toolkit might be just the thing you are looking for.

FWTK Components

So, what exactly do you get when you download the toolkit? Documentation from TIS states that the toolkit consists of three components:

- Design Philosophy
- Configuration Practices and Verification Strategies
- Software tools

Although the last item in this list might be what you consider to be the most important part of the kit, that isn't necessarily so. To make good use of the tools the kit provides, you need really understand what you are doing with the tools. The "design philosophy" component of the kit sets forth several important principles. For example, when you implement a firewall, you should configure it so that no host from an untrusted network (for example, the Internet) will be able to make a direct connection to any network services that are running with privileges on your network. Any network services that you do provide should be done with applications that are simply coded, and not large complex applications that are difficult to understand and, thus, prone to bugs. When you have configured the firewall, you should be able to test it thoroughly so that you can have confidence in your expectations from it.

Configuration practices, the second component, means that you should configure the firewall with respect to your network's architecture and security policies. In Chapter 4, "Firewall Security Policy and Firewall Design Strategies," I discussed common firewall strategies, such as the dual-homed host, screened host, and screened subnet. Techniques for creating a demilitarized zone so that network services could be offered by bastion hosts that were outside your LAN, yet not directly on the Internet, were also discussed. You need to understand which strategy will work best in your environment before you start using the tools provided by FWTK.

An example of the configuration practices you will find in the toolkit is the FTP service. To enhance the security of anonymous FTP, the toolkit describes how to use another component, `netacl`, to provide a more secure version of this service.

The software tools that are included in the toolkit are the following:

- `netacl` to provide for Telnet, Finger, and network access control lists.

- `smap` and `smapd` to provide for a secure SMTP service.

- `ftp-gw` to provide a proxy server for FTP.

- `tn-gw` to provide a proxy server for Telnet.

- `rlogin-gw` to provide a proxy server for Rlogin.

- `plug-gw` to provide a general-purpose proxy service.

- `authd` to provide an authentication service to enhance "strong authentication" practices.

- `telnetd` A Telnet server that can be used to manage the firewall.

- `login-sh` An enhanced login program that provides support for secure logins using token authenticators, such as smart cards.

- `syslogd` A replacement of the traditional UNIX logging daemon.

The rest of this chapter will discuss some of the more useful of these components in more detail.

netacl

The `netacl` program provided in the toolkit functions as an access control program. This program is supplied in the toolkit so you can

---

What Is a Crystal Box?

The term "black box" is usually used to describe a system where the input and output are known, but the internal workings of the system are not. This is not the philosophy used with the toolkit. Instead, it is developed as a "crystal box." Instead of compiling the components and keeping the source code secret, it is made available to anyone who wants to examine it.

The thought behind this move is that if the code for the toolkit components is known—both to users and to the hackers that will try to defeat it—it will be easy for bug fixes to be made and distributed throughout the Internet. Instead of waiting for a vendor to respond to a new security threat, the users who support the toolkit on the Internet can quickly develop a patch or workaround and make it available to all.

allow some network services to be used on the firewall in a more secure manner. For example, you can use netacl to run the Telnet server on the firewall, but set up rules which allow only certain hosts—the network administrator's workstation, for example—to make use of it. Because of the way in which netacl can be configured, you can even specify a different Telnet daemon for different users. While you are using the Telnet service as an example, you can use netacl to run a variety of other network services on the firewall host. Because netacl can be used to provide the administrator network access to the firewall, I will discuss it before looking at the proxy applications that come with the toolkit.

Like other toolkit proxies, the netacl program uses a file called /usr/local/etc/netperm-table to decide whether or not a service is allowable based on the IP address or hostname of the source of the request. To understand how netacl works, first look at how network services are usually started.

On UNIX systems the inetd daemon is responsible for starting network services, which are configured in the /etc/inetd.conf file. This file contains a list of services and information that the inetd daemon needs to provide the service. Table 14.1 describes the fields for each line in the configuration file.

Table 14.1 Fields in the */etc/inetd* Configuration File

Field Name	Description
Name	The name of the service, such as "FTP" or "telnet." This name is used as a cross-reference into the /etc/services file, which contains the port number for each service.
Data type	Stream, datagram or dgram, to indicate a connection-oriented (stream) or connectionless protocol for the service.
Protocol	The network transport protocol used by the service, such as TCP or UDP. Protocols are defined in the /etc/protocols file.
Wait-state	"wait" or "nowait." If wait, the inetd daemon will wait to start a process for a request and then wait until it finishes before servicing another request. If nowait, the daemon will start a process for a request and then continue to listen on the socket for other requests and service them.

Field Name	Description
UID	The UserID (UID) under which the service process will run.
Server	The name of the server program that the inetd daemon starts to service the request.
Process arguments	Command line arguments passed to the service program. The name of the service task is always specified as the first argument.

As you can see in Figure 14.1, the inetd daemon runs as a background process and listens for network requests. To make a request, a packet is sent to the server that includes both the sender's IP address as well as a *port* number. The port number is used by the daemon to decide which service is being requested. The file /etc/services is used to look up the port number, and once the name of the service is known, the daemon can then use the information found in the /etc/inetd.conf file to determine if the service is allowed on this server and, if so, what program to run to satisfy the request.

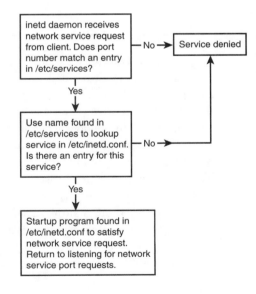

FIGURE 14.1
The inetd daemon listens for network service requests and starts the program used to satisfy the request.

SEE ALSO

➤ *For more information about how ports are used by TCP and UDP, see page 49*

➤ *For a list of well known TCP and UPD ports, go to page 395*

Restart inetd After You Edit the /etc/inetd. conf File!

Because the inetd dae-mon only reads its configu-ration file when it is started, you will need to restart the daemon (or reboot the system) after you make edits to the /etc/inetd.conf file.

netacl Does Not Support UDP

The netacl application can only be used for services which use TCP. It cannot be used for UDP-based ser-vices. This is because it is almost impossible to reli-ably verify the origin of a UDP packet. If you want to make use of UDP-based services, use a TCP wrap-per application instead.

Listing 14.1 shows an example of a portion of the /etc/inetd.conf file.

Listing 14.1 Example of the */etc/inetd.conf* File

```
#
#       /etc/inetd.conf
#
ftp         stream    tcp     nowait   root     /usr/etc/in.ftpd
in.ftpd
telnet      stream    tcp     nowait   root     /usr/etc/in.telnetd
➥in.telnetd
shell       stream    tcp     nowait   root     /usr/etc/in.rshd
login       stream    tcp     nowait   root     /usr/etc/in.rlogind
➥in.rlogind
tftp        dgram     udp     wait     root     /usr/etc/in.tftpd
➥in.tftpd
finger      stream    tcp     nowait   nobody   /usr/etc/in.fingerd
➥in.fingerd
. . .
#
# end
```

In this listing, you can see that common network services, such as FTP and telnet, are provided by the firewall by running the associ-ated program. There is a very important bit of functionality missing from this file, however. There is no method of access control. The inetd daemon simply does what an entry in this file tells it to do. It has no mechanism for deciding whether or not a particular host making a request should really be allowed to make use of the service. This is left up to the usual system authentication procedures, which involve a username and password stored in the /etc/passwd file. Because this method of authentication is not a terribly strong one—the telnet service passes usernames and passwords as clear text which can be intercepted, for example—this simple method is not really a secure method for offering services on the firewall host.

To make up for this lack of access control, the netacl program is used. To use netacl with a network service, you must edit this file. Instead of calling the in.ftpd program to satisfy an FTP request, you would call the netacl program instead and let it handle the rest of the process of starting up a server daemon for the requesting host. A sample entry in the `/etc/ineted.conf` file for the FTP service would be the following:

```
ftp        stream   tcp     nowait   root     /usr/local/etc/netacl
➥in.ftpd
```

As you can see from this example, the Server field in the `/etc/inetd.conf` file now calls the `netacl` program instead of the FTP server program. The argument passed to `netacl` is the name of the service. There is still one more step that must be done, however, before `netacl` can start the server program. It must look up in the `/usr/local/etc/netperm-table` file to find an entry for the FTP service to decide whether it is allowed to run for the requesting host and, if so, what program will be run to provide the service and what userID (UID) it will run under. In Figure 14.2, you can see that the process merely adds a few steps to the regular process used to start a network service.

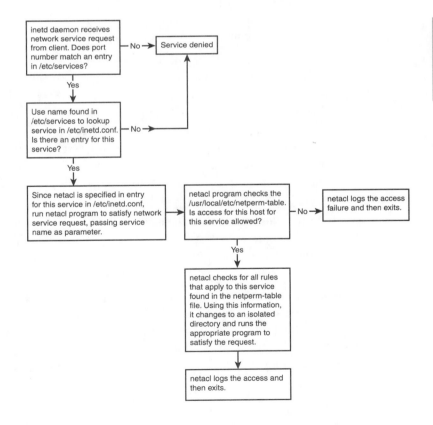

FIGURE 14.2
The `netacl` program is called by `inetd` to satisfy the service request.

The Configuration File: */usr/local/etc/netperm-table*

When the netacl program is started by inetd, it doesn't immediately start running the requested service that is passed to it as a command line argument. Instead, it takes this single argument and uses it to look up information about the service in a database of rules that you define in the /usr/local/etc/netperm-table. You can think of this file as the central source of configuration information for all the proxies that make up the toolkit. As soon as netacl (or another proxy application from the toolkit) is executed, it reads its configuration information from this file and stores it in memory. Thus, after the application uses chroot to change to a different directory, for example, the information is still available to it and the file does not have to be accessible to the running service. Using this method ensures that a bug in a service program cannot be used to hack into the netperm-table file.

Each line of text in the netperm-table file is called a *rule*. Each rule can apply to one or more toolkit applications. Each rule is composed of two major components:

How Long Can a Rule Be?

The maximum size of a rule depends on the operating system you are using, but the general idea is that the rule must fit on one line. There is no "line continuation character" that you can use to let a rule span across multiple lines. For most systems, the maximum size that a line can be is usually 1,024 bytes.

- **Keyword**   This is the name of the application(s) that the rule applies to. This name is composed of the text the name of the service, which you can obtain by looking in the /etc/services file. When used with the netacl application, the name is composed of the text "netacl-" plus the name of the service. The name portion of the rule is separated from the rest of the rule by a colon (:) character. Separate multiple names on the line with commas. You can also use wildcards to specify multiple applications.

- **Attribute** *valuelist*   This is the actual text which defines the rule for the application it is associated with. The attribute part is a configuration parameter for the application and is followed by one or more values for that parameter.

You can insert comments into the file that can help to make these single-line entries easier to understand. Use the "#" character at the beginning of the line to indicate a comment. Also, when an application reads this file to obtain the rules that apply to it, it reads the file from top to bottom and maintains the order in which rules appear.

This means that if you create two rules that apply to the same thing, only the first one will be used. When making changes to this file, be sure to read all entries so that you can avoid creating a duplicate rule by mistake. A duplicate rule does not mean two rules that apply to the same proxy application. As a matter of fact, it is often necessary to create several rules that are used by the same proxy. One rule might be used to define the hosts that can use the proxy, whereas another rule might be used to define the directory that the proxy will change to when it is invoked. An example of a duplicate rule would be to create two rules that both define the directory specification. In that case, only the first directory definition would be used.

Another important concept to remember is that when matching attribute values for a hostname or IP address, the comparison is done based on whether the rule contains only numeric characters (and the period character) or if it contains alphabetic characters that indicate a hostname. Consider these two sample rules:

```
netacl-in.ftpd:  permit-hosts yoko.twoinc.com -exec /usr/etc/
➥in.ftpd
```

or

```
netacl-in.ftpd:  permit-hosts 140.176.177.69 -exec /usr/etc/
➥in.ftpd
```

In the first instance, the rule contains a hostname so the application will retrieve the name of the host making the request and use it to match against the rule. In the second case, the rule contains only numeric characters and the period character, so the requesting host's IP address is used for the comparison. In general, you should always use the second format. Why? Because it is a very simple matter to use DNS spoofing to make the requesting host's name appear to something different from what it actually is.

You can use wildcards in a rule so that it can apply to multiple hosts. For example, instead of creating a large number of rules to cover every host on a network that you will permit (or deny) access to, you could use a format similar to the following:

```
netacl-in.ftpd:  permit-hosts 140.176.177.* -exec/usr/etc/in.ftpd
```

In this case, the rule would allow all hosts in the 140.176.177.0 network to use the application that is being launched by `netacl`.

What Are Unknown Hosts?

When resolving an IP address to its associated hostname, the text "unknown" is returned if the reverse lookup fails. You can use the text "unknown" in a rule instead of a hostname or an IP address. An example of this would be to use the "deny-" modifier with "unknown" to prevent these hosts from using the proxy.

In the preceding examples, the modifier "permit-" was used with the "hosts" attribute. The "permit-" and "deny-" modifiers can be used with some of the attributes that you can use in rules. The attributes, which can be used within the file, depend on the application that the rule applies to. The manual pages ("man pages") that are supplied with the toolkit specify the attributes that can be used for each application. In the examples you just looked at, the "hosts" attribute was used (permit-hosts). The ftp-gw proxy also allows the use of the attribute denial-msg *file*, which is used to specify the file containing the text that is returned to the user who is denied access to the application by the rule.

In addition, some applications allow you to specify options to the rule using the "-" character. In the case of the ftp-gw proxy (which is supplied in the toolkit), the following example shows the use of the -log option:

```
ftp-gw: hosts 140.176.177.* -log {retr stor}
```

Note that in this example the "netacl-" text is not prefixed to the name keyword at the start of the rule. This is because it is the ftp-gw application proxy that the rule applies to. This rule does not apply to using netacl to execute the usual FTP daemon for the operating system. Also, this rule does not permit or deny a host from using the application. Instead, it defines logging options for all hosts coming from the 140.176.177.0 network. The parameters enclosed by braces ({retr stor}) specify that these actions (when performed by the hosts named in the rule) by the FTP proxy will be logged. Thus, although the most obvious purpose of rules in the netperm-table file might be to control access, you can also use rules to configure options for the service that is run.

Table 14.2 lists the keywords that can be used to configure netacl in the netperm-table file.

Table 14.2 Configuration Attribute Keywords Used with the *netacl* Program

Keyword	Description
hosts *hosts*	Specifies a hosts permission rule. You can use permit- and deny- with this keyword.
-exec *program* [args]	Specifies the executable program that will be run for the service this rule applies to. Must be the last option in the rule. When using netacl, there must be an -exec option in every rule.

Keyword	Description
-user *userid*	Specifies the user (either numeric UID or text of user-name). This user must be present in the /etc/passwd file.
-chroot *directory*	The directory that netacl will chroot to *before* it invokes the executable for the service. Because the chroot is done before the service is executed, the executable (specified by the -exec option) must be in a path relative to this directory.
Timeout *seconds*	The number of seconds that the daemon can be idle before it will be disconnected. FTP timeouts are typically set from 300 seconds (5 minutes) to 3600 seconds (1 hour). You might want to use a value on the lower end when using FTP through a firewall so that connections do not stay open for long periods of time.

Keywords and options that can be used with each proxy application provided by the toolkit are listed in the sections that follow for each proxy.

Configuring Proxy Services

The toolkit provides "pass-through" proxies for the most commonly used TCP/IP network services. Each of these applications should be configured by placing rules into the netperm-table file, just as you did for netacl. Note that the first part of the rule, the name portion, will be the name of the server and should *not* be prefixed with netacl-.

FTP: *ftp-gw*

The ftp-gw proxy allows you to provide a pass-through proxy application for the FTP network service. By configuring the proxy (with rules you create in the netperm-table file), you can provide access control (which hosts can use the service) and logging options and block selected destinations. The ftp-gw proxy first changes to an isolated empty directory, so it does not, in itself, present a security risk on the firewall. The proxy does no local I/O (other than to read information from the netperm-table configuration file).

Table 14.3 lists the options you can use in the netperm-table file to configure the ftp-gw proxy.

Running ftp-gw and the Other Proxies as Daemon Processes

The ftp-gw proxy, along with the other proxies in the toolkit, can run as a daemon process, in which case you should place an entry into the /etc/rc.local file. For example, when ftp-gw is started in this manner it will listen on the standard FTP port—port 21. To change the port to a non-standard port, use the command line option -daemon *port*.

Table 14.3   Configuration Attribute Keywords Used with the *ftp-gw* Proxy

Keyword	Description
authserver *host port*	Use this to specify the name of a host running an authentication server and the port used for the service.
denial-msg *filename*	Use this to point to a file which contains the text presented to users who are denied access to the ftp-gw proxy. A default message will be generated if you do not use this option.
dendest-msg *filename*	Use this to point to a file which contains the text presented to users who are trying to access a destination they are not permitted to access. A default message will be generated if you do not use this option.
hosts *hosts*	Use this to specify one or more hosts and options for those hosts.
directory *directory*	Use this option to specify the directory that the proxy will use as its root directory before it begins to provide the service to the user.
groupid *group*	Use this to specify the group that the proxy will use when it runs.
help-msg *file*	Use this to point to a file that will be presented to the user when they use the help command. If this option is not used, the proxy will display a list of commands.
timeout *seconds*	Use this to specify the number of seconds that the proxy can remain idle before it disconnects.
userid *user*	Use this to specify the username or user ID (UID) that the proxy will run under.
welcome-msg *filename*	This points to a file containing the text of a welcome message to present to users. If this option is not used, a default message will be generated.

As you can see, the ftp-gw proxy application has many more attributes than the netacl program. However, the configuration process becomes even more complicated when you find out that the hosts attribute has a number of options you can use. These options are listed in Table 14.4. When you use these options with the `hosts` attribute, don't forget to start each one with the "`-`" character, as shown in the table.

Table 14.4   Options for the *hosts* Attribute

Option	Description
-noinput	Use this to specify that the proxy will not accept input over a port. When an attempt is made, the connection will be closed.
-nooutput	Use this to specify that the proxy will not transmit output over a port. When an attempt is made, the connection will be closed.
-log *operation* or -log {*operation1 operation2...*}	This option controls logging for the hosts it is associated with. You can specify one or more FTP daemon operations using this option.
-authall	\If this option is used, the proxy will not allow any FTP operation to be performed (other than `quit`), until the user has been authenticated to the server.
-auth *operation* or -auth {*operation1 operation2 ...*}	The FTP operations you specify with *this option will not be permitted until* the user has been authenticated to the server.
-dest *destination* or -dest {*destination1 destination2 ...*}	This option specifies valid destinations that the user can FTP to. Use the "!" character to negate a destination. *Destination* can be in the form of an IP address or domain name, and either can contain wildcards.
-deny *operation* or -deny {*operation1 operation2 ...*}	Use this option to specify one or more FTP operations that are not allowed. If you do not use this option, all FTP commands are available to the user.

When you look at all the items you can use in the `netperm-table` file to configure the `ftp-gw` proxy server, it might look overwhelming at first. However, most of the time you will usually only use a small number of options. Some of the options listed in Table 14.4 will require that you do a little further research. Specifically, to get a list of the FTP operations that can be specified using the `-log`, `-auth`, and `-deny` options, use the manual pages on your UNIX system. Although it is quite a long list, some of the more typical ones you might recognize are the retr and stor operations, which retrieve and store files, respectively.

After all that, now look at a few examples of configuration rules in netperm-table file that you can create the following:

```
ftp-gw:     welcome-msg      /usr/local/etc/ftp-welcome.txt
ftp-gw:     denial-msg       /usr/local/etc/ftp-denial.txt
ftp-gw:     help-msg         /usr/local/etc/help-ftp.txt
ftp-gw:     timeout 2400
ftp-gw:     permit-hosts 140.176.177.*
ftp-gw:     permit-hosts * -authall -log {retr stor }
```

In these examples, you can see how to specify text files for the welcome, denial, and help messages. The timeout value for a connection is set to 2400 seconds, after which an idle connection will be dropped. Hosts from the network 140.176.177.0 are allowed access to the proxy, whereas all others (*) must be authenticated for all operations, and retrieve and store (get/put) operations will be logged.

After the user has connected to the proxy server, the ftp> prompt is displayed, after the welcome message if you have created one. As you can see in Figure 14.3, at this prompt the user then needs to use the user command to specify the host that they want to connect to. The format of the command is the following:

user *username@hostname*

where *username* is a valid username for the target *hostname*, which is the computer that the FTP proxy will make a connection to.

For example, for the remote user to use FTP to get files from or put files to the server named karma, using the username smithj, they would first use their FTP client to establish a session with the firewall proxy and from there specify the server that they wanted to interact with the following:

```
popeye> ftp firewall.ono.com
Connected to firewall.ono.com
[welcome message, and so on]
ftp> user smithj@karma
```

After the proxy application makes a connection to the karma host and passes it the username smithj, it will then prompt for the password for the smithj username.

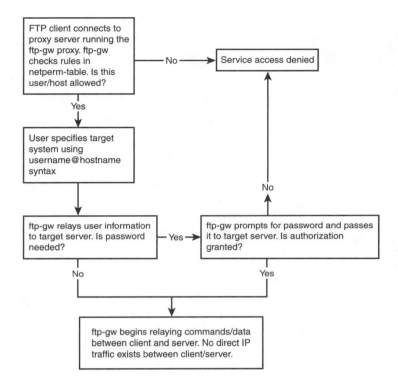

FIGURE 14.3
The ftp-gw application relays information between the client and the target FTP server.

Remember, this is a proxy application. This means that the remote user can never directly send an IP packet from his computer to the host computer specified in the user command. The proxy server receives requests (and all IP packets) from the remote system and then, at the application level, interacts with the destination FTP site for the remote user.

This two-step process might seem a bit cumbersome, but the extra step is really nothing compared to the security the proxy can provide for the network.

Remote Logins and Telnet: *tn-gw* and *rlogin-gw*

The tn-gw proxy server application works in a similar manner to the ftp-gw proxy application. You configure the application using similar attribute keywords in the netperm-table file. As a matter of fact, you use the same keywords to configure tn-gw that you do for ftp-gw (listed in the previous section in Table 14.3), except that there are two additional keywords you can use. Table 14.5 shows the additional attribute keywords you can use for the `tn-gw` proxy application.

Table 14.5 Configuration Attribute Keywords Used with the *tn-gw* Proxy

Keyword	Description
Prompt *prompt*	Use this keyword to specify the prompt that is presented to the user by the Telnet proxy server when it is in command mode. If you use a prompt that contains spaces, it is usually required that you place the text within quotes.
Xforwarder *program*	Use this keyword to specify the location of the executable program that the Telnet proxy will pass requests for the X proxy. In most cases, this specifies the location of the X proxy.

The options that you can use with the `hosts` keyword is a much smaller set than those used with the `ftp-gw` proxy. Obviously, some of the FTP proxy application keywords, such as `-log` *operation* are specific to FTP. Telnet doesn't have a set of operations it can perform. It merely provides a remote terminal session between the remote user and the target system.

The `-dest` option works the same way it does for the `ftp-gw` application. Use it to specify one or more destinations to which access is granted. Don't forget that wildcards are permitted, and you can use the "!" character before a destination to negate a destination.

Additionally, two other options can be used with the `hosts` attribute keyword:

- `-auth` Use this to specify that the user must authenticate using a valid user ID/password before they can use the gateway.

- `-passok` Use this option to specify that the user is allowed to change their password (when connecting from the host that the rule applies to).

Once connected to the Telnet proxy server the user can then use the `connect` command to make a connection to a particular host. Again, remember that no IP traffic actually passes directly from the remote user to the target system. The proxy server receives data from the remote user and then acts on their behalf to make requests of the target system's Telnet daemon.

Table 14.6 lists the commands that the user can issue once connected to the `tn-gw` proxy server.

Table 14.6 Commands Recognized by the *tn-gw* Proxy Server

Command	Description
connect *host* [*port*]	Connects the user in a Telnet session to the specified host (and port, if specified). You can use either a hostname or IP address for *host*.
exit or quit	Just what it says! Exits the Telnet proxy server.
Help or ?	Displays help text.
password	Allows the user to change their strong authentication password. This can only be done from hosts listed in the `netperm-table` file.
timeout *seconds*	Use this to override the timeout value specified in the `netperm-table` file.
x-gw [*hostname:display* [*.screennumber*]]	This command invokes the X11 proxy to connect the user to the specified host and display.

Similar to the Telnet service, `rlogin` can be used to get to the command prompt of a remote system so that you can execute commands. Unlike Telnet, though, `rlogin` does not require that the user authenticate to the service running on the remote system. Instead, access is controlled by use of the `hosts.equiv` and `.rhosts` files. Depending on which of these files is used, access is granted if the requesting host's name (or IP address) or the requesting user's name is found in these files.

SEE ALSO

➤ *For more information about the various "r" services which make use of the* `host.equiv` *and* `.rhosts` *files and why these services might present a security risk, see page 60*

The `rlogin-gw` proxy gateway that you can compile from the toolkit is configured almost exactly the same as the `tn-gw` proxy gateway. The attribute keywords and options are the same. The command set that the end-user can use when they connect to the proxy is also the same. The main difference between the two is that you must configure the `hosts.equiv` or `.rhosts` files on the target system so that they "trust" the firewall host, and not the host computer that the remote user comes from. Like the Telnet `tn-gw` proxy, you can specify rules in the `netperm-table` file regarding which hosts are allowed to use the proxy. You can also require that the remote users first authenticate themselves to the firewall before they are allowed to continue on to establish a remote login on the target computer.

The "r" services were originally designed to keep from having to send clear-text passwords across the network. That is why the `hosts.equiv` and `.rhosts` files are used. The services' security is based on the ability of one computer to trust another. By using strong authentication with the `rlogin-gw`, you can protect against username and password interception when the remote user authenticates themselves to the firewall. However, although the firewall proxy can protect you against misuse of these services from outside of your firewall-secured network, remember that the firewall can do nothing to protect you from misuse by users on the internal network. In general, the "r" services are not that good an idea if you have a large number of users and require tight security on your network.

SMTP: *smap*

Of all the programs that have been misused over the years by taking advantage of known bugs and other coding problems, one of the most notorious is `sendmail`. For example, if the programmer does not check user entry to be sure that the data entered will fit into the buffer which has been set aside, it is possible to overwrite not only the buffer space, but also to overwrite the program code itself. When this happens, the results might be unpredictable—the program will usually crash resulting in a denial of service attack. Or, if the attacker is a little more clever, the code which has overwritten the original program might execute instead. Because `sendmail` runs under root in most cases, this can be disastrous, giving the executing code access to the entire system.

This is what happened with the infamous "Internet Worm" fiasco about ten years ago, which used `sendmail` to compromise thousands and thousands of systems in a very short time. Since then, attempts have been made to patch and repair the program. However, because of its large size (20,000 plus lines) and complexity, it can be difficult to ever certify that this application can be used by itself in a secure manner. Another reason that sendmail (and many other mailer programs) can present a security problem is that they usually run with system-level permissions. Thus, when a bug is exploited, it is possible to open up the system such that normal resource protections are not a barrier.

The toolkit provides to programs that are used to help make the delivery of email a little safer. They are smap and smapd. When you use these programs, you do not have to make any changes to your actual mailer program or its configuration file. Instead, you configure smap and smapd, which work to relay mail traffic between an outside mailer and the regular mailer you use on your network.

The mechanics of how these two programs work is quite simple. The smap client program is started when the system boots and listens in on the SMTP port (usually port 25, as defined in the /etc/services file) for mail requests. When a mail message is delivered to the smap daemon, it does not make any attempt to forward the message to its recipient. Instead, it writes the message to a directory. Periodically, the smapd server daemon wakes up and looks to see if there are any files in this directory. If so, smapd then is responsible for calling the actual mailer program, such as sendmail, which then delivers the message to its final destination. After a message has been forwarded to the mailer program, smapd then deletes it from the directory used for temporary storage.

By placing smap and smapd between the internal and external SMTP mailer programs, no contact is ever made directly through the firewall. Although I have discussed it in many different places in this book, I think it is important again to emphasize that the smap and smapd proxy programs can do nothing at all to protect you from viruses or other programs that can be sent into your system via email. All these two programs do is to block the misuse of the sendmail (or other mailer program) so that it cannot be exploited to compromise your systems or network.

The configuration attribute keywords that you use in the netperm-table file are shown in Table 14.7 for smap and Table 14.8 for smapd.

Table 14.7 Configuration Attribute Keywords Used with the *smap* Client Proxy Application

Keyword	Description
directory *directory*	Use this keyword to specify the directory that smap uses for its root directory before it begins to process mail. This directory will also be used as the temporary storage area for messages that smapd will pick up.
groupid *group*	This keyword is used to specify the name of the group that smap will run under.
timeout *seconds*	The number of seconds that can elapse with no activity before the smap proxy will disconnect.
userid *user*	This keyword is used to specify the userID that the smap proxy runs under.

Table 14.8 Configuration Attribute Keywords Used with the *smapd* Server Proxy Application

Keyword	Description
badadmin *user*	When smapd cannot deliver mail, it will send it to the user specified by this keyword. The value for this keyword can be an actual username or an alias.
baddir *directory*	When smapd cannot deliver mail, it will place it in the directory specified by this keyword. The directory should be located on the same device as the spool directory (specified using the directory keyword) and should have the same owner and permissions as the regular spool directory.
directory *directory*	Use this keyword to specify the directory that smapd uses for its root directory before it begins to process mail. This directory will also be used as the temporary storage area for messages that smapd will pick up.
executable *program*	This is a required keyword and is used to specify the name of the smapd program itself. To deliver mail to the mailer program, smapd will fork and exec a new copy of itself for each message it handles.
groupid *group*	This keyword is used to specify the name of the group that smap will run under.

Keyword	Description
maxchildren *children*	Use this keyword to limit the number of child processes that smapd uses when handling messages.
sendmail *program*	Use this keyword to specify the path for the mailer program used on the inside of your network.
wakeup *seconds*	Use this keyword to specify the number of seconds that the smapd server sleeps before it wakes up to check the spool directory for messages. The default value if this keyword is not used is 60 seconds.
userid *user*	This keyword is used to specify the user ID that the smap proxy runs under.

Whereas all the other toolkit proxies can be run either from the inetd.conf file on a connection-by-connection basis, these two programs should be handled a little differently. The smap client program should be started up when the system boots. This is usually done by placing an entry in the /etc/rc.local file. For example:

```
/usr/local/etc/smapd
```

The smapd server application can also be started in this manner, as can all the proxies, unless you are using an old version of the toolkit.

Configuring Other Services: *plug-gw*

To handle other services that the toolkit does not have a proxy for (such as NNTP—the Network News Transport Protocol), you can use the plug-gw proxy program. Unlike the other proxies in the toolkit, plug-gw doesn't have built-in commands that can be used for any particular service. For example, the tn-gw proxy allows the user to use the connect command to connect to a remote server on the internal LAN after they have been authenticated to the firewall. When using plug-gw, however, all that is provided is a "pipe" that can connect an external source to an internal source so that a service can be tunneled through the firewall. The security that plug-gw provides is to block any IP traffic from traveling directly through the firewall, which is what a proxy does. Additional security is provided because plug-gw, like the other proxies in the toolkit, also performs logging so that you can review what kind of traffic is flowing through the firewall. By exchanging data at the application level, plug-gw simply "plugs" the two sides of the data pipe together.

Configure the Firewall in DNS to Handle Mail

Don't forget to check the DNS configuration for your domain to ensure that an MX (mail exchanger) record exists that sends SMTP traffic to the firewall where you are running smap. For more information about DNS, see Chapter 2, "Introduction to the TCP/IP Suite."

For each service you want to use with `plug-gw`, a separate daemon process is created. You can configure `plug-gw` to start from the `inetd.conf` file when a connection is detected, or you can configure it to run from the `/etc/rc.local` file. To have the `inetd` daemon start the proxy, create an entry similar to the following:

```
nntp    stream    tcp    nowait    root    /usr/local/etc/plug-gw
➥plug-gw 119
```

In this example, the proxy is used to handle requests for Internet newsgroups. You can look in the `/etc/services` file and find that port 119 (the last entry on the line) is the port number for NNTP. This value is passed along with `plug-gw` itself as arguments to the `plug-gw` proxy. As was shown in Table 14.1, the first field in this entry is the name of the service that the `inetd` daemon is to start in response to a connection attempt. Remember also that `inetd` only knows the port that the request is asking for, not the name of the service. The file `/etc/services` is used as a cross-reference for ports and the names of services associated with them.

If you decide to run `plug-gw` as a daemon, you can use two command line arguments to start it:

■ `-daemon port [or service name]`

■ `-version`

The first argument is used to specify the port or service that `plug-gw` will be performing proxy functions for, whereas the second argument will cause information about the version of the proxy to be echoed to standard output.

As with all proxies in the toolkit, the `netperm-table` is used to configure `plug-gw`. Table 14.9 lists the attribute keywords that can be used.

Table 14.9 Configuration Attribute Keywords Used with *plug-gw*

Keyword	Description
groupid *group*	Use this to specify the group under which the proxy runs.
port *portid hosts*	Use this to specify the port number of the service and a list of hosts that can use the service.
timeout *seconds*	Number of seconds the proxy can remain idle before disconnecting.
userid *user*	Use this to specify the user that the proxy will run under.

In addition to these attribute keywords, there are several options that you need to use to specify how the connection will be made by `plug-gw`. These options are the following:

- `-plug-to` *host* This option is used to indicate the host on the internal LAN that `plug-gw` will connect the incoming service request to. This option is mandatory.

- `-privport` Use this option to specify that a reserved port number will be used on the host that is providing the service. This option is usually used for security purposes.

- `-port` *portid* This option is used to specify the port number on the internal host. If you do not specify this option, the port number of the request is used by default. This option is very useful when you want to run several instances of `plug-gw` to handle duplicate copies of the service. For example, if your network needs to use more than one external news source, you can configure each internal news host to use a different port. If you used the same port, `plug-gw` would try to connect each of the internal servers to the same external news host.

Now look at an example entry in `netperm-table` for `plug-gw`:

```
plug-gw:   port 119 140.176.115.*    -plug-to 198.22.43.122
```

This simple entry will host all computers on the 140.176.115.0 network to connect to an external news host that uses the IP address of 198.22.43.122. Note that after the `plug-gw:` identifier at the start of the line is the port number (119) that is used to identify the service. Remember that although the other proxies provided by the toolkit were for specific services, `plug-gw` is a neutral service and protocol, so you must tell it which services it will handle requests for. Because the `-port` option was not used after the host address at the end of the line, the default port (119) will also be used for the external connection.

Take the next two configuration examples, for instance:

```
plug-gw:   port 2119 140.176.115.*    -plug-to 198.22.43.122
➡-port 119
plug-gw:   port 2120 140.176.115.*    -plug-to 198.22.43.123
➡-port 119
```

Here the -port option is used. Why? Because the default would be either port 2119 or 2120, and neither of these would be valid for a news server on the Internet. These two examples show how you can configure the proxy so that you can use two different external news servers to provide news service to clients on the internal LAN. In this case, you would need to configure news clients to use either port 2119 or 2120, depending on which external server you wanted them to be connected to. Note also that when you configure clients for the news service you use the IP address of the firewall, not the external news server, because the client computers should connect to the proxy which then forwards requests to the external server.

If you use this method to start multiple instances of plug-gw to provide a service on multiple ports, you need to make sure that the /etc/services file contains entries for the new ports. For the example you just looked at, you would add the following lines:

```
nntp-a     2119/tcp     readnews    untp    # Internet news server
➥NNTP
nntp-b     2120/tcp     readnews    untp    # Internet news server
➥NNTP
```

You would also have to create two entries in the inetd.conf file so that the inetd daemon would know to respond to requests on these ports using plug-gw:

```
nntp-a     stream     tcp    nowait    root    /usr/local/etc/plug-gw
➥plug-gw 2119
nntp-a     stream     tcp    nowait    root    /usr/local/etc/plug-gw
➥plug-gw 2120
```

Lastly, remember that although plug-gw can be a useful tool to provide proxy services for many different kinds of services, it is not always a good idea to use it indiscriminately. New services and protocols are being developed and springing up on the Internet all the time. You should remember that the firewall is constructed based on your site's security policies. Don't simply plug new services into the firewall whenever a user makes a request, thinking that the proxy will keep anything bad from happening. You need first to understand how the service or protocol works. Then, based on just how important the service is to the user, make a decision. Evaluate the risk! Compare this with the benefits to be gained!

Other FWTK Components

In addition to the proxy services that I have covered in this chapter, the toolkit also provides authentication services, a replacement for the UNIX `syslogd` daemon, and several tools that can be used to test security on your system.

The `authd` service, for example, can be configured to work with `ftp-gw` and `tn-gw` to provide additional security by forcing users to authenticate to the firewall before using them. `Authd` can be configured to work with several different kinds of authentication services that are already in widespread use.

The version of `syslogd` found in the toolkit is an extended version of the regular daemon, but allows you to specify search patterns in the configuration file and to invoke specific programs when a particular event occurs. Thus, you can, in effect, perform real-time scanning on the events sent to the `syslogd` daemon. Instead of having to sit at a terminal and watch for messages, however, you can configure `syslogd` to shut down the system in the event of a serious security breach.

Installing the Toolkit on a Bastion Host

The toolkit comes in source code format and is written using the C programming language. This means that after you download the toolkit you need to compile it on your local system before you can use it. Included with the download you will find several read-me files that need to be reviewed before you start. Before you start to compile toolkit components on your system, read the tutorials that can be found at `www.fwtk.org` to find out specific examples for your UNIX variant. You might also want to subscribe to the mailing list that is devoted to FWTK. To do this, simply send an email to `majordomo@ex.tis.com` and make the body of the message nothing but the text "subscribe fwtk-users."

Remember also that the firewall you build is only going to be as secure as the host on which it runs. This host is usually called a bastion host.

SEE ALSO

➤ *In Chapter 6, "Using a Bastion Host" (page 131), I cover a lot of territory on how to secure a system so that it can be used for this purpose. The topics covered there range from limiting services that run on the system and removing unnecessary user accounts to turning off IP forwarding and rebuilding the kernel.*

Do not simply install the toolkit on a fresh UNIX installation and depend on it as a secure firewall. Read Chapter 6 first!

Summary

The Trusted Information Systems Internet Firewall Toolkit is a freely available set of components that can be used to construct a firewall on a highly secured UNIX system that resides at the perimeter of your network. These tools allow you to create a firewall that provides all the standard network services, such as Telnet, FTP, and email. In addition, the `plug-gw` proxy makes it easy to connect client and server applications through the firewall when no standard proxy exists.

The toolkit is not a tool to be used by everyone. Only an experienced UNIX administrator with a good knowledge of TCP/IP should attempt to make use of the toolkit components to secure a network. This is because the proxy allows you to finely tune which services are allowed through the firewall. If you do not understand the network services provided by the TCP/IP suite and how they are configured on a typical UNIX system, you will find it difficult to use the toolkit to create a firewall which you can trust to be secure.

Because the toolkit is supported only by other users, you will not be able to depend on the backing of a vendor when you need help. Keep this in mind when making a decision on whether this firewall solution is right for you.

chapter

15

SOCKS

SOCKS V4 and SOCKS V5 •

SOCKSified Applications •

SOCKSCap •

How to Get SOCKS •

SOCKS Support •

SOCKS V4 and SOCKS V5

SOCKS Request For Comments (RFC) Documents

Since version 5, SOCKS has been discussed by several RFCs. If you want to know more about the details of how SOCKS works, this would be a good place to start. You can download copies of the following RFCs from the NEC Web site devoted to SOCKS, www.socks.nec.com.

RFC 1928, "SOCKS Protocol Version 5," sets for the basic protocol and describes how it differs from version 4.

RFC 1929, "Username/Password Authentication for SOCKS V5," describes a method for using clear-text username and passwords with SOCKS.

RFC 1961, "GSSAPI authentication for SOCKS V5," describes a more secure method for authentication for use with SOCKS.

In addition, at the NEC Web site, you will also find many Internet Drafts that cover other aspects of the protocol and its implementation. There are also older Internet Drafts that describe version 4 of the protocol.

SOCKS is a protocol that can be used to create proxy connections through a firewall. Originally developed by David Koblas and Ying-Da Lee at NEC Systems Laboratory, SOCKS has been made a standard by a number of Request for Comments (RFC) documents and is widely used on the Internet. The SOCKS protocol can be used to allow a host on one side of the SOCKS server to interact with a host on the other side, subject to authentication, without passing IP packets directly between them.

Remember that SOCKS is a protocol. Whether a particular firewall provides SOCKS server support depends on the vendor. Client software that supports a SOCKS connection is widely available. For older applications, NEC provides several alternatives, including a library of functions that can be used to recompile an application to "SOCKSify" the application and a DLL for Windows systems called SocksCap that can intercept calls to WinSock networking functions.

If you are curious about the technology, you can download reference versions of SOCKS from NEC, along with a few client utilities that use the protocol.

Version 4

SOCKS is a simple protocol. In V4, the protocol does three basic tasks:

- Connection request exchange
- Setup of proxy circuit
- Relay application data

These simple steps allow the client to set up a circuit through the SOCKS server that can be used to relay application network traffic based on TCP.

The *CONNECT* Request

To begin a connection, the client application sends a CONNECT request to the SOCKS server. This request contains several fields:

- **Version Number** This 8-bit field contains the version number, which is 4 for this version.

- **SOCKS Command Code**   This 8-bit field is used for a code that indicates the function of the packet. A value of 1 indicates a connect request.

- **Destination Port**   This 16-bit field is the port number on the target server that the client wants to connect to.

- **Destination IP Address**   This 32-bit field is the IP address of the target server that the client wants to connect to.

- **User ID**   This is a variable length field that contains a userID that is valid on the target server.

After the SOCKS server consults its rules and determines that the connection is allowable, the server attempts to connect to the target server using the IP address and port number supplied by the client. After this succeeds (or fails), the SOCKS server returns a packet to the client, including the following:

- **Version number**   This 8-bit field is the version number of the reply code and should be 0.

- **SOCKS Result Code**   The value in this 8-bit field indicates the success or failure of the CONNECT request.

If this messages contains a failure code, the SOCKS server terminates its connection to the client after sending this reply. Otherwise, the server stands ready to relay data between the client and server applications (see Figure 15.1).

The *BIND* Request

After a client application has successfully used the CONNECT request to establish a proxied connection to a target application server, the BIND request can be used to inform the SOCKS server that the client wants to set up an incoming connection from the application server. The contents of the BIND request packet is the same as the CONNECT request, except that the SOCKS Command Code should be 2. If the SOCKS server, after consulting its rules, decides that the connection can be allowed, it returns a reply packet to the client that is similar to the reply to the CONNECT request. The SOCKS server allocates a socket to be used to listen for the application server connection and returns a reply to the client application with two additional fields of data:

- **Destination Port**   This is the port allocated on the SOCKS server to receive data from the application server.

Where Does the Name SOCKS Come From?

The name SOCKS was not drawn out of a hatful of suggestions. Instead, it comes from the internal development name that was used during its inception: SOCK-et-S.

How Is a SOCKS Server Configured?

SOCKS is a protocol. Vendors can choose to implement configuration details however they want. The SOCKS V5 Reference Implementation from NEC, for example, uses a configuration file called /etc/socks5.conf on the server and /etc/libsocks5.conf on the client. Check the documentation for your firewall to see if it includes SOCKS support.

- **Destination IP Address**   This is the IP address of the adapter on the SOCKS server that receives data from the application server. This is necessary if the SOCKS server has more than one network adapter. If the value of this field is 0, the client uses the same address as the original CONNECT connection to the SOCKS server.

FIGURE 15.1
For a connection request, a SOCKS server must verify its configuration before connecting to the target server.

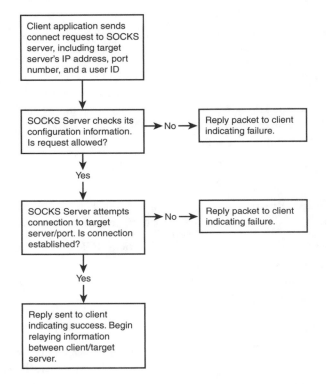

The client application uses this socket information to format a request to the target application server. The application server then opens a connection with the SOCKS server, using this socket. The SOCKS server checks to see that this second connection comes from the same host that was identified in the original BIND request and, if so, sends another reply packet to the client application telling it that the connection has been established (see Figure 15.2).

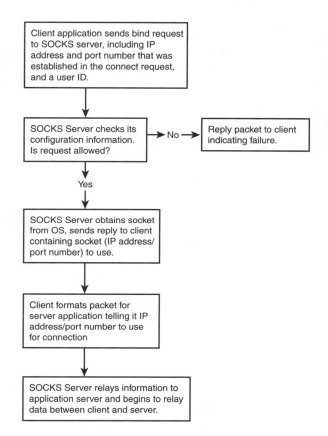

FIGURE 15.2
Once connected, the client can use a BIND request to inform the SOCKS server that it wants an incoming connection from the target server.

As you can see, although the SOCKS protocol can be used to create a client/server connection through the firewall, the SOCKS protocol itself does not perform any application-specific checks. In this manner, it operates much like a packet filter. The SOCKS server can be configured to permit or deny certain hosts, networks, and so on, but it does not get into the details of whether specific functions of an application can be allowed. That functionality is up to the application that is coded to use the SOCKS protocol. Unlike a packet filter, however, SOCKS does not pass IP packets directly between the client and server applications. No direct IP connection exists between the two.

Version 5

The newest version of the SOCKS protocol adds support for authentication and for creating UDP proxies in addition to TCP. Support for domain names and IPv6 addressing is also part of the new specification.

SEE ALSO

➤ *For more information about IPv6, the Next Generation IP, see Chapter 21, "Firewalls and Beyond," page 381*

In SOCKS V4, when the client application sent in a CONNECT request, a value for a userID was included in the request. This information is used by the SOCKS server when it consults its rules to decide whether the connection can be allowed. SOCKS can also use the functionality of the IDENT protocol to try to verify the username of the client making a request. However, actual authentication over the proxied connection between the client and server is not affected by SOCKS V4. That is, if you use FTP through a SOCKS connection and the FTP client sends the username/password data as clear text, security can be compromised if the text is intercepted.

SOCKS V5 adds support for authentication methods in a generalized manner by using a specification framework that provides for the use of arbitrary authentication protocols in the initial socks connection setup.

After the client connects to the SOCKS server, it sends a message that identifies the version of the SOCKS protocol and one or more "methods" than can be used for authentication. Although the packet format provides for up to 255 different methods, only a few are defined at this point. The SOCKS server selects one of the methods supplied by the client and returns a message to the client indicating the method chosen. Values for methods are controlled by the Internet Assigned Numbers Authority (IANA), and currently are the following:

- No authentication required (0)
- GSS-API (1)
- USERNAME/PASSWORD (2)
- IANA (3–127)

- Reserved for private methods (128–254)
- No acceptable methods (255)

After the client has received this message, the client and the SOCKS server then enter into a negotiation phase that is specific to the authentication method chosen.

The SOCKS V5 Request Format

Although similar to the V4 format, the SOCKS V5 format provides for more information. The Version Number field should be set to 5. The SOCKS Command Code field now has three values:

- 1   CONNECT
- 2   BIND
- 3   UDP ASSOCIATE

A new field is used to indicate the type of IP address. This 8-bit value should be 1 if the address is an IPV4 style address, 3 if the address field contains a domain name, and 4 if the address field contains an IPv6-type of address. The Destination Address field contains the actual address, in a format indicated by the Address Type field. The Destination Port field is the same as in version 4, indicating the target port for the service the client wants to connect. The size of the Destination Address field depends on the type of address. If a fully-qualified domain name is used, the first octet of the address field (8 bits) is a value that indicates the length (in octets) of the domain name that follows in the address field.

The UDP Associate Function

Again, the version field of the reply message is now 5 instead of 4. The SOCKS Result Code field provides for the same results as in version 4, but it adds a few new ones. The reply message also contains fields for address type and address as in the request format.

In addition to CONNECT and BIND requests, SOCKS V5 offers a new service to allow UDP proxies to be created. In the UDP ASSOCIATE request packet, the client tells the server the port and IP address that the client wants to use for the association. The reply packet returned by the server tells the client the port number and IP address where it must send packets for the connection. Relaying UDP traffic is done

SOCKS V5 Authentication Methods

Two other Request For Comments documents detail two of the methods that the SOCKS V5 protocol can use for authentication. These are the following:

RFC 1929, "Username/Password Authentication for SOCKS V5," is an authentication method using clear-text for exchanging the user-name and password values and is not a secure method.

RFC 1961, "GSS-API Authentication Method for SOCKS Version 5," describes using the GSS-API for authentication and for other uses such as encapsulating IP traffic. GSS-API is further discussed in RFCs 1508 and 1509.

UDP Fragmentation

The SOCKS V5 protocol has a field in the UDP request header that can be used to indicate when a packet has been fragmented. This is an optional feature that might not be implemented in all SOCKS servers.

differently from TCP traffic, however. Instead of simply receiving packets from one side of the connection and relaying them to the other, each packet that the client sends to the SOCKS server for UDP has a UDP request header attached to it. This request header includes the standard fields used in request/replies for SOCKS and, it also includes the desired destination port and IP address.

Because UDP is a connectionless, unreliable protocol that doesn't provide for acknowledgement of packets received, the SOCKS server does not inform the client whether a packet is forwarded or dropped.

SOCKSified Applications

If you have the source code for an application that doesn't yet support SOCKS, it is possible that you can "SOCKSify" the application by recompiling it using a library of functions provided with the SOCKS V5 Reference Implementation from NEC. The library includes routines that are functionally equivalent to standard BSD socket functions but that implement the SOCKS protocol.

At the NEC SOCKS Web site, you can find detailed instructions for the minor modifications that need to be made to the existing code and how to link the code with the SOCKS library functions. Following is the URL for this link:

www.socks.nec.com/how2socksify.html

SocksCap

SocksCap can be used on Windows systems to enable applications to work through a SOCKS firewall without requiring any modification to the original application. SocksCap intercepts calls to networking services by WinSock clients and sends them to a SOCKS server instead. Several versions of SocksCap exist, in 16- and 32-bit formats. For Windows 95 or Windows 98, you can use either version, depending on the client applications that are used with SOCKS. For Windows NT, only the 32-bit version can be used.

Note that SocksCap does not replace WinSock; it merely changes some of the functionality.

To download SocksCap, start at the following Web site:

www.socks.nec.com

How to Get SOCKS

At the NEC Web site, you can find a large amount of information about the SOCKS protocols. As for client software, you can check with the vendor if you are unsure, but many new applications come with support for SOCKS built in. If the application you want to use does not have the ability to work with a SOCKS proxy server, there are several alternatives, such as recompiling the application in a "SOCKSified" manner, as discussed earlier, or using SOCKSCap or some other SOCKS library-based solution.

Most major firewall products also support SOCKS. If strong authentication is important for security at your site—which it should be— be sure to check the documentation to see whether the product is based on SOCKS V4 or V5.

In addition to commercial implementations of SOCKS, NEC has available for download the SOCKS V5 Reference Implementation. This comes in source code format and you can get it from the following site:

`ftp.nec.com/pub/socks/socks5`

This package also has client applications for Telnet, FTP, finger, whois, archie, ping, and traceroute.

There is also an implementation that has been created by Hewlett Packard for internal use. You can download this SOCKS server from the following site:

`ftp.cup.hp.com/diskt/socks`

SOCKS Support

You should be able to get support for any good commercial firewall product from the vendor who produces it. This support, however, is probably limited to configuration issues and minor troubleshooting. If you want to dig further into the technical aspects of SOCKS or stay up-to-date on new developments about this protocol or applications based on it, there are three SOCKS-specific mailing lists you can subscribe to. To subscribe, send an email message to

`Majordomo@socks.nec.com`

Do not use a subject line for the message; instead, include text similar to the following as the body of the message:

Subscribe *<list> you@address.com*

For *list*, specify which list (SOCKS, SOCKS5, or SOCKSCAP).

Summary

The SOCKS protocol is an example of how new protocols and services are being developed to respond to the rapidly growing Internet. As security needs increase, a framework such as SOCKS can be used by many different vendors to create applications that can work together in a standardized manner. In the next chapter, you will look at another proxy solution that is available on the Internet: SQUID, a proxy server with caching as its main objective.

chapter

16

SQUID

What Is SQUID? •

Where to Get SQUID •

Installing and Configuring SQUID •

Managing SQUID •

Configuring Clients to Use SQUID •

What Is SQUID?

SQUID is a caching proxy server. If you will recall, one of the first uses for a proxy server was to cache frequently visited Web pages so that valuable bandwidth could be conserved. This was more prominent during the earlier days of the Internet before there were many commercial sites. When the Internet was used mostly for scientific and educational uses, many investigators used the same resource for information, downloading the information over and over each time any access was made. By keeping copies of frequently accessed, mostly static, data available on a local server, one response from the Web site resource could be used to satisfy a number of local users.

Caching proxy servers work by keeping copies of recently accessed objects that were retrieved from the Internet in a local disk or memory cache. If another request for the same object comes along a short time later, the proxy server can use its local copy of the data instead of having to send another request to the original URL of the object.

The SQUID cache proxy application is freely available from the Internet under the GNU license. Although SQUID can be downloaded free from the Internet, do not mistake it for a simple product with few features. Instead, SQUID has a rich feature set and can be successfully employed on a small or large network to provide caching services. Some important features of SQUID are the following:

- Proxy services and caching for the HTTP and FTP protocols, and SSL.
- Hierarchical organization so multiple cache servers can be configured to work together using the standard Internet Caching Protocol (ICP).
- Transparent operation for users.
- Access controls.
- DNS lookup caching.
- HTTP server acceleration.

SQUID is a complex product that has many configuration options. In this chapter, you will briefly look at how to install SQUID and get it up and running using default values for configuration. If you are interested in evaluating SQUID for use in your firewall, it would be a good idea to carefully review the SQUID FAQ first to get a more detailed understanding of the complex configuration commands that can be used to manage SQUID.

Where to Get SQUID

If you want to download SQUID, you can visit the SQUID Web site. However, if you are using Linux, you might first want to check your operating system documentation. Many Linux variants come with the SQUID source code and some even include the compiled binary code. At the Web site, though, you will also find the official SQUID FAQ, a good User's Guide, and other documentation that would be helpful to anyone using SQUID on a production basis. So, even if you already have SQUID on your system, the official Web site can still be a valuable resource. The URL for the SQUID site is the following:

www.squid-cache.org

At the time this book is being published, the most recent version of SQUID is version 2.3. Previous versions are still available for download, however.

Installing and Configuring SQUID

To install SQUID, it is a good idea to first create a user account that the proxy server will be run under. Do *not* install or run SQUID under root. The only files that SQUID needs to have access to are its configuration files and the files and directories used to store cached objects. The recommended practice is to create a squid user account and a directory (/usr/local/squid) for the account and use this to run SQUID. When you unpack the tar file and compile the SQUID source code, use this account so that it will own the files when you are finished.

Choosing a SQUID Server

When deciding on a server to use for the SQUID installation, be sure to choose a system that has plenty of memory and an efficient disk system. Because caching involves short-term storage of objects that are downloaded from the Internet, using multiple disks for SQUID cache directories improves performance. Using a RAID disk subsystem can enable you to further speed up the process. The speed of the CPU does not affect performance as much as the amount of memory does. The more memory you can afford, the better response users will see. It is recommended that at least 128MB of memory be used for a SQUID server, though 256MB or more is better.

Installing the Software

Installing SQUID is a simple matter. After you create a user account that SQUID will be run under, log in to that account, then unpack the compressed files, execute a few commands to compile the code, and create directories and indexes that SQUID will use.

Installing SQUID

1. Create a directory to store the SQUID source files in:

   ```
   # mkdir -p /usr/local/squid/src
   ```

2. Set your default to the directory you just created and unpack the compressed file that contains the SQUID source:

   ```
   # gzip -cd squid-2.3.STABLE2-src.tar.gz | tar xv
   ```

   This command also creates several new subdirectories. The /doc directory contains useful information, of course, and you should be sure to check out the files here, especially any readme files that might contain information about updates or recent notices.

3. Use the configure command to start an automatic process that will examine your server:

   ```
   # ./configure
   ```

4. Use the SQUID make file to compile the source, and after a successful compilation, use the install parameter to install SQUID:

   ```
   # make
   # make install
   ```

   These commands will install SQUID in several directories that will be created under the /usr/local/squid directory, including the bin, etc, cache, and logs subdirectories.

5. A default copy of the configuration file /usr/local/squid/etc/ squid.conf is created. You can use this copy of the file or use a text editor to modify entries in this file. For example, if you do

not want SQUID to store cached objects in the default /usr/local/squid/cache directory, but on another disk instead, you can edit the file to change this.

6. Use the squid command to create directories used to index stored data:

```
# /usr/local/bin/squid -z
```

7. Finally, use the squid command to start a background process that will listen for requests on SQUID's default port 3128. Check the log file /usr/local/bin/logs/cache.log to determine whether any errors have occurred.

When the squid command is executed with no parameters, it starts a parent background process that then spawns a child process. The child process does the actual work of the program. If for any reason the child process exits, the parent then spawns a new one. You can check the syslog message files to look for entries made by SQUID when it starts or restarts a process. If you notice that this is happening often, check the SQUID log file named cache.log to try to resolve the problem.

To determine whether SQUID is functioning as you expect, configure a client, such as Internet Explorer, to use SQUID and then try to browse the Web. When you are sure that all is well, add a command to your system's startup files to start SQUID when the system boots.

Managing SQUID

To make changes to the current SQUID configuration, you need to edit the configuration file and then invoke the squid command to apply the changes. After making any changes to the squid.conf file, use the following command to apply the changes you have made:

```
/usr/local/bin/squid -k reconfigure
```

The *squid.conf* file

This file is the main configuration file for SQUID, and it is usually located at /usr/local/squid/etc/squid.conf. This file contains information such as the HTTP port that SQUID will use. You don't have to worry about creating this file from scratch. When you execute the

---

Using the configure Script

In the example showing how to compile SQUID, notice that you had to run the configure script after the source had been uncompressed, but before you compiled it. The configure script evaluates your system and creates make files, among other things. This script file takes several parameters that can be used to govern how it works. For example, you can tell configure to use a different directory for SQUID other than its default of /usr/local/squid. To find out more about the parameters you can use with the configure script, enter

./configure--help.

---

configure script, the make install commands that a default copy of this file will be automatically created for you. The parameters that you can modify in this file are numerous, and the best way to get started is to simply read through the file. The default file that is created is heavily commented throughout, making much of it easy to follow. Some of it does get more involved, however. Before you start to make changes here, I suggest that you first read through the SQUID FAQ, which is more up-to-date than the User's Guide. In addition to answering questions about tuning the SQUID server through this file, you can also learn how to configure access control lists (ACLs) to control which objects can or cannot be accessed or which users or hosts are allowed to use the SQUID server.

The default squid.conf file can be used as is if you simply want to use SQUID as a caching server and do not care about user or URL access controls. The SQUID FAQ can be downloaded from the SQUID Web site at www.squid-cache.org.

The *squid* Command

To start the SQUID cache server, you only need to execute the squid command. However, the syntax for this command is actually quite complicated. When you become used to using SQUID, you can explore some of the additional things that you can do. Some of the important command-line parameters for squid are the following:

- -a *port*   Designates that SQUID use a different port number for listening for HTTP requests. The default is 3128.

- -d *error-level*   Sets the level for debugging messages sent to stderr.

- -f   Designates an alternative squid.conf configuration file.

- -h   Displays help information.

- -k reconfigure   Sends SQUID the HUP signal telling it to re-read its configuration file.

- -k rotate   Sends SQUID the USR1 signal. This causes SQUID to rotate log files (close the current one, rename it, and open a new file).

- -k shutdown   Sends SQUID a TERM signal, telling it to shut down. SQUID waits for a short amount of time to let current connections finish before shutting down.

- `-k interrupt`   Sends SQUID an INT signal telling it to shut down immediately.

- `-k kill`   Sends SQUID a KILL signal. This causes SQUID to exit at once without performing any file cleanup activity. This should be used only when all else fails.

- `-k debug`   Sends SQUID the USR2 signal. Until the next USR2 signal is sent, SQUID generates full debugging messages.

- `-k check`   Sends SQUID a ZERO signal to check to see if the process is actually running. Check the exit status variable for the shell you are using to find the results.

- `-s`   Tells SQUID to send only level 0 debugging messages to syslog.

- `-u`   Used to specify an alternative port number for SQUID to use for listening for incoming ICP messages. The default is port 3130.

- `-v`   Tells SQUID to display its version number.

- `-z`   Used to created swap directories.

- `-D`   Suppresses DNS testing. If not used, SQUID tries to check for a few well-known DNS host names to check whether DNS is functioning properly when it starts up.

- `-F`   Used to rebuild the cache in the "foreground." This causes the cache to be rebuilt faster, but HTTP requests are not serviced while this is occurring.

- `-N`   Tells SQUID to not run as a background process. This is useful for testing if you want the process to run on your terminal.

- `-R`   Tells SQUID to not set the `SO_REUSEADDR` option on sockets.

- `-V`   This enables virtual host support for the httpd-accelerator mode.

- `-X`   Tells SQUID to use full debugging mode when it reads the configuration file.

- `-Y`   Use this to allow caches to rebuild faster when using mostly child caches.

Many of these parameters are useful for debugging and will probably never be used by most ordinary SQUID administrators. The actual commands you will most likely use will be simple ones, such as `squid` by itself to simply start the application. You might want to find out whether SQUID is still running. To do so, type the following:

```
# squid -k check
```

After you execute this command, check the error status variable for the shell you are using to check for an error. To run SQUID as a foreground process so you can troubleshoot, use the following:

```
# squid -N
```

SQUID Log Files

SQUID uses several log files. These are the following:

- `cache.log` This file contains information relating to the SQUID server itself, including general error messages and information about starting and stopping SQUID.

- `access.log` This file keeps track of client requests made to the SQUID server. Analyzing this file can tell you which are the most popular Web sites that your clients are visiting.

- `store.log` This log file tracks data that is being added to or removed from the cache. Because this file can become quite large, you might want to consider disabling it. To do so, add `cache_store_log none` to the `squid.conf` file.

- `swap.state` This log file keeps track of every cache object that is written to disk, such as the file the object is held in and a timestamp for the last time the object was verified to be current. SQUID re-reads this log file when it starts up.

The data you find in each file is pretty intuitive. For example, the `access.log` file supports a native format, or you can use the CERN standard format for HTTP access logs. HTTP status codes used in all log files conform to those defined in Request For Comments (RFC) 2068. In addition to the `cache.log` file, SQUID also sends logging messages to `syslogd`. When troubleshooting problems with the server, check both `cache.log` and the log files maintained by `syslogd`.

Log files under SQUID can become quite large and should be monitored periodically. To manage large log files, *rotate* them and save the old log files offline. To rotate log files, use the following command:

```
# squid -k rotate
```

When this command is executed, SQUID closes log files, renames them with a numeric extension (for example, `.0` or `.1`), and opens a new file. When you get used to the volume of data collected in these log files, you can automate the process by creating a `cron` job to do this for you.

What Is the SQUID Cache Hierarchy?

SQUID can work by itself as a standalone caching proxy server, or you can use multiple SQUID servers, configured in parent-child relationships. Using a hierarchical organization of SQUID servers can be more efficient for a large site than using a single SQUID server.

In the cache hierarchy, you can find both parent and child (sibling) cache servers. A SQUID server can query either a sibling or a parent server for an object that it does not have in its own cache.

A server first attempts to retrieve a requested object by looking in its own local cache. If the object is not found there, it sends UDP queries to servers it knows as siblings. If no sibling is able to supply a copy of the object, the server next contacts a parent in the hierarchy, if one is available. If the parent does not have a copy of the object, the parent then retrieves the object from the Web and returns a copy to the sibling that requested it. As you can see, the interaction between siblings and parents is similar, but not quite the same. Although a SQUID server can query either a parent or a sibling for a copy of an object, only the parent attempts to retrieve it from the Web if it does not have a current copy. Siblings simply return a message indicating failure if they do not have a copy.

To configure the server to use a parent or sibling cache server, make entries into the `squid.conf` file. For example:

```
cache_peer parent.twoinc.com    parent 3128 3130
```

This entry tells SQUID that a parent exists, called `parent.twoinc.com`, that the server should use for queries that it and its siblings cannot satisfy. Alternatively, you could use the following:

```
cache_peer child1.twoinc.com    sibling 3128 3130
```

This tells the SQUID server that it can use a child (sibling) server called `child1.twoinc.com` to query when it does not have the object in its own cache.

Analyzing SQUID Log Files

The log files produced by SQUID can become quite large and difficult to make any sense of. For example, reading through `access.log` to locate a particular user's Web usage can be a tedious chore if the file is large. At the SQUID Web site, you can find links to other applications that people have developed that can be useful for analyzing the data produced by SQUID.

What Is the Internet Cache Protocol (ICP)?

This protocol is used by caching proxy servers to communicate with each other. Request for Comments (RFC) document 2186, "Internet Cache Protocol (ICP) Version 2," describes the standard for version 2 of the ICP protocol. In this document, you will find information about the message format that is used. If you want to learn even more about how ICP works, see also RFC 2187, "Application of Internet Cache Protocol (ICP), Version 2." This RFC goes beyond the message format and describes how servers use the protocol for issuing queries and replies or for retrieving objects from neighboring caches.

Configuring Clients to Use SQUID

Most modern browsers are able to work with proxy servers. For example, to configure Internet Explorer to use a SQUID server to satisfy HTTP, FTP, and gopher requests, use the following steps.

Configuring Internet Explorer for SQUID

1. While in Internet Explorer, click the Tools menu, and then select Internet Options.

2. When the Internet Options dialog box appears, click the Connections tab and then the LAN Settings button.

3. When the Local Area Network (LAN) Settings dialog box appears, click the Advanced button. This brings up the Proxy Settings dialog box, which can be used to designate proxy servers.

4. For each network protocol that you want the client to use the SQUID server for, enter the IP address or the fully-qualified DNS name of the SQUID server in the field labeled Proxy Address to Use. In the Port field, enter the port number that the SQUID server listens on (by default, 3128).

5. Click the OK button on each dialog box to close it.

Configuring Netscape Navigator for SQUID

1. While in Netscape Navigator, select Network Preferences from the Edit menu.

2. Select Advanced and then Proxies from the Category tree menu.

3. Select the radio button labeled Manual Proxy Configuration and then click the View button.

4. For each network protocol that you want the client to use the SQUID server for, enter the IP address or the fully-qualified DNS name of the SQUID server in the field labeled Proxy Address to Use. In the Port field, enter the port number that the SQUID server listens on (by default, 3128).

5. Click the OK button on each dialog box to close it.

To find out how to configure your particular product, use the help function and search for "proxy." If your client is not proxy-enabled, you might want to consider that now is the time to update to a newer product!

Summary

SQUID is a free caching proxy server that runs on UNIX (and
Linux) platforms. SQUID can be used by itself as a standalone server
or in conjunction with a hierarchy of other SQUID servers. You can
even use SQUID in a hierarchy of other caching servers if they support the ICP protocol. In the next chapter, you will look at two other
applications that can be acquired for no charge that you can use to
help build a firewall: `ipfwadm` and `ipchains` on Linux.

chapter
17

Using *ipfwadm* and *ipchains* on Linux

What Are `ipfwadm` and `ipchains`? ●

Installing and Configuring `ipfwadm` ●

Installing and Configuring `ipchains` ●

What Are *ipfwadm* and *ipchains*?

The Linux operating system comes with packet filtering capabilities built into the kernel. The `ipfwadm` and `ipchains` programs can be used to manage the firewall and accounting rules that are set up in the kernel. Using these programs, you are able to create sets of rules that can be used to filter IP packets that are being received by the host, being sent by the host, or being forwarded from one network adapter to another by the host (routing). Each rule specifies certain criteria, such as the IP addressing information or protocol type, and then an action to be taken if a packet matches the rule. For example, based on IP address, the rules can be configured to accept an incoming packet or to drop the packet. Thus, by using a Linux system configured as a dual-homed bastion host, you can create a packet filter for the firewall without having to bear the cost of purchasing special software or a new router.

SEE ALSO

➤ *For a detailed introduction to the concepts involved in packet filtering, see Chapter 5, "Packet Filtering", page 109.*

It should be cautioned at the start, however, that you need good Linux administrative and TCP/IP skills if you are going to start using `ipfwadm` or `ipchains`. Compiling and installing the source code is not difficult, but you should thoroughly understand the complex syntax for these utilities and test your configuration before declaring your efforts a success.

In this chapter, you will look at the syntax for each of these utilities and offer a few words of advice. If you are going to pursue using `ipfwadm` or `ipchains`, I would advise you to visit the various Web sites devoted to these utilities and review the advice and examples you find there. Remember that Linux and its associated products are essentially developed in an open environment and support usually comes from Internet newsgroups and mailing lists. If you are using a commercial distribution of Linux, such as Red Hat or Caldera, discuss what support the vendor can offer for `ipfwadm` and `ipchains` before committing yourself to making it an important link in your security. You can visit Red Hat at `www.redhat.com` and Caldera at `www.caldera.com`.

SEE ALSO

➤ *Packet filtering is not in itself an adequate solution for a complete firewall. When combined with other applications, such as the Trusted Information Systems Internet Firewall Toolkit (FWTK), however, the packet filtering capabilities of the Linux kernel can be used to create a very good firewall. For more information on the TIS FWTK, see Chapter 14, "Using the TIS Internet Firewall Toolkit", page 263.*

Installing and Configuring *ipfwadm*

The first utility you will look at in this chapter is ipfwadm. It was based on the original ipfw code that was part of BSD UNIX.

Installing ipfwadm is a simple matter of obtaining the source and using the make file to compile and install the software. Although it's a simple matter to obtain the code, installing and managing it is another matter. Most experienced Linux administrators find this chore to be easy. If you are new to the operating system, you probably will not. ipfwadm does not come with a graphical user interface, so it is necessary to learn and fully understand the syntax of the commands that are used to set up and manage the rules.

Obtaining *ipfwadm*

You can download the source code for ipfwadm, as well as binaries for some systems, from the home Web page that has been set up by X/OS Experts in Open Systems BV:

http://www.xos.nl/linux/ipfwadm/

To use ipfwadm, you need to be using a Linux kernel that is version 1.2.1 or greater. The newest version of ipfwadm is 2.3.0, and this works only with Linux kernel versions from 1.3.66 up to 2.0.36. If you are using one of the newer kernels, you have to use the ipchains utility instead.

The features that you are able to use for a specific version also depend on the version of the Linux kernel you are using. Check the readme document that is included with the download to get more specific information about versions and features that work with them.

Installing *ipfwadm*

After you have downloaded the source, use a compression utility to unpack the files. For example:

```
gzip -c -d ipfwadm_2.3.0.tar.gz | tar xvf -
```

Next, use the `make` file to compile and install the software. Set the default to the directory you used for the source and enter the following:

```
make ipfwadm
make install
```

The last `make` command creates the following directories:

- `/sbin/ipfwadm`
- `/usr/man/man8/ipfwadm.8`
- `/usr/man/man4/ipfw.4`

After this simple installation, you next need to create rules based on the security policy for your site. To create or manage rules, you use the `ipfwadm` command.

Using *ipfwadm* Commands

There are four categories for rules that you can manage using `ipfwadm`:

- **IP input firewall**   Rules for incoming IP packets on a network interface
- **IP output firewall**   Rules for outgoing IP packets on a network interface
- **IP forwarding firewall**   Rules for forwarding IP packets from one interface to another
- **IP packet accounting**   Rules for selecting packets that will increment byte counters used for accounting purposes

Filtering via these rules is supported for the TCP, UDP, and ICMP protocols.

SEE ALSO

➤ *What are the TCP, UPD and ICMP protocols? For more information about these basic protocols, see Chapter 2, "Introduction to the TCP/IP Protocol Suite", page 25.*

The syntax for the `ipfwadm` command is as follows:

`ipfwadm -category command parameters [options]`

There are five parameters that you can use on the command line for *category*, which is used to specify which set of rules the command will apply to. These are the following:

- `-A` *direction*   Accounting rules, with an optional *direction* being `in`, `out`, or `both`. If no direction is specified, the default is both directions.
- `-I`   Input firewall rules.
- `-O`   Output firewall rules.
- `-F`   Forwarding firewall rules.
- `-M`   IP masquerading management. This option can be used with `-l` for listing rules information or with `-s` for setting time-out values.

Following the category, you must next indicate a command that specifies a specific action to be performed for that category. The valid commands are the following:

- `-a` *policy*   Use this command to append one or more rules to the end of the list. For firewall chains, use one of the following values for *policy*: `accept`, `deny`, or `reject`. For accounting chains, do not use a policy value.
- `-i` *policy*   This command inserts one or more rules into the list. Use the same values for *policy* as with the `-a` command.
- `-d` *policy*   This command deletes one or more rules in the list. Use the same syntax you would for the `-a` or `-i` commands. The first rule matching the syntax is deleted.
- `-l`   This command lists all the rules in the list.
- `-z`   This command resets the byte counters for all rules in a list. You can use the `-l` and `-z` commands together. In that case, the byte values are zeroed after they are first displayed by the list command.
- `-f`   This command flushes the list of rules.
- `-p` *policy*   This command can be used to change the default policy for the selected firewall. Again, *policy* should be `accept`, `reject`, or `deny` and should be used only with the firewall rules,

not the accounting category. The default policy for a firewall is what is used when no matching rule is found for a packet.

- `-s tcp tcpfin udp` This command is used to change the timeout values used in masquerading. You must use all three parameters and specify values in seconds. The first value (*tcp*) is the timeout value for TCP sessions, the second (*tcpfin*) is the timeout value for TCP sessions which have received a FIN packet, and the third (*udp*) is the timeout value for UDP packets. This command can be used only with the `-M` category to manage masquerading. If you only want to change the timeout value for one or two categories, use zeros for those that you want to remain unchanged.

- `-c` This command can be used to check whether an IP packet would have been passed or rejected by the rules. This command can be used only with the `-I`, `-O`, and `-F` categories.

- `-h` This is the help command.

Of these commands, you can use *policy* (that is, accept, reject or deny) only with the firewall categories. Policy values are not valid for the accounting category because commands for this category do not enforce any policy, but merely perform statistical accounting functions. Note that the `-p policy` command can be used to specify a default policy for a particular firewall category. This default policy value is used when no other rule in the category matches an IP packet that is being evaluated. Thus, you can set up specific rules to match situations that you are aware of and use the default policy to deny (or allow) all other packets.

Parameters

When managing rules, you insert, append, or delete them. To use these commands, you need to further specify information that is needed to create or identify the rule for deletion. Remember the syntax for the ipfwadm command:

```
ipfwadm -category command parameters [options]
```

So far, I have discussed the category, which selects the list of rules to manage, and the command, which performs an action on the specified list. For the insert, append, and delete commands, you can use the following parameters:

The Difference Between reject **and** deny

You can instruct ipfwadm to respond in two ways for packets that will not be allowed to pass through. You can reject packets or you can deny packets. If you use the reject policy with a rule, packets that are not accepted result in an ICMP *host unreachable* message being sent back to the client that originated the packet. If you use the deny policy, the packet is dropped, but no message is sent back to the source.

- **-P** *protocol*   This can be `tcp`, `udp`, `icmp`, or `all` to specify the protocol that the rule will match. The default is `all`. For example, a rule with -P `tcp` applies only to TCP packets, whereas -P `udp` creates a rule that applies only to UDP packets.

- **-S** *address[/mask][port ...]*   This is used to indicate the source specification. For *address*, use a hostname, network name, or an IP address. For *mask*, use a network mask. For *port*, specify one or more port numbers or an ICMP type for the ICMP protocol.

- **-D** *address[/mask][port ...]*   This is used to indicate the destination specification. The syntax is the same as used for the -S parameter, except that you cannot use ICMP types for the destination address.

- **-V** *address*   This is used to optionally specify the interface that the packet is received on or is being sent to. For *address*, you can use a hostname or an IP address.

- **-W** *name*   This is used to optionally specify the name of the interface on which a packet is received or is being sent to.

Options

Finally, on the command line, there are several options you can use to further narrow down the rule. These are the following:

- **-b**   Designates bi-directional mode, which means the rule matches packets in either direction.

- **-e**   This option is used only with the list command and causes it to show extended output.

- **-k**   This option is used to match TCP packets that have the ACK bit set. This is used only with rules for the TCP protocol.

- **-m**   This option causes packets accepted for forwarding to be masqueraded using the host's address instead of the address from which the packet originated.

- **-n**   This option causes output to be in numeric format instead of text, where applicable. For example, IP addresses are displayed instead of hostnames.

- **-o**   This option turns on kernel logging of matching packets.

- **-r** *port*   This option redirects packets to a local socket.

- -t *andmask xormask*   This option is used to specify a mask used to modify the TOS field in the IP header.

- -v   This option causes the command to result in verbose output.

- -x   This option causes exact numbers to be displayed for counters. By default, numbers are rounded to multiples of 1,000 (1K) or multiples of 1000K.

- -y   This option causes TCP packets with the SYN bit and the ACK bit cleared to be matched by the rule.

With this long list of options, along with the numerous commands you can use for each category, the syntax for the ipfwadm command can seem overwhelming. However, when you begin to experiment with the command, it becomes easier. Observe the following example:

```
ipfwadm -Fle
```

This command will display (l for list) all rules for forwarding (F) in extended format (e). The next two commands will list rules for incoming packets (I), and outgoing packets (O), respectively, using extended format (e), and showing addresses and port numbers in numeric format (n):

```
ipfwadm -Inle
ipfwadm -Onle
```

It is a good idea to begin creating rules by setting the default policies for each firewall category. To set the default policy for IP packet forwarding, for example, you can use:

```
ipfwadm -F -p deny
```

Here the -p deny option is used to set the default policy to deny for IP forwarding (-F). A Linux system with two network adapters installed usually forwards packets from one adapter to the other if the packet is not destined for the local host. Setting the default policy to deny forwarding is a good idea if you are using the host as a firewall. Remember that that although deny and reject are similar, using reject causes an icmp message to be returned to the originator of the packet. For a highly secure firewall, giving out no information is better than giving out anything at all.

It is probably a good idea to go ahead and set the default policy for each of the firewall categories to deny before any other rules. Because the -p *policy* command only sets the default, using this command at the start of the file does not immediately match a packet and cause it to be denied. Instead, it sets the default policy so that the packet is denied if it passes through the remainder of the rules without a match being found. To set the default policy for the incoming and outgoing firewall categories, simply substitute -I or -O in the previous example for -F.

After you have started off by denying access by default, you can then start to create rules that specify which hosts you will allow to pass through each network interface. The rules you construct depend on the actual IP addresses used on your network and your Internet connection. For a good set of examples, an excellent document to see is the IPFWADM FAQ. This FAQ can be found at the following site:

http://www.dreamwvr.com/ipfwadm/ipfwadm-faq.html

Place *ipfwadm* Rules in a Startup File

After you have created a list of rules that you want to use, you can place them into one of your system's startup boot files so that the rules become effective when the system boots. For example, you can place the rules at the end of the r.local file.

Installing and Configuring *ipchains*

Earlier in this chapter, I said that ipfwadm works only with Linux kernels up to version 2.0.36. For newer Linux kernels (version 2.1.102 and above), you need to use the newer utility, ipchains. This utility is a rewrite of both the Linux IP firewall code and the ipfwadm utility. The result is a more flexible utility that can be used to manage packet filtering on Linux systems. If you want to check to see whether your Linux version includes the necessary kernel support for the new ipchains packet filtering utility, look for the file /proc/net/ip_fwchains. If this file exists on your system, you are ready to go. If not, you can check the ipchains official Web site to see whether a patch exists. If not, you will have to upgrade to a newer Linux kernel.

Obtaining *ipchains*

You can download `ipchains` from its official Web site:

`www.rustcorp.com/linux/ipchains`

Here, you will find the source code, as well as binaries for several UNIX variants. There are also links to several versions of a HOW-TO document and instructions for subscribing to several mailing lists that discuss `ipchains`.

How *ipchains* Differs from *ipfwadm*

Just as `ipfwadm` was an improvement on the original `ipfw` utility, `ipchains` is an improvement on the `ipfwadm` utility. These two utilities are similar in that they both are used to manage lists of rules that are applied to IP packets encountered by the host system. There are a few differences, however:

- The syntax has been improved. In `ipchains` capital letters are used for commands, whereas lowercase letters now are used for options.

- In addition to the built-in lists—or chains—of rules, `ipchains` enables you to create user-named lists. Creating your own named list of rules makes it easier to test configurations easily. If you make a mistake, all you need to do is delete (or change) the list you have created. If you continually manipulate rules in one of the built-in chains, you might get lost in the jumble and forget what it was that worked in the first place!

- An operator has been added that can be used to negate a value (the `!` operator).

- Processing for packet fragments has been improved.

- The "accounting" list of rules no longer exists.

- Support for new protocols (in addition to TCP, UDP, and ICMP) is provided.

- Counters are larger (64-bit up from 32-bit).

- In addition to ICMP *types*, ICMP *codes* are also supported.

There are other differences, which will become obvious if you are moving from using `ipfwadm` to using `ipchains`. In the next few sections, you will look at the syntax used for `ipchains`.

Creating and Deleting Chains

ipchains works in a similar manner to ipfwadm, except that it adds new functionality and support for additional protocols. For ipchains, there are three built-in lists of rules, called *chains*, that can be used to decide how to treat an incoming or outgoing IP packet on the host:

- **Input chain**   Rules for managing packets coming in from a network adapter on the host.
- **Output chain**   Rules for managing packets being sent out through a network adapter on the host.
- **Forward chain**   Rules for forwarding packets from one adapter to another.

In Figure 17.1, you can see a list of rules that make up an Input Chain. When an IP packet arrives on a network adapter, it is processed against each rule in this list.

Input Chain
Rule 1   no match
Rule 2   no match
Rule 3   no match
Rule 4   Match - target is to deny access
Rule 5   ignored
Rule 6   ignored
Rule 7   ignored
Rule 8   ignored
Rule 9   ignored
End of list

FIGURE 17.1
Each IP packet arriving on a network adapter is checked against each rule in the Input Chain.

In this figure, nothing in the IP packet information matches any of the first three rules. However, a match is found for rule four, which causes the IP packet to be dropped.

The MASQ and REDIRECT Targets

In addition to the `accept`, `deny`, and `reject` targets, you can also use `masq` and `redirect` with the `ipchains` command. `masq` enables you to use the IP masquerading feature of the Linux kernel, and `redirect` enables you to send the IP packet to a socket on the local host. For more information about using these features with the `ipchains` command, visit the `ipchains` home Web site and look at the examples found in the FAQ, or search for the Linux Mas-querade HOW-TO documents.

In addition to these chains, you can also use the `ipchains` command to create your own user-named chains. A user-defined chain can be the target of a rule you create in one of the three built-in chains. This can be useful for grouping sets of rules for testing or for use in more than one chain.

Each rule that you add to a particular chain is used to evaluate an IP packet. If the packet does not match the criteria specified by the first rule, the next rule is examined. When a matching rule is found, the rule specifies a target for the packet. The target can be one of the keywords, `accept`, `deny`, `reject`, or `return`, or it can be a name of a user-defined chain. If the latter is the case, the rules in the user-defined chain are used to continue evaluating the IP packet. If a matching rule is found in the user-defined chain, the target for that rule is used to continue the process. If no matching rule is found in a user-defined chain, processing for the IP packet continues with the next rule in the original chain that follows the rule that was used to send the packet to the user-defined chain.

In Figure 17.2 you can see an example of using a user-defined chain.

FIGURE 17.2
The target of a rule can be a user-defined chain that contains additional rules to be checked.

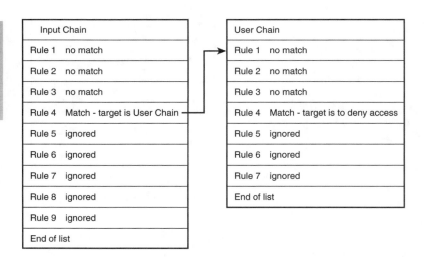

Input Chain	
Rule 1	no match
Rule 2	no match
Rule 3	no match
Rule 4	Match - target is User Chain
Rule 5	ignored
Rule 6	ignored
Rule 7	ignored
Rule 8	ignored
Rule 9	ignored
End of list	

User Chain	
Rule 1	no match
Rule 2	no match
Rule 3	no match
Rule 4	Match - target is to deny access
Rule 5	ignored
Rule 6	ignored
Rule 7	ignored
End of list	

Here, a match is found for the IP packet in rule number 4 on the
Input Chain. The target of the rule is not ACCEPT, DENY or REJECT.
Instead, it is a user-defined chain. Thus, after matching rule number
4, processing continues on the user-defined chain. In that chain, the
first three rules do not contain matching criteria. However, at rule
number 4, a match is found, and the target is to deny access. When
processing continues in a user-defined chain, there is no requirement
that a match be found for the packet in that chain. In Figure 17.3,
you can see another example of jumping to a user-defined chain.

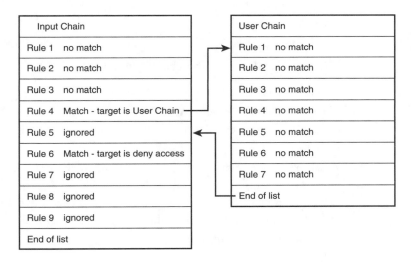

FIGURE 17.3
If no match is found in a
user-defined chain, pro-
cessing resumes back in
the original chain.

Here, the user-defined chain was the target of a rule in the Input
Chain. However, no match was found for the packet in the user-
defined chain, so processing resumed in the Input Chain at the next
rule. Finally, in the Input Chain, a match was found at rule number
6, which denies access.

If the IP packet falls through all the rules of the chain without a
match occurring, the default policy of the chain is used to decide the
packet's fate. Again, it is a good idea to set a default policy for each
chain.

The return target can be used to stop processing rules and jump to the end of the chain. If a return is used in one of the built-in chains, jumping to the end of the chain results in the built-in chain's default policy being applied to the packet. If a return is encountered in a user-defined chain, jumping to the end of that chain results in processing resuming with the next rule in the built-in chain from which the user-defined chain was called.

Managing Chains

The ipchains syntax for creating chains or managing rules in a chain is pretty straightforward:

```
ipchains command parameters [options]
```

The basic commands to manage chains are the following:

- -N *chain*   Creates a new chain named *chain*.

- -X *chain*   Deletes a chain. All rules for the chain must be deleted before you can delete the chain. You cannot delete built-in chains.

- -P *chain target*   Sets the policy for a built-in chain. User-defined chains do not have a default policy. When the end of a user-defined chain is reached with no match, processing resumes in the built-in chain that called the user-defined chain.

- -L *chain*   Lists the rules in a chain.

- -F *chain*   Flushes all rules from a chain.

- -Z *chain*   Resets packet and byte counters for all rules of the chain.

Managing Rules

As you can see, these commands can be used to manipulate the chains themselves. To manage the rules for each chain, use the following commands with ipchains:

- -A *chain rule*   This command appends a new rule to a chain.

- -I *chain rule-number rule*   This command inserts a rule in a chain. Rules are numbered. Specify the location where the rule will be inserted by using *rule-number*.

- -R *chain rule-number rule*   This command replaces an existing rule (specified by *rule-number*).

- -D *chain rule* or -D *chain rule-number*   Deletes a rule by rule-number or by the first rule matching *rule*.

As you can see, the delete command (ipchains -D) can delete a rule. You can specify the rule to delete just as you did with the add command (ipchains -A), but simply use the -D in place of the -A. If you want to use rule numbers, first use the list command (ipchains -L) to list the rules, and then use the appropriate number with the delete command.

So far, you have seen how to create and manage chains and the commands to add or manage rules. The parameters (in lowercase, you will note) that you can use to specify the actual rules are the following:

- -s *source*   Indicates the source IP address. This can be an actual host or network address or hostname or network name.

- -d *destination*   Indicates the destination IP address.

- -p *protocol*   Indicates the protocol. Use names (tcp, udp, icmp, or all) or protocol number (as defined in /etc/protocols).

- -i *interface*   Indicates the network interface.

- -j *target*   Jumps to target. This is used to indicate the target action taken if the IP packet matches the rule. The target can be one of the standard targets (for example, accept, deny, reject), or it can be the name of a user-defined chain of rules. Note that if you do not specify a target, the rule does not affect how the packet is handled. The rule does, however, cause counters associated with the rule to be incremented for accounting purposes.

- -f   This parameter indicates that the rule applies only to fragmented packets after the first fragment.

When you use the -s and -d parameters to specify an address, you can use an IP address or a host or network name. When you specify an address, you can also specify the network mask and port number. When you specify an IP address, you can specify the exact address, or you can specify a range of addresses. There are two ways to specify a range:

- Use the / symbol to specify a mask. The text 140.176.122.0/255.255.255.0 matches any IP packet where the address ranges from 140.176.122.0 to 140.176.122.255. The mask

255.255.255.0 indicates that the first three bytes of the address are significant.

- Use a whole number to indicate the number of 1s in the address. Remember that the 1 value is used in a mask to allow a bit position to be significant. Thus, the text 140.176.122.0/24 is the same as 140.176.122.0/255.255.255.0 because a string of 24 1s in binary (111111111111111111111111100000000) is the same as 255.255.255.0 when expressed in dotted-decimal notation.

To specify a port number, simply place it after the address on the command line. To specify a range of ports, use the : character. When specifying a range of ports, if you omit one of the ports, ipchains assumes a default value. The default value for the beginning port number is 0, whereas the default value for the end of the range is 65535. Thus

```
1024:1050
```

would specify all ports between 1024 and 1050, whereas

```
:1023
```

would specify all ports between 0 and 1023.

Putting this all together, look at a few examples:

```
ipchains –A input –s 140.176.200.254 –j DENY
```

In this example, you add a rule (-A) to the input chain that looks to match packets with a source address (-s) of 140.176.200.254. Packets that match this rule are sent (-j) to the standard target DENY, which means that the packet is dropped with no ICMP message returned to the sender.

```
ipchains –A output –p TCP –d 0.0.0.0/0 8080 –j REJECT
```

In this example, a packet being sent outbound (output chain) using the TCP protocol (-p) for any destination address (0.0.0.0/0) for port 8080 would be rejected. The REJECT target means that ipchains would send an ICMP message back to the sender of the packet.

Other Command Options

In addition to the basic syntax you have examined so far, ipchains provides for a few more options you can specify on the command line. These are the following:

- -b Bidirectional flag. This option means that two rules are be created instead of just one. The second rule is the same as the first, but the source and destination specifications is reversed for the second rule.

- -v Verbose flag. This causes the list command to display additional output.

- -n Numeric output. Addresses and port numbers are shown in numeric format. The default is to use text (for example, hostnames) when known.

- -l Logging flag. This option causes kernel logging of packets to be turned on.

- -o [*maxsize*] This option is used, mostly by developers, to cause packets that match to be copied to a user device for further examination. If used, *maxsize* limits the number of bytes copied form each packet.

- -m *markvalue* This option is used to mark packets with a 32-bit unsigned value. This option is useful for kernel hackers and is not used much at this time.

- -t *andmask ormask* This option is used to modify the TOS (type of service) field in the IP header. The TOS field is bitwise ANDed with the first mask and then the result is bitwise XORed with the second mask.

- -x This option causes counters to be displayed numerically instead of in rounded number format.

- -y This option causes packets that have the SYN bit set and the ACK and FIN bits cleared, to match the rule. This option is used with the TCP protocol to specify packets that are requesting a connection.

Some of these options are for convenience, such as the -b option, which enables you to create two rules at the same time. The -y option is very useful for blocking TCP connection attempts. The following example could be used to match incoming TCP connections from host 140.176.200.1:

```
ipchains A input -p TCP -s 140.176.200.1 -y
```

Another interesting trick to remember is to use the ! negate operator. For example:

```
ipchains -A output -p TCP ! 140.176.200.1 www
```

This rule states that all hosts can send www packets on the outbound chain with the exception of the host with the address 140.176.200.1. You can also negate other parts of the rule. For example, if you had placed the negation operator directly before the www port specification, all hosts could send out any kind of packet except for www packets.

Using Scripts to Save Rules

There are two commands you can use with ipchains to save rules to a file and restore them. These are ipchains-save and ipchains-restore. These are actually script files to perform the functions for you. For example:

```
ipchains-save > firewallrules
```

This saves all the currently defined rules in all chains to the file firewallrules. Use the -v option with this command, and it displays the name of each chain as its rules are being saved. The default policy for the standard built-in chains is also saved with this command.

To restore, use the other script file:

```
ipchains-restore < firewallrules
```

Again, the -v option causes the names of each chain to be displayed as the rules are restored. You can also use the -f option. This causes the restore script to prompt you to skip or flush any user-defined chains as it comes to them.

Further Information About *ipchains*

The ipchains utility is an advance on the ipfwadm utility in the capabilities offered. In this chapter, you have looked only at the basic command syntax and have seen how ipchains works to filter IP packets through lists of rules. To become proficient in using Linux as a packet filter, you should do further reading into the matter. As it stands, the ipchains utility could be the subject of an entire book!

To make matters easier, visit the home page for the ipchains utility (www.rustcorp.com/linux/ipchains). In addition, check out the various Linux HOWTO documents, especially "Linux IPCHAINS-HOWTO", by Paul Russell. You can download this document from this site:

```
http://metalab.unc.edu/mdw/HOWTO/IPCHAINS-HOWTO.html
```

Don't forget that `ipchains` is a user-supported product, and you can often find answers to your questions by looking in the various newsgroups or by subscribing to the mailing lists associated with `ipchains`.

Summary

The Linux operating system contains code already built into the kernel that can be used for packet filtering. The `ipfwadm` and `ipchains` utilities are used as interfaces into this packet filtering system. For earlier versions of Linux, use `ipfwadm`. For newer kernel versions, use `ipchains`. Although both of these utilities use a syntax that will be difficult for those new to it, you can't beat the price. If you have not yet installed Linux on a system at your site, be sure to use a newer version so that you can make use of the enhanced features that `ipchains` has over `ipfwadm`.

Because of this packet filtering capability, a Linux system can be a valuable addition to a firewall. Remember that in addition to packet filtering, you will also need a proxy application solution of some sort in order to have a complete firewall.

chapter

18

Microsoft Proxy Server

Overview of Microsoft Proxy
Server

Installing and Configuring
Microsoft Proxy Server 2.0

Client Software Configuration Issues

Overview of Microsoft Proxy Server

When the first version of Microsoft Proxy Server was released, it was lacking in some features that made it an incomplete product for use as a firewall. Version 2.0 has added dynamic packet filtering and other new features that make the Proxy Server a good solution for many situations. It can be used in small LANs, where the caching functionality might help cut back on Internet bandwidth usage and where security management issues are minor. It can also be used to create arrays of Proxy Servers that can help manage Internet services in a large network.

The main features you will find in version 2.0 include the following:

- **Virtual Private Network (VPN)**   This provides for encrypted networking for clients in the field that need to connect to the company network.

- **Caching**   By caching frequently accessed objects, the Proxy Server can help reduce bandwidth usage on your Internet connection.

- **Application Proxies**   These proxies can help protect clients that need to access services on the Internet. Proxies prevent a direct exchange of IP packets between the client and the Internet and instead act as a man-in-the-middle to make requests for clients.

- **Address translation**   By using one of the reserved address ranges on your internal LAN, you can get by with a smaller assigned address space and also allow the Proxy Server to hide internal addresses of clients.

- **Dynamic Packet Filtering**   You can enable this for each proxy service to further enhance security. Ports are opened and closed dynamically as needed so the administrator doesn't have to create a complex set of rules involving a lot of ports.

- **Reverse Hosting**   You can use the Proxy Server to present Web pages to the Internet that in reality are coming from Web servers on your internal LAN.

The MS Proxy Server provides support for three kinds of proxies:

- WinSock Proxy
- SOCKS Proxy
- Web Proxy

The combination of packet filtering and proxy services, along with logging and alerting features of this package, makes MS Proxy Server a good candidate for consideration as a host-based firewall. The WinSock and SOCKS Proxy capabilities mean that there are a lot of client/server applications available that will work with MS Proxy Server. The application-level Web Proxies include support for Web browsing (HTTP and HTTP-S), file transfers (FTP), and the Gopher protocol.

SEE ALSO
➤ *For more information about the SOCKS Proxy, see page 291*

In this chapter, you will go over the setup process used to install the Proxy Server and then look at how configuration is done by walking through the configuration of the Web Proxy Service.

Installing and Configuring Microsoft Proxy Server 2.0

There are several prerequisites that need to be taken care of before you can install MS Proxy Server 2.0 on a Windows NT Server platform.

One prerequisite is Internet Information Server 3.0. If you install Windows NT 4.0 Server from scratch on a host, which you should if you are creating a secure platform for use as a proxy server, you also have to install a service pack before installing the proxy server. At a minimum, install Service Pack 3, which upgrades the Internet Information Server to version 3.0. To take advantage of other patches and additions that have been made to NT 4.0, it is advisable to instead update to the latest service pack. Because service packs are cumulative, you only have to install the latest one, not all those that came before it.

> **Where to Find Windows NT Service Packs**
>
> Depending on where you got your Windows NT source CDs, you might have a CD that includes the latest service pack. Although Service Pack 3.0 is sufficient to get your Internet Information Server upgraded to IIS 3.0, it's probably best to read about and then install the latest service pack. To get it, go to the following site:
>
> `www.microsoft.com/downloads/`

Converting FAT Partitions to NTFS Partitions

It is easy to convert a partition to NTFS. When you install Windows NT, the setup program prompts you to format the disk you are using for an installation partition as an NTFS partition. If you are setting up Windows NT Server on a platform for use as a Proxy Server, performing the conversion during setup for the operating system makes sense. However, if you have already installed NT and have a partition that is either FAT or FAT32, you can use the **CONVERT** command to change the file system to NTFS:

```
C:\> CONVERT D:
/FS:NTFS
```

If you use this command on the drive currently containing the operating system, you have to reboot the system before the command completes.

As always, before making any significant change to a system, don't forget to do a full backup of the affected drive before you convert it! You can never be sure that nothing will go wrong. For example, while your drive is being converted, a power failure could cause the system to crash and become corrupted, resulting in the loss of data.

Another prerequisite is that you have a file partition that uses NTFS, the Windows NT File System. A DOS partition (FAT or FAT32) cannot be used for the cached files the Proxy Server creates. If you have installed the NT Server operating system on a FAT partition, you should convert it to NTFS for the security benefits that NTFS provides. If you are choosing to use a different partition for installing the Proxy Server, that partition also needs to be converted to NTFS before you can continue.

A few other things to do before installing are the following:

- Use Windows NT Server installed in a server-only mode, not as a domain controller. A domain controller by default holds sensitive information, such as a copy of the SAM database where user accounts and domain trust relationships are stored. You don't want that kind of information on a Proxy Server.

- To make use of the packet filtering capabilities that version 2.0 offers, use a host with two network interfaces installed—one connected to the internal LAN and one connected to the Internet. By using two network interfaces and therefore isolating the internal network completely from a direct IP connection to the Internet, you make your Proxy Server a choke point that all traffic must pass through. A savvy user is not able to reconfigure his workstation to bypass the Proxy Server and talk directly to your external router.

Running Setup

When you execute the setup program for MS Proxy Server, the first few dialog boxes are the standard ones you usually see for applications that install on Windows NT Server—the Software License and Copyright dialog boxes. After that, you are prompted to enter the CD key for the software. Then, the Setup program begins to ask questions about the proxy software installation to be performed.

Installing Proxy Server

1. The Installation Options dialog box (Figure 18.1) enables you to change the disk drive and folder that will be used for the installation of the Proxy Server. Click Change Folder to do this.

FIGURE 18.1
Use the Installation Options dialog box to change the folder or to select which applications to install.

2. The Installation Options (large button) in this dialog box can be used to select which components of the Proxy Server you want to install, as is shown in Figure 18.2. For a first installation, choose all three.

FIGURE 18.2
You can select to install the documentation and Administration Tool along with the Proxy Server software.

3. The next dialog box prompts you to select a drive to hold the cache files (Figure 18.3). Remember that this drive must be formatted using the NTFS file system. You can also use this dialog box to set the size of the cache. Leave this at the default for a first installation.

4. The next dialog box (Figure 18.4) enables you to enter one or more ranges of addresses that are used on the internal LAN. If you use the Construct Table button in this dialog box, the setup program enables you to select address ranges that it finds in the server's routing table (Figure 18.5).

FIGURE 18.3
Select the partition (disk drive) to be used for the cache files and set the initial size of the cache file area.

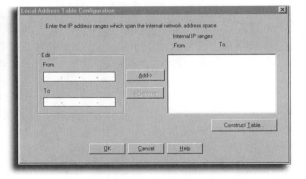

FIGURE 18.4
To define the internal LAN address space, enter the start and end of an address range and click Add.

FIGURE 18.5
You can add address ranges from the local routing table, or you can select a private address range.

Selecting a private address range can give you a large address space that is not used directly on the Internet. The Proxy Server uses network address translation (NAT) to provide this function. If you use the routing table option, Setup prompts you to edit out any address ranges that appear to come from outside your LAN. This can be caused by current Internet connections.

5. The next dialog box enables you to configure some client information. Clients can connect to the server either by name or IP address. You can decide that clients will connect to port 80 to contact the Proxy Server or specify the URL for a proxy configuration file to load more complex configurations on clients.

If the Configure Web browsers check box is selected, you can choose the Configure button and then enter a URL for use by clients that autoconfigure Proxy Server information. If you click the Properties button, you are enabled to specify domains or specific hosts that should not be proxied (see Figure 18.7). This can not only be used to allow local clients to directly access services within the LAN, but also to use the Proxy Server for all Internet related services.

6. The Access Control dialog box (Figure 18.8) next enables you to enable access control for clients. Select to enable access control for either or both WinSock or the Web Proxy services.

7. Finally, a few files are copied, a notice tells you that you can configure packet filtering using the administration tool, and a final dialog box tells you that MS Proxy Server has been successfully installed.

When the installation is complete, reboot the computer so that all changes take effect. You can then start to examine the tools that are available for managing the Proxy Server and look at some of the items that you can configure and manage.

339

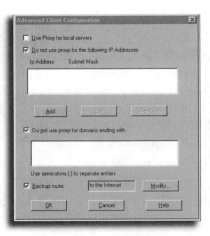

FIGURE 18.7
For automatic client setup, you can select local servers or domains that will not use the Proxy Server.

FIGURE 18.8
Enable access control using this dialog box.

Using the Internet Service Manager.

After you have installed the Proxy Server, you will find a new folder called Microsoft Proxy Server located in the Programs folder. The Internet Service Manager found in this folder is the application that is used to manage the services of the Proxy Server. To start, stop, or pause a service, simply highlight it and then select Start, Stop, or Pause from the Properties menu.

To configure a service, you can highlight it and then select Service Properties from the Properties menu, or you can simply right-click the service and then select Service Properties from the submenu that appears.

Packet Filter Properties

You can set up packet filtering, either static or dynamic, by using the Properties page for the SOCKS, WinSock, or Web Proxy services in the Microsoft Internet Service Manager utility. In this example, you will see the process using the WinSock service.

Setting Up Packet Filtering

1. Click Start, Programs, Microsoft Proxy Server, Internet Service Manager.

2. The main window of the utility (Figure 18.9) displays the running services.

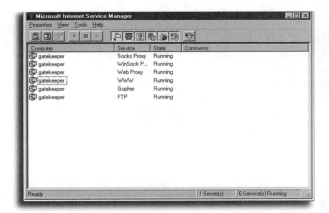

FIGURE 18.9
The Internet Service Manager shows the running proxy services.

Right-click the SOCKS Proxy, WinSock Proxy, or the Web Proxy to bring up the service properties sheets. In Figure 18.10, you can see an example of the WinSock Proxy's properties sheets.

3. Click the Security button to bring up the Security property sheets, the first of which is titled Packet Filters (see Figure 18.11).

To enable dynamic packet filtering, select both the check boxes on this page: Enable Packet Filtering on External Interface and Enable Dynamic Packet Filtering of Microsoft Proxy Server Packets.

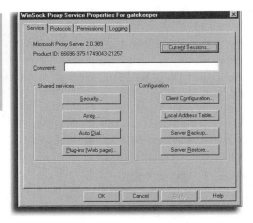

FIGURE 18.10
To enable packet filtering, select the Security button on the Service property sheet.

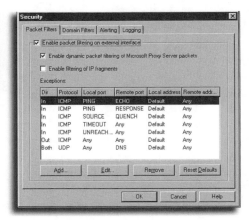

FIGURE 18.11
You can enable packet filtering using this dialog box.

4. In the Exceptions field, you're able to add rules to create exceptions to the dynamic packet filter, or you can remove or modify those that are listed here by the default configuration. Use the Add button to add a rule for a specialized service, for example. The dialog box that appears (shown in Figure 18.12) enables you to configure a packet filter rule based on protocol, direction (inbound or outbound traffic), and source and destination ports.

5. Using this dialog box, you can configure very specific packet filtering rules. You can set up a fixed or dynamic port for both the source and destination ports and a single external host or hosts on the Internet. Use this dialog box to set up special connections where a port must be specified and a dynamically selected port

will not work. When finished adding a rule, click the OK button. Continue using the Add button to enter additional rules.

6. When finished, click OK on the Packet Filter Properties page to exit.

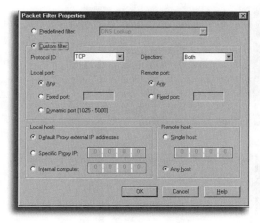

FIGURE 18.12
You can configure static or dynamic ports using this dialog box.

The ability to set up very explicit rules for a packet filter, by service, gives you a lot of room for flexibility. You can choose to enable dynamic packet filtering, stick with static rules, or use both.

Web Proxy Service Properties

In Figure 18.13, you can see the properties pages for the Web Proxy service. Again, you can use the Security button on the Service property page to enable packet filtering for the proxy, as discussed for the WinSock Proxy Server in the previous section.

There are some other interesting items you can control using the properties sheets, and in this section, you will look at some of them using the Web Proxy as an example. Grouped under Shared Services are four buttons that are used to manage services offered by the proxy.

Configuring Auto Dial

The Auto Dial feature lets the Proxy Server automatically dial an Internet connection when it is associated with a service. Click the Auto Dial button on the Service property sheet to bring up the Configuration property sheet for Auto Dial (see Figure 18.14).

Dynamic packet filtering by MS Proxy Server starts when a client makes a request for a service by using a WinSock Proxy. The proxy client connects to the MS Proxy Server that authenticates the user and then creates a socket using a random port number. The packet filter manager is passed this port number and then allows the outbound packets and incoming expected packets to pass through the filter for this session and application. When the client terminates the connection, the port is closed and cannot be used by another application.

FIGURE 18.13
The properties page for the Web Proxy service enables you to control access and management issues.

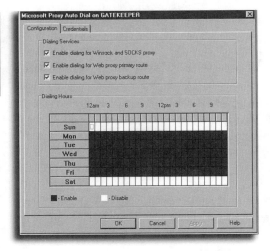

FIGURE 18.14
Select the hours and days for which autodialing will be in effect.

Here, you can use the mouse to select, by one hour increments, the hours and days that the Auto Dial feature will be active. The Dialing Services selections at the top of this dialog box allow you to enable autodialing for SOCKS, WinSock, and the Web Proxy services. If you select the tab at the top to bring up the Credentials property sheet, you can then select a dial-up account to use for the connection and enter the authentication information required for the account (see Figure 18.15).

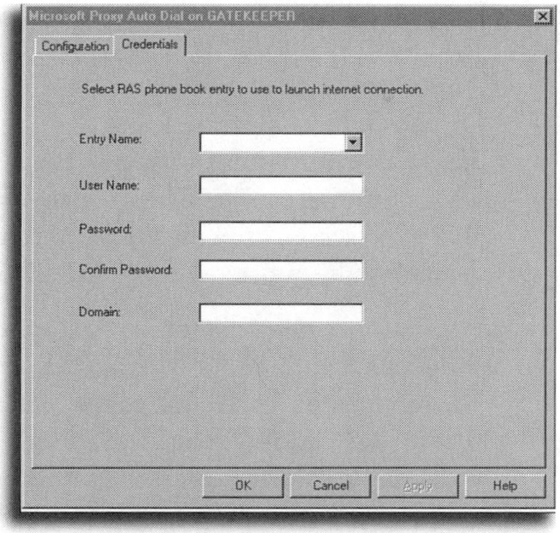

FIGURE 18.15
You can select an existing dial-up account or enter information for a new one.

Joining an Array of Proxy Servers

The Array button under Shared Services enables you to join an array of Proxy Servers so that they can exchange information. After you click the Array button, a dialog box displays any current array configurations. You can then use the Add button to join another array. The Join Array dialog box prompts you to enter the name of another computer. If a new array is being created, another dialog box prompts for a name for the array.

Using several MS Proxy Servers operating together as an array can help distribute the load when you have a large client base making use of proxied services. Servers that are in the same array use peer-to-peer communications to exchange information. An array also provides fault-tolerance because the loss of a single Proxy Server won't stop all Internet access. It is also possible to perform some management functions on more than one server at a time if they are associated as members of an array.

Third-Party Plug-ins

The Plugs button found under Shared Services on the Service property page enables you to download components for MS Proxy Server from third-party developers. Using this option enables you to specify the URL that points to the plug-in Web page. From there, you can choose the plug-in to be installed.

Configuration Management on the Service Property Page

On the right side of the Service property page for the Web Proxy Service are a group of buttons beneath the Configuration heading. These buttons can be used to change configuration information about the server or clients, similar to the dialog boxes that were presented during the product installation.

For example, the Client Configuration button brings up a dialog box shown in Figure 18.6 earlier in this chapter. You can use this dialog box to change how clients connect to the Proxy Server (by name or IP address) and to set up client configuration information such as which addresses are accessed by the Proxy Server.

The Local Address Table button brings up the dialog box you saw during the setup process, shown in Figure 18.4. Here, you can specify the address ranges that will be used for computers on the internal protected LAN.

The Server Backup button enables you to select a directory that is used for backing up the Proxy Server configuration information. The Server Restore button enables you to perform a partial or full restoration of the configuration information from a previous backup file.

Managing Permissions For the Web Proxy Services

The Permissions tab brings up the Permissions property page for the Web Proxy Server. In Figure 18.16, you can see this page enables you to select a service (using the Protocol field) and associate users or user groups with permissions to make use of the service by using the Edit button.

The Protocol field enables you to select the FTP Read, Gopher, Secure, and WWW services. When you click the Edit button, a dialog box appears that shows current permissions, if any, for the service. The Add button can then be used to get to a standard Windows NT Add Users and Groups dialog box (Figure 18.17). Here, you can select by user group or use the Show Users button to select individual user accounts.

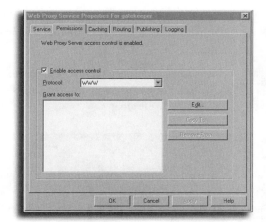

FIGURE 18.16
The Permissions property page can be used to control access to the Web Proxy services.

FIGURE 18.17
Select users or user groups that you want to grant access to the Web Proxy.

Remember to be careful when granting access to a proxy application for an entire user group. If only a portion of a group needs access or if users from different groups need access, it might make better sense to create a new user group and make each of these users members of the new group.

Managing the Caching Properties of the Service

A Proxy Server performs a security service when it masks the identity of internal hosts that need to connect to an Internet service. A Proxy Server also can be used to enhance performance for these services by keeping copies of frequently accessed objects available in a local cache. Repetitive requests for these objects that can be satisfied from the cache save on valuable bandwidth used for the Internet connection.

How long an object stays in the cache can be managed by using the Caching property page. Figure 18.18 show this property page for the Web Proxy Service.

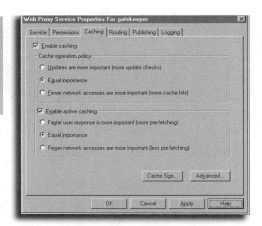

FIGURE 18.18
The Caching property page can be used to manage how log objects stay in the cache.

To enable caching for the service, select the Enable Caching check box, at the top of the page. Next, you can select a general policy to be used for caching objects for this service, or you can use the Advanced button to determine how objects are cached.

Under Cache Expiration Policy, you can choose from one of three general policies:

- **Updates Are More Important (More Update Checks)** This selection causes the Proxy Server to download the object more frequently.

- **Fewer Network Accesses Are More Important (More Cache Hits)** This option is used to improve user response time. The cache is used more to satisfy requests.

- **Equal Importance** This option causes the server to operate in a manner that balances the first and last of these options.

For most purposes, you should probably use the Equal Importance selection here first and, depending on response from users, change this later to one of the other options. If the data that users access changes infrequently, the third option saves on Internet bandwidth usage. Objects such as vendor documentation fit into this category, although users viewing financial data that changes rapidly might not like this because it requires more frequent updates.

The Advanced button enables you to specify the size of objects that are cached and to more precisely control the objects' time-to-live (TTL)—how long it remains in the cache until it is no longer valid. Figure 18.19 shows the Advanced Cache Policy dialog box.

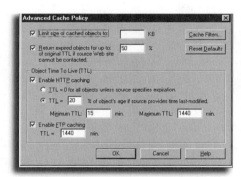

FIGURE 18.19
The Advanced Cache Policy dialog box provides more precise control over how objects are cached.

To limit the size of objects stored in the cache, select the check box at the top of the page and fill in a value (in KB) for the maximum size. The second check box can be used to instruct the Proxy Server to keep using an expired cache entry to satisfy user requests for a while longer if the original Web site cannot be contacted.

Although the Proxy Server itself usually determines which objects are cached, based on usage, you can specify that certain URLs are always to be included in the cache by using the Cache Filters button. This brings up a dialog box that you can use to enter URLs one at a time.

Grouped under Object Time To Live (TTL) are several items that can be used to control how long objects stay in the cache for HTTP and FTP services. First, you must enable caching for HTTP and FTP by selecting the appropriate check box for the service.

Under Enable HTTP Caching, you can select that the TTL value is 0 unless the source of the data specifies an expiration time, or you can select the second radio button to specify a percentage of an object's age based on the last time it was modified. Again, this information must be supplied by the host server. The last two fields for HTTP enable you to specify the minimum and maximum amount of time (in minutes) that objects can be found unexpired in the cache.

Routing Within Proxy Arrays

The Routing property page enables you to manage how client requests are handled by Proxy Servers in an array. You can specify that requests are sent directly to the Internet, to another upstream Proxy Server, or to another array. If you have several Proxy Servers operating in an array, you might be able to balance performance by having some be responsible for one service while others provide other services. By configuring how client requests are routed, you can quickly direct their requests to a Proxy Server that can satisfy them. If you are not using an array, you do not need to use this property page.

Using the Publishing Property Page

The MS Proxy Server can allow clients on the Internal LAN to publish Web pages through the Proxy Server. This protects the internal clients from potential hacking from outside the LAN while still enabling you to create a Web presence. The Proxy Server acts as a front-end for all your Web servers.

The Publishing property page of the Web Proxy Service is shown in Figure 18.20. Select the Enable Web Publishing check box if you want to allow clients to make use of this service.

At the top of this page are three radio buttons that determine what is done with incoming requests. In the lower half of this page, you can specify exceptions to this choice. For example, you can specify that all incoming HTTP requests be discarded (or ignored) and then specify a few exceptions for only those Web servers you will allow through the firewall. You can also route the request to a local Web server (the IIS service running on the local node) or to another Web server. These two selections are also modified by any exceptions you specify.

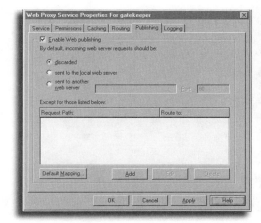

FIGURE 18.20
You can use this property page to allow clients to publish Web pages through the Proxy Server.

To specify an exception, use the Add button. This brings up the Mapping dialog box, where you can enter two pieces of information to create a mapping:

- **The request path** The URL of the Web server the request is being sent to.

- **URL** The URL of the Web server that will satisfy the request.

By using this mapping feature, it is easy to direct incoming requests to a different URL, again helping to hide information about your internal network from the outside world.

Setting Real Time Alerts and Logging Options

Logging and alerts are some of the more important features of a firewall. Regardless of how well your security policy is created, you can never be totally sure that things are not getting past the firewall that should be looked at. Log files and alerts can help you respond quickly to a suspicious event and provide you with the data needed to help track down the offender.

In Figure 18.21, the Logging property page for the Web Proxy Service is shown.

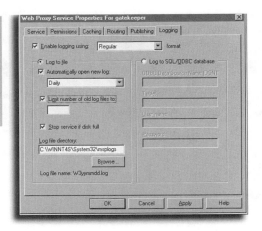

FIGURE 18.21
The Logging property page can be used to set up log files or to send logging to an ODBC-compliant database.

To allow logging for the service, select the Enable Logging Using check box and then use the drop-down menu to select either Regular or Verbose format. Verbose format causes more information to be logged, whereas Regular format causes only a subset of the available information to be logged.

There are two methods you can employ for logging: log files or a database. To send logging events to an ODBC-compliant database, select the Log to SQL/ODBC Database radio button and fill in the source and authentication information. When using this option, you should first have consulted with the database administrator so that the table(s) you require could have been created.

If you select the Log to File radio button, you can further specify some management parameters:

- **Automatically open new log**   Under this selection, you can specify that a new log file be created every day, once a week, or once a month.

- **Limit number of old log files to**   When a new log file is created, the existing log file is renamed so it can be saved for archive purposes. Use this selection to limit the number of old log files that are kept.

- **Stop service if disk full**   Use this option if you want the proxy service to stop servicing users when the log file disk becomes full.

At the bottom of the page, you can select the location for the log files. Note that the naming convention is the service, plus the date in yymmmdd format. Log files ideally should be kept around for as long as you have space. If security is of the highest importance in your network, you should make it a regular procedure to copy archived log files produced by the Proxy Server to another location so that they can be regularly saved offline. It might take weeks or months after a break-in before the damage becomes evident. This can happen because of a Trojan horse program, for example. Being able to look back to find out how the break-in occurred or how your configuration failed to prevent the intrusion can help you prepare for the future.

To configure an email alert, use the Service tab under Shared Services in the Internet Service Manager. Here, you can select the type of event that will generate an alert. Select the check box Send SMTP Mail. You can then configure the email account that will receive messages.

In the Security dialog box, select the Alerting tab. Next, click Configure Mail. The Configure Mail Alerting dialog box pops up and prompts you for the name of a mail server. For security purposes, be sure to specify an internal mail server. You should not trust an external mail server to report on events. In the Send Mail To field, enter the email address to which alert emails will be sent. In the From Address field, enter a valid email address that you will recognize as coming from your Proxy Server system. Click OK when finished. To test the email alerts, click the Test button and then OK, both of which are found on the Alerting tab in the Security dialog box.

Client Software Configuration Issues

Most modern Internet software that runs on a Windows platform understands how to talk to a Proxy Server. Netscape and Microsoft's Internet Explorer both have options that allow them to use Proxy Servers for Internet services. For example, to specify a Proxy Server for Internet Explorer (IE), first obtain the names or addresses and ports used for Proxy Servers from your network administrator and then perform the following steps.

Using Proxy Servers for Internet Services

1. In Internet Explorer, select Internet Options from the View menu. The Internet Options property sheets are displayed.

2. Select the Connection property sheet by clicking Connection at the top of the property page. (See Figure 18.22.)

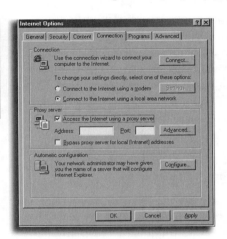

FIGURE 18.22
Use the Connection property page to configure the client for a Proxy Server.

Select the Access the Internet Using a Proxy Server check box. If only one Proxy Server is used for all Internet services, enter the address and port number used here.

3. If you want to specify different servers or ports for each service, click the Advanced button. This brings up the Proxy Settings dialog box (see Figure 18.23).

   You can also specify exceptions that will not use the Proxy Server. These can be, for example, internal Web servers that do not reside on the Internet. Local LAN clients can access these directly with no security issues involved because they do not have to go through the firewall.

4. When you have finished configuring proxy information, you can click the OK button, and the settings will take effect.

In a large network, it would be tedious to have to enter a lot of proxy information for each client. Instead, you can usually write a setup script for the clients and let them instead specify the URL for a Web page that can be accessed to run the setup script. In Figure 18.22,

you can see that Internet Explorer enables you to do this by using
the Configure button located at the bottom of the property sheet
under Automatic Configuration.

FIGURE 18.23
Here, you can specify a
different Proxy Server for
each Internet service the
client will use.

Automatic configuration capabilities vary from one browser to
another, but they generally enable you to set not only proxy configuration data, but also other parameters, such as a default home page
for the user. Check the documentation for your browser (or an
administrator's kit if there is one) for further information about creating setup files for clients.

Summary

A Proxy Server can be used to shield clients from the external network. By hiding information about your clients and network, the
Proxy Server makes the hacker's job more difficult. In this chapter,
you have looked at a popular product: Microsoft's Proxy Server.
This is not the only Proxy Server on the market, but due to the
popularity of the Windows platform, this one will most likely be
around for a while, especially with a large company behind it to
provide support.

chapter
19

The Elron CommandView Firewall

Overview •

Installing CommandView Firewall •

The CommandView Firewall
Manager Application •

Managing User Services •

Where to Go from Here •

Overview

The Elron CommandView Firewall is a flexible, easy to manage commercial firewall product that can be used on large and small networks to create a secure connection to the Internet. CommandView consists of a firewall service and a separate manager application that can be run on the same computer or on another host. In addition to the basic network services such as FTP and email, CommandView enables you to offer many other services and even enables you to configure your own service if you do not find the one you need in the firewall's predefined list.

This chapter covers the basic installation of the firewall service and the manager application and shows you how to configure basic services. Covering all the available configuration options and services offered by this firewall would fill an entire book, so this chapter should be considered just an introduction. For example, in addition to providing for a large number of network services, CommandView enables you to use Network Address Translation (NAT) or to create Virtual Private Networks (VPNs) so that you can create a secure, encrypted channel of communication over an insecure network such as the Internet. Because CommandView is based on industry standards, you will find that it can be configured to operate with other vendors' products. For example, CommandView supports the IP Authentication Header and Encapsulating Security Payload (ESP) protocols.

SEE ALSO
➤ *For more information about the IP Authentication Header and ESP, See Chapter 10, "Virtual Private Networks (VPNs) and Tunneling," page 211*

SEE ALSO
➤ *For more information about Network Address Translation (NAT), see Chapter 7, "Application Gateways and Proxy Servers," page 157*

Installing CommandView Firewall

To install the CommandView firewall, you need to have a Windows NT 4.0 (the current version is incompatible with Windows 2000) computer and should have first installed at least Service Pack 3. The system that runs the Firewall SMLI Engine service should be equipped with the following:

Evaluate First!

Try before you buy. You can download a trial version of CommandView firewall from the following Web site:

www.elronsoftware.com

Should You Buy Elron CommandView?

At the start, I should tell you that I did not select the Elron CommandView Firewall for use as an example in this book because I recommend it. Indeed, I'd rather you use the information contained in this book to make your own intelligent purchasing decision. There are literally hundreds of other competing products to choose from. Although I do not specifically endorse Elron, I did choose it because it is representative of many other products that can be easily installed, configured, and managed. I would like to thank the folks at Elron Software, however, for their help in answering some of the questions that arose as this chapter was written.

- A Pentium processor running at 166MHz or better
- At least 64MB of memory (128MB is better)
- 500MB of disk space
- Two network adapters (10Mb, 100Mb, or 10/100Mb)

If you want to create a demilitarized zone (DMZ), you need three network adapters.

SEE ALSO

➤ *For more information about using a DMZ, see Chapter 4, "Firewall Security Policy and Firewall Design Strategies," page 85*

You can also run the Firewall Manager application on the same system. Alternatively, you can install the manager application on another Windows NT 4.0 system or on a Windows 95 or Windows 98 computer. If you choose to use a separate computer for the manager application, be sure that both hosts are on the same network segment and IP subnet. Remember that it is a good security practice to place firewall devices in a secure location—such as in a locked closet or computer room—which means that installing the manager application on another, more accessible host, makes sense. The minimum requirements for a system running the manager application are the following:

- Windows 95, Windows 98, or Windows NT 4.0
- 32MB of memory
- 50MB of disk space
- WinSock 2.0–compliant TCP/IP stack

Before you start to run the setup program, you should first review the network adapter cards installed in the system and record the number assigned to them.

Reviewing the Adapter Cards

1. Click Start, Settings, and then Control Panel. Double-click the Network Applet.

2. Click the Protocols tab, and then highlight the TCP/IP Protocol. Click Properties.

3. On the Properties page for TCP/IP (Figure 19.1), you can see the pull-down menu labeled Adapter. There should be an entry in this menu for each network adapter on the system. Click the down arrow on the menu to see each adapter and record the number associated with it.

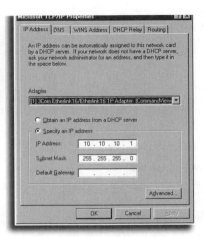

FIGURE 19.1
Use the Adapter drop-down menu to list and record the network adapters installed in the system.

Running the Setup Program

To begin the setup program, insert the CommandView CD in the computer's hard drive. The setup program should autostart. Alternatively, you can run the program by manually executing the SETUP.EXE program if the CD is loaded on a network drive.

Running the Setup Program

1. The first few screens cover information about installation pre-requisites and licensing. After you read these screens, you can click the Next or Yes button to continue.

2. The dialog box (Figure 19.2) prompts you for the type of instal-lation. A Typical installation installs both the firewall service and the manager application. Select Custom if you want to install only the service or the manager application. A Welcome dialog box appears. Click Next to continue.

3. A dialog box prompts you for the target directory for the instal-lation. You can change this or accept the default and then click Next to continue.

4. The Setup Type dialog box (Figure 19.3) then prompts you for the kind of firewall architecture to create, using either two net-work adapters for the basic firewall or three network adapters to create a DMZ. For this sample installation, I chose the two adapter selection.

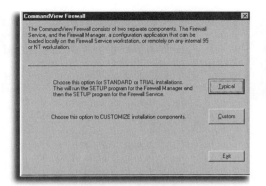

FIGURE 19.2
Select a Typical installation to install the firewall service and the manager application.

FIGURE 19.3
You can install CommandView firewall using two or three network adapters.

5. A dialog box titled Select Program Folder appears. Click Next to continue if you want to use the default to create an Elron CommandView folder, or select an existing folder and click Next.

6. The Setup Complete dialog box informs you that the manager application has been installed. Click the Finish button. If you had elected to install both applications when beginning the setup process, the setup program now begins the installation of the firewall service.

7. The first dialog box for the service setup prompts you again for the type of firewall: two or three network adapters. Select the same type that you did for the manager application.

8. Another dialog box prompts you for the destination for the installation of the firewall software. Either change the default location listed or accept the default. Click Next to continue.

9. The next dialog box lists the system's network adapters. You need to use your cursor to drag and drop each adapter to its location in the firewall architecture. For example, if adapter number one is the adapter that connects to the internal network, drag it to the icon labeled Internal Network. When you are finished, click the Save button. When prompted by Setup, reboot the computer.

When the computer reboots and you log in, a New Firewall Installation screen appears and prompts you through the remaining configuration process for the firewall. You don't need to configure the manager application, so if you have only installed the manager application and not the actual firewall service, click the Cancel button. Otherwise, to continue the configuration, click Next to continue the configuration process.

The configuration wizard walks you through configuring the firewall policy of several popular services, such as WWW, email, and FTP. First, however, you need to configure one or more ranges of addresses on the internal network that will be grouped together for policy purposes. In Figure 19.4, you can see the dialog box used for this purpose.

FIGURE 19.4
Use this dialog box to create one or more address ranges.

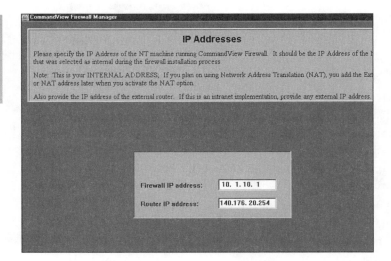

For each service, you can decide what type of access to allow. For example, for the WWW service, you can enable or disable outbound access for all the addresses you included in the address ranges created for the internal network adapter. If you prefer, you can create a custom policy that enables you to specify individual IP addresses that are allowed access. The other services are configured in a similar manner, with dialog boxes that are specific to the service.

In addition to configuring policies for network services, the wizard enables you to set up email notifications for significant firewall events. In Figure 19.5, you can see the Set Notification Command dialog box. If you want to set up email notifications, click the Enable E-Mail notification check box. If you do not want email notifications, leave this check box blank. The remaining fields enable you to enter the necessary information, such as the address of your email server. You can also enter an email address that will appear as the sender of the email notifications. In the example in Figure 19.5, the account firewall@twoinc was selected for this.

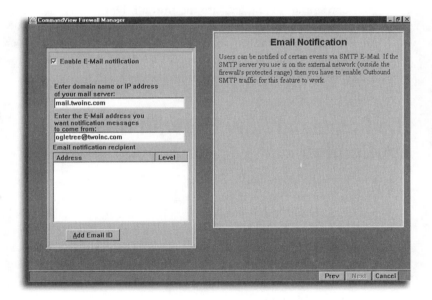

FIGURE 19.5
Enter the name or address of the mail server to use and the name of the email account from which the mail notifications will be sent.

Click the Add Email ID button. Another dialog box, titled Create Email Rule (see Figure 19.6), then prompts you to enter the email address to which the notification will be sent and enables you to then select the severity level of logging for which you want to be notified. Events at that severity level or higher are sent to the email address you enter. Click OK to add the account and return to the previous dialog box.

FIGURE 19.6
Enter the email account that will receive notifications and select the severity level.

FIGURE 19.6
Enter the email account that will receive notifications and select the severity level.

You can continue to set up one or more email accounts using this dialog box by clicking the Add Email ID button (refer to Figure 19.5) for each.

After the configuration process is complete, you are prompted to save your configuration and activate the firewall. Don't worry if you are not exactly sure of how you want the firewall to be configured at this time. The wizard is useful for a quick setup after the firewall has been installed, but you can always go back later, using the manager utility, to make further configuration decisions.

The CommandView Firewall Manager Application

The firewall service and the manager application are separate programs. You can run them on the same computer or on different computers. Although the firewall service must be run on a Windows NT computer, the manager application can be run on a workstation running NT or Windows 95/98. The manager application is used to control the firewall. For example, if you decide later that you want to change the firewall policies that you initially created, you can do so using this program.

When you first launch the manager application, you are prompted for a firewall that the application will attach to and a password for that firewall. You can use the manager application to control more than one installation of the firewall service, so you must first select the one you want to manage at this time. The first time the program is run for a particular firewall, you should select the Default Password checkbox. When the program is running, you can set your own password to protect the program from unauthorized users.

In Figure 19.7, you see the manager application, which displays the Master Security Plan that was last saved. This is the configuration that you created with the setup wizard or the current configuration if you have already used the manager application to make changes.

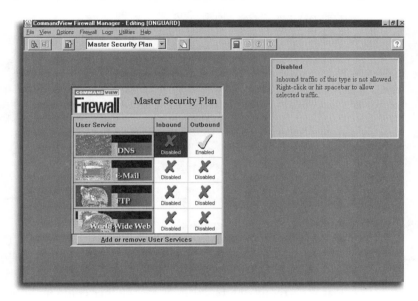

FIGURE 19.7
The CommandView Firewall Manager is used to control the firewall service.

File Menu and View Menu

The File menu enables you to perform a wide variety of management functions. Table 19.1 lists the menu options and gives a brief description of their usage.

Table 19.1 File Manager Options

Menu Option	Description
Attach to Firewall	Attaches to a specific firewall for management purposes.
Detach From Firewall	Breaks the current firewall connection.

continues...

Table 19.1 Continued

Menu Option	Description
Configure New Firewall	Starts the Express Configuration of a new firewall.
Retrieve Plan from Firewall	Gets the plan file for the currently active firewall.
Save Plan to Firewall	Saves the current configuration to the firewall as the Master Security Plan. Restarts the firewall to have this take effect.
Load Plan from File	Loads a saved configuration (a file with the extension .OGM).
Save Plan to File	Saves a configuration to a file (with an .OGM extension).
Print MSP Summary	Prints a summary of the Master Security Plan (MSP), showing user services with inbound/outbound status.
Print MSP Details	Prints a detailed list of the current Master Security Plan.
Exit	Exits the Firewall Manager application.

The Master Security Plan

The settings you specify for the Master Security Plan are stored in a file. You can create multiple plans. This is convenient if you want to test a particular configuration and save it for later testing or examination. Each configuration is saved in a file (with an extension of .OGM). The master Security Plan, which is the plan currently running on the firewall, is saved in a file called ONGUARD.OGM and is found in the directory C:\Program Files\ Elron Software\ FirewallManager\ Onguard. If you save multiple firewall configurations, they are stored in this directory by default, but you can change that to a custom directory if you want.

As you can see, this menu enables you to perform some very basic functions, such as changing the firewall that you are managing. Use the attach and detach options to switch between firewalls. The load and save options enable you to view the configuration of the firewall plan that is currently in effect or to manage other configurations and save them to a file. If you want to change the Master Security Plan, use the Save Plan to Firewall option and then use the Firewall Menu to restart the firewall so that the plan will take effect.

The View menu contains even more options, enabling you to display the Master Security Plan in a brief or detailed format or to save it to a text file so that you can print it out. Other options enable you to edit address ranges, select encryption methods, manage encryption keys, and so on. This menu is also where you can elect to add or modify your notification commands so that you are notified when significant events occur.

Firewall Menu Options

The Firewall Menu contains only a few options. Table 19.2 lists these along with a description of their usage.

Table 19.2   Firewall Menu Options

Menu Option	Description
Set Date/Time	Just what it says!
Set Password	Use this option to change the password for the firewall service you are managing.
SMXP Encryption Key	The firewall uses a default key for encryption purposes unless you set one here.
Check Alive	This option checks to see if the firewall is active at this time.
Ping Router	Use this option to determine whether the firewall can contact the default gateway or external router that connects to the Internet.
ReStart	Restarts the firewall you are managing.
	Note that this option reboots the computer, but you can specify a time at which it will occur.
Upgrade	This option is used for upgrading the firewall after you have already upgraded the manager application. The system needs to be rebooted afterwards.

The options that you will most likely use the most are the Set Password and ReStart options. Remember that the first time you connect to a newly installed firewall service, there is no password set. That is why you select the Default Password check box. As soon as you have set up a new firewall, go straight to this menu and create a password for it. Even though you might be running the manager application on a computer that you consider to be secure, you should still be concerned about the password. Why? Because the password applies to the firewall service, not the manager program or the computer it runs on. If you do not set a password, it would be a simple matter for someone who has a little knowledge about it to obtain a copy of the manager application, install it on another computer, attach to your firewall service (using the default password option), and make changes.

Set the password immediately! Change it frequently! Of course, as with all passwords, make it a good one, and don't write it down!

Logs Menu Options

This menu is used to examine the log files kept by the firewall service. The log files are Events, Traps, and Statistics. After you select one of these log files, you can then use other options to sort log records or to create filters so that you can pare down the information to only what you want to have captured in the log files. The Sort and Filter options are not available until you first select the log file you want to manage.

Managing User Services

Earlier in this chapter, a configuration wizard was used to create the initial firewall policy for basic services. The CommandView Firewall is not limited to just WWW, FTP, or email. In fact, the firewall enables you to offer over 25 user services that are already defined. You can also create a new user service if you do not find what you are looking for. Some of the predefined services include (but are not limited to) the following:

- AOL
- Citrix
- CompuServe
- IPX
- IRC
- LDAP
- NetBIOS
- News

As you can see, the services that can be used with the CommandView firewall cover a lot of territory. Ordinary services you expect, such as FTP, email, and news are there, as well as services for IPX and LDAP. If you have Novell servers on your network, you can provide access to them through the firewall. If you are currently upgrading your network to Windows 2000 servers, you might want to investigate configuring the LDAP service for the firewall because LDAP is the primary wire protocol used to access the Active Directory.

To add one of these services to your firewall's Master Security Plan, click the button titled Add or Remove User Services. This button appears at the bottom of the manager application window when you first launch the application. The Select User Service for Master Security Plan dialog box (see Figure 19.8) then enables you to choose the service and add it to the plan. Highlight the service you want to add and click the Select Button. The service then appears in the User Services Selected field on the right side of the dialog box.

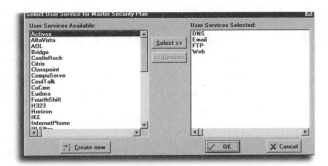

FIGURE 19.8
Select services to add to the Master Security Plan using this dialog box.

To remove a service from the plan, highlight it and click the Remove button. You can also simply double-click a service to add or remove it, depending on its current status. When you are finished managing services, click OK. The Master Security Plan now shows the new service configuration. If you have added a new service, it is disabled until you set a policy for it.

Where to Go from Here

CommandView is a good example of a typical commercial firewall product. If you want to further investigate it, go to Elron's Web site, listed at the start of this chapter, download an evaluation copy, and install it yourself. As a matter of fact, if you are new to firewalls, it would probably be a good idea to look around at other products and, for those who offer an evaluation, do the same. Each time you run through the setup and management of a product, you will become more aware of the features that can best be used in your environment. Go ahead and download several. You can use the demo copies to make presentations to upper management or to your co-workers who will be working with the firewall software.

Summary

The Elron CommandView firewall is a good example of a full-featured commercial firewall product. If you do not have the stomach to tackle configuring a firewall using utilities such as TCP Wrappers or the TIS Internet Firewall Toolkit, a product such as Elron will make your day. When you decide on what products you will use for creating a firewall, there are several factors that need to be considered. Of course, one of the most important factors is whether the product will provide the network services you require. An equally important factor is the support you will be able to get from the vendor. Elron, like many other good commercial firewall products, is backed up by a vendor that provides good technical support. So, if you do not have the inhouse technical expertise to fiddle with the bits and bytes of configuration files or compilation make files, a solution such as the Elron CommandView Firewall is a good choice.

chapter

20

Firewall Appliances

What Is a Firewall Appliance?   •

Pricing a Firewall Appliance   •

What Is a Firewall Appliance?

Throughout this book, firewalls have been discussed as complex systems that use packet filtering, application and circuit-level gateways, strong authentication, and other techniques to protect your network. In some chapters, you have been cautioned about not attempting to install a particular product (such as the TIS Internet Firewall Toolkit) unless you possess considerable skills in UNIX system administration and TCP/IP. Most of the freely downloadable firewall components and security utilities that you can download from the Internet require that you compile them on your local system and then spend time fiddling with configuration details.

For a business that is large enough to support a staff of employees to manage the network and handle users, managing a firewall is probably no big deal. It just requires that one or more persons with the necessary skills take responsibility for monitoring and maintaining the firewall. For a small business or perhaps a home office where there are only one or two servers, a few workstations, and an Internet connection, it might not be financially possible to hire someone to do nothing but manage a firewall. In this small environment, it is likely that all the applications are off-the-shelf packages and that there are no programming or real system management skills in any of the employees.

In this kind of situation, how do you safely connect to the Internet? Does a small business have to remain dependent on their Internet provider for all their security needs?

A new breed of firewall product has recently been gaining a lot of notice in the press. The term *firewall appliance* has been coined to refer to these all-in-one Internet security solutions. The many products that claim to be in this new class of firewalls vary considerably from each other in features, price, and effectiveness. However, most of the products claiming to be firewall appliances have the following features:

- Quick, easy installation. Some advertise plug-and-play.
- Simple management interface. Possibly remote management capability.
- Self-contained in one device.

- Works with multiple interfaces, from dial-up phone lines to Ethernet and possibly T1.

- Default security policies so the user doesn't have to understand all of the details.

- Packet filtering and application proxy functionality.

- Network Address Translation (NAT) functionality.

- Easy-to-use reporting capabilities, usually with a set of canned reports. Alerting capabilities.

- Virtual Private Networking (VPN) capabilities.

- Good vendor support.

Quick, Easy Installation

One of the best selling features of firewall appliances is their easy installation. The user should be able to simply plug her network into one interface on the firewall appliance, plug the Internet connection into the other, and answer a few simple questions. There should be no complicated configuration files that need to be edited. The user should not have to understand, in any great detail, how IP addressing works or how to subnet a network address. The configuration should be conducted by a wizard program that can prompt the user for a few simple questions.

The configuration process should enable you to specify, in a general way, a security policy for the network. The whole installation process, from unpacking the box to using the device, should not take any longer than an hour for most devices. If the time it takes to set up a firewall appliance exceeds one hour, calling the device an appliance might be a misnomer.

Simple Management Interface

After the installation is complete, there should be little that you need to do to manage the device. Many firewall appliances do not even have a system console—a monitor—that you can use. Instead, the trend is toward remote management capabilities. An HTML-based Web interface is the usual route, but be sure that the communication channel between the firewall appliance and the management console is an encrypted one. For this purpose, the appliance should support a standard form of encryption, such as DES or Secure Sockets Layer (SSL).

Large and Small Firewall Appliances

Although the market for firewall appliances in the next few years is going to grow dramatically as more small business enterprises begin to use them for Internet connections, there also exists a market for high-end systems that are self-contained and easy to manage. For example, Cisco and Lucent both make products that are billed as firewall appliances but that cost over $10,000. Obviously, these "appliances" are not geared toward the small business owner. Instead, they are being targeted at network administrators who operate large networks. Although the term firewall appliance makes it sound like the product is a simple device like a toaster, that does not mean that it is an inexpensive, disposable device. The term appliance is intended to connote not price, but ease of use.

The interface should be graphical. A command-line interface, with complex syntax and long lines of cryptic commands, is not the way to go with a simple device such as a firewall appliance. You should be able to point-and-click to perform most actions. Producing a report should be a simple matter of selecting it from a menu and, perhaps, entering a date or other bit of information that will be used to produce the report.

Self-Contained Device

To be plug-and-play, a firewall appliance is contained in a single box, usually the size of an ordinary PC or smaller. Some hardware platforms for firewall appliances actually are PCs that use either a proprietary operating system or a hardened version of a standard operating system. For example, the Interceptor firewall appliance from Technologic uses an operating system that is based on the BSD/OS from Berkeley Software Design, Inc. (BSDI). This is a UNIX-based operating system. The Lucent Managed Firewall appliance uses Lucent's Inferno operating system, which contains embedded code for the firewall functions.

There are several that use an operating system that is contained on a floppy disk or CD-ROM. Using a read-only CD-ROM ensures that files of the operating system used by the firewall appliance cannot be overwritten. There are some devices that take this even further. The PERMIT firewall appliances from TimeStep have no moving parts at all. This solid-state firewall appliance keeps the operating system in memory, along with its version of the Check Point FireWall-1 software.

When evaluating competing products, keep in mind that simplicity is the design goal for a firewall appliance, so there should be no complicated user manual instructing you to make decisions about installing the software components.

Multiple Network Interfaces

In a small environment, your connection to the Internet is likely to be a dial-up phone line, ISDN, or possibly a Digital Subscriber Line (DSL) connection. Most firewall appliances are able to work with any of these. Higher-end models, with high-end prices, include connections for T1 lines. Check the details in the vendor's documentation to be sure that the device you purchase is able to connect to your network and Internet connection without needing special adapters or other hardware.

Although the typical manner in which a firewall is installed in a small office usually makes use of only two interfaces, some firewall appliances give you an extra interface for use as a DMZ, as you can see in Figure 20.1.

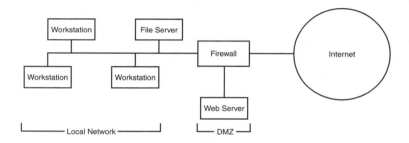

FIGURE 20.1
A third network interface enables you to place servers in a demilitarized zone (DMZ).

This feature is important if your small business manages its own Web server. Although the trend today is to outsource the hosting of a Web site, that solution might not be the most suited to your business model. Maintaining a simple Web site, using modern development tools, doesn't have to be a time-consuming process involving lots of skilled programmers. Applications such as Microsoft FrontPage can be used to create very complex Web sites, but they can also be used to create simple, easy-to-manage ones. When a firewall appliance gives you the option of using a third interface to separate the Web server (or other server providing a network service), this greatly enhances the security of your local network that is connected to the other adapter.

Default Security Policies

In Chapter 4, "Firewall Security Policy and Firewall Design Strategies," you learned that before you can implement a firewall, you first must create a security policy for your site and then design a security policy that applies to the firewall itself. Although a firewall appliance won't take away all the details involved in this task, it can simplify them. Using a wizard program to set up a firewall configuration makes the initial installation process an easy task. Several of the firewall appliances I have seen recently have a set of built-in security policies that can be understood using ordinary English, instead of complicated technical language. The user can quickly make a determination about which policy to use and then let the wizard configure the appropriate rules on the firewall.

The Lucent Managed Firewall appliance enables you to create separate *virtual security zones* for different groups of hosts so that a particular policy can be applied to each group. This can be done on a single firewall appliance or with a group of them managed from a central location. When changes are made to a security policy, they can be propagated immediately to all the devices that are being managed together.

If you do not have time to delve into the intricacies of firewall rules, services, port numbers, and so on, a predetermined set of security policies that you can easily understand is a benefit.

Packet Filtering and Application Proxies

A good firewall performs both packet filtering and application proxy functions. Check to see that the network services that you use are included as proxy applications for the device. There should also be a generic circuit-level gateway capability for other services. Packet filtering capabilities should be implemented using stateful packet filtering techniques.

Of course, it goes without saying that a modern firewall appliance makes these services available transparently to clients.

SEE ALSO

➤ *For more information about packet filters, see Chapter 5, "Packet Filtering", page 109*

➤ *For more information about how proxy servers operate, see Chapter 7, "Application Gateways and Proxy Servers," page 157*

Network Address Translation (NAT)

Does your Internet provider use DHCP to dynamically assign you an IP address for your Internet connection, or do you have a dedicated subnet of addresses that are valid on the Internet? If you use a dial-up connection, it is most likely that DHCP is used. If that is the case, you are not guaranteed to the same IP address every time you call, so your firewall appliance needs to be able to cope with this. Be sure that the device doesn't require that you statically assign an address to the adapter connected to the Internet. Indeed, for a dial-up connection of this sort, be sure that the appliance supports the PPP protocol.

SEE ALSO

➤ *Network Address translation is covered in more detail in "Network Address Translators (NATs)", in Chapter 7, "Application Gateways and Proxy Servers", page 166*

If you do not have a dedicated subnet of addresses that you can use to assign IP configuration information to workstations on the local network, you have to use one of the reserved private address ranges set aside by IANA for this purpose. This means that the firewall appliance has to support Network Address Translation (NAT) for clients on your network to be able to interact with servers on the Internet.

If the appliance supports NAT, another good feature to look for is a DHCP server in the appliance itself. By combining the DHCP server into the firewall appliance, you do not have to set up yet another computer to perform this service. Because one of the goals of using a low-cost firewall appliance is to minimize management chores, keeping multiple services in one place makes sense.

Reporting and Alerting

Because a firewall appliance is targeted for use by those who do not possess a lot of TCP/IP or networking experience, the reporting and alerting capabilities of the device are very important. The appliance should come with robust reporting capabilities so that you can configure specific reports after you become familiar with the firewall. It should also be equipped with a number of prewritten, canned reports that make it easy to understand the data that the reports represent.

For example, you might want a report that would show you the top Web sites visited by your users or maybe a report that shows you just the Web sites visited by one user. Network traffic statistics are important for capacity planning, so reports in this area should contain information that can help you decide when the Internet connection is becoming saturated and needs to be changed to a bigger pipe.

Reports that show possible break-in attempts or other forms of attack are also important.

A good firewall appliance should be capable of alerting you to suspicious activity or the detection of a possible intrusion, by both email and pager. If the firewall appliance also supports the Simple Network Management Protocol (SNMP), that's a good feature, but it is more useful in a larger organization where a centralized management team controls more than one firewall, perhaps for remote offices.

Virtual Private Networking (VPN)

For any business that has users who travel, creating a secure communications link between the mobile employee and the home office is important. For businesses that have several offices in different geographical locations, a secure link is also important. Using a virtual private network (VPN) link enables you to forgo the costs of dedicated leased lines or long distance charges from modem use. Instead, you can create an encrypted channel of communications between offices by using the same firewall appliance at each end. If the vendor uses a standard method for creating a VPN instead of a proprietary one, you will find that a firewall appliance might even be able to establish an encrypted link with another vendor's product.

For mobile users, the firewall should support a standard such as Microsoft's Point-to-Point Tunneling Protocol (PPTP) because that capability is found in the Windows operating systems. Because the VPN software is built into clients such as these, there is no need to use another firewall at the mobile user's end of the connection.

SEE ALSO

➤ *For more information about PPTP and Virtual Private Networks, see Chapter 10, "Virtual Private Networks (VPNs) and Tunneling," page 211*

Pricing a Firewall Appliance

The term firewall appliance is being applied to a wide range of products. There are very low-cost products—under $1,000—and there are some that cost more than $10,000. Some work as standalone products, whereas others can be used in numbers to support multiple locations. The price that you pay, however, does not always directly correlate with the functionality that you get. It is important to read documentation and sales literature thoroughly and to ask questions when making a purchase of this sort.

Check also for pricing for technical support and updates. No firewall, appliance or otherwise, is a static product that never needs to change. The threats that can target your network from the Internet are evolving and changing every day. Software updates for the firewall appliance are only as good as the vendor who produces the product. So, when evaluating competing products, take into consideration the one-time purchase price as well as the long-term support commitment. Make sure that the vendor is in the business for the long haul and that support includes a 24-hour hotline that can provide help in an emergency.

Firewall appliances can deceive some users. If you think about it as simply another device to hook up to the network and forget about, you do not fully understand how important a firewall is—and what it does—is for your network.

Summary

Firewall appliances are basically a computer-in-a-box that has been configured to perform a specific function: act as a firewall to guard the gateway between your network and the Internet. When shopping around for an appliance such as this, be sure to check the documentation to first determine if the product offers the features that you feel are necessary to guard your network. If you are unsure of some of the terminology used by a vendor, use this book as a technology reference and then call their support hotline and ask questions!

Firewall appliances are a very hot product right now. It appears that what was once a complicated process has now been reduced to a plug-and-play appliance. In the next chapter, you will look at some topics that relate to the future of Internet security and what place firewalls will have in that future.

chapter 21

Firewalls and Beyond

It's All About the Internet •

New Functionality •

Home Computers •

Virtual Private Network Clients •

IPv6: The Next Generation IP Protocol •

It's All About the Internet

If the Internet did not exist, about the only people you would probably be likely to hear talking about a firewall would be a building contractor or, perhaps, a network security technician working for the military. However, the Internet is a reality, and millions of people use it everyday for everything from simple email messages to complex financial transactions. The Internet is a growing organism. New technologies are developing every day and, with them, new security vulnerabilities. Because of this, you can expect to see many changes in the next few years when it comes to firewalls. New protocols, such as IPv6, will present new tools for implementing security and will also most likely introduce new threats. New threats will require new methods for protection. New protocols, new threats—these will require new functionality for firewalls.

In this chapter, you will look at a few possibilities for new developments in firewalls. You will also briefly review the next generation IP protocol (IPv6) that is in the future of anyone who is connected to the Internet.

New Functionality

Current firewalls work by using two basic methods I have discussed throughout this book: packet filtering and application proxying. As firewalls develop, they will continue to acquire new functionality. When you shop around today and compare different firewall products, you will find that there are many "value-added" features that can distinguish one product from another. New features that are being incorporated into firewalls include the following:

- New implementations of stateful packet filtering or dynamic packet filtering to better enable UDP applications through a firewall.

- Virus scanning. Scan for viruses at the firewall instead of waiting until the virus hits the user's computer.

- Intrusion detection, or the ability to detect suspicious activity and respond to it. Responses could include alerting an administrator or increasing the level of logging during the suspected activity.

- Stronger authentication techniques, such as hardware tokens and one-time use passwords, will become a very important feature of firewalls in the next few years.

- Management capabilities. Administrators should not have to construct complicated sets of rules using the syntax of stone-age routers. Graphical interfaces and wizards will become common for simplifying management and configuration tasks.

SEE ALSO

➤ *For more information about packet filtering, see Chapter 5, "Packet Filtering," page 109. For more information about application proxies, see Chapter 7, "Application Gateways and Proxy Servers," page 157*

Vendors of firewall products will continue to differentiate their product by trying to add new features. It might be a good idea to evaluate vendors before you start to evaluate products. If the technology is one that is going to be changing rapidly in the next few years (and this is true of firewalls), you want to be in business with a vendor that will be around a year from now. You want to be doing business with a vendor that will continue to develop and grow their product.

Firewall Integration

It is easy to think of a firewall as a single choke point that can be used to monitor traffic between your network and the Internet. In practice, many large organizations deploy multiple firewalls. These can be used to secure multiple connections to the Internet, or to secure connections between departments or with customers or other business partners. Managing multiple firewalls in this kind of situation could become a tiresome chore indeed.

New firewall products should be configured so that they can be managed centrally, preferably by using an easy-to-understand graphical interface. The development of standardized application programming interfaces (APIs) that work with established security standards and protocols will help make the integration of products from different vendors easier. By using standards, it will be possible for firewall products to be managed just like many other network devices, using SNMP, RMON, or possibly an extension to these developed specifically for firewalls.

Firewall Testing

One of the biggest difficulties faced by an administrator who has just deployed a firewall is determining how well the firewall functions. During the setup process, you have to make decisions about how the firewall is to be configured. Complex sets of rules, especially on a router, can be difficult to grasp and can lead to holes in security. Without some method of testing the firewall, how can you ever be sure of what level of protection you are really getting?

One way is to simply wait until something really bad happens and then fix the problem. This is not, of course, the preferred way to test the firewall. Instead, vendors need to provide applications that can be used from both sides of the firewall to probe for security holes and present the data in a format that the administrator can easily understand. Although it is possible for an experienced network and UNIX administrator to use utilities such as COPS and SATAN to probe their network, many administrators do not have the necessary skills to use these tools. Vendors that can provide thorough testing software to use with their products will find many eager customers.

SEE ALSO

➤ *You can get COPS and SATAN and use them to help evaluate the security profile of your network. These utilities, along with others, are discussed in Appendix B, "Other Security Tools You Can Use," page 445*

Home Computers

Until very recently little thought was given to providing a firewall type of product for home use. At home the most a user had to worry about was the problem of downloading a virus or a Trojan horse program. A whole industry has grown up to provide virus protection to the masses. With the dial-up nature of most home Internet connections, most home users are not on the Internet for a long enough duration to allow a probing hacker to get into their system.

With the advent and deployment of Digital Subscriber Line (DSL) technology, however, this is changing. Cable modems are becoming a popular way to connect to the Internet. When compared to dial-up modem access, there is an important difference. When you disconnect from a dial-up modem, you are disconnected from the Internet.

When you use a cable modem, there is no dial-up to begin the connection. Instead, you are always online. Even when you are not sitting at the computer browsing the Internet, if the computer is powered-up and booted, it is possible for an intruder to infiltrate your computer.

Some of the more recent hacker tools, such as the distributed denial-of-service attack tools, make use of tens or hundreds of unsuspecting computers to launch an attack on a target. The hacker seeks out hosts that are online and have minimal security protections in place. When you think about it, home computers are ideal for this.

SEE ALSO

➤ *For more information about distributed denial-of-service attack tools, such as Tribe Flood Network and Stacheldraht, see "Denial of Service Attacks," in Chapter 3, "Security and the Internet," page 69*

At this time there are several products showing up that are geared to the home computer user. You can expect to see more products of this kind in the near future. Until then, consider powering off your home computer or disconnecting it from your cable provider's connection when it is not being used if you are a DSL user!

Virtual Private Network Clients

Some of the technology that you mainly think of as being associated with firewalls is being moved into the client operating system. For example, firewalls are commonly used to create a virtual private network (VPN) between two networks, so that clients and servers on the two networks can securely communicate across an insecure network—the Internet, for example. Microsoft developed VPN software for use in Windows NT 4.0 with its remote access service. With Windows 2000, Microsoft has extended its VPN capabilities by incorporating new protocols, such as IPSec and L2PT, in addition to its original implementation using PPTP.

SEE ALSO

➤ *For more information about IPSEC, PPTP and L2PT, see Chapter 10, "Virtual Private Networks (VPNs) and Tunneling," page 211*

Firewalls that use proprietary technology for VPNs can establish a secure channel only with other devices that use the same technology.

Newer firewalls, and those that you can expect to see in the coming years, will instead use standard protocols. Because of this, you will be able to create VPNs between firewalls that come from different vendors. Because standard protocols will be used, you can also expect to see more development in the client area, allowing individual hosts to create VPNs between themselves and the firewall and, perhaps, between themselves and another host, bypassing the firewall entirely.

IPv6: The Next Generation IP Protocol

The IPv6 Forum and IPv6.org

There are several Web sites devoted to the next generation IP protocol. At www.ipv6.org you will find a Web site that contains links to the IPv6 FAQ, specification documents, a mailing list, and other information.

The IPv6 Forum is a consortium of vendors and others that promote the adoption and use of IPv6. You can visit their Web site at www.ipv6forum.com.

Of all the new technologies that you can expect to be using in just a few years, one stands out that will have a large impact on firewall construction. That is the next generation of the IP protocol.

The current version of the Internet Protocol, version 4 (or IPv4), is almost 20 years old, and it is beginning to show its age. The total address space that IPv4 provides for is being rapidly exhausted. Hacker technology is continually finding new ways to exploit weaknesses in the protocol and services that use it. Newer services could be better built if the protocol, which underlies the Internet, were a little more robust. For all these reasons and more, it should be very obvious that the next generation IP protocol, version 6 (IPv6) is in the near future. Work on IPv6 was started in the early 1990s, and the first proposed standard was approved in November, 1994, in Request For Comments (RFC) 1752, "The Recommendation for the IP Next Generation Protocol."

The move to IPv6 will not be a dramatic one but instead will be an evolutionary one. IPv6 can interoperate with IPv4, so a gradual period of peaceful coexistence will most likely take place while IPv6 is deployed.

The IPv6 Header

The new IP header has a fixed length of 40 bytes. By using a fixed-length header, network devices can be created that can process packets much faster than when having to deal with variable-length headers. The new header, as you can see in Figure 21.1, contains fewer fields than the IPv4 header.

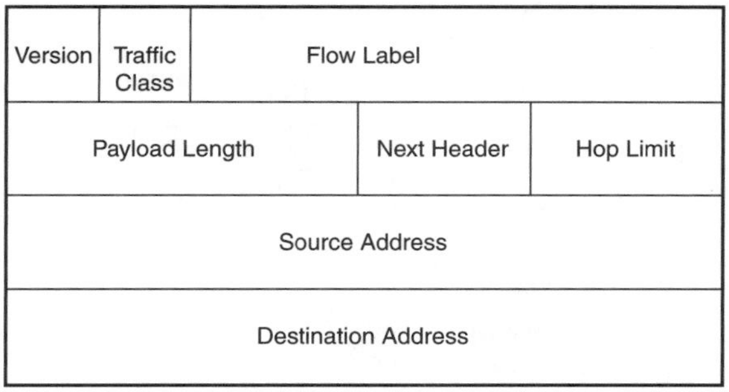

FIGURE 21.1
The IPv6 header is fixed at 40 bytes.

In addition to its smaller number of fields, the next most obvious change made to the IPv6 header is the large address fields. A full 128 bits is used for both the source and destination address fields. This should give the Internet enough addresses to uniquely identify every grain of sand on the planet. That should be enough to last for at least a few more years.

SEE ALSO

➤ *The IPv4 Header and its fields are discussed in detail in Chapter 2, "Introduction to the TCP/IP Protocol Suite," page 25*

Fields that were included in the IPv4 header but that will not be used in the IPv6 header include the following:

- Fragmentation-related fields, such as Fragment Offset and Identification Fields, and the Don't Fragment and More Fragments flags
- Checksum field
- Options field

To increase the speed of processing, packet fragmentation was dropped from IPv6. If a packet is too large for a router to forward it across the next network link, it will not be split into smaller packets and then reassembled at the receiving end. Instead, the packet will be dropped, and a new ICMP message ("Packet Too Big") will be sent back to the sender, who can then create smaller packets for transmission.

In another attempt to increase packet processing speed, IPv6 does not have a checksum field for the header. For each router that an IPv4 packet traverses, this field needs to be recalculated because the

Interoperation of IPv4 and IPv6

How will IPv4 and IPv6 nodes be able to work together on the same network? There are two methods proposed at this time. The first is to create the new IPv6 systems so that they will use two different protocol stacks, one for Ipv4 and one for IPv6, depending on the node with which they are communicating. The second method is to tunnel IPv6 packets inside of IPv4 packets when sending data from one IPv6 machine to another, through a route that contains IPv4 machines.

TTL field is decremented at each hop. Because the data link layer that is below IP performs a checksum function and because upper-level protocols such as TCP and UDP also perform this function, removing it from the IP header is expected to cause no problems.

The Options field is another matter. Although this variable-length field has been removed from the IP header so that the IP header can now be set to fixed-length, this does not mean that option processing has been removed entirely. Instead, if options are to be used in the packet, the Next Header field, which usually designates another protocol such as TCP or UDP, can be used to specify options instead. If this is the case, the options information is contained in the payload data section of the packet, and the Next Header field identifies it. Again, by removing options processing from the header and thus allowing for a fixed-length header, processing of IP packets can be done much more quickly.

SEE ALSO

➤ *For more information about the Internet Control Message Protocol (ICMP), see "The Internet Message Control Protocol (ICMP)," in Chapter 2, "The TCP/IP Protocol Suite," page 34*

The fields that will be in the new Ipv6 header include the following:

- **Version**   This four-bit field is used, as in IPv4, to specify the version of the IP protocol. For IPv6, the value will always be 6.

- **Traffic Class**   This eight-bit field serves a purpose similar to the type of service (TOS) field in the IPv4 header, though the implementation is not yet ironed out.

- **Flow Label**   This field will be used to identify different *flows*, or streams of traffic, that the sender wants to receive special handling. The exact definition of what constitutes a flow is not yet fully defined. It could be traffic from a user who is paying a higher rate for a service, or it could be used to identify traffic used for audio or video feeds.

- **Payload Length**   This value is a 16-bit field that specifies the number of bytes that follow the header field.

- **Next Header**   This field uses the same protocol numbers as IPv4, and it is used to specify the higher-level protocol that IP will deliver the packet to for further processing.

- **Hop Limit**   The maximum hops allowed for the packet. Each router decrements this field by one. When this field reaches zero, the packet is dropped.

The New ICMP

The Internet Control Message Protocol is used by IP for various functions. The most widely known use of the protocol is the PING utility, which uses echo messages to determine whether a remote network host is reachable. Just as the IP protocol is undergoing a transformation, the ICMP protocol will also be enhanced to keep up with the times. In addition to changes made because of IPv6, ICMP will also have the functionality of the Internet Group Management Protocol (IGMP) merged into it. In Request For Comments (RFC) 2463, "Internet Control Message Protocol (ICMPv6) for the Internet Protocol Version 6 (IPv6)," you can find a discussion of the changes made to ICMP.

- **Source Address**   A 128-bit field identifying the source of the packet.
- **Destination Address**   A 128-bit field identifying the destination of the packet.

Extension Headers

In the fixed-length 40-byte header, the Next Header field is used to indicate the type of header that will be found at the start of the IP packet's data field. Remember that IP usually encapsulates a higher level protocol, such as TCP or UDP, and these protocols each have their own header information. By using a fixed-length IP header, processing by routers and other network hosts can be made to work much faster. Because some fields were omitted from the header, however, another method needs to be used to provide for the functionality that is lost.

For this purpose, there are several types of *extension headers*, which can also show up at the beginning of the data portion of the IP packet. The Next Header field will identify an extension header just as it would if the next header were for a higher-level protocol. The basic extension headers that can be used include the following:

- Hop-by-Hop Options
- Fragmentation
- Routing
- Authentication
- Security Encapsulation
- Encapsulating Security Payload
- Destination Options

The first type of extension header, hop-by-hop options, is identified in the Next Header field by a value of 0. This header is used for information that every system in the packet's path needs to examine. The only option defined at this time is one that provides for a Jumbo Payload—that is, an IP packet that is larger than 65,535 bytes. When you look at the format for the hop-by-hop extension header (Figure 21.2), you can see that it contains a Next Header field just like the IPv6 header. This provides for multiple extension headers, each pointing to the next.

How Many IPv4 Addresses?

In theory, it is possible to address over 16 million networks and over 4 billion individual hosts using the IPv4 addressing mechanism. Because there are already over 6 billion people on the earth and as more and more addresses are allocated, it is easy to see how the address pool will quickly become exhausted in the near future. Remember that each person doesn't have to have just one address. As more devices, such as cell phones and personal digital assistants, become Internet capable, it will become commonplace for a single person to make use of many addresses.

389

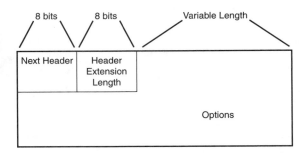

FIGURE 21.2
The hop-by-hop extension header format.

The Fragmentation extension header, identified by a value of 44 in the Next Header field, is used when the source of a packet realizes that it must fragment the message to send it through the network. Remember that in IPv6, there are no provisions for fragmenting a packet while it is being routed through the network. This function was removed to speed up the processing of IP packets. Any fragmentation done for a message will now be done at the source of the packet, and this extension header is used to store information about the process so that the host on the receiving end can correctly reassemble the message.

The Routing Options extension header (Next Header field value of 43) works in a manner similar to source routing in IPv4. This header is used to specify one or more nodes that a packet should visit on its journey through the network.

The Destinations Options header (Next Header field value of 60) is used to store information that only the destination node needs to examine.

➤ *The extension headers relating to security and authentication are defined by other Request For Comments documents. For example, the Authentication Header and Encapsulating Security Payload are defined in RFCs 2402 and 2406. For more information about these and other security related protocols, see Chapter 10, "Virtual Private Networks (VPNs) and Tunneling," page 211*

A value of 59 in the Next Header field indicates that there are no more extension headers to be examined. If the Payload Length value specifies that there are additional bytes that contain headers, they will be ignored when a header with this value is found.

IPv6 Addressing

As you can probably imagine, by jumping from 32 bits to 128 bits, the addressing space for IPv6 will be astronomically larger than that for IPv4.

IPv6 will have three basic address types:

- **Unicast**   An address that uniquely identifies a specific network interface.

- **Anycast**   An address that is used by more than one interface. A packet that is routed to an anycast address will be sent to the closest interface (as determined by the routing protocol being used) that is assigned this address.

- **Multicast**   This address type also identifies an address that is assigned to more than one interface. However, unlike an anycast address, a packet sent to a multicast address is sent to all interfaces that are assigned this address.

Whereas a unicast address uniquely identifies a network interface, a single interface can have multiple unicast addresses. Broadcast addresses are gone. Instead, that functionality has been incorporated into the multicast address type.

Unlike IPv4, addresses for IPv6 will be classless. That is, there will be no identification of class A, B, or C addresses. The format for the actual address is also a little more complicated than the IPv4 format. For additional details you should read Request For Comments (RFC) 2373, "IP Version 6 Addressing Architecture."

The Transition to IPv6

The next generation IP protocol has been under development for many years now. The expected exhaustion of the IPv4 address space has been put off by a few years with the advent of such technology as Network Address Translation. However, the benefits to be expected from IPv6 go beyond a simple expansion of the address space, so the eventual adoption of IPv6 is in our future.

To reiterate, it is expected that there will be no immediate, all-at-once, cut-over to IPv6. Instead, the transition will be gradual, with network devices designed to work with both IPv4 and IPv6. RFC

1993, "Transition Mechanism for IPv6 Hosts and Routers," discusses the two methods that are being considered. The first method uses network devices with dual protocol stacks that can respond to either IPv4 or IPv6. The second provides for the tunneling of an IPv6 datagram inside an IPv4 packet.

Summary

Ten years ago, if you had mentioned creating a firewall for your network not many people would have known what you were talking about. Of course, ten years ago if you had said you were going to connect your network to the Internet, not many people would have known what you were talking about.

Today, the Internet is spreading rapidly and will soon be as pervasive as the telephone network. The opportunities to incorporate networking technology into all sorts of everyday devices will generate entire new technologies and industries in the near future. As technology progresses, new security vulnerabilities will be discovered. To keep up with this, firewall technology will have to change. As IPv6 and other new protocols are implemented, new security techniques will be introduced. As security becomes more an issue for all concerned, firewall products will begin to become more common in the home computing environment.

Appendixes

TCP and UDP Common Ports   395

Other Security Tools You Can Use   445

Additional Resources   455

Appendix
A

TCP and UDP Common Ports

Understanding Ports

Computers on the Internet use the TCP/IP suite of network protocols to communicate with each other. Each computer, then, needs to have its own unique IP address so that it can be uniquely identified on the Internet. If only one channel of communication was needed between two computers, the IP address would be the only information necessary to allow applications on computers to talk to one another. However, what happens when more than one application on a computer needs to communicate with applications on one or more other computers? Obviously, there needs to be another mechanism that can be used to help identify the target of a network packet.

Port numbers are used for this additional identification. The destination IP address in a packet specifies the remote computer system that the packet will travel to. The port number, which is also found in the packet header, tells the recipient computer what *application* the packet is intended for. To make an analogy, the IP address is similar to a building's mailing address. Using the mailing address, you will get your letter delivered to the correct building. If you want to get the letter delivered quickly to Bob Smith who can be found on the fourth floor, you would also want to include his office or suite number as part of the address. This number is similar to a port.

The range of port numbers is from 0 to 65535. Ports 0 through 1023 are called *well-known ports* and are assigned by the Internet Assigned Numbers Authority (IANA) organization. The use for these ports has been defined in several Request For Comment documents (most recently RFC 1700), and they don't change frequently. Table A.1 provides a list of these ports and a short description of their usage.

Because well-known ports are usually accessible on a given system by a privileged process or privileged users, it is important when configuring a firewall that you understand what each port is used for so that you can decide which ports you need to block. The Telnet utility generally uses port 23. Note that some more secure versions of a particular utility might use a different port from the ordinary unsecure version of the utility. The documentation that comes with such an application should be able to give you this information.

Ports numbered from 1024 to 65535 are not governed by the IANA. These ports are called *registered ports* and can be used by almost any user process on the system.

In most cases, the User Datagram Protocol (UDP) and Transmission Control Protocol (TCP) use the same port for a particular port. This isn't required, however, so when you are using this table, be sure to check the protocol for each port when looking up its use.

Table A.1 TCP and UDP Well-known Port Numbers

Service	Port Number	Protocol	Description
	0	tcp	Reserved
	0	udp	Reserved
tcpmux	1	tcp	TCP Port Service Multiplexer
tcpmux	1	udp	TCP Port Service Multiplexer
compressnet	2	tcp	Management Utility
compressnet	2	udp	Management Utility
compressnet	3	tcp	Compression Process
compressnet	3	udp	Compression Process
rje	5	tcp	Remote Job Entry
rje	5	udp	Remote Job Entry
echo	7	tcp	Echo
echo	7	udp	Echo
discard	9	tcp	Discard
discard	9	udp	Discard
systat	11	tcp	Active Users
systat	11	udp	Active Users
daytime	13	tcp	Daytime (RFC 867)
daytime	13	udp	Daytime (RFC 867)
qotd	17	tcp	Quote of the Day
qotd	17	udp	Quote of the Day
msp	18	tcp	Message Send Protocol
msp	18	udp	Message Send Protocol
chargen	19	tcp	Character Generator
chargen	19	udp	Character Generator

continues...

397

APPENDIX A TCP and UDP Common Ports

Table A.1 Continued

Service	Port Number	Protocol	Description
ftp-data	20	tcp	File Transfer [Default Data]
ftp-data	20	udp	File Transfer [Default Data]
ftp	21	tcp	File Transfer [Control]
ftp	21	udp	File Transfer [Control]
ssh	22	tcp	SSH Remote Login Protocol
ssh	22	udp	SSH Remote Login Protocol
telnet	23	tcp	Telnet
telnet	23	udp	Telnet
	24	tcp	Any private mail system
	24	udp	Any private mail system
smtp	25	tcp	Simple Mail Transfer
smtp	25	udp	Simple Mail Transfer
nsw-fe	27	tcp	NSW User System FE
nsw-fe	27	udp	NSW User System FE
msg-icp	29	tcp	MSG ICP
msg-icp	29	udp	MSG ICP
msg-auth	31	tcp	MSG Authentication
msg-auth	31	udp	MSG Authentication
dsp	33	tcp	Display Support Protocol
dsp	33	udp	Display Support Protocol
	35	tcp	Any private printer server
	35	udp	Any private printer server
time	37	tcp	Time
time	37	udp	Time
rap	38	tcp	Route Access Protocol
rap	38	udp	Route Access Protocol
rlp	39	tcp	Resource Location Protocol
rlp	39	udp	Resource Location Protocol
graphics	41	tcp	Graphics

Service	Port Number	Protocol	Description
graphics	41	udp	Graphics
name	42	tcp	Host Name Server
name	42	udp	Host Name Server
nameserver	42	tcp	Host Name Server
nameserver	42	udp	Host Name Server
nicname	43	tcp	Who Is
nicname	43	udp	Who Is
mpm-flags	44	tcp	MPM FLAGS Protocol
mpm-flags	44	udp	MPM FLAGS Protocol
mpm	45	tcp	Message Processing Module [recv]
mpm	45	udp	Message Processing Module [recv]
mpm-snd	46	tcp	MPM [default send]
mpm-snd	46	udp	MPM [default send]
ni-ftp	47	tcp	NI FTP
ni-ftp	47	udp	NI FTP
auditd	48	tcp	Digital Audit Daemon
auditd	48	udp	Digital Audit Daemon
tacacs	49	tcp	Login Host Protocol (TACACS)
tacacs	49	udp	Login Host Protocol (TACACS)
re-mail-ck	50	tcp	Remote Mail Checking Protocol
re-mail-ck	50	udp	Remote Mail Checking Protocol
la-maint	51	tcp	IMP Logical Address Maintenance
la-maint	51	udp	IMP Logical Address Maintenance
xns-time	52	tcp	XNS Time Protocol
xns-time	52	udp	XNS Time Protocol
domain	53	tcp	Domain Name Server
domain	53	udp	Domain Name Server
xns-ch	54	tcp	XNS Clearinghouse
xns-ch	54	udp	XNS Clearinghouse

continues...

APPENDIX A TCP and UDP Common Ports

Table A.1 Continued

Service	Port Number	Protocol	Description
isi-gl	55	tcp	ISI Graphics Language
isi-gl	55	udp	ISI Graphics Language
xns-auth	56	tcp	XNS Authentication
xns-auth	56	udp	XNS Authentication
	57	tcp	Any private terminal access
	57	udp	Any private terminal access
xns-mail	58	tcp	XNS Mail
xns-mail	58	udp	XNS Mail
	59	tcp	Any private file service
	59	udp	Any private file service
	60	tcp	Unassigned
	60	udp	Unassigned
ni-mail	61	tcp	NI MAIL
ni-mail	61	udp	NI MAIL
acas	62	tcp	ACA Services
acas	62	udp	ACA Services
whois++	63	tcp	whois++
whois++	63	udp	whois++
covia	64	tcp	Communications Integrator (CI)
covia	64	udp	Communications Integrator (CI)
tacacs-ds	65	tcp	TACACS-Database Service
tacacs-ds	65	udp	TACACS-Database Service
sql*net	66	tcp	Oracle SQL*NET
sql*net	66	udp	Oracle SQL*NET
bootps	67	tcp	Bootstrap Protocol Server
bootps	67	udp	Bootstrap Protocol Server
bootpc	68	tcp	Bootstrap Protocol Client
bootpc	68	udp	Bootstrap Protocol Client
tftp	69	tcp	Trivial File Transfer

Service	Port Number	Protocol	Description
tftp	69	udp	Trivial File Transfer
gopher	70	tcp	Gopher
gopher	70	udp	Gopher
netrjs-1	71	tcp	Remote Job Service
netrjs-1	71	udp	Remote Job Service
netrjs-2	72	tcp	Remote Job Service
netrjs-2	72	udp	Remote Job Service
netrjs-3	73	tcp	Remote Job Service
netrjs-3	73	udp	Remote Job Service
netrjs-4	74	tcp	Remote Job Service
netrjs-4	74	udp	Remote Job Service
	75	tcp	Any private dial out service
	75	udp	Any private dial out service
deos	76	tcp	Distributed External Object Store
deos	76	udp	Distributed External Object Store
	77	tcp	Any private RJE service
	77	udp	Any private RJE service
vettcp	78	tcp	vettcp
vettcp	78	udp	vettcp
finger	79	tcp	Finger
finger	79	udp	Finger
http	80	tcp	World Wide Web HTTP
http	80	udp	World Wide Web HTTP
www	80	tcp	World Wide Web HTTP
www	80	udp	World Wide Web HTTP
www-http	80	tcp	World Wide Web HTTP
www-http	80	udp	World Wide Web HTTP
hosts2-ns	81	tcp	HOSTS2 Name Server
hosts2-ns	81	udp	HOSTS2 Name Server

continues...

Table A.1 Continued

Service	Port Number	Protocol	Description
xfer	82	tcp	XFER Utility
xfer	82	udp	XFER Utility
mit-ml-dev	83	tcp	MIT ML Device
mit-ml-dev	83	udp	MIT ML Device
ctf	84	tcp	Common Trace Facility
ctf	84	udp	Common Trace Facility
mit-ml-dev	85	tcp	MIT ML Device
mit-ml-dev	85	udp	MIT ML Device
mfcobol	86	tcp	Micro Focus Cobol
mfcobol	86	udp	Micro Focus Cobol
	87	tcp	Any private terminal link
	87	udp	Any private terminal link
kerberos	88	tcp	Kerberos
kerberos	88	udp	Kerberos
su-mit-tg	89	tcp	SUMIT Telnet Gateway
su-mit-tg	89	udp	SUMIT Telnet Gateway
dnsix	90	tcp	DNSIX Securit Attribute Token Map
dnsix	90	udp	DNSIX Securit Attribute Token Map
mit-dov	91	tcp	MIT Dover Spooler
mit-dov	91	udp	MIT Dover Spooler
npp	92	tcp	Network Printing Protocol
npp	92	udp	Network Printing Protocol
dcp	93	tcp	Device Control Protocol
dcp	93	udp	Device Control Protocol
objcall	94	tcp	Tivoli Object Dispatcher
objcall	94	udp	Tivoli Object Dispatcher
supdup	95	tcp	SUPDUP
supdup	95	udp	SUPDUP
dixie	96	tcp	DIXIE Protocol Specification

Service	Port Number	Protocol	Description
dixie	96	udp	DIXIE Protocol Specification
swift-rvf	97	tcp	Swift Remote Virtual File Protocol
swift-rvf	97	udp	Swift Remote Virtual File Protocol
tacnews	98	tcp	TAC News
tacnews	98	udp	TAC News
metagram	99	tcp	Metagram Relay
metagram	99	udp	Metagram Relay
newacct	100	tcp	[unauthorized use]
hostname	101	tcp	NIC Host Name Server
hostname	101	udp	NIC Host Name Server
iso-tsap	102	tcp	ISO-TSAP Class 0
iso-tsap	102	udp	ISO-TSAP Class 0
gppitnp	103	tcp	Genesis Point-to-Point Trans Net
gppitnp	103	udp	Genesis Point-to-Point Trans Net
acr-nema	104	tcp	ACR-NEMA Digital Imag. & Comm. 300
acr-nema	104	udp	ACR-NEMA Digital Imag. & Comm. 300
cso	105	tcp	CCSO name server protocol
cso	105	udp	CCSO name server protocol
csnet-ns	105	tcp	Mailbox Name Nameserver
csnet-ns	105	udp	Mailbox Name Nameserver
3com-tsmux	106	tcp	3COM-TSMUX
3com-tsmux	106	udp	3COM-TSMUX
rtelnet	107	tcp	Remote Telnet Service
rtelnet	107	udp	Remote Telnet Service
snagas	108	tcp	SNA Gateway Access Server
snagas	108	udp	SNA Gateway Access Server

continues...

Table A.1 Continued

Service	Port Number	Protocol	Description
pop2	109	tcp	Post Office Protocol - Version 2
pop2	109	udp	Post Office Protocol - Version 2
pop3	110	tcp	Post Office Protocol - Version 3
pop3	110	udp	Post Office Protocol - Version 3
sunrpc	111	tcp	SUN Remote Procedure Call
sunrpc	111	udp	SUN Remote Procedure Call
mcidas	112	tcp	McIDAS Data Transmission Protocol
mcidas	112	udp	McIDAS Data Transmission Protocol
ident	113	tcp	
auth	113	tcp	Authentication Service
auth	113	udp	Authentication Service
audionews	114	tcp	Audio News Multicast
audionews	114	udp	Audio News Multicast
sftp	115	tcp	Simple File Transfer Protocol
sftp	115	udp	Simple File Transfer Protocol
ansanotify	116	tcp	ANSA REX Notify
ansanotify	116	udp	ANSA REX Notify
uucp-path	117	tcp	UUCP Path Service
uucp-path	117	udp	UUCP Path Service
sqlserv	118	tcp	SQL Services
sqlserv	118	udp	SQL Services
nntp	119	tcp	Network News Transfer Protocol
nntp	119	udp	Network News Transfer Protocol
cfdptkt	120	tcp	CFDPTKT
cfdptkt	120	udp	CFDPTKT
erpc	121	tcp	Encore Expedited Remote Pro.Call
erpc	121	udp	Encore Expedited Remote Pro.Call
smakynet	122	tcp	SMAKYNET
smakynet	122	udp	SMAKYNET

Service	Port Number	Protocol	Description
ntp	123	tcp	Network Time Protocol
ntp	123	udp	Network Time Protocol
ansatrader	124	tcp	ANSA REX Trader
ansatrader	124	udp	ANSA REX Trader
locus-map	125	tcp	Locus PC-Interface Net Map Ser
locus-map	125	udp	Locus PC-Interface Net Map Ser
nxedit	126	tcp	NXEdit
nxedit	126	udp	NXEdit
locus-con	127	tcp	Locus PC-Interface Conn Server
locus-con	127	udp	Locus PC-Interface Conn Server
gss-xlicen	128	tcp	GSS X License Verification
gss-xlicen	128	udp	GSS X License Verification
pwdgen	129	tcp	Password Generator Protocol
pwdgen	129	udp	Password Generator Protocol
cisco-fna	130	tcp	Cisco FNATIVE
cisco-fna	130	udp	Cisco FNATIVE
cisco-tna	131	tcp	Cisco TNATIVE
cisco-tna	131	udp	Cisco TNATIVE
cisco-sys	132	tcp	Cisco SYSMAINT
cisco-sys	132	udp	Cisco SYSMAINT
statsrv	133	tcp	Statistics Service
statsrv	133	udp	Statistics Service
ingres-net	134	tcp	INGRES-NET Service
ingres-net	134	udp	INGRES-NET Service
epmap	135	tcp	DCE endpoint resolution
epmap	135	udp	DCE endpoint resolution
profile	136	tcp	PROFILE Naming System
profile	136	udp	PROFILE Naming System
netbios-ns	137	tcp	NETBIOS Name Service

continues...

Table A.1   Continued

Service	Port Number	Protocol	Description
netbios-ns	137	udp	NETBIOS Name Service
netbios-dgm	138	tcp	NETBIOS Datagram Service
netbios-dgm	138	udp	NETBIOS Datagram Service
netbios-ssn	139	tcp	NETBIOS Session Service
netbios-ssn	139	udp	NETBIOS Session Service
emfis-data	140	tcp	EMFIS Data Service
emfis-data	140	udp	EMFIS Data Service
emfis-cntl	141	tcp	EMFIS Control Service
emfis-cntl	141	udp	EMFIS Control Service
bl-idm	142	tcp	Britton-Lee IDM
bl-idm	142	udp	Britton-Lee IDM
imap	143	tcp	Internet Message Access Protocol
imap	143	udp	Internet Message Access Protocol
uma	144	tcp	Universal Management Architecture
uma	144	udp	Universal Management Architecture
uaac	145	tcp	UAAC Protocol
uaac	145	udp	UAAC Protocol
iso-tp0	146	tcp	ISO-IP0
iso-tp0	146	udp	ISO-IP0
iso-ip	147	tcp	ISO-IP
iso-ip	147	udp	ISO-IP
jargon	148	tcp	Jargon
jargon	148	udp	Jargon
aed-512	149	tcp	AED 512 Emulation Service
aed-512	149	udp	AED 512 Emulation Service
sql-net	150	tcp	SQL-NET
sql-net	150	udp	SQL-NET
hems	151	tcp	HEMS
hems	151	udp	HEMS

Service	Port Number	Protocol	Description
bftp	152	tcp	Background File Transfer Program
bftp	152	udp	Background File Transfer Program
sgmp	153	tcp	SGMP
sgmp	153	udp	SGMP
netsc-prod	154	tcp	NETSC
netsc-prod	154	udp	NETSC
netsc-dev	155	tcp	NETSC
netsc-dev	155	udp	NETSC
sqlsrv	156	tcp	SQL Service
sqlsrv	156	udp	SQL Service
knet-cmp	157	tcp	KNET VM Command Message Protocol
knet-cmp	157	udp	KNET VM Command Message Protocol
pcmail-srv	158	tcp	PCMail Server
pcmail-srv	158	udp	PCMail Server
nss-routing	159	tcp	NSS-Routing
nss-routing	159	udp	NSS-Routing
sgmp-traps	160	tcp	SGMP-TRAPS
sgmp-traps	160	udp	SGMP-TRAPS
snmp	161	tcp	SNMP
snmp	161	udp	SNMP
snmptrap	162	tcp	SNMPTRAP
snmptrap	162	udp	SNMPTRAP
cmip-man	163	tcp	CMIP TCP Manager
cmip-man	163	udp	CMIP TCP Manager
cmip-agent	164	tcp	CMIP TCP Agent
smip-agent	164	udp	CMIP TCP Agent
xns-courier	165	tcp	Xerox
xns-courier	165	udp	Xerox

continues...

Table A.1 Continued

Service	Port Number	Protocol	Description
s-net	166	tcp	Sirius Systems
s-net	166	udp	Sirius Systems
namp	167	tcp	NAMP
namp	167	udp	NAMP
rsvd	168	tcp	RSVD
rsvd	168	udp	RSVD
send	169	tcp	SEND
send	169	udp	SEND
print-srv	170	tcp	Network PostScript
print-srv	170	udp	Network PostScript
multiplex	171	tcp	Network Innovations Multiplex
multiplex	171	udp	Network Innovations Multiplex
cl/1	172	tcp	Network Innovations CL/1
cl/1	172	udp	Network Innovations CL/1
xyplex-mux	173	tcp	Xyplex
xyplex-mux	173	udp	Xyplex
mailq	174	tcp	MAILQ
mailq	174	udp	MAILQ
vmnet	175	tcp	VMNET
vmnet	175	udp	VMNET
genrad-mux	176	tcp	GENRAD-MUX
genrad-mux	176	udp	GENRAD-MUX
xdmcp	177	tcp	X Display Manager Control Protocol
xdmcp	177	udp	X Display Manager Control Protocol
nextstep	178	tcp	NextStep Window Server
nextstep	178	udp	NextStep Window Server
bgp	179	tcp	Border Gateway Protocol
bgp	179	udp	Border Gateway Protocol
ris	180	tcp	Intergraph

Service	Port Number	Protocol	Description
ris	180	udp	Intergraph
unify	181	tcp	Unify
unify	181	udp	Unify
audit	182	tcp	Unisys Audit SITP
audit	182	udp	Unisys Audit SITP
ocbinder	183	tcp	OCBinder
ocbinder	183	udp	OCBinder
ocserver	184	tcp	OCServer
ocserver	184	udp	OCServer
remote-kis	185	tcp	Remote-KIS
remote-kis	185	udp	Remote-KIS
kis	186	tcp	KIS Protocol
kis	186	udp	KIS Protocol
aci	187	tcp	Application Communication Interface
aci	187	udp	Application Communication Interface
mumps	188	tcp	Plus Five's MUMPS
mumps	188	udp	Plus Five's MUMPS
qft	189	tcp	Queued File Transport
qft	189	udp	Queued File Transport
gacp	190	tcp	Gateway Access Control Protocol
gacp	190	udp	Gateway Access Control Protocol
prospero	191	tcp	Prospero Directory Service
prospero	191	udp	Prospero Directory Service
osu-nms	192	tcp	OSU Network Monitoring System
osu-nms	192	udp	OSU Network Monitoring System
srmp	193	tcp	Spider Remote Monitoring Protocol
srmp	193	udp	Spider Remote Monitoring Protocol

continues...

409

APPENDIX A TCP and UDP Common Ports

Table A.1 Continued

Service	Port Number	Protocol	Description
irc	194	tcp	Internet Relay Chat Protocol
irc	194	udp	Internet Relay Chat Protocol
dn6-nlm-aud	195	tcp	DNSIX Network Level Module Audit
dn6-nlm-aud	195	udp	DNSIX Network Level Module Audit
dn6-smm-red	196	tcp	DNSIX Session Mgt Module Audit Redir
dn6-smm-red	196	udp	DNSIX Session Mgt Module Audit Redir
dls	197	tcp	Directory Location Service
dls	197	udp	Directory Location Service
dls-mon	198	tcp	Directory Location Service Monitor
dls-mon	198	udp	Directory Location Service Monitor
smux	199	tcp	SMUX
smux	199	udp	SMUX
src	200	tcp	IBM System Resource Controller
src	200	udp	IBM System Resource Controller
at-rtmp	201	tcp	AppleTalk Routing Maintenance
at-rtmp	201	udp	AppleTalk Routing Maintenance
at-nbp	202	tcp	AppleTalk Name Binding
at-nbp	202	udp	AppleTalk Name Binding
at-3	203	tcp	AppleTalk Unused
at-3	203	udp	AppleTalk Unused
at-echo	204	tcp	AppleTalk Echo
at-echo	204	udp	AppleTalk Echo
at-5	205	tcp	AppleTalk Unused
at-5	205	udp	AppleTalk Unused
at-zis	206	tcp	AppleTalk Zone Information
at-zis	206	udp	AppleTalk Zone Information
at-7	207	tcp	AppleTalk Unused

Service	Port Number	Protocol	Description
at-7	207	udp	AppleTalk Unused
at-8	208	tcp	AppleTalk Unused
at-8	208	udp	AppleTalk Unused
qmtp	209	tcp	The Quick Mail Transfer Protocol
qmtp	209	udp	The Quick Mail Transfer Protocol
z39.50	210	tcp	ANSI Z39.50
z39.50	210	udp	ANSI Z39.50
914c/g	211	tcp	Texas Instruments 914C/G Terminal
914c/g	211	udp	Texas Instruments 914C/G Terminal
anet	212	tcp	ATEXSSTR
anet	212	udp	ATEXSSTR
ipx	213	tcp	IPX
ipx	213	udp	IPX
vmpwscs	214	tcp	VM PWSCS
vmpwscs	214	udp	VM PWSCS
softpc	215	tcp	Insignia Solutions
softpc	215	udp	Insignia Solutions
CAIlic	216	tcp	Computer Associates Int'l License Server
CAIlic	216	udp	Computer Associates Int'l License Server
dbase	217	tcp	dBASE UNIX
dbase	217	udp	dBASE UNIX
mpp	218	tcp	Netix Message Posting Protocol
mpp	218	udp	Netix Message Posting Protocol
uarps	219	tcp	Unisys ARPs
uarps	219	udp	Unisys ARPs
imap3	220	tcp	Interactive Mail Access Protocol, V3
imap3	220	udp	Interactive Mail Access Protocol, V3

continues...

411

Table A.1 Continued

Service	Port Number	Protocol	Description
fln-spx	221	tcp	Berkeley rlogind with SPX
authfln-spx	221	udp	Berkeley rlogind with SPX
authrsh-spx	222	tcp	Berkeley rshd with SPX auth
rsh-spx	222	udp	Berkeley rshd with SPX auth
cdc	223	tcp	Certificate Distribution Center
cdc	223	udp	Certificate Distribution Center
masqdialer	224	tcp	masqdialer
masqdialer	224	udp	masqdialer
direct	242	tcp	Direct
direct	242	udp	Direct
sur-meas	243	tcp	Survey Measurement
sur-meas	243	udp	Survey Measurement
dayna	244	tcp	Dayna
dayna	244	udp	Dayna
link	245	tcp	LINK
link	245	udp	LINK
dsp3270	246	tcp	Display Systems Protocol
dsp3270	246	udp	Display Systems Protocol
subntbcst_tftp	247	tcp	SUBNTBCST_TFTP
subntbcst_tftp	247	udp	SUBNTBCST_TFTP
bhfhs	248	tcp	bhfhs
bhfhs	248	udp	bhfhs
rap	256	tcp	RAP
rap	256	udp	RAP
set	257	tcp	Secure Electronic Transaction
set	257	udp	Secure Electronic Transaction
yak-chat	258	tcp	Yak Winsock Personal Chat
yak-chat	258	udp	Yak Winsock Personal Chat
esro-gen	259	tcp	Efficient Short Remote Operations

Service	Port Number	Protocol	Description
esro-gen	259	udp	Efficient Short Remote Operations
openport	260	tcp	Openport
openport	260	udp	Openport
nsiiops	261	tcp	IIOP Name Service over TLS/SSL
nsiiops	261	udp	IIOP Name Service over TLS/SSL
arcisdms	262	tcp	Arcisdms
arcisdms	262	udp	Arcisdms
hdap	263	tcp	HDAP
hdap	263	udp	HDAP
bgmp	264	tcp	BGMP
bgmp	264	udp	BGMP
http-mgmt	280	tcp	http-mgmt
http-mgmt	280	udp	http-mgmt
personal-link	281	tcp	Personal Link
personal-link	281	udp	Personal Link
cableport-ax	282	tcp	Cable Port AX
cableport-ax	282	udp	Cable Port AX
rescap	283	tcp	rescap
rescap	283	udp	rescap
novastorbakcup	308	tcp	Novastor Backup
novastorbakcup	308	udp	Novastor Backup
entrusttime	309	tcp	EntrustTime
entrusttime	309	udp	EntrustTime
bhmds	310	tcp	bhmds
bhmds	310	udp	bhmds
asip-webadmin	311	tcp	AppleShare IP WebAdmin
asip-webadmin	311	udp	AppleShare IP WebAdmin
vslmp	312	tcp	VSLMP
vslmp	312	udp	VSLMP

continues...

Table A.1 Continued

Service	Port Number	Protocol	Description
magenta-logic	313	tcp	Magenta Logic
magenta-logic	313	udp	Magenta Logic
opalis-robot	314	tcp	Opalis Robot
opalis-robot	314	udp	Opalis Robot
dpsi	315	tcp	DPSI
dpsi	315	udp	DPSI
decauth	316	tcp	decAuth
decauth	316	udp	decAuth
zannet	317	tcp	Zannet
zannet	317	udp	Zannet
pkix-timestamp	318	tcp	PKIX TimeStamp
pkix-timestamp	318	udp	PKIX TimeStamp
ptp-event	319	tcp	PTP Event
ptp-event	319	udp	PTP Event
ptp-general	320	tcp	PTP General
ptp-general	320	udp	PTP General
pip	321	tcp	PIP
pip	321	udp	PIP
rtsps	322	tcp	RTSPS
rtsps	322	udp	RTSPS
pdap	344	tcp	Prospero Data Access Protocol
pdap	344	udp	Prospero Data Access Protocol
pawserv	345	tcp	Perf Analysis Workbench
pawserv	345	udp	Perf Analysis Workbench
zserv	346	tcp	Zebra server
zserv	346	udp	Zebra server
fatserv	347	tcp	Fatmen Server
fatserv	347	udp	Fatmen Server
csi-sgwp	348	tcp	Cabletron Management Protocol

Service	Port Number	Protocol	Description
csi-sgwp	348	udp	Cabletron Management Protocol
mftp	349	tcp	mftp
mftp	349	udp	mftp
matip-type-a	350	tcp	MATIP Type A
matip-type-a	350	udp	MATIP Type A
matip-type-b	351	tcp	MATIP Type B
matip-type-b	351	udp	MATIP Type B
bhoetty	351	tcp	bhoetty
bhoetty	351	udp	bhoetty
dtag-ste-sb	352	tcp	DTAG
dtag-ste-sb	352	udp	DTAG
bhoedap4	352	tcp	bhoedap4
bhoedap4	352	udp	bhoedap4
ndsauth	353	tcp	NDSAUTH
ndsauth	353	udp	NDSAUTH
bh611	354	tcp	bh611
bh611	354	udp	bh611
datex-asn	355	tcp	DATEX-ASN
datex-asn	355	udp	DATEX-ASN
cloanto-net-1	356	tcp	Cloanto Net 1
cloanto-net-1	356	udp	Cloanto Net 1
bhevent	357	tcp	bhevent
bhevent	357	udp	bhevent
shrinkwrap	358	tcp	Shrinkwrap
shrinkwrap	358	udp	Shrinkwrap
tenebris_nts	359	tcp	Tenebris Network Trace Service
tenebris_nts	359	udp	Tenebris Network Trace Service
scoi2odialog	360	tcp	scoi2odialog
scoi2odialog	360	udp	scoi2odialog

continues...

Table A.1 Continued

Service	Port Number	Protocol	Description
semantix	361	tcp	Semantix
semantix	361	udp	Semantix
srssend	362	tcp	SRS Send
srssend	362	udp	SRS Send
rsvp_tunnel	363	tcp	RSVP Tunnel
rsvp_tunnel	363	udp	RSVP Tunnel
aurora-cmgr	364	tcp	Aurora CMGR
aurora-cmgr	364	udp	Aurora CMGR
dtk	365	tcp	DTK
dtk	365	udp	DTK
odmr	366	tcp	ODMR
odmr	366	udp	ODMR
mortgageware	367	tcp	MortgageWare
mortgageware	367	udp	MortgageWare
qbikgdp	368	tcp	QbikGDP
qbikgdp	368	udp	QbikGDP
rpc2portmap	369	tcp	rpc2portmap
rpc2portmap	369	udp	rpc2portmap
codaauth2	370	tcp	codaauth2
codaauth2	370	udp	codaauth2
clearcase	371	tcp	Clearcase
clearcase	371	udp	Clearcase
ulistproc	372	tcp	ListProcessor
ulistproc	372	udp	ListProcessor
legent-1	373	tcp	Legent Corporation
legent-1	373	udp	Legent Corporation
legent-2	374	tcp	Legent Corporation
legent-2	374	udp	Legent Corporation
hassle	375	tcp	Hassle

Service	Port Number	Protocol	Description
hassle	375	udp	Hassle
nip	376	tcp	Amiga Envoy Network Inquiry Proto
nip	376	udp	Amiga Envoy Network Inquiry Proto
tnETOS	377	tcp	NEC Corporation
tnETOS	377	udp	NEC Corporation
dsETOS	378	tcp	NEC Corporation
dsETOS	378	udp	NEC Corporation
is99c	379	tcp	TIA/EIA/IS-99 modem client
is99c	379	udp	TIA/EIA/IS-99 modem client
is99s	380	tcp	TIA/EIA/IS-99 modem server
is99s	380	udp	TIA/EIA/IS-99 modem server
hp-collector	381	tcp	hp performance data collector
hp-collector	381	udp	hp performance data collector
hp-managed-node	382	tcp	hp performance data managed node
hp-managed-node	382	udp	hp performance data managed node
hp-alarm-mgr	383	tcp	hp performance data alarm manager
hp-alarm-mgr	383	udp	hp performance data alarm manager
arns	384	tcp	A Remote Network Server System
arns	384	udp	A Remote Network Server System
ibm-app	385	tcp	IBM Application
ibm-app	385	udp	IBM Application
asa	386	tcp	ASA Message Router Object Def.
asa	386	udp	ASA Message Router Object Def.
aurp	387	tcp	Appletalk Update-Based Routing Pro.
aurp	387	udp	Appletalk Update-Based Routing Pro.
unidata-ldm	388	tcp	Unidata LDM Version 4
unidata-ldm	388	udp	Unidata LDM Version 4

continues...

417

APPENDIX A   TCP and UDP Common Ports

Table A.1   Continued

Service	Port Number	Protocol	Description
ldap	389	tcp	Lightweight Directory Access Protocol
ldap	389	udp	Lightweight Directory Access Protocol
uis	390	tcp	UIS
uis	390	udp	UIS
synotics-relay	391	tcp	SynOptics SNMP Relay Port
synotics-relay	391	udp	SynOptics SNMP Relay Port
synotics-broker	392	tcp	SynOptics Port Broker Port
synotics-broker	392	udp	SynOptics Port Broker Port
dis	393	tcp	Data Interpretation System
dis	393	udp	Data Interpretation System
embl-ndt	394	tcp	EMBL Nucleic Data Transfer
embl-ndt	394	udp	EMBL Nucleic Data Transfer
netcp	395	tcp	NETscout Control Protocol
netcp	395	udp	NETscout Control Protocol
netware-ip	396	tcp	Novell Netware over IP
netware-ip	396	udp	Novell Netware over IP
mptn	397	tcp	Multi Protocol Trans. Net.
mptn	397	udp	Multi Protocol Trans. Net.
kryptolan	398	tcp	Kryptolan
kryptolan	398	udp	Kryptolan
iso-tsap-c2	399	tcp	ISO Transport Class 2 Non-Control over TCP
iso-tsap-c2	399	udp	ISO Transport Class 2 Non-Control over TCP
work-sol	400	tcp	Workstation Solutions
work-sol	400	udp	Workstation Solutions
ups	401	tcp	Uninterruptible Power Supply

Service	Port Number	Protocol	Description
ups	401	udp	Uninterruptible Power Supply
genie	402	tcp	Genie Protocol
genie	402	udp	Genie Protocol
decap	403	tcp	decap
decap	403	udp	decap
nced	404	tcp	nced
nced	404	udp	nced
ncld	405	tcp	ncld
ncld	405	udp	ncld
imsp	406	tcp	Interactive Mail Support Protocol
imsp	406	udp	Interactive Mail Support Protocol
timbuktu	407	tcp	Timbuktu
timbuktu	407	udp	Timbuktu
prm-sm	408	tcp	Prospero Resource Manager Sys. Man.
prm-sm	408	udp	Prospero Resource Manager Sys. Man.
prm-nm	409	tcp	Prospero Resource Manager Node Man.
prm-nm	409	udp	Prospero Resource Manager Node Man.
decladebug	410	tcp	DECLadebug Remote Debug Protocol
decladebug	410	udp	DECLadebug Remote Debug Protocol
rmt	411	tcp	Remote MT Protocol
rmt	411	udp	Remote MT Protocol
synoptics-trap	412	tcp	Trap Convention Port
synoptics-trap	412	udp	Trap Convention Port
smsp	413	tcp	SMSP
smsp	413	udp	SMSP

continues…

Table A.1 Continued

Service	Port Number	Protocol	Description
infoseek	414	tcp	InfoSeek
infoseek	414	udp	InfoSeek
bnet	415	tcp	BNet
bnet	415	udp	BNet
silverplatter	416	tcp	Silverplatter
silverplatter	416	udp	Silverplatter
onmux	417	tcp	Onmux
onmux	417	udp	Onmux
hyper-g	418	tcp	Hyper-G
hyper-g	418	udp	Hyper-G
ariel1	419	tcp	Ariel
ariel1	419	udp	Ariel
smpte	420	tcp	SMPTE
smpte	420	udp	SMPTE
ariel2	421	tcp	Ariel
ariel2	421	udp	Ariel
ariel3	422	tcp	Ariel
ariel3	422	udp	Ariel
opc-job-start	423	tcp	IBM Operations Planning and Control Start
opc-job-start	423	udp	IBM Operations Planning and Control Start
opc-job-track	424	tcp	IBM Operations Planning and Control Track
opc-job-track	424	udp	IBM Operations Planning and Control Track
icad-el	425	tcp	ICAD
icad-el	425	udp	ICAD

Service	Port Number	Protocol	Description
smartsdp	426	tcp	smartsdp
smartsdp	426	udp	smartsdp
svrloc	427	tcp	Server Location
svrloc	427	udp	Server Location
ocs_cmu	428	tcp	OCS_CMU
ocs_cmu	428	udp	OCS_CMU
ocs_amu	429	tcp	OCS_AMU
ocs_amu	429	udp	OCS_AMU
utmpsd	430	tcp	UTMPSD
utmpsd	430	udp	UTMPSD
utmpcd	431	tcp	UTMPCD
utmpcd	431	udp	UTMPCD
iasd	432	tcp	IASD
iasd	432	udp	IASD
nnsp	433	tcp	NNSP
nnsp	433	udp	NNSP
mobileip-agent	434	tcp	MobileIP-Agent
mobileip-agent	434	udp	MobileIP-Agent
mobilip-mn	435	tcp	MobilIP-MN
mobilip-mn	435	udp	MobilIP-MN
dna-cml	436	tcp	DNA-CML
dna-cml	436	udp	DNA-CML
comscm	437	tcp	comscm
comscm	437	udp	comscm
dsfgw	438	tcp	dsfgw
dsfgw	438	udp	dsfgw
dasp	439	tcp	dasp
dasp	439	udp	dasp
sgcp	440	tcp	sgcp

continues...

421

Table A.1 Continued

Service	Port Number	Protocol	Description
sgcp	440	udp	sgcp
decvms-sysmgt	441	tcp	decvms-sysmgt
decvms-sysmgt	441	udp	decvms-sysmgt
cvc_hostd	442	tcp	cvc_hostd
cvc_hostd	442	udp	cvc_hostd
https	443	tcp	http protocol over TLS/SSL
https	443	udp	http protocol over TLS/SSL
snpp	444	tcp	Simple Network Paging Protocol
snpp	444	udp	Simple Network Paging Protocol
microsoft-ds	445	tcp	Microsoft-DS
microsoft-ds	445	udp	Microsoft-DS
ddm-rdb	446	tcp	DDM-RDB
ddm-rdb	446	udp	DDM-RDB
ddm-dfm	447	tcp	DDM-RFM
ddm-dfm	447	udp	DDM-RFM
ddm-ssl	448	tcp	DDM-SSL
ddm-ssl	448	udp	DDM-SSL
as-servermap	449	tcp	AS Server Mapper
as-servermap	449	udp	AS Server Mapper
tserver	450	tcp	TServer
tserver	450	udp	TServer
sfs-smp-net	451	tcp	Cray Network Semaphore server
sfs-smp-net	451	udp	Cray Network Semaphore server
sfs-config	452	tcp	Cray SFS config server
sfs-config	452	udp	Cray SFS config server
creativeserver	453	tcp	CreativeServer
creativeserver	453	udp	CreativeServer
contentserver	454	tcp	ContentServer
contentserver	454	udp	ContentServer

Service	Port Number	Protocol	Description
creativepartnr	455	tcp	CreativePartnr
creativepartnr	455	udp	CreativePartnr
macon-tcp	456	tcp	macon-tcp
macon-udp	456	udp	macon-udp
scohelp	457	tcp	scohelp
scohelp	457	udp	scohelp
appleqtc	458	tcp	apple quick time
appleqtc	458	udp	apple quick time
ampr-rcmd	459	tcp	ampr-rcmd
ampr-rcmd	459	udp	ampr-rcmd
skronk	460	tcp	skronk
skronk	460	udp	skronk
datasurfsrv	461	tcp	DataRampSrv
datasurfsrv	461	udp	DataRampSrv
datasurfsrvsec	462	tcp	DataRampSrvSec
datasurfsrvsec	462	udp	DataRampSrvSec
alpes	463	tcp	alpes
alpes	463	udp	alpes
kpasswd	464	tcp	kpasswd
kpasswd	464	udp	kpasswd
digital-vrc	466	tcp	digital-vrc
digital-vrc	466	udp	digital-vrc
mylex-mapd	467	tcp	mylex-mapd
mylex-mapd	467	udp	mylex-mapd
photuris	468	tcp	proturis
photuris	468	udp	proturis
rcp	469	tcp	Radio Control Protocol
rcp	469	udp	Radio Control Protocol
scx-proxy	470	tcp	scx-proxy

continues...

423

APPENDIX A TCP and UDP Common Ports

Table A.1 Continued

Service	Port Number	Protocol	Description
scx-proxy	470	udp	scx-proxy
mondex	471	tcp	Mondex
mondex	471	udp	Mondex
ljk-login	472	tcp	ljk-login
ljk-login	472	udp	ljk-login
hybrid-pop	473	tcp	hybrid-pop
hybrid-pop	473	udp	hybrid-pop
tn-tl-w1	474	tcp	tn-tl-w1
tn-tl-w2	474	udp	tn-tl-w2
tcpnethaspsrv	475	tcp	tcpnethaspsrv
tcpnethaspsrv	475	udp	tcpnethaspsrv
tn-tl-fd1	476	tcp	tn-tl-fd1
tn-tl-fd1	476	udp	tn-tl-fd1
ss7ns	477	tcp	ss7ns
ss7ns	477	udp	ss7ns
spsc	478	tcp	spsc
spsc	478	udp	spsc
iafserver	479	tcp	iafserver
iafserver	479	udp	iafserver
iafdbase	480	tcp	iafdbase
iafdbase	480	udp	iafdbase
ph	481	tcp	Ph service
ph	481	udp	Ph service
bgs-nsi	482	tcp	bgs-nsi
bgs-nsi	482	udp	bgs-nsi
ulpnet	483	tcp	ulpnet
ulpnet	483	udp	ulpnet

Service	Port Number	Protocol	Description
integra-sme	484	tcp	Integra Software Management Environment
integra-sme	484	udp	Integra Software Management Environment
powerburst	485	tcp	Air Soft Power Burst
powerburst	485	udp	Air Soft Power Burst
avian	486	tcp	avian
avian	486	udp	avian
saft	487	tcp	saft Simple Asynchronous File Transfer
saft	487	udp	saft Simple Asynchronous File Transfer
gss-http	488	tcp	gss-http
gss-http	488	udp	gss-http
nest-protocol	489	tcp	nest-protocol
nest-protocol	489	udp	nest-protocol
micom-pfs	490	tcp	micom-pfs
micom-pfs	490	udp	micom-pfs
go-login	491	tcp	go-login
go-login	491	udp	go-login
ticf-1	492	tcp	Transport Independent Convergence for FNA
ticf-1	492	udp	Transport Independent Convergence for FNA
ticf-2	493	tcp	Transport Independent Convergence for FNA
ticf-2	493	udp	Transport Independent Convergence for FNA
pov-ray	494	tcp	POV-Ray
pov-ray	494	udp	POV-Ray

continues...

APPENDIX A TCP and UDP Common Ports

Table A.1 Continued

Service	Port Number	Protocol	Description
intecourier	495	tcp	intecourier
intecourier	495	udp	intecourier
pim-rp-disc	496	tcp	PIM-RP-DISC
pim-rp-disc	496	udp	PIM-RP-DISC
dantz	497	tcp	dantz
dantz	497	udp	dantz
siam	498	tcp	siam
siam	498	udp	siam
iso-ill	499	tcp	ISO ILL Protocol
iso-ill	499	udp	ISO ILL Protocol
isakmp	500	tcp	isakmp
isakmp	500	udp	isakmp
stmf	501	tcp	STMF
stmf	501	udp	STMF
asa-appl-proto	502	tcp	asa-appl-proto
asa-appl-proto	502	udp	asa-appl-proto
intrinsa	503	tcp	Intrinsa
intrinsa	503	udp	Intrinsa
citadel	504	tcp	citadel
citadel	504	udp	citadel
mailbox-lm	505	tcp	mailbox-lm
mailbox-lm	505	udp	mailbox-lm
ohimsrv	506	tcp	ohimsrv
ohimsrv	506	udp	ohimsrv
crs	507	tcp	crs
crs	507	udp	crs
xvttp	508	tcp	xvttp
xvttp	508	udp	xvttp
snare	509	tcp	snare

Service	Port Number	Protocol	Description
snare	509	udp	snare
fcp	510	tcp	FirstClass Protocol
fcp	510	udp	FirstClass Protocol
passgo	511	tcp	PassGo
passgo	511	udp	PassGo
exec	512	tcp	remote process execution;
comsat	512	udp	
biff	512	udp	used by mail system to notify users
login	513	tcp	remote login a la telnet
who	513	udp	maintains data bases showing who's
shell	514	tcp	cmd
syslog	514	udp	
printer	515	tcp	spooler
printer	515	udp	spooler
videotex	516	tcp	videotex
videotex	516	udp	videotex
talk	517	tcp	like tenex link, but across
talk	517	udp	like tenex link, but across
ntalk	518	tcp	
ntalk	518	udp	
utime	519	tcp	unixtime
utime	519	udp	unixtime
efs	520	tcp	extended file name server
router	520	udp	local routing process (on site)
ripng	521	tcp	ripng
ripng	521	udp	ripng
ulp	522	tcp	ULP
ulp	522	udp	ULP
ibm-db2	523	tcp	IBM-DB2

continues...

Table A.1 Continued

Service	Port Number	Protocol	Description
ibm-db2	523	udp	IBM-DB2
ncp	524	tcp	NCP
ncp	524	udp	NCP
timed	525	tcp	timeserver
timed	525	udp	timeserver
tempo	526	tcp	newdate
tempo	526	udp	newdate
stx	527	tcp	Stock IXChange
stx	527	udp	Stock IXChange
custix	528	tcp	Customer IXChange
custix	528	udp	Customer IXChange
irc-serv	529	tcp	IRC-SERV
irc-serv	529	udp	IRC-SERV
courier	530	tcp	rpc
courier	530	udp	rpc
conference	531	tcp	chat
conference	531	udp	chat
netnews	532	tcp	readnews
netnews	532	udp	readnews
netwall	533	tcp	for emergency broadcasts
netwall	533	udp	for emergency broadcasts
mm-admin	534	tcp	MegaMedia Admin
mm-admin	534	udp	MegaMedia Admin
iiop	535	tcp	iiop
iiop	535	udp	iiop
opalis-rdv	536	tcp	opalis-rdv
opalis-rdv	536	udp	opalis-rdv
nmsp	537	tcp	Networked Media Streaming Protocol
nmsp	537	udp	Networked Media Streaming Protocol

Service	Port Number	Protocol	Description
gdomap	538	tcp	gdomap
gdomap	538	udp	gdomap
apertus-ldp	539	tcp	Apertus Technologies Load Determination
apertus-ldp	539	udp	Apertus Technologies Load Determination
uucp	540	tcp	uucpd
uucp	540	udp	uucpd
uucp-rlogin	541	tcp	uucp-rlogin
uucp-rlogin	541	udp	uucp-rlogin
commerce	542	tcp	commerce
commerce	542	udp	commerce
klogin	543	tcp	
klogin	543	udp	
kshell	544	tcp	krcmd
kshell	544	udp	krcmd
appleqtcsrvr	545	tcp	appleqtcsrvr
appleqtcsrvr	545	udp	appleqtcsrvr
dhcpv6-client	546	tcp	DHCPv6 Client
dhcpv6-client	546	udp	DHCPv6 Client
dhcpv6-server	547	tcp	DHCPv6 Server
dhcpv6-server	547	udp	DHCPv6 Server
afpovertcp	548	tcp	AFP over TCP
afpovertcp	548	udp	AFP over TCP
idfp	549	tcp	IDFP
idfp	549	udp	IDFP
new-rwho	550	tcp	new-who
new-rwho	550	udp	new-who
cybercash	551	tcp	cybercash

continues...

Table A.1 Continued

Service	Port Number	Protocol	Description
cybercash	551	udp	cybercash
deviceshare	552	tcp	deviceshare
deviceshare	552	udp	deviceshare
pirp	553	tcp	pirp
pirp	553	udp	pirp
rtsp	554	tcp	Real Time Stream Control Protocol
rtsp	554	udp	Real Time Stream Control Protocol
dsf	555	tcp	
dsf	555	udp	
remotefs	556	tcp	rfs server
remotefs	556	udp	rfs server
openvms-sysipc	557	tcp	openvms-sysipc
openvms-sysipc	557	udp	openvms-sysipc
sdnskmp	558	tcp	SDNSKMP
sdnskmp	558	udp	SDNSKMP
teedtap	559	tcp	TEEDTAP
teedtap	559	udp	TEEDTAP
rmonitor	560	tcp	rmonitord
rmonitor	560	udp	rmonitord
monitor	561	tcp	
monitor	561	udp	
chshell	562	tcp	chcmd
chshell	562	udp	chcmd
nntps	563	tcp	nntp protocol over TLS SSL (was snntp)
nntps	563	udp	nntp protocol over TLS SSL (was snntp)
9pfs	564	tcp	plan 9 file service
9pfs	564	udp	plan 9 file service
whoami	565	tcp	whoami

Service	Port Number	Protocol	Description
whoami	565	udp	whoami
streettalk	566	tcp	streettalk
streettalk	566	udp	streettalk
banyan-rpc	567	tcp	banyan-rpc
banyan-rpc	567	udp	banyan-rpc
ms-shuttle	568	tcp	microsoft shuttle
ms-shuttle	568	udp	microsoft shuttle
ms-rome	569	tcp	microsoft rome
ms-rome	569	udp	microsoft rome
meter	570	tcp	demon
meter	570	udp	demon
meter	571	tcp	udemon
meter	571	udp	udemon
sonar	572	tcp	sonar
sonar	572	udp	sonar
banyan-vip	573	tcp	banyan-vip
banyan-vip	573	udp	banyan-vip
ftp-agent	574	tcp	FTP Software Agent System
ftp-agent	574	udp	FTP Software Agent System
vemmi	575	tcp	VEMMI
vemmi	575	udp	VEMMI
ipcd	576	tcp	ipcd
ipcd	576	udp	ipcd
vnas	577	tcp	vnas
vnas	577	udp	vnas
ipdd	578	tcp	ipdd
ipdd	578	udp	ipdd
decbsrv	579	tcp	decbsrv
decbsrv	579	udp	decbsrv

continues...

431

APPENDIX A TCP and UDP Common Ports

Table A.1 Continued

Service	Port Number	Protocol	Description
sntp-heartbeat	580	tcp	SNTP HEARTBEAT
sntp-heartbeat	580	udp	SNTP HEARTBEAT
bdp	581	tcp	Bundle Discovery Protocol
bdp	581	udp	Bundle Discovery Protocol
scc-security	582	tcp	SCC Security
scc-security	582	udp	SCC Security
philips-vc	583	tcp	Philips Video-Conferencing
philips-vc	583	udp	Philips Video-Conferencing
keyserver	584	tcp	Key Server
keyserver	584	udp	Key Server
imap4-ssl	585	tcp	IMAP4+SSL (use 993 instead)
imap4-ssl	585	udp	IMAP4+SSL (use 993 instead)
password-chg	586	tcp	Password Change
password-chg	586	udp	Password Change
submission	587	tcp	Submission
submission	587	udp	Submission
cal	588	tcp	CAL
cal	588	udp	CAL
eyelink	589	tcp	EyeLink
eyelink	589	udp	EyeLink
tns-cml	590	tcp	TNS CML
tns-cml	590	udp	TNS CML
http-alt	591	tcp	FileMaker, Inc. - HTTP Alternate (see Port 80)
http-alt	591	udp	FileMaker, Inc. - HTTP Alternate (see Port 80)
eudora-set	592	tcp	Eudora Set
eudora-set	592	udp	Eudora Set
http-rpc-epmap	593	tcp	HTTP RPC Ep Map

Service	Port Number	Protocol	Description
http-rpc-epmap	593	udp	HTTP RPC Ep Map
tpip	594	tcp	TPIP
tpip	594	udp	TPIP
cab-protocol	595	tcp	CAB Protocol
cab-protocol	595	udp	CAB Protocol
smsd	596	tcp	SMSD
smsd	596	udp	SMSD
ptcnameservice	597	tcp	PTC Name Service
ptcnameservice	597	udp	PTC Name Service
sco-websrvrmg3	598	tcp	SCO Web Server Manager 3
sco-websrvrmg3	598	udp	SCO Web Server Manager 3
acp	599	tcp	Aeolon Core Protocol
acp	599	udp	Aeolon Core Protocol
ipcserver	600	tcp	Sun IPC server
ipcserver	600	udp	Sun IPC server
urm	606	tcp	Cray Unified Resource Manager
urm	606	udp	Cray Unified Resource Manager
nqs	607	tcp	nqs
nqs	607	udp	nqs
sift-uft	608	tcp	Sender-Initiated Unsolicited File Transfer
sift-uft	608	udp	Sender-Initiated Unsolicited File Transfer
npmp-trap	609	tcp	npmp-trap
npmp-trap	609	udp	npmp-trap
npmp-local	610	tcp	npmp-local
npmp-local	610	udp	npmp-local
npmp-gui	611	tcp	npmp-gui
npmp-gui	611	udp	npmp-gui
hmmp-ind	612	tcp	HMMP Indication

continues...

433

Table A.1 Continued

Service	Port Number	Protocol	Description
hmmp-ind	612	udp	HMMP Indication
hmmp-op	613	tcp	HMMP Operation
hmmp-op	613	udp	HMMP Operation
sshell	614	tcp	SSLshell
sshell	614	udp	SSLshell
sco-inetmgr	615	tcp	Internet Configuration Manager
sco-inetmgr	615	udp	Internet Configuration Manager
sco-sysmgr	616	tcp	SCO System Administration Server
sco-sysmgr	616	udp	SCO System Administration Server
sco-dtmgr	617	tcp	SCO Desktop Administration Server
sco-dtmgr	617	udp	SCO Desktop Administration Server
dei-icda	618	tcp	DEI-ICDA
dei-icda	618	udp	DEI-ICDA
digital-evm	619	tcp	Digital EVM
digital-evm	619	udp	Digital EVM
sco-websrvrmgr	620	tcp	SCO WebServer Manager
sco-websrvrmgr	620	udp	SCO WebServer Manager
escp-ip	621	tcp	ESCP
escp-ip	621	udp	ESCP
collaborator	622	tcp	Collaborator
collaborator	622	udp	Collaborator
aux_bus_shunt	623	tcp	Aux Bus Shunt
aux_bus_shunt	623	udp	Aux Bus Shunt
cryptoadmin	624	tcp	Crypto Admin
cryptoadmin	624	udp	Crypto Admin
dec_dlm	625	tcp	DEC DLM
dec_dlm	625	udp	DEC DLM
asia	626	tcp	ASIA
asia	626	udp	ASIA

Service	Port Number	Protocol	Description
passgo-tivoli	627	tcp	PassGo Tivoli
passgo-tivoli	627	udp	PassGo Tivoli
qmqp	628	tcp	QMQP
qmqp	628	udp	QMQP
3com-amp3	629	tcp	3Com AMP3
3com-amp3	629	udp	3Com AMP3
rda	630	tcp	RDA
rda	630	udp	RDA
ipp	631	tcp	IPP (Internet Printing Protocol)
ipp	631	udp	IPP (Internet Printing Protocol)
bmpp	632	tcp	bmpp
bmpp	632	udp	bmpp
servstat	633	tcp	Service Status update (Sterling Software)
servstat	633	udp	Service Status update (Sterling Software)
ginad	634	tcp	ginad
ginad	634	udp	ginad
rlzdbase	635	tcp	RLZ Dbase
rlzdbase	635	udp	RLZ Dbase
ldaps	636	tcp	ldap protocol over TLS SSL (was sldap)
ldaps	636	udp	ldap protocol over TLS SSL (was sldap)
lanserver	637	tcp	lanserver
lanserver	637	udp	lanserver
mcns-sec	638	tcp	mcns-sec
mcns-sec	638	udp	mcns-sec
msdp	639	tcp	MSDP

continues...

APPENDIX A TCP and UDP Common Ports

Table A.1	Continued		
Service	Port Number	Protocol	Description
msdp	639	udp	MSDP
entrust-sps	640	tcp	entrust-sps
entrust-sps	640	udp	entrust-sps
repcmd	641	tcp	repcmd
repcmd	641	udp	repcmd
esro-emsdp	642	tcp	ESRO-EMSDP V1.3
esro-emsdp	642	udp	ESRO-EMSDP V1.3
sanity	643	tcp	SANity
sanity	643	udp	SANity
dwr	644	tcp	dwr
dwr	644	udp	dwr
pssc	645	tcp	PSSC
pssc	645	udp	PSSC
ldp	646	tcp	LDP
ldp	646	udp	LDP
dhcp-failover	647	tcp	DHCP Failover
dhcp-failover	647	udp	DHCP Failover
rrp	648	tcp	Registry Registrar Protocol (RRP)
rrp	648	udp	Registry Registrar Protocol (RRP)
aminet	649	tcp	Aminet
aminet	649	udp	Aminet
obex	650	tcp	OBEX
obex	650	udp	OBEX
ieee-mms	651	tcp	IEEE MMS
ieee-mms	651	udp	IEEE MMS
udlr-dtcp	652	tcp	UDLR_DTCP
udlr-dtcp	652	udp	UDLR_DTCP
repscmd	653	tcp	RepCmd
repscmd	653	udp	RepCmd

Service	Port Number	Protocol	Description
aodv	654	tcp	AODV
aodv	654	udp	AODV
tinc	655	tcp	TINC
tinc	655	udp	TINC
spmp	656	tcp	SPMP
spmp	656	udp	SPMP
mdqs	666	tcp	
mdqs	666	udp	
doom	666	tcp	doom Id Software
doom	666	udp	doom Id Software
disclose	667	tcp	campaign contribution disclosures - SDR Technologies
disclose	667	udp	campaign contribution disclosures - SDR Technologies
mecomm	668	tcp	MeComm
mecomm	668	udp	MeComm
meregister	669	tcp	MeRegister
meregister	669	udp	MeRegister
vacdsm-sws	670	tcp	VACDSM-SWS
vacdsm-sws	670	udp	VACDSM-SWS
vacdsm-app	671	tcp	VACDSM-APP
vacdsm-app	671	udp	VACDSM-APP
vpps-qua	672	tcp	VPPS-QUA
vpps-qua	672	udp	VPPS-QUA
cimplex	673	tcp	CIMPLEX
cimplex	673	udp	CIMPLEX
acap	674	tcp	ACAP
acap	674	udp	ACAP
dctp	675	tcp	DCTP

continues...

Table A.1 Continued

Service	Port Number	Protocol	Description
dctp	675	udp	DCTP
vpps-via	676	tcp	VPPS Via
vpps-via	676	udp	VPPS Via
vpp	677	tcp	Virtual Presence Protocol
vpp	677	udp	Virtual Presence Protocol
ggf-ncp	678	tcp	GNU Gereration Foundation NCP
ggf-ncp	678	udp	GNU Generation Foundation NCP
mrm	679	tcp	MRM
mrm	679	udp	MRM
entrust-aaas	680	tcp	entrust-aaas
entrust-aaas	680	udp	entrust-aaas
entrust-aams	681	tcp	entrust-aams
entrust-aams	681	udp	entrust-aams
xfr	682	tcp	XFR
xfr	682	udp	XFR
corba-iiop	683	tcp	CORBA IIOP
corba-iiop	683	udp	CORBA IIOP
corba-iiop-ssl	684	tcp	CORBA IIOP SSL
corba-iiop-ssl	684	udp	CORBA IIOP SSL
mdc-portmapper	685	tcp	MDC Port Mapper
mdc-portmapper	685	udp	MDC Port Mapper
hcp-wismar	686	tcp	Hardware Control Protocol Wismar
hcp-wismar	686	udp	Hardware Control Protocol Wismar
asipregistry	687	tcp	asipregistry
asipregistry	687	udp	asipregistry
realm-rusd	688	tcp	REALM-RUSD
realm-rusd	688	udp	REALM-RUSD
elcsd	704	tcp	errlog copy/server daemon
elcsd	704	udp	errlog copy/server daemon

Service	Port Number	Protocol	Description
agentx	705	tcp	AgentX
agentx	705	udp	AgentX
borland-dsj	707	tcp	Borland DSJ
borland-dsj	707	udp	Borland DSJ
entrust-kmsh	709	tcp	Entrust Key Management Service Handler
entrust-kmsh	709	udp	Entrust Key Management Service Handler
entrust-ash	710	tcp	Entrust Administration Service Handler
entrust-ash	710	udp	Entrust Administration Service Handler
cisco-tdp	711	tcp	Cisco TDP
cisco-tdp	711	udp	Cisco TDP
netviewdm1	729	tcp	IBM NetView DM/6000 Server/Client
netviewdm1	729	udp	IBM NetView DM/6000 Server/Client
netviewdm2	730	tcp	IBM NetView DM/6000 send/tcp
netviewdm2	730	udp	IBM NetView DM/6000 send/tcp
netviewdm3	731	tcp	IBM NetView DM/6000 receive/tcp
netviewdm3	731	udp	IBM NetView DM/6000 receive/tcp
netgw	741	tcp	netGW
netgw	741	udp	netGW
netrcs	742	tcp	Network based Rev. Cont. Sys.
netrcs	742	udp	Network based Rev. Cont. Sys.
flexlm	744	tcp	Flexible License Manager
flexlm	744	udp	Flexible License Manager
fujitsu-dev	747	tcp	Fujitsu Device Control
fujitsu-dev	747	udp	Fujitsu Device Control
ris-cm	748	tcp	Russell Info Sci Calendar Manager

continues...

439

Table A.1 Continued

Service	Port Number	Protocol	Description
ris-cm	748	udp	Russell Info Sci Calendar Manager
kerberos-adm	749	tcp	kerberos administration
kerberos-adm	749	udp	kerberos administration
rfile	750	tcp	
loadav	750	udp	
kerberos-iv	750	udp	kerberos version iv
pump	751	tcp	
pump	751	udp	
qrh	752	tcp	
qrh	752	udp	
rrh	753	tcp	
rrh	753	udp	
tell	754	tcp	send
tell	754	udp	send
nlogin	758	tcp	
nlogin	758	udp	
con	759	tcp	
con	759	udp	
ns	760	tcp	
ns	760	udp	
rxe	761	tcp	
rxe	761	udp	
quotad	762	tcp	
quotad	762	udp	
cycleserv	763	tcp	
cycleserv	763	udp	
omserv	764	tcp	
omserv	764	udp	
webster	765	tcp	

Service	Port Number	Protocol	Description
webster	765	udp	
phonebook	767	tcp	phone
phonebook	767	udp	phone
vid	769	tcp	
vid	769	udp	
cadlock	770	tcp	
cadlock	770	udp	
rtip	771	tcp	
rtip	771	udp	
cycleserv2	772	tcp	
cycleserv2	772	udp	
submit	773	tcp	
notify	773	udp	
rpasswd	774	tcp	
acmaint_dbd	774	udp	
entomb	775	tcp	
acmaint_transd	775	udp	
wpages	776	tcp	
wpages	776	udp	
multiling-http	777	tcp	Multiling HTTP
multiling-http	777	udp	Multiling HTTP
wpgs	780	tcp	
wpgs	780	udp	
concert	786	tcp	Concert
concert	786	udp	Concert
qsc	787	tcp	QSC
qsc	787	udp	QSC
mdbs_daemon	800	tcp	
mdbs_daemon	800	udp	

continues...

441

APPENDIX A   TCP and UDP Common Ports

Table A.1   Continued

Service	Port Number	Protocol	Description
device	801	tcp	
device	801	udp	
fcp-udp	810	tcp	FCP
fcp-udp	810	udp	FCP Datagram
itm-mcell-s	828	tcp	itm-mcell-s
itm-mcell-s	828	udp	itm-mcell-s
pkix-3-ca-ra	829	tcp	PKIX-3 CA/RA
pkix-3-ca-ra	829	udp	PKIX-3 CA/RA
rsync	873	tcp	rsync
rsync	873	udp	rsync
iclcnet-locate	886	tcp	ICL coNETion locate server
iclcnet-locate	886	udp	ICL coNETion locate server
iclcnet_svinfo	887	tcp	ICL coNETion server info
iclcnet_svinfo	887	udp	ICL coNETion server info
accessbuilder	888	tcp	AccessBuilder
accessbuilder	888	udp	AccessBuilder
cddbp	888	tcp	CD Database Protocol
omginitialrefs	900	tcp	OMG Initial Refs
omginitialrefs	900	udp	OMG Initial Refs
xact-backup	911	tcp	xact-backup
xact-backup	911	udp	xact-backup
ftps-data	989	tcp	ftp protocol, data, over TLS/SSL
ftps-data	989	udp	ftp protocol, data, over TLS/SSL
ftps	990	tcp	ftp protocol, control, over TLS/SSL
ftps	990	udp	ftp protocol, control, over TLS/SSL
nas	991	tcp	Netnews Administration System

Service	Port Number	Protocol	Description
nas	991	udp	Netnews Administration System
telnets	992	tcp	telnet protocol over TLS SSL
telnets	992	udp	telnet protocol over TLS SSL
imaps	993	tcp	imap4 protocol over TLS SSL
imaps	993	udp	imap4 protocol over TLS SSL
ircs	994	tcp	irc protocol over TLS SSL
ircs	994	udp	irc protocol over TLS SSL
pop3s	995	tcp	pop3 protocol over TLS/SSL (was spop3)
pop3s	995	udp	pop3 protocol over TLS/SSL (was spop3)
vsinet	996	tcp	vsinet
vsinet	996	udp	vsinet
maitrd	997	tcp	
maitrd	997	udp	
busboy	998	tcp	
puparp	998	udp	
garcon	999	tcp	
applix	999	udp	Applix ac
puprouter	999	tcp	
puprouter	999	udp	
cadlock	1000	tcp	
ock	1000	udp	
surf	1010	tcp	surf
surf	1010	udp	surf
	1023	tcp	Reserved
	1023	udp	Reserved

Appendix

B

Other Security Tools You Can Use

This appendix contains Web links to many different programs that might prove useful to a network administrator concerned about the security of the local network. Some of these tools are referenced in other books and online resources, whereas others are not. I have tried to locate download sites that are current for each tool. Some of the sources I have checked before include links that are now stale. For example, the CERT Web site used to allow downloads of Crack and TCP Wrappers. These packages are no longer maintained in their archive. If you find that any of the links contained in this appendix no longer work, please do two things:

- Use a search engine to try to locate the software elsewhere.
- Send me an email (ogletree@bellsouth.net) so I can update future versions of this book!

Password Utilities

As mentioned in Chapter 3, "Security and the Internet," one of the first lines of defense for any computer system is the username and password that is used in the login process. For that reason, hackers have developed much expertise in the area of discovering passwords. Because many users still do not take seriously the job of creating a hard-to-guess password and many system administrators still do not take seriously the job of enforcing a good password policy, hackers don't really have to do much work in this area today. If you are reading this book, I can only assume that you do take this matter seriously, so the first thing this appendix points you to are a few programs you can use to enhance password security. Remember that good passwords are a necessity on both firewall bastion hosts and on the servers and workstations that are on your LAN.

Crack

Hey, if it's good enough for hackers, it's good enough for me! This is the good old standard password-cracking program, written by Alex Muffett, that has caused so many problems for system administrators for many years now. However, like any good tool, if used for the proper reasons, it can be quite valuable. Because users are notoriously famous for using easy-to-guess passwords, it only makes sense that you should use the same utility that many hackers use. Check your system on a periodic basis to find out whether you do have any user accounts that are susceptible to making a break-in an easy job.

You can download Crack from the following site:

`http://www.nomoresecrets.net/download/download.html`

This site also has downloads for many other tools a security conscious administrator can use.

Computer Oracle and Password System (COPS)

COPS is made up of several different programs that can be used to locate well-known security problems in UNIX systems. It was written by Dan Farmer, who is one of the authors of *How to...by Breaking Into It*.

You can download COPS from the following sites:

`http://www.nomoresecrets.net/download/download.html`

or

`http://ciac.llnl.gov/ciac/ToolsUnixSysMon.html`

or

`http://www.auscert.org.au/Information/Tools/other_tools.html`

Perl Cops—Perl Implementation of COPS

This tool is similar to COPS but is written in Perl by Steve Romig. You can find Perl Cops at the following site:

`ftp://coast.cs.purdue.edu/pub/tools/unix/cops-perl.tar`

Tiger

This is a collection of system-monitoring scripts that is similar in function to COPS. Tiger was written to help improve security for systems at Texas A & M University that were being accessed by computers outside the campus network. You can find Tiger at the following site:

`http://ciac.llnl.gov/ciac/ToolsUnixSysMon.html`

There is also a mailing list for Tiger. To subscribe, send an email to the following site with the words `subscribe tiger` as the message body:

`majordomo@net.tamu.edu`

Tools Used for Network Monitoring

The utilities in this section relate to the network. Some, such as ARGUS, can be used to monitor IP traffic on the network, whereas others, such as SWATCH, are used to manage log files so that you can keep track of what is happening on the network.

ARGUS

This is an IP auditing tool, written by Carter Bullard and Chas DeFatta, that can be used to analyze IP transactions.

You can download ARGUS from the following sites:

`ftp://ftp.sei.cmu.edu/pub/argus`

or

`http://www.auscert.org.au/Information/Tools/other_tools.html`

Simple WATCHer (SWATCH)

SWATCH is a utility written by Stephen Hansen and Todd Atkins that can be used to make log file management an easier chore. SWATCH can filter out certain events and take actions based on things that it finds. It can be used to remove ordinary entries that are simply taking up room in the file. You can download SWATCH from the following site:

`ftp://ftp.stanford.edu/general/security-tools/swatch`

Internet Security Scanner (ISS)

ISS, written by Christopher Klaus, can be used to probe one or more IP addresses to look for well-known system security problems.

You can download ISS from the following sites:

```
ftp://ftp.iss.net/pub/iss/
```

or

```
http://www.nomoresecrets.net/download/download.html
```

Security Administrator Tool for Analyzing Networks (SATAN)

This popular tool was mentioned briefly in Chapter 12, "Firewall Tools Available on the Internet." It is mentioned again here in case you skipped that chapter. Although you need to have good UNIX system administration and TCP/IP networking skills to configure and benefit from using SATAN, it is an excellent configurable tool.

You can find SATAN at the following sites:

```
http://ciac.llnl.gov/ciac/ToolsUnixNetSec.html
```

or

```
http://www.nomoresecrets.net/download/download.html
```

Courtney—Is SATAN Looking at You?

Because SATAN can be used to probe for network vulnerabilities, it is often used not only by respectable network administrators, but also by those less-than-respectable persons who want to cause you lots of grief. Yes, it's those hackers again. The utility named Courtney can be used to monitor your network, let you know whether SATAN is being used against you, and try to identify the source of the scan.

You can download Courtney from the following sites:

```
http://ciac.llnl.gov/ciac/ToolsUnixNetMon.html
```

or

```
http://www.auscert.org.au/Information/Tools/other_tools.html
```

Gabriel—Another SATAN Detector

This is another tool that, like Courtney, can be used to determine whether the SATAN tool is probing your network.

Gabriel can be downloaded from the following site:

`http://ciac.llnl.gov/ciac/ToolsUnixNetMon.html`

Merlin—Front End Utility

Merlin is not a security tool in itself, but it provides a front-end graphical user interface for some of the more popular tools, such as SATAN, COPS, and Tripwire.

You can download Merlin from the following site:

`ftp://ciac.llnl.gov/pub/ciac/sectools/unix/merlin/merlin.tar.gz`

ifstatus—Locate Promiscuous Network Interfaces

When run in promiscuous mode, a network adapter card will pass all packets it finds on the wire up the protocol stack. In effect, this is the mode an Ethernet sniffer uses to capture all network traffic for analysis. It can also be used by someone who is sniffing about your network, possibly intercepting passwords and other important data. Use `ifstatus`, written by Dave Curry, to locate network adapters operating in this mode on your network.

You can download `ifstatus` from the following site:

`ftp://coast.cs.purdue.edu/pub/tools/unix/ifstatus/ifstatus.tar.Z`

NID—Network Intrusion Detector

This utility from the Computer Security Technology Center is composed of several tools that can detect network intrusions. It can also be used to determine whether valid users are attempting to do things they're not supposed to do.

You can download NID from the following site:

`http://ciac.llnl.gov/ciac/ToolsUnixNetMon.html`

tcpdump

This is a utility written by Van Jacobson that can be used with an Ethernet adapter operating in promiscuous mode to capture and examine packets from the network. Filtering capabilities make it easier to narrow down your search. For those who cannot afford a high-end (read that to mean expensive) network protocol analyzer, this might be a good substitute.

You can download `tcpdump` from the following site:

`http://ciac.llnl.gov/ciac/ToolsUnixGeneral.html`

System Health-Check Tools

The programs in this section can be used to perform a checkup to see whether your system has any glaring security holes.

Secure_Sun

This is a program, written by David Safford, that can check many SunOS machines for common security problems.

You can download `Secure_Sun` from the following site:

`http://www.cerias.purdue.edu/coast/archive/Archive_Indexing.html`

trojan.pl

This is a program that examines all executables in a search path, looking for possible Trojan Horse programs that can be executed by root.

This program can be downloaded from the following site:

`http://www.cerias.purdue.edu/coast/archive/data/categ50.html`

Tripwire

This utility can be used to preserve the integrity of your file systems. Tripwire stores information about files and directories in a database so that you can discover whether important system files have been modified when you perform scans at a later time.

You can download Tripwire from the following sites:

`http://www.tripwiresecurity.com/`

or

`ftp://info.cert.org/pub/tools/tripwire/`

MD5

MD5 can be used to produce a 128-bit message digest of files on your system. By comparing the "fingerprint" produced to previous scans, you can determine whether important system files have been modified.

For more information about MD5, you can also check out Request For Comments 1321.

You can download MD5 from the following site:

```
ftp://info.cert.org/pub/tools/md5/
```

lsof (List Open Files)

This small utility, written by Vic Abell, can be used to display open files on a UNIX system and tell you which processes have them opened.

You can download lsof from the following site:

```
ftp://vic.cc.purdue.edu/pub/tools/unix/lsof/
```

Replacements for Popular Programs

Many UNIX commands contain bugs or other problems that can be used to your disadvantage. Replacements or patches are available for some of these.

smrsh—*sendmail* Restricted Shell Program

Written by the original author of sendmail, smrsh helps protect against some of the problems caused by this 20,000 line program. This program is included in sendmail starting with version 8.7.1 (and can be found in the /smrsh subdirectory). Note that smrsh doesn't fix all of the problems with sendmail, and if you are using a really old copy, it would be a very good idea to update to the newest version.

You can download smrsh from the following site:

```
ftp://ftp.uu.net/pub/security/smrsh/
```

fingerd—Replacement for the *finger* Program

Written by Mike Shanzer, this version of the `finger` command adds
logging and access control lists.

This program can be downloaded from the following site:

`http://www.cerias.purdue.edu/coast/archive/Archive_Indexing.html`

sfingerd—Another Replacement for the *finger* Program

This is a small, safe `finger` program written by Laurent Demailly.

This program is also downloadable from the following site:

`http://www.cerias.purdue.edu/coast/archive/Archive_Indexing.html`

PortMap V3

Written by Wietse Venema, who was also responsible for TCP
Wrappers, this is a replacement of the portmapper program. It
includes an access control that is similar to that used by TCP
Wrappers.

You can download this program from the following site:

`http://www.cerias.purdue.edu/coast/archive/Archive_Indexing.html`

SRA—Secure RPC Authentication for Telnet and FTP

This utility comes from Texas A & M University and provides for
secure encrypted authentication across the network for Telnet and
FTP, which usually send passwords as clear text.

This utility is available for download at the following site:

`http://www.cerias.purdue.edu/coast/archive/Archive_Indexing.html`

Authd—Authentication Server Daemon

Request for Comments 931 describes a server daemon that can be
used to provide a username for connections across a network. If a
system supports RFC 931, remote systems can interrogate the server
daemon to find out who is actually using a network connection. This

can provide greater security because the information can be recorded in log files or used by access control programs.

You can download Authd from the following site:

```
http://www.cerias.purdue.edu/coast/archive/Archive_Indexing.html
```

su—Dummy *su* Program

When a hacker uses su to get information about users on your system, fool him instead with this dummy version of the program that instead can alert you that it is being used. This program was written by Shawn F. McKay.

This program can be downloaded from the following site:

```
http://www.cerias.purdue.edu/coast/archive/Archive_Indexing.html
```

ssh—The Secure Shell Package

Although it is widely understood that the r* tools (such as rsh and rlogin) present a security problem on the network, it is hard to do away with them when users get used to their convenience. The utilities included in the ssh package add strong authentication and encryption to these tools so that you can continue to provide your users with the convenience and functionality.

You can download ssh from the following site:

```
ftp://ftp.cs.hut.fi/pub/ssh/
```

Appendix

C

Additional Resources

No single book can ever contain all the information that you need to configure a good firewall, much less maintain it. One of the reasons is that the Internet is growing so rapidly, and new protocols and services are constantly being developed. You need to be aware of these new developments so that you can determine whether your firewall is properly configured to handle them. Another reason that you need additional resources is that applications, protocols, and operating systems are not perfect. New bugs or security holes are being discovered all the time. If you don't know that you have a security hole in your firewall, you obviously won't be protected!

This appendix contains an assortment of other places you can go to get additional information about the topics covered in this book as well as places you can use to stay updated on security issues as they are discovered. Once again, because the Internet is expanding and changing every day, you might find that a URL in this appendix no longer works. That is the price you pay for progress! If you find that you cannot locate the resource listed here by the URL that is included, you might try simply using a good search engine (such as `www.altavista.com`) to see whether the resource is still available, using a different URL.

This appendix does not list vendors of firewall products. This is because it is beyond my ability to evaluate every product and determine each product's usefulness. The last thing I want to do is to try to tell you what product to purchase. No author can do that because authors do not know anything about your network, and you need to make a determination of what you need based on what you already have. Instead, you will find here sites that are dedicated to security issues that you can use to further educate yourself.

In case you haven't figured it out yet, you should also consider visiting the home page of the vendor whose operating system or application you use. The vendor itself can usually provide important information and, hopefully, patches or other means that can be used to remedy any problems that have been discovered.

www.first.org   Forum of Incident Response and Security Teams

This organization has members from incident response teams from government, commercial, and academic sites. At this site, you will find many documents relating to security issues. In addition, you can also find here the addresses for several email mailing lists that are for members only. However, if you do not want to become a member of FIRST, you can still subscribe to their public mailing list, which is used for discussions related to security issues as well as for releasing new security advisories.

To subscribe, send an email with "subscribe first-info" as the body of your email text to `first-majordomo@first.org`.

www.sans.org/giac.htm   The SANS Institute

The Systems Administration, Networking, and Security (SANS) Institute is an organization of over 62,000 professionals who work as system, security, or network administrators. This organization maintains a Web site that will help you find up-to-date information about malicious behavior and tools that you can use to improve security at your site. Their Global Incident Analysis Center (GIAC) tracks security holes and methods that you can use to patch them. If you are looking for a new job, they even have a salary survey you can look at.

In addition to their Web presence, SANS also offers training courses that might be helpful to you or others at your site and various tools and resources that can be used to help improve your security. There is also an annual SANS conference that usually lasts for a week. In addition, SANS hosts a smaller get-together called SANS SNAP. SNAP stands for System and Network Assurance Program and consists of several multi-day courses in security-related issues.

www.cert.org The CERT Coordination Center

This URL takes you to the Web site for the Computer Emergency Response Team (CERT for short). This organization, which is based at Carnegie-Mellon University's Software Engineering Institute, issues advisories on newly discovered forms of attack and is one of the better sites dedicated to this purpose. CERT was created after the infamous Internet Worm wreaked havoc on the Internet in 1988. At this site, you can sign up for their mailing list to help you stay on top of current security issues relating to the Internet.

There are several other worldwide sites that use the CERT name. You might want to visit them also to compare information about the advisories, training, and other resources offered:

- `www.cerias.purdue.edu/pcert/pcert.html` The Purdue Computer Emergency Response Team (PCERT) is, as you can probably guess, located at Purdue University.

- `www.nic.surfnet.nu/surfnet/security/cert-nl.html` This site (located in the Netherlands, Europe) is a member of the Global Forum of Incident Response and Security Teams.

- `www.cert.dfn.de/eng` This Web page is the CERT organization in Denmark. The site has only limited pages in English, but it can be a good resource for all you wonderful Danish people who bought this book!

- `www.cert.lu` This is the Web page for the CERT organization in Luxembourg, Europe.

- `www.auscert.org.au` This is the Web page for the CERT organization in Australia.

- `www.afcert.csap.af.mil` The Air Force Computer Emergency Response Team is the United States Air Force CERT organization located at Kelly Air Force Base.

- `www.infosec.nosc.mil/infosec.html` Still another United States military site, this is the URL for the United States Navy's CERT Web page.

Also, of course, don't forget that if you happen to be the one who discovers a new form of attack, use the CERT site to file a report so that others can be made aware!

www.microsoft.com

No doubt you have heard many reports over the past few years about newly discovered bugs or other security problems with operating systems (Windows 98, Windows NT, and Windows 2000) as well as applications (Internet Explorer, for example) produced by Microsoft. If you make use of their products, you can rest assured that Microsoft tries to stay on top of things, and if you want to do the same, you can visit their Web site and sign up for their security email newsletter. To subscribe, go to www.microsoft.com and click the Subscribe button on the toolbar at the top of the Web page. Fill in your information, and you will start receiving emails on a regular basis.

You might also want to go to www.microsoft.com/security, which is a Web page at Microsoft that is devoted to security issues. From there, you can download the latest updates for Microsoft products and get more information about specific products.

www.securityportal.com

This is the Web page of an Internet service provider that also provides a lot of information about security issues that relate to the Internet. You can visit this page to subscribe to their Security Portal Weekly Newsletter. Although this is a commercial site, they also offer a discussion forum and news about late-breaking security events.

www.ntsecurity.net

This site is, as you can probably guess, devoted to security issues that relate to the Windows NT (now Windows 2000) operating system and related products. It is sponsored by *Windows 2000 Magazine* (formerly *Windows NT Magazine*, published by Duke Communications

International Inc.). If you use Windows products, you should really consider visiting this site because it has a lot of resources and, of course, an email mailing list to which you can subscribe. This author also heartily recommends that, if you use Windows operating systems, you should also subscribe to the magazine, which is perhaps the best of those currently published for Windows.

www.l0pht.com

This Web site is the home of the L0pht Heavy Industries organization. As this book is being written, this organization of hackers(?) has just joined forces with a startup firm called @Stake. When a security-oriented company joins forces with a group of hackers, what will result? Well, as the news has shown for several years now, the guys at L0pht have been very good at seeking out security flaws in major operating systems. By combining forces with a company that specializes in security issues, who knows what the result will be? However, be sure to visit their Web site to make use of the voluminous resources they provide.

The Firewalls Mailing List

This is an email mailing list that has a lot of postings. If you have questions, want to provide answers, or just want to keep abreast of new topics that relate to firewalls, their architecture, and other security issues, you should subscribe to this mailing list.

To subscribe, send the command `subscribe firewalls` in the body of an email message (not on the "Subject:" line) to the following address:

`majordomo@greatcircle.com`

A digest is also available if you don't want to look at each individual message. To subscribe to the digest, send the command `subscribe firewalls-digest` in the body of an email message to the same address.

You can also access the archives of this mailing list and other valuable material by using the following URL:

`ftp://ftp.greatcircle.com/pub/firewalls/index.html`

http://waldo.wi.mit.edu/WWW/tools/ security/www-security-faq/index.html

The World Wide Web Security FAQ (frequently asked questions) can be found at this URL. If you are operating a Web server, this FAQ might be of some help when you are setting it up.

www.cerias.purdue.edu/coast   Computer Operations, Audit and Security Technology (COAST)

This Web site is managed by the Computer Sciences department at Purdue University. Here, you will find a newsletter mailing list and an assortment of reports and papers on computer security matters. The COAST archive contains voluminous amounts of information, from white papers and software tools to links to other security sites.

ciac.llnl.gov   Computer Incident Advisory Capability

This U.S. Department of Energy Web site is hosted by the Computer Security Technology Center for Lawrence Livermore National Laboratory. Although it serves as a central point to disseminate information about new security issues, you will also find many other resources here, including a virus database and a listing of hoaxes—or security threats that really aren't!

Several of the security utilities listed in Appendix B, "Other Security Tools You Can Use," can be downloaded from this site.

www.fedcirc.gov   Federal Computer Incidence Response Capability

At yet another federal government Web site, you will find a variety of resources relating to computer and network security. This site also has available for download many of the utilities listed in Appendix B, such as ISS, SATAN, and COPS. One particularly good document

461

you can obtain at this site is "Practices For Securing Critical Information Assets," written by the Critical Infrastructure Assurance office. This document looks at network security overall, from computer viruses to physical security issues. Although it was developed with U.S. federal agencies in mind, it can be an excellent tool for briefing co-workers, especially upper management, about the necessity of maintaining good network security.

www.nsi.org/compsec.html   The National Security Institute's Security Resource Net

This is another good Web site that you can use to download security tools and papers. From this site, you can also order a number of CSI's (Computer Security Institute) guides that cover specific areas of security, such as virus prevention and email security issues. They aren't inexpensive, but they are worth the price for the information they can provide.

xforce.iss.net/maillists/otherlists.php3

This site contains a very good list of mailing lists related to computer and network security. Each mailing list is described, and instructions for subscribing are given for each list.

INDEX

Symbols

: (colon), 272, 328
! (exclamation point), 280
- (hyphen), 274
(number sign/pound symbol), 184, 272
. (period), 53
? command, 281
/ (slash) symbol, 327
%% variable, 261
3DES, 202

A

-A *chain rule* command, 326
-A *direction* parameter, 317
-a *policy* command, 317
-a *port* command-line parameter, 306
A record type, 57
%A variable, 260
AAAA record type, 57
accept keyword, 324
accept target, 324
acceptable usage statements (security policies), 88-90
access control, 243, 254-255
access control lists (routers), 126-127
access control programs, 267. *See also* netacl
Access the Internet Using a Proxy Server check box, 354
access.log file, 308
accessing encrypted files (PGP), 232
account names, 64
accounts (user), 303
ACK bit, 123-124
ACK Flag field, 70
actions, 182-184
adapter cards (network), reviewing, 359

Add Email ID button, 363
Add or Remove User Services button, 369
Add Users and Groups dialog box, 150, 191, 346
adding public keys to key rings, 231
additional resources, 456
    CERT Coordination Center, 458-459
    COAST (Computer Operations, Audit and Security) Web site, 461
    Federal Computer Incidence Response Capability Web site, 461-462
    Firewalls mailing list, 460
    Forum of Incident Response and Security Teams, 457
    L0pht Heavy Industries Web site, 460
    Microsoft sites, 459
    Microsoft Web sites, 459
    National Security Institute's Security Resource Net Web site, 462
    NT security, 460
    SANS (System Administration, Networking, and Security) Institute, 457
    Security Portal Web site, 459
    U.S. Department of Energy Web site, 461
    World Wide Web Security FAQ Web site, 461
Address Mask Reply message type, 35
Address Mask Request message type, 35

Address Resolution Protocol. *See* ARP
address space (LANs), increasing with NAT, 170
address translation, 11
Address Type field, 297
address vectoring, 11, 170-171
addresses
    broadcast, 40-41
    dotted-decimal notation, 36-37
    hardware, 33, 36
    IP, 32-36
        assigning, 376-377
        classes. See IP addresses, classes
        length, 36
        specifying, 327-328
        translating, 33
    IPv6, 391
    loopback, 40
    MAC, 33-36
    multicast, 40-41
    physical, 36
    private networks, 40
    specifying, 327
    subdividing (subnet masks), 43
    subnet, calculating, 43-44
    unicast, 40, 391
Administrative Tools command (Programs menu), 189
Administrative Tools folder, 189
Administrative Tools menu commands
    Event Viewer, 194
    User Manager, 189
Advanced command (Category menu), 310

Advanced menu commands
(Proxies), 310
advisory bulletins, finding,
75
aggressive mode, 219
AH (Authentication Header),
217-221
alerting capabilities (firewall
appliances), 377-378
Alerting tab, 353
alerts, 351-353
ALL keyword, 259
allocating sockets, 293
altavista, 456
altavista Web site, 456
anonymous FTP, 52
anonymous FTP sites, 15
Anycast address, 391
Application event log file,
193
application gateways, 96,
158-161, 296
  advantages and disadvan-
    tages, 161
  blocking IP traffic, 158-159,
    163
  disabling routing, 160-161
  proxy server, 264
Application layer, 27, 30
application proxies, 10, 17,
96, 376
application proxy gateway,
96-100
application proxying, 382
application-level gateways,
167
application-specific log files,
196
applications, 274
  netacl, 270
  proxy, 296
  removing unnecessary files
    from bastion hosts,
    141-142
  SOCKSifying, 247, 298
architectures (firewalls), 93
Argus, 448
Argus Web site, 448
ARP (Address Resolution
Protocol), 26, 33-34

ARP broadcast method, 34
arp command, 34
ARP table, 34
arpa organizational domain,
53
Array button, 345
arrays (Proxy servers), joining, 345
ASCII Armor, 232
assigning IP addresses,
376-377
asymmetric encryption. See
public key encryption
AT (network address translation), 21
Attach to Firewall command
(Command View File
menu), 365
attribute *valuelist*, 272
attribute values, matching,
273
attributes, host, 274, 277,
280
Audit command (Policies
menu), 189
Audit Policy dialog box,
189-191
Audit These Events radio
button, 189
auditing, 178, 181, 196
  bastion hosts, configuring,
    152
  IP (Argus), 448
  login failures, 180
  printer usages, 193
  success logins, 180
  syslog utility (UNIX),
    181-182. See also syslog
    configuration file
  Windows NT, 188-189
    disabling, 190
    Event Viewer, 188
    setting up events to audit.
    See events, auditing
Auditing button, 191
auditing policies, setting up,
191
auditing. See also log files;
logging
-auth option, 280

authd, 246, 267, 289,
453-454
Authd Web site, 454
authentication, 200, 383
  GSS-API, 297
  support, 296
  VPNs, 214
Authentication Data field,
221
authentication extension
header, 389
Authentication Header (AH),
217, 219-221
Authentication Server
Protocol, 262
authentication methods
(SOCKS V5), 297
Authentication Server
Daemon patches (Authd),
453-454
authserver *host port* keyword,
276
Auto Dial button, 343
AutoDial, 343-344
automating
  log file reviewing, 180
  UNIX tasks, 187

B

-b command-line option,
319, 329
backdoors, creating, 81
badadmin *user* command,
284
baddir *directory* command,
284
basic NAT (Network
Address Translation),
167-168
bastion hosts, 18, 98, 104,
132
  auditing and logging, con-
    figuring, 152
  compromised bastion hosts,
    154-155
  configuring, 132-133
  installing FWTK, 289-290
  proxy software, running,
    153-154

removing unnecessary applications and files, 141-142

secure operating systems, installing from scratch, 133-134

UNIX daemon processes, 135-137

UNIX network configuration files, 138

UNIX resource permissions, 142-146
  owner values, changing, 145-146
  permission values, changing, 145-146
  permission values, viewing, 143-144
  SGID (Set Group ID), 144-145
  SUID (Set User ID), 144-145

Windows NT services, 139-140

Windows NT resource permissions, 147-152
  modifying, 150-152
  special permissions, 147
  standard permissions, 148
  viewing on files/directories, 148-149

bidirectional flag, 329
BIND (Berkeley Internet Name Domain), 53. *See also* **DNS**
BIND requests, 293-294, 297
black box, 267
blocking Internet access, 171-172
Blowfish, 202
Blowfish Web site, 202
boolean logic subnet masks, 42
bootp protocol, 36
broadcast addresses, 40-41
broadcast methods (ARP), 34
broadcasts, 41
BSDI (BSD/OS), 374

built-in proxy servers, 174-175
bulletins (CIAC-2319), 75
buttons
  Add Email ID, 363
  Add or Remove User Services, 369
  Array, 345
  Auditing, 191
  Auto Dial, 343
  Cache Filters, 349
  Certificates, 209
  Client Configuration, 346
  LAN Settings, 310
  Local Address Table, 346
  Plugs, 345
  Search, 192
  Security, 341
  Server Backup, 346
  Server Restore, 346
  Show Users, 192, 346
  View, 310
bytes, 46

C

-c command, 318
%c variable, 260
CA (Certificate Authority), 206, 219
cable modems, 384
cache file, 56
Cache Filters button, 349
cache hierarchy (SQUID), 309
cache servers, 248
  child, 309
  parent, 309
  sibling, 309
  SQUID, 306
cache.log file, 308
caching, 11
caching properties, managing, 347-350
Caching property page, 347-349
caching proxy servers, 248, 302. *See also* **SQUID**
caching servers, 11, 247
caching-only servers (DNS), 55

calculating
  subnet addresses, 43-44
  subnet values, 43
Caldera Web site, 314
calls, intercepting (WinSock networking functions), 292, 298
capabilities, dial-in/dial-out, 187
Category blocking, 172
Category menu commands (Advanced), 310
centralized user databases, 66
CERN standard format, 308
CERT (Computer Emergency Response Team), 458
CERT Coordination Center Web sites, 458-459
Certificate Authority (CA), 206, 219
Certificate dialog box, 209
Certificate Path tab, 209
certificates
  digital, 218
  issuing, 207
Certificates button, 209
CH (CHAOS) class, 60
chains, 323-326. *See also* **rules**
  creating, 326
  Forward, 323
  Input, 323
  managing, 326
  Output, 323
  user-defined, 324-325
Change Settings field, 195
changing default configuration file (syslog), 182
Check Alive command (CommandView Firewall menu), 367
check boxes
  Access the Internet Using a Proxy Server, 354
  Enable Caching, 348
  Enable Dynamic Packet Filtering on Microsoft Proxy Server Packets, 341

Enable E-Mail Notification, 363
Enable Logging Using, 352
Enable Packet Filtering on External Interface, 341
Enable Web Publishing, 350
Failure, 189
Replace Auditing on Existing Files, 191
Replace Auditing on Subdirectories, 191
Send SMTP Mail, 353
Success, 189
checking Web pages for encryption, 209
child cache servers, 309
child processes, 305
child servers, 248
chmod command, 145
choosing servers (SQUID), 303-304
chown command, 145
-chroot *directory* **keyword, 275**
CIAC-2319 bulletin, 75
ciphertext, 200
circuit-level gateways, 167, 296
Class A addresses, 38
Class B addresses, 39
Class B subnet masks, 42
Class C addresses, 39
Class D addresses, 40
Class E addresses, 40
Class field, 60
classes
CH (CHAOS), 60
HS (Hesiod), 60
IP address, 36-37
Class A, 38
Class B, 39
Class C, 39
Class D, 40
Class E, 40
determining, 37-38
option, 48
classical proxies, 162-166
Client Configuration button, 346

client requests, handling, 350
client/server connections, establishing (SOCKS server), 292-295
clients, configuring to use SQUID, 310
CNAME record type, 58-59
COAST (Computer Operation, Audit and Security Technology) Web site, 461
code, linking to SOCKS library functions, 298
code listings (/etc/inetd.conf file example), 270
codes (ICMP), 322
colon (:), 272, 328
com organizational domain, 53
combining firewall strategies, 97-100
dual-homed hosts, 98-99
screened hosts, 100
Command Code field (SOCKS V5), values, 297
command-line options
-b, 319, 329
-e, 319
ipchains, 328
ipfwadm command, 319-320
-k, 319
-l, 329
-m, 319
-m *markvalue*, 329
-n, 319, 329
-o, 319
-o [*maxsize*], 329
-r *port*, 319
-t *andmask ormask*, 329
-t *andmask xormask*, 320
-v, 320, 329
-x, 320, 329
-y, 320, 329
command-line parameters (squid command), 306-308
-a *port*, 306
-D, 307
-d *error-level*, 306

-f, 306-307
-h, 306
-k, 306
-k check, 307
-k debug, 307
-k interrupt, 307
-k kill, 307
-k rotate, 306
-k shutdown, 306
-N, 307
-R, 307
-s, 307
-u, 307
-V, 307
-X, 307
-Y, 307
-z, 307
CommandView Firewall
downloading trial version, 358
File menu, 365-366
Firewall menu, 367-368
installing, 358-359
Log menu, 368
manager application, 364-365
setup program, running, 360-364
View menu, 366
commands
?, 281
-A *chain rule*, 326
-a *policy*, 317
Administrative Tools menu
Event Viewer, 194
User Manager, 189
Advanced menu (Proxies), 310
arp, 34
badadmin *user*, 284
baddir *directory*, 284
-c, 318
Category menu (Advanced), 310
chmod command, 145
chown command, 145
connect, 280
connect *host*, 281
-D *chain rule*, 327

-D *chain rule-number rule*, 327

-d *policy*, 317

dbmgr, 249

directory *directory*, 284

Edit menu (Network Preferences), 310

executable *program*, 284

exit, 281

-F *chain*, 326

-f *policy*, 317

File menu
Attach to Firewall, 365
Configure New Firewall, 366
Detach From Firewall, 365
Exit, 366
Load Plan from File, 366
Print MSP Details, 366
Print MSP Summary, 366
Properties, 191
Retrieve Plan from Firewall, 366
Save Plan to File, 366
Save Plan to Firewall, 366
Settings, 195

finger, 186

Firewall menu
Check Alive, 367
Ping Router, 367
Restart, 367
Set Date/Time, 367
Set Password, 367
SMXP Encryption Key, 367
Upgrade, 367

groupid *group*, 284-286

-h, 318

Help, 281

-I *chain rule-number rule*, 326

-i *policy*, 317

ipchains-restore, 330

ipchains-save, 330

ipfwadm, 317-321

Keys menu (New Key), 235

-l, 317

-L *chain*, 326

last, 186

Log menu (Security), 194

make, 316

make install, 306

managing chains, 326

managing rules, 326-327

maxchildren *children*, 285

Microsoft Proxy Server menu (Internet Service Manager), 341

-N *chain*, 326

-P *chain target*, 326

-p *policy*, 318

password, 281

PGP, 231

PGP menu (PGPkeys), 235

PING, 35

Policies menu (Audit), 189

port *portid hosts*, 286

Programs menu
Administrative Tools, 189
Microsoft Proxy Server, 341
PGP, 235
Windows NT Explorer, 191

Properties menu (Service Properties), 340

ps, 139, 188

quit, 281

-R *chain rule-number rule*, 326

rwho, 186

-s *tcp tcpfin udp*, 318

sendmail *program*, 285

shell, 260-261

squid, 305-308

su, 187

timeout *seconds*, 281, 284-286

tn-gw proxy server, 281

Tools menu (Internet Options), 310

touch (UNIX), 161

TRACEROUTE, 35

UNIX
replacement/patches. See replacements (UNIX commands)
patches (UNIX commands), 452

userid *user*, 284-286

View menu (Internet Options), 354

wakeup *seconds*, 285

who, 186

-X *chain*, 326

x-gw, 281

-z, 317

-Z *chain*, 326

comments, inserting into files, 272

communicating between child and parent servers (SQUID), 248

comparing
FWTK and Gauntlet firewall, 265-266
ipfwadm and ipchains, 322

compatibility of IPv4 and IPv6, 387

compiling source code (UNIX PCP install), 229

components
FWTK, 266, 289
configuration practices, 267
design philosophy, 266
software tools, 266-267
system tools, 267
PGP, selecting, 233-234
PGP Command Line, 234
PGP Eudora Plugin, 233
PGP Key Management, 233
PGP Microsoft Exchange/Outlook Plugin, 234
PGP Microsoft Outlook Express Plugin, 234
PGP User's Guide, 234
PGPnet Virtual Private Networking, 233

compromised bastion hosts, 154-155

Computer Emergency Response Team (CERT), 458

Computer Incident Advisory Capability Web site, 75

Computer Oracle and Password System (COPS), 447

computers
host, crashing (denial-of-service attacks), 70
physical security, 67
configuration files (syslog)
changing, 182
facility names, 183
reviewing, 184-185
sending messages to other computers, 184-185
severity levels, 183
configuration Practices (FWTK), 267
configurations (SOCKS servers), 293
Configure Mail Alerting dialog box, 353
Configure New Firewall command (CommandView File menu), 366
configure script, 305
configuring
auditing and logging (bastion host), 152
bastion hosts, 132-133
clients to use SQUID, 310
email alerts, 353
firewall for mail (DNS), 285
firewalls, 26
ftp-gw proxy, 277-279
ipchains, 321
packet filters, 48
packet-filtering routers, 32
PGP (Windows NT), 235-237
plug-gw, 286
proxy information, 354
proxy servers, 275
squid, 248, 303
syslogd, 182
TCP Wrappers, 256-257
hosts.allow file, 258-261
hosts.deny file, 258-261
inetd.conf file, 257-258
connect command, 280
connect *host* command, 281
CONNECT requests, 292-293, 297

connection methods, three-way handshake, 70-71
connections
client/server, establishing (SOCKS server), 292-295
control (PPTP), 223-224
dial-up, 212
physical, evaluating, 35
Connections tab, 310
contents (key rings), viewing, 231
control connections (PPTP), 223-224
controlling
network connections, 28
sessions, 29
COPS (Computer Oracle and Password System), 447
COPS Web sites, 447
Courtney, 449
Courtney Web sites, 449
Crack, 446-447
Crack Web site, 447
cracking passwords, 80
crashing host computers (denial-of-service attacks), 70
Create Email Rule dialog box, 363
creating
backdoors, 81
chains, 326
digital signatures (PGP), 232
firewall policies, 16
rules, 273
secure channels, 212
security policies, 14-16
selectors, 184
UDP proxies, 296-297
user accounts (SQUID), 303
user-defined chains, 324
VPNs, 212-213
cron daemon, 187
cryptographic algorithms, 218
cryptography, 200
crystal box, 267
custom proxies, creating, 166

D

-D *address*[/*mask*][*port...*] parameter, 319
-D *chain rule* command, 327
-D *chain rule-number* command, 327
-D command-line parameter, 307
-d *destination* parameter, 327
-d *error-level* command-line parameter, 306
-d *policy* command, 317
%d variable, 261
daemons, 134
cron, 187
inetd, 255, 258, 268-270
mountd daemon, 137
rpcbind daemon, 137
sendmail, 256
syslog, 182
syslogd, 256
talkd daemon, 136
tcpd (TCP Wrappers), 255, 258
UNIX daemon processes, 135-137
inetd.conf configuration file, 135-136
NFS (Network File System), 137
DARPA (Defense Advanced Research Projects Agency), 245, 264
data
encrypting, 200. *See also* IKE; PPTP
messages, 117
stream of data, 117
transmitting (PPTP tunnels), 224
Data Encryption Standard (DES), 202
data integrity, 200, 205-207
Data Link layer, 28
data streams, encrypting, 207
Data type field, 257, 268
database files, 56
databases
login, 65
password, 65

SAM (Security Accounts Manager), 65
user (centralized), 66
Datagram Length field, 46
datagrams, 32, 45, 48. *See also* **packets**
dbmgr command, 249
decrypting
files (PGP), 237-238
keys, 203
default configuration file (syslog), changing, 182
Defense Advanced Research Projects Agency (DARPA), 245, 264
defining
environment variables, 229
source routing, 48
deleting
log files, 180
public keys to key rings, 231
rules, 327
delivering email, 15, 283. *See also* **SMTP**
demilitarized zone. *See* **DMZ**
dendest-msg *filename* **keyword, 276**
denial-msg *filename* **keyword, 276**
denial-of-service attacks, 69
crashing host computers, 70
distributed, 74-76
overloading limited resources, 69-70
preventing, 70
reconfiguring hosts/network information, 70
deny keyword, 324
deny policy, 318
deny target, 324
deny- modifier, 274
DES (Data Encryption Standard), 202
design philosophy (FWTK), 266
designing firewalls, 86-93
firewall policies, 91-93
security policies, 86-91
acceptable usage statements, 88-90

discussing specifics with employees, 90-91
incident reporting and response, 105-106
network connection policy, 87-88
strategies, 93-100, 102-105
application proxy gateway, 96-97
bastion hosts, 104
combining strategies, 97-100
packet filters, 94-96
sacrificial hosts, 104-105
screened subnet architecture, 101-103
Destination Address field, 47, 297, 389
destination extension header, 389-390
Destination IP Address field
BIND request, 294
CONNECT Request, 293
Destination Port field
BIND request, 293
CONNECT Request, 293, 297
Destination Unreachable message types, 35, 73
Detach from Firewall command (CommandView File menu), 365
Details tab, 209
determining classes (IP addresses), 37-38
/dev/klog device, 182
/dev/log socket, 182
devices (/dev/klog), 182
DHCP (Dynamic Host Configuration Protocol), 36, 376
dial-in capabilities, 187
dial-out capabilities, 187
dial-up connections, 212
dialog boxes
Add Users and Groups, 150, 191, 346
Audit Policy, 189-191
Certificates, 209
Configure Mail Alerting, 353

Create Email Rule, 363
Directory Auditing, 191-192
Directory Permissions (Windows NT), 149-152
Event Log Settings, 195
Installation Options (MS Proxy Server setup), 336
Internet Options, 310
Join Array, 345
Key Generation Wizard, 235
Local Area Network (LAN) Settings, 175, 310
Proxy Settings, 174, 310, 354
Security, 353
Select Components, 233
Select Program Folder, 361
Select User Service for Master Security Plan, 369
Service dialog box (Windows NT), 139
Set Notification Command, 363
Setup Complete, 361
Setup Type, 360
Special Directory Access (Windows NT), 152
Diffie-Hellman/DSS encryption, 237
digital certificates, 206-207, 218
digital signatures, 79, 204-206, 232
Digital Subscriber Line (DSL), 384
directories (Windows NT), 148-149
Directory Auditing dialog box, 191-192
directory *directory* **command, 284**
directory *directory* **keyword, 276**
Directory Permissions dialog box (Windows NT), 149-152
disabling events auditing (Windows NT), 190

distributed denial-of-service attacks, 74-76
DMZ (demilitarized zone), 18, 98, 101-103, 267
DNS (Domain Name Service), 33
DNS (Domain Name System), 52-54
    configuring firewall for mail, 285
    hierarchy, 54
    root domain, 53
DNS information (classical proxies), 165-166
DNS lookup server, 248
DNS record types, 57-59
DNS resource records, 56-57
DNS servers
    caching-only, 55
    files, 56
    primary, 54-55
    secondary, 54-55
dnsserver, 248
Do Not Audit radio button, 190
documents (RFC). See RFC documents
domain controllers (Windows NT Server), 191
Domain Name field, 58
Domain Name Service (DNS), 33
Domain Name System. See DNS
domain names (support), 296
domains, 53
Don't Fragment (DF) field, 46
dotted-decimal notation, 36-37
downloading
    CommandView Firewall (trial version), 358
    ipchains, 322
    ipfwadm, 315
    SOCKS server, 299
    SOCKS V5 Reference Implementation, 299

SocksCap, 298
SQUID, 303
TCP Wrappers, 244
Drawbridge, 248-249
Drawbridge Filter Compiler, 249
Drawbridge Filter Engine, 249
Drawbridge Manager, 249
Drawbridge Web site, 250
/drop sudirectory (/rules directory), 251
DSL (Digital Subscriber Line), 384
dual-homed hosts, 98-99, 127
dynamic address assignments, 167
Dynamic Host Configuration Protocol (DHCP), 36, 376
dynamic packet filtering, 125, 341, 382

E

-e command-line option, 319
Echo Reply message type, 35, 72
Echo Request message type, 35, 72
Edit menu commands (Network Preferences), 310
editing files
    hosts.allow, 244
    hosts.deny, 244
    inetd.conf, 243
edu organizational domain, 53
educating users about security, 80-81
Elron CommandView Firewall. See CommandView Firewall
email
    delivering, 283. See also SMTP
    forging, 78-79
    spoofing, 79
Email Address field, 58
email alerts, configuring, 353

embedded content, 172
Enable Caching check box, 348
Enable Dynamic Packet Filtering on Microsoft Proxy Server Packets check box, 341
Enable E-Mail Notification check box, 363
Enable Logging Using check box, 352
Enable Packet Filtering on External Interface check box, 341
Enable Web Publishing check box, 350
enabling event auditing, 191-192
encapsulating security payload extension header, 389
Encapsulating Security Payload (ESP), 217, 221
encapsulation, 32
encrypted files, accessing (PGP), 232
encrypting
    data, 200, 217, 222. See also IKE; PPTP
    data streams, 207
    files (PGP), 231-232, 237-238
encryption, 201
    3DES (Data Encryption Standard), 202
    Blowfish, 202
    checking Web pages for, 209
    DES (Data Encryption Standard), 202
    Diffie-Hellman/DSS, 237
    IDEA (International Data Encryption Algorithm), 202
    PGP. See PGP
    private key (asymmetric), 203
    public key (asymmetric), 66, 201-203, 228. See also PGP
    RSA, 237
    single key (symmetric), 201-202
    Slipjack, 202

encryption software, PGP (Pretty Good Privacy). *See* PGP

endpoints, 49

ensuring secure connections, 82

environment variables, defining, 229

ESP (Encapsulating Security Payload), 217, 221

establishing client/server connections (SOCKS server), 292-295

/etc/inetd.conf file, 268-270

/etc/inted configuration file, 257

/etc/networks file (UNIX), 138

/etc/passwd file, 270

/etc/protocols file (UNIX), 138

/etc/services file, 138, 255

/etc/syslog.conf, 182. *See also* syslog configuration file

/etc/utmp file, 186

Ethernet 802 frame format, 32

evaluating
    IP packets, 324
    physical connections, 35

event icons, 194-195
    exclamation point in yellow circle, 194
    "I" in blue circle, 194
    key, 195
    padlock, 195
    stop sign, 194

Event Log Files, 191

Event Log Settings dialog box, 195

Event Log Wrapping radio buttons, 195

Event Viewer, 188, 193-195

Event Viewer command (Administrative Tools menu), 194

events
    auditing (Window NT), 189
    disabling, 190
    Event Viewer, 193-194

Print Manager, 191
Properties Sheet, 189
setting up policies, 191
User Manager, 189-191
Windows NT Explorer, 189-192

failure, logging, 189
File and Object Access, 190
Logon and Logoff, 190
Process Tracking, 190-191
Restart, Shutdown, and System, 190
Security Policy Changes, 190
success, logging, 189
Use of User Rights, 190
User and Group Management, 190

EXCEPT operator keyword, 259

exchanging keys, 202, 218

exclamation point (!), 280

exclamation point in yellow circle icon, 194

-exec *program* keyword, 274

executable *program* command, 284

exit command, 281

Exit command (CommandView File menu), 366

Expire Rate field, 59

Explorer (Windows NT)
    modifying permissions, 150-151
    viewing permissions on files/directories, 148-149

extension headers (IPv6), 389-390

F

-F *chain* command, 326

-f command-line parameter, 306-307

-f option, 330

-F parameter, 317, 327

-f *policy* command, 317

facility names (syslog configuration file), 183

/facts sudirectory (/rules directory), 251

Failure check box, 189

failure events, logging, 189

Farmer, Dan and Wietse Venema, "Improving the Security of Your Site by Breaking Into It", 13-14, 251

FAT partitions, converting to NTFS partitions, 336

FDDI frame format, 32

Federal Computer Incidence Response Capability Web site, 461-462

fields
    ACK Flag, 70
    Address Type, 297
    AH, 220-221
    BIND Request, 293-294, 297
    Change Settings, 195
    Class, 60
    CONNECT Request, 292-293, 297
    Data type, 257, 268
    Destination Address, 297, 389
    Destination Port, 297
    Domain Name, 58
    Don't Fragment (DF), 46
    Email Address, 58
    /etc/inetd.conf file, 268-269
    /etc/inted configuration file, 257
    Expire Rate, 59
    FIN Flag, 71
    fixed-length headers (IPv6), 387-389
    Flags, 76
    Flow Label, 388
    Fragment Offset, 76
    Hop Limit, 388
    Identification, 76
    IN, 58-60
    IP headers
        Datagram Length, 46
        Destination Address, 47
        Flags, 46
        Fragment Offset, 46
        Header Checksum, 47
        Identification, 46

Internet Header Length (IHL), 45
Options, 47
Padding, 47
protecting, 219-220
Protocol, 47
Source Address, 47
Time to Live (TTL), 47
Type of Service, 46
Version, 45
Maximun Log Size, 195
Minimum TTL, 59
Name, 257, 268
Next Header, 388
Payload Length, 388
Port, 310
Primary Server, 58
Process arguments, 257, 269
Protocol, 257, 268
Proxy Address to Use, 310
Refresh Rate, 59
reply code (Version Number), 293
Retry Rate, 59
Sequence Number, 70
Serial Number, 59
Server, 257, 269
SOA, 58
SOA records, 58-59
Source Address, 82, 389
SYN Flag, 70
Traffic Class, 388
UDP ASSOCIATE Request (SOCKS V5 Command Code), 297
UID, 257, 269
Version, 388
Version Number, 297
Wait-state, 257, 268
File and Object Access event, 190
File menu commands
Command View Firewall, 365-366
Attach to Firewall, 365
Configure New Firewall, 366
Detach From Firewall, 365

Exit, 366
Load Plan from File, 366
Print MSP Details, 366
Print MSP Summary, 366
Retrieve Plan from Firewall, 366
Save Plan to File, 366
Save Plan to Firewall, 366
Properties, 191
Settings, 195
File Transfer Protocol. *See* FTP
files
access.log, 308
cache, 56
cache.log, 308
comments, inserting, 272
configuration, syslog. *See* syslog configuration file
database, 56
decrypting (PGP), 237-238
default configuration (syslog), changing, 182
DNS servers, 56
encrypted, accessing, 232
encrypting (PGP), 231-232, 237-238
/etc/inetd.conf file, 268-270
/etc/inted configuration, 257
/etc/passwd, 270
/etc/services, 255
/etc/utmp, 186
hosts files, 166
hosts.allow, 257
configuring, 258-261
editing, 244
hosts.deny, 257
configuring, 258-261
editing, 244
hosts.equiv, 61-62, 281
inetd.conf, 255-256
configuring, 257-258
editing, 243
inetd.conf configuration file (UNIX), 135-136
keys.asc, 230
lastlog, 186
log, 106-107, 178-179, 196, 353

application-specific, 196
deleting, 180
Event, 191
managing, 195
reviewing, 178-181, 193-194
SQUID, 308-309
make, 304
netperm-table, 272. *See also* rules
network configuration files (UNIX), 138
password, 65
permissions, viewing (Windows NT), 148-149
removing unnecessary files from bastion hosts, 141-142
reverse lookup, 56
.rhosts, 61-62, 281
shadow password file (UNIX), 134
squid.conf, 248, 305-306
store.log, 308
swap.state, 308
syslogd.conf, 256
transferring between computers, 51
/usr/adm/wtmp, 186
/var/adm/aculog, 187
/var/log/cron, 187
filtering packets, 110-116, 314-315, 376, 382
ACK bit, 123-124
advantages/disadvantages, 128-129
dangerous services, 115-116
Drawbridge, 248-250
dynamic packet filtering, 125
hardware and software packet filters, 126-127
ICMP packets, 124-125
IP header information, 116-117
ports, 120-122
Proxy Server, 341-343
rules, 113-115
screened subnets, 112
screened-host configuration, 111
sockets, 120

stateful packet filtering, 95
stateless packet filtering, 95, 125
SYN bit, 123
TCP header information, 117-119
UDP header information, 120
where to use packet filters, 110-113
FIN Flag field, 71
finding advisory bulletins, 75
finger, 261
finger replacements, 453
finger command, 186
finger utility (UNIX), 136
fingerd, 453
fingerd Web site, 453
firewall appliances, 18, 126, 372-373
alerting capabilities, 377-378
application proxies, 376
installing, 373
Interceptor, 374
Lucent Managed Firewall, 374-376
managing, 373-374
NAT support, 377
network interfaces, 374-375
packets, filtering, 376
PERMIT, 374
plug-and-play, 374
pricing, 378-379
reporting capabilities, 377-378
security policies, 375-376
selecting, 378-379
VPN, 378
Firewall menu (CommandView Firewall), 367-368
Firewall menu commands
Check Alive, 367
Ping Router, 367
Restart, 367
Set Date/Time, 367
Set Password, 367
SMXP Encryption Key, 367
Upgrade, 367

firewall policies, 91-93
Firewall Toolkit. See FWTK
firewalls, 11-12. *See also*
application proxies; packet filters; security
additional resources, 456
CERT Coordination Center, 458-459
COAST (Computer Operations, Audit and Security Technology) Web site, 461
Federal Computer Incidence Response Capability Web site, 461-462
Firewalls mailing list, 460
Forum of Incident Response and Security Teams, 457
L0pht Heavy Industries Web site, 460
Microsoft Web sites, 459
National Security Institute's Security Resource Net Web site, 462
NT security, 460
SANS (System Administration, Networking, and Security) Institute, 457
U.S. Department of Energy Web site, 461
World Wide Web Security FAQ Web site, 461
address translation, 11
address vectoring, 11
architectures, 93
benefits, 21
caching, 11
CommandView. *See* CommandView Firewall
configuring, 26
configuring for mail (DNS), 285
designing
application proxy gateway, 96-97
bastion hosts, 104
combining strategies, 97-100
firewall policies, 91-93

packet filters, 94-96
sacrificial hosts, 104-105
screened subnet architecture, 101-103
security policies, 86-91, 105-106
Elron CommandView Firewall. *See* CommandView Firewall
Gauntlet, 244, 265-266
home computers, 384-385
integrating, 383
limitations, 21-22
maintaining, 23-24
NAT (network address translation), 21
new functionality, 382-383
policies, creating, 16
restricting Internet access, 11
selecting, 18-20
TCP Wrappers, 254-255
access control, 254-255
configuring, 256-261
limitations, 261-262
logging, 255-256
obtaining, 256
tcpd daemon, 255
testing, 384
Firewalls mailing list, 460
fixed-length headers (IPv6), 386-389
flags
bidirectional, 329
logging, 329
More Fragments (MF), 46
verbose, 329
Flags field, 46, 76
Flow Label field, 388
folders, Administrative Tools, 189
forging email, 78-79
Forum of Incident Response and Security Teams Web site, 457
Forward chains, 323
FQDN (fully-qualified domain name), 54
Fragment Offset field, 46, 76
fragmentation (UDP), 298

fragmentation extension
header, 389-390
fragmenting packets, 298
frame formats, 32
Free Software Foundation,
302
Free Software Foundation
Web site, 302
FreeBSD, 249-250
FreeBSD Web site, 250
freeware, 242
frequency, exchanging keys,
218
FTP (File Transfer
Protocol), 15, 26, 51, 254
disadvantages, 51-52
patches (SRA), 453
FTP services (UNIX), 135
FTP sites (anonymous), 15,
52
ftp-gw, 267
ftp-gw proxy, 275
configuring, 277-279
keywords, 276-277
ftp-qw, 245
fully-qualified domain name
(FQDN), 54
FWTK (Firewall Toolkit),
97, 244-246, 264, 315
authd, 246
comparing to Gauntlet firewall, 265-266
components, 266-267, 289
ftp-qw, 245
installing (bastion hosts),
289-290
history of, 264
login-sh, 246
netacl, 245
obtaining, 264-265
plug-qw, 245
rloginqw, 245
smap, 245
smapd, 245
syslogd, 246
telnetd, 246
tn-qw, 245
FWTK Web site, 264, 289

G

Gabriel, 449
Gabriel Web site, 450
gatekeepers, 110
gateways
application, 264, 296. See
also application proxy;
proxy server
circuit-level, 296
proxy (rlogin-gw), 281-282
Gauntlet firewall, 244,
265-266
generating public/private key
pairs
UNIX PCP install, 229-230
Windows NT PCP install,
235-237
geographical domains, 53
GIAC (Global Incident
Analysis Center), 457
GNU, 302
gov organizational domain, 53
groupid group command,
284-286
groupid group keyword, 276
GSS-API, 297

H

-h command, 318
-h command-line parameter,
306
%h variable, 261
hackers, 79
handling client requests, 350
handshake protocols, SSL
(Secure Sockets Layer),
207-208
hardening computers for
bastion hosts, 133
secure operating systems,
installing from scratch,
133-134
UNIX daemon processes,
135-137
UNIX network configura-
tion files, 138
Windows NT services,
139-140

hardware addresses, translating, 33, 36
hardware and software packet
filters, 126-127
Header Checksum field, 47
header fields (IP), protecting,
219-220
headers
extension (IPv6), 389-390
fixed length (IPv6), 386-389
IP, 45-47
IP header information,
116-117
TCP, 70
TCP header information
117-119
UDP header information 120
Help command, 281
help-msg file keyword, 276
hierarchy (DNS), 54
HINFO record type, 58
history of FWTK, 264
home computer security,
384-385
Hop Limit field, 388
hop-by-hop options extension
header, 389
host computers, crashing
(denial-of-service attacks),
70
hostnames, 34
hosts, 36
bastion, 18, 104, 132
auditing and logging, configuring, 152
compromised bastion hosts,
154-155
configuring, 132-133
installing FWTK on,
289-290
proxy software, running,
153-154
removing unnecessary applications and files, 141-142
secure operating systems,
installing from scratch,
133-134
UNIX daemon processes,
135-137
UNIX network configuration
files, 138

UNIX resource permissions, 142-146
Windows NT resource permissions, 147-152
Windows NT services, 139-140
dual-homed hosts, 98-99, 127
reconfiguring (denial-of-service attacks), 70
sacrificial, 18
sacrificial hosts, 104-105
screened hosts, 100
trusted, 83
hosts attribute, 274, 277, 280
hosts files, 166
hosts *hosts* keyword, 274-276
hosts keyword, 280
hosts.allow file, 257
configuring, 258-261
editing, 244
hosts.deny file, 257
configuring, 258-261
editing, 244
hosts.equiv file, 61-62, 281
Hosttype sudirectory (/rules directory), 251
HS (Hesiod) class, 60
hyphen (-), 274

I

-I *chain rule-number rule* command, 326
"I" in blue circle icon, 194
-i *interface* parameter, 327
-I parameter, 317
-i *policy* command, 317
IANA (Internet Assigned Numbers Authority), 49, 296, 396
ICMP (Internet Control Message Protocol), 34-36, 388
codes, 114, 322
message types, 35, 72-73
packets, 35, 124-125
source quench messages, 124
types, 322

icons, event, 194-195
exclamation point in yellow circle, 194
"I" in blue circle, 194
key, 195
padlock, 195
stop sign, 194
ICP (Internet Cache Protocol), 248, 309
IDEA (International Data Encryption Algorithm), 202
IDENT protocol, 296
Identification field, 46, 76
IETF (Internet Engineering Task Force), 222
IETF Web site, 209
ifstatus, 450
ifstatus Web site, 450
IKE (Internet Key Exchange), 217-219
IKE SA, 219
improving performance, 12
"Improving the Security of Your Site by Breaking Into It" (Dan Farmer and Wietse Venema), 13-14, 251
IN field, 58-60
incident reporting and response procedures (security policies), 105-106
inetd, 243
inetd daemon, 255, 268-270
inetd daemon server, 136
inetd.conf configuration file (UNIX), 135-136
inetd.conf file, 243, 255-256
configuring, 257-258
editing, 243
Information Reply message type, 35-36
Information Request message type, 35-36
Input chains, 323
inserting comments into files, 272
Installation Options dialog box (MS Proxy Server setup), 336

installing
Drawbridge, 249
firewall appliances, 373
firewalls (CommandView Firewall), 358-359
FWTK bastion host, 289-290
ipchains, 321
ipfwadm, 316
Microsoft Proxy Server, 335-339
NTFS partitions, 336
service packs, 335
setup program, 336
PGP, 229
UNIX, 229-230
Windows NT, 233-234
secure operating systems from scratch, 133-134
SQUID, 303-305
int organizational domain, 53
integrating firewalls, 383
intercepting
calls (WinSock networking functions), 292, 298
network communications, 81-82
packets, 82
Interceptor firewall appliance, 374
interfaces (network), firewall appliances, 374-375
International Data Encryption Algorithm (IDEA), 202
International Standardization Organization (ISO), 26
Internet, 382
access
blocking, 171-172
restricting, 11
screening, 171-172
security, 12-14
security policies, creating, 14-16
uses, 14-15
Internet Assigned Numbers Authority (IANA), 49, 296, 396

Internet Cache Protocol (ICP), 248, 309
Internet Control Message Protocol. *See* ICMP
Internet Daemon, 243. *See also* inetd
Internet Engineering Task Force (IETF), 222
Internet Header Length (IHL) field, 45
Internet Key Exchange (IKE), 217-219
Internet Options command
    Tools menu, 310
    View menu, 354
Internet Options dialog box, 310
Internet Protocol. *See* IP
Internet Security Association and Key Management Protocol (ISAKMP), 217-219
Internet Security Scanner (ISS), 448-449
Internet service (Proxy Server), 353-355
Internet Service Manager, 340
Internet Service Manager command (Microsoft Proxy Server menu), 341
intrusion detection, 382
IP (Internet Protocol), 31-32, 69, 82-83, 254, 386
IP address classes, 36-37
    Class A, 38
    Class B, 39
    Class C, 39
    Class D, 40
    Class E, 40
    determining, 37-38
IP addresses, 34-36
    assigning, 376-377
    dotted-decimal notation, 36-37
    length, 36
    specifying, 327-328
    translating, 33
IP addressing, 32-33

IP auditing tools, 448
IP forwarding, 98, 160
IP forwarding firewall rule, 316
IP header fields, protecting, 219-220
IP header information, 116-117
IP headers, 45-47
IP input firewall rule, 316
IP layer, 45
IP output firewall rule, 316
IP packet accounting rule, 316
IP packets, 45, 82, 324
IP spoofing, 47, 114
ipchains, 314-315, 330-331
    chains, 323-326
    command-line options, 328
    comparing to ipfwadm, 322
    configuring, 321
    downloading, 322
    installing, 321
ipchains Web site, 322, 330
ipchains-restore command, 330
ipchains-save command, 330
ipfw, 315
ipfwadm, 314-315, 330
    commands, 317-318
    comparing to ipchains, 322
    downloading, 315
    installing, 316
    parameters, 318-319
    rules, 316
    Web site, 315
ipfwadm command, 319-321
ipfwadm rules, 321
IPSec protocol suite, 216-217
IPv4, 216, 386-387
IPv6, 216, 386, 391-392
    addresses, 391
    compatibility with IPv4, 387
    extension headers, 389-390
    fixed-length headers, 386-389
IPv6 addressing (support), 296
IPv6 Forum Web site, 386
IPv6 Web site, 386

ISAKMP (Internet Association and Key Management Protocol), 217-219
ISO (International Standardization Organization), 26
ISS (Internet Security Scanner), 448-449
ISS Web sites, 449
issuing certificates, 207

J-K

-j *target* parameter, 327
Join Array dialog box, 345
joining
    Proxy server arrays, 345
    VPNs, 213
-k check command-line parameter, 307
-k command-line option, 319
-k command-line parameter, 306
-k debug command-line parameter, 307
-k interrupt command-line parameter, 307
-k kill command-line parameter, 307
-k rotate command-line parameter, 306
-k shutdown command-line parameter, 306
Kerberos, 66
key data, 218
Key Generation Wizard, 235, 238
Key Generation Wizard dialog box, 235
key icon, 195
key rings, 230-231
key servers, 230
key size, specifying, 229
key size prompt, 229
key user ID prompt, 229
keys, 201
    decrypting, 203
    exchanging, 202, 218
    naming, 229
    public, 231
    storing, 230

Keys menu commands (New Key), 235
keys.asc file, 230
keyword, 272
keywords, 274-275
accept, 324
ALL, 259
authserver *host port*, 276
-chroot *directory*, 275
denial-msg *filename*, 276
deny, 324
directory *directory*, 276
EXCEPT, 259
-exec *program*, 274
ftp-gw proxy, 276-277
groupid *group*, 276
help-msg *file*, 276
hosts, 280
hosts *hosts*, 274-276
KNOWN, 259
LOCAL, 259
PARANOID, 259
plug-gw, 286
prompt *prompt*, 280
reject, 324
return, 324
smap, 284
smapd, 284-285
Timeout *seconds*, 275-276
tn-gw proxy, 280
UNKNOWN, 259
-user *userid*, 275
userid *user*, 276
welcome-msg *filename*, 276
Xforwarder *program*, 280
KNOWN keyword, 259
Koblas, David, 292

L

-L *chain* command, 326
-l command, 317
-l command-line option, 329
L0pht Heavy Industries Web site, 460
L2TP (Layer Two Tunneling Protocol), 225
labels, 56
LAN Settings button, 310

LANs (Local Area Networks), 64
address space, increasing with NAT, 170
LAN information, hiding with NAT, 169
security, 64
physical safeguards, 67
resource protections, 66-67
user authentication, 64-66
last command, 186
lastlog file, 186
Layer Two Tunneling Protocol (L2TP), 225
layers, 27-28
Application, 27, 30
Data Link, 28
IP, 45
Logical Link Control (LLC), 28
Media Access Control (MAC), 28
Network, 28-29
Physical, 27-28
Presentation, 27, 30
Session, 29
Transport, 29
leased-lines, 212
Lee, Ying-Da, 292
length of IP addresses, 36
Length field, 220
library functions (SOCKS), linking code to, 298
Lightweight Internet Cache Protocol (ICP), 248, 309
limited resources, overloading (denial-of-service attacks), 69-70
linking code to SOCKS library functions, 298
Linux, 181
List Open Files (lsof), 452
Load Plan from File command (CommandView File menu), 366
Local Address Table button, 346
Local Area Network (LAN) Settings dialog box, 175, 310

Local Area Networks. *See* LANs
LOCAL keyword, 259
locating promiscuous network interfaces, 450
log files, 106-107, 178-179, 196, 351-353
Application event, 193
application-specific, 196
deleting, 180
Event, 191
managing (Windows NT), 195
reviewing, 178-181, 193-194
Security event, 193-194
SQUID, 308-309
System event, 193
UNIX, 185-187
Log menu (CommandView firewall), 368
Log menu commands (Security), 194
Log to File radio button, 352
Log to SQL/ODBC Database radio button, 352
logging, 255-256, 351-353
bastion hosts, configuring, 152
events, 189
proxy servers, 173
Regular format, 352
TCP Wrapper (syslogd daemon), 244
Verbose format, 352
logging flag, 329
logging in remotely, 50
Logging property page, 351
Logical Link Control (LLC) layer, 28
login databases, 65
login failures, auditing, 180
login-sh, 246, 267
Logon and Logoff event, 190
loopback address, 40
loose source routing, 48
lsof (List Open Files), 452
lsof Web site, 452
Lucent Managed Firewall firewall appliance, 374-376

M

-m command-line option, 319

-m *markvalue* command-line option, 329

-M parameter, 317

MAC addresses, 33-36

mailing lists
Firewalls, 460
SOCKS, 299-300
Tiger, 448

main mode, 218

maintaining firewalls, 23-24

make commands, 316

make file, 304

make install command, 306

man pages, 274

manager application (CommandView Firewall), 364-365

managing
caching properties, 347-350
chains, 326
firewall appliances, 373-374
log files (Windows NT), 195
rules, 326-327
SQUID, 305
user services, 368-369

manual pages, 274

Manual Proxy Configuration radio button, 310

masq target, 324

master secret, 208

Master Security Plan, 365-366

matching attribute values, 273

maxchildren *children* command, 285

Maximum Log Size field, 195

MB record type, 58

MD5, 452

Media Access Control (MAC) layer, 28

Merlin, 450

Merlin Web site, 450

message digest, 205

message types
Address Mask Reply, 35
Address Mask Request, 35
Destination Unreachable, 35, 73
Echo Reply, 35, 72
Echo Request, 35, 72
ICMP, 35
Information Reply, 35-36
Information Request, 35-36
Parameter Problem, 35
Redirect, 72-73
Redirect Message, 35
Source Quench, 35
Time Exceeded, 35
Timestamp Reply, 35
Timestamp Request, 35

messages
data, 117
sending to other computers (syslog configuration file), 184-185

MG record type, 58

Microsoft Point-to-Point Tunneling Protocol. *See* PPTP

Microsoft Proxy Server. *See* Proxy Server

Microsoft Proxy Server command (Programs menu), 341

Microsoft Proxy Server menu commands (Internet Service Manager), 341

Microsoft Web sites, 134, 459
security, 459
service pack downloads, 335

mil organizational domain, 53

MINFO record type, 58

Minimum TTL field, 59

models, layers, 27-28

modes
aggressive, 219
main, 218
quick, 219
transport, 221
tunnel, 221

modifiers
deny-, 274
permit-, 274

monitoring
network components, 64
network traffic, 81-82
networks (tools), 448
Argus, 448
Courtney, 449
Gabriel, 449
ifstatus, 450
ISS (Internet Security Scanner), 448-449
Merlin, 450
NID (Network Intrusion Detector), 450
SATAN (Security Administrator Tool for Analyzing Networks), 449
SWATCH (Simple WATCHer), 448
tcpdump, 450

More Fragments (MF) flag, 46

mountd daemon, 137

MR record type, 58

multicast addresses, 40-41, 391

multiple screened subnets, 104

MX record type, 58

N

-N *chain* command, 326

-n command-line option, 319, 329

-N command-line parameter, 307

%n variable, 261

Name field, 257, 268

naming keys, 229

NAPT (Network Address Port Translation), 168-169

NAT (Network Address Translation), 166-171, 377
basic NAT, 167-168
comparing to address vectoring, 170-171
dynamic address assignments, 167
LANs (local area networks), 169-170

NAPT (Network Address Port Translation), 168-169

static address assignments, 167

support (firewall appliances), 377

NAT (Network Address Translation) functionality, 373

National Security Institute's Security Resource Net Web site, 462

NDS (Novell Directory Services), 66

net organizational domain, 53

netacl, 245, 267-271, 274-275

netacl application, 270

NetBIOS protocol (Windows NT), 140

netd daemon, restarting, 258

netperm-table file, 272. *See also* rules

network monitoring tools. *See* tools, monitoring networks

network adapter cards, reviewing, 359

Network Address Port Translation (NAPT), 168-169

Network Address Translation. *See* NAT

Network Address Translation (NAT) functionality, 373

Network applet (Windows NT), 139

Network Associates Web site, 228

network communications, intercepting, 81-82

network components, monitoring, 64

network configuration files (UNIX), 138

network connection policy (security policies), 87-88

network connections, controlling, 28

Network File System (NFS), 115, 137

network information, reconfiguring (denial-of-service attacks), 70

Network Information Center (NIC), 47

Network Information Services (NIS), 65, 115

network interfaces
    firewall appliances, 374-375
    promiscuous, locating, 450

Network Intrusion Detector (NID), 450

Network layer, 28-29

network masks, specifying, 327

Network News Transport Protocol (NNTP), 285

Network Preference command (Edit menu), 310

network protocols
    security concerns, 68
    TCP/IP, 254

network security (firewall appliances), 375

network traffic, monitoring, 81-82

networking functions (WinSock), intercepting calls, 292, 298

networking models (OSI), 26-28

networks
    DNS information, 165-166
    hosts files, 166
    private (addresses), 40
    security policies, creating, 14-16

New Key command (Keys menu), 235

Next Header field, 220, 388

NFS (Network File System), 115, 137

NIC (Network Information Center), 47

NID (Network Intruder Detector), 450

NID Web site, 450

NIS (Network Information Service), 65, 115

NNTP (Network News Transport Protocol), 285

nodes (network connections), controlling, 28

nonrepudiation, 205

notation (dotted-decimal), 36-37

Novell Directory Services (NDS), 66

NS record type, 58-59

NT security Web site, 460

NTFS partitions, 336

NULL record type, 58

number sign/pound symbol (#), 184, 272

numeric output, 329

O

-o command-line option, 319

-O parameter, 317

-o [*maxsize*] command-line option, 329

Oakley key exchange method, 217-218

obtaining
    FWTK, 264-265
    TCP Wrappers, 256

Open System Interconnect (OSI), 26

operating systems
    secure operating systems, installing from scratch, 133-134
    selecting firewalls, 19-20

operator keywords (EXCEPT), 259

option classes, 48

option numbers, 48

options
    -auth, 280
    -f, 330
    -passok, 280
    -plug-to *host*, 287
    -port portid, 287
    -privport, 287
    -v, 330
    hosts attribute, 277, 280
    plug-gw, 287

Options field, 47

org organizational domain, 53
organizational domains, 53
OSI (Open System Interconnect), 26
OSI networking model, 26-28
output, numeric, 329
Output chains, 323
overloading limited resources (denial-of-service attacks), 69-70
owner values (UNIX resource permissions), changing, 145-146

P

-P *chain target* command, 326
-p *policy* command, 318
-P *protocol* parameter, 319, 327
%p variable, 261
packet filtering, 382
 dynamic, 341, 382, 341
 Proxy Server, 341-343
 stateful, 382
packet filtering routers, 127
packet filters, 10, 17, 47-48, 72, 94-96, 110-116
 ACK bit, 123-124
 advantages/disadvantages, 128-129
 combining with application proxy gateway, 97-100
  dual-homed hosts, 98-99
  screened hosts, 100
 configuring, 48
 dangerous services, 115-116
 dynamic packet filtering, 125
 hardware and software packet filters, 126-127
 ICMP packets, 124-125
 IP header information, 116-117
 ports, 120-122
 rules
  conventions, 114-115
  creating, 113-115
 screened subnets, 112

 screened-host configuration, 111
 sockets, 120
 stateless packet filters, 125
 SYN bit, 123
 TCP header information, 117-119
 UDP header information, 120
 where to use packet filters, 110-113
packet fragmentation, 76-78
packet headers, 10
packet-filtering routers, configuring, 32
packets, 69. *See also* **datagrams**
 filtering, 314-315, 376
  Drawbridge, 248-250
  dynamic, 382
  stateful, 382
 fragmenting, 298
 ICMP, 35
 ICMP packets, 124-125
 intercepting, 82
 IP, 82
 reply, 297
 request (UDP ASSOCIATE), 297
 transferring, 31-32
Padding field, 47
padlock icon, 195
Parameter Problem message type, 35
parameters
 -A direction, 317
 -D *address*[*/mask*][*port...*], 319
 -d *destination*, 327
 -F, 317, 327
 -I, 317
 -i *interface*, 327
 -j *target*, 327
 -M, 317
 -O, 317
 -P *protocol*, 319, 327
 -S *address*[*/mask*][*port...*], 319
 -s *source*, 327
 -V *address*, 319
 -W *name*, 319

 command-line (squid command), 306-308
 ipfwadm, 318-319
 rules, specifying, 327
PARANOID keyword, 259
parent background processes, 305
parent cache servers, 309
parent servers, 248
partitions, FAT/NTFS, 336
pass phrase prompts, 229
pass phrases, 229-230
-passok option, 280
password command, 281
password databases, 65
password files
 shadow, 65
 synchronizing, 65
password security (password utilities), 446
password utilities
 COPS (Computer Oracle and Password System), 447
 Crack, 446-447
 Perl COPS (Computer Oracle and Password System), 447
 Tiger, 447-448
passwords, 65, 80
patches (UNIX commands), 452
 Authentication Server Daemon (Authd), 453-454
 r* tools (ssh), 454
 sendmail (smrsh), 452
 su (dummy program), 454
 Telnet/FTP (SRA), 453
Payload Length field, 388
PCERT (Purdue Computer Emergency Response Team) Web site, 458
performance, improving, 12
period (.), 53
Perl COPS (Computer Oracle and Password System), 447
Perl COPS Web site, 447
Permission tab, 346
permission values (UNIX resource permissions)
 changing, 145-146
 viewing, 143-144

permissions (resource permissions). *See* resource
permissions
permissions array (UNIX
resource permissions), 143
Permissions property page,
346-347
PERMIT firewall appliance,
374
permit- modifier, 274
PGP (Pretty Good Privacy)
encryption software, 203,
212, 228, 231-232
  components, selecting,
  233-234
  configuring (Windows NT),
  235-237
  decrypting files, 237-238
  digital signatures, creating,
  232
  encrypted files, accessing,
  232
  encrypting files, 237-238
  installing, 229
    UNIX, 229-230
    Windows NT, 233-234
PGP command (Programs
menu), 235
PGP Command Line com-
ponent, 234
pgp commands, 231
PGP Eudora Plugin compo-
nent, 233
PGP Key Management com-
ponent, 233
PGP menu commands
(PGPkeys), 235
PGP Microsoft
Exchange/Outlook Plugin
component, 234
PGP Microsoft Outlook
Express Plugin component,
234
PGP User's Guide compo-
nent, 234
PGP window, 235
PGPkeys command (PGP
menu), 235
PGPnet Virtual Private
Networking component,
233

phrases, pass, 229-230
physical addresses, 36
physical connections, evaluating, 35
Physical layer, 27-28
physical outages, 22
PING, 72-73, 388
PING command, 35
PING of Death, preventing,
74
Ping Router command
(CommandView Firewall
menu), 367
plug-and-play firewall appliances, 374
plug-gw, 267, 285-288
  configuring, 286
  keywords, 286
  options, 287
  starting, 286
plug-gw gateway, 166
plug-qw, 245
-plug-to *host* option, 287
Plugs button, 345
Point-to-Point protocol
(PPP), 222, 377
Point-to-Point Tunneling
protocol. *See* PPTP
policies
  deny, 318
  firewalls, creating, 16
  reject, 318
  security, 12-16
Policies menu commands
(Audit), 189
policy values, 318
Port field, 310
port numbers, 49, 269,
327-328, 396
port *portid hosts* command,
286
-port portid option, 287
PortMap V3, 453
PortMap V3 Web site, 453
portmapper program
replacements (PortMap
V3), 453
ports, 396-397. *See also* protocols
  packet filters, 120-122
  privileged ports, 121

range, 327-328
registered, 50, 396
TCP, 49
UDP, 49
well-known, 49-50, 396
pound symbol/number sign
(#), 184, 272
power outages, 22
PPP (Point-to-Point protocol), 222, 377
PPTP (Point-to-Point
Tunneling protocol), 214,
222-223, 378
PPTP control connections,
223-224
PPTP tunnels, 222-224
premaster secret, 208
Presentation layer, 27, 30
Pretty Good Privacy encryption software. *See* PGP
encryption software
preventing
  denial-of-service attacks, 70
  PING of Death, 74
  SYN flooding, 71-72
pricing firewall appliances,
378-379
Primary Server field, 58
primary servers (DNS),
54-55
Print Manager, 191
Print MSP Details command
(CommandView File
menu), 366
Print MSP Summary com-
mand (CommandView File
menu), 366
printers
  auditing usages, 193
  Properties Sheet, 189
privacy, 200
private key (asymmetric)
encryption, 203
private networks, addresses,
40
privileged ports, 121
-privport option, 287
Process arguments field,
257, 269
Process Tracking event,
190-191

Programs menu commands
Administrative Tools, 189
Microsoft Proxy Server, 341
PGP, 235
Windows NT Explorer, 191
promiscuous network inter-
faces, locating, 450
prompt *prompt* **keyword, 280**
prompts, 229-230
properties caching, manag-
ing, 347-350
Properties command (File
menu), 191
Properties menu commands
(Service Properties), 340
Properties Sheet, 189, 193
property pages
Caching, 347-349
Logging, 351
Permissions, 346-347
Publishing, 350-351
Routing, 350
Service, 346
protecting
IP header fields, 219-220
passwords, 80
Protocol field, 47, 257, 268
protocol stacks, 26
protocol suites, 26, 216-217
protocols. *See also* **ports**
ARP (Address Resolution
Protocol), 26, 33-34
bootp, 36
FTP, 26, 51-52
handshake (SSL), 207-208
ICMP (Internet Control
Messages Protocol), 34-36
IDENT, 296
IP (Internet Protocol),
31-32, 69, 386
NetBIOS protocol
(Windows NT), 140
network (TCP/IP), 254
NFS (Network File
System), 137
PPP (Point-to-Point proto-
col), 222, 377
PPTP (Point-to-Point
Tunneling protocol), 214,
222

record (SSL), 207
SMTP (Simple Mail
Transfer Protocol), 60
SOCKS, 292
SSL (Secure Sockets Layer),
203, 207-209, 212
TCP (Transmission Control
Protocol), 32, 70-71
TCP/IP. *See* TCP/IP
TFTP, 52
TLS (Transfer Layer
Security), 209
UDP, 26, 33
proxies
application, 10, 17, 96, 376
application proxy, 96
classical proxies, 162-166
custom proxies, creating,
166
ftp-gw, 275
configuring, 277-279
keywords, 276-277
Remote Login, 281
rlogin, 281
Telnet, 279
tn-gw, 279-280
transparent proxies,
163-165
UDP, creating, 296-297
Proxies command (Advanced
menu), 310
Proxy Address to Use field,
310
proxy applications, 296
proxy gateways (rlogin-gw),
281-282
proxy information, configur-
ing, 354
Proxy Server, 96-97, 158,
160-161, 247, 264, 296,
334-335. *See also* **applica-**
tion proxy, application
gateway
advantages/disadvantages,
161
arrays, joining, 345
blocking
Internet access, 171-172
IP traffic, 158-159, 163
built-in proxy servers,
174-175

caching, 302
Caching property page,
347-349
configuring, 275
custom proxies, creating, 166
disabling routing, 160-161
installing, 334-337, 339
NTFS partitions, 336
service packs, 335
setup program, 336
Internet service, 353-355
Internet Service Manager,
340
logging, 173
Logging property page, 351
packet filtering, 341-343
Permission property page,
346-347
Proxy server arrays, joining,
345
Publishing property page,
350-351
Routing property page, 350
screening Internet access,
171-172
Service property page, 346
third-party plug-ins, 345
tn-gw (commands), 281
transparent access to network
services, 174-175
Web Proxy service, 343-344
Proxy Settings dialog box,
174, 310, 354
proxy software, running on
bastion hosts, 153-154
ps command, 139, 188
PTR record type, 58-59
public key (asymmetric)
encryption, 66, 201-203,
228. *See also* **PGP**
public keys, 231
public/private key pairs, gen-
erating
UNIX PGP install, 229-230
Windows NT PGP install,
235-237
publishing to the Web, 350
Publishing property page,
350-351

Q-R

quick mode, 219
quit command, 281

-R *chain rule-number rule* command, 326
-R command-line parameter, 307
-r *port* command-line option, 319
r services (UNIX), 135
r utilities, 60-61
r* tools (ssh patches), 454
radio buttons
    Audit These Events, 189
    Do Not Audit, 190
    Event Log Wrapping, 195
    Log to File, 352
    Log to SQL/ODBC, 352
    Manual Proxy Configuration, 310
random typing prompt, 230
ranges, specifying, 327-328
RAS (remote access server), 214
rcp utility, 61
reconfiguring hosts/network information (denial-of-service attacks), 70
record protocols, SSL (Secure Sockets Layer), 207
record types, 57-59
records, 182
    actions, 182-184
    resource, 56-57
    selectors, 182-184
    SOA (Start of Authority), 56-59
Red Hat Web site, 314
Redirect Message message type, 35
Redirect message types, 72-73
redirect target, 324
Refresh Rate field, 59
registered ports, 50, 396
Regular logging format, 352
reject keyword, 324
reject policy, 318
reject target, 324

relaying traffic (UDP), 297-298
remote access server (RAS), 214
remote login, 15. *See also* Telnet
Remote Login proxy, 281
Remote Monitoring (RMON), 64
remotely logging in, 50
Replace Auditing on Existing Files check box, 191
Replace Auditing on Subdirectories check box, 191
replacements (UNIX commands), 452-453
reply code (Version Number field), 293
reply packets, 297
reporting capabilities (firewall appliances), 377-378
reports, 377
Request for Comments documents. *See* RFC documents
request formats (SOCKS V5), 297
request headers (UDP), 298
request packets (UDP ASSOCIATE), 297
request paths, 351
requests
    BIND, 293-294
    CONNECT (SOCKS V4), 292-293
Reserved field, 220
resource permissions
    UNIX, 142-146
        owner values, changing, 145-146
        permission values, changing, 145-146
        permission values, viewing, 143-144
        SGID (Set Group ID), 144-145
        SUID (Set User ID), 144-145
    viewing on files/directories, 148-149

Windows NT, 147-152
    modifying, 150-152
    special permissions, 147
    standard permissions, 148
resource protection, 66-67, 181
resource records, 54-57
resources (limited), overloading (denial-of-service attacks), 69-70
Restart command (CommandView Firewall menu), 367
Restart, Shutdown, and System event, 190
restarting inetd daemon, 258, 270
restoring rules, 330
restricting Internet access, 11
Retrieve Plan from Firewall command (CommandView File menu), 366
Retry Rate field, 59
return keyword, 324
return target, 326
reverse lookup file, 56
reverse name lookup, 265
reviewing
    log files, 178-181, 193-194
    network adapter cards, 359
    syslog configuration file, 184-185
rexec utility, 61
RFC (Request for Comments) documents, 292
    Address Allocation for Private Networks (RFC 1918), 40
    Application of Internet Cache Protocol (ICP), Version 2 (RFC 2187), 248
    The Authentication Header (RFC 1826), 216
    Authentication Protocol (RFC 931), 261-262
    Domain Names—Implementation and Specification (RFC 1035), 56

The ESP DES-CBC Transform (RFC 1829), 216

GSS-API (RFC 1508/RFC 1509), 297

GSS-API Authentication Method for SOCKS V5 (RFC 1961), 292, 297

HTTP status codes used in log files (RFC 2068), 308

Identification Protocol (RFC 1413), 262

Internet Cache Protocol (ICP), Version 2 (RFC 2186), 248

Internet Control Message Protocol (ICMPv6) for the Internet Protocol Version 6 (IPv6) (RFC 2463), 388

Internet Security Association and Keyed Management Protocol (ISAKMP) (RFC 2048), 217-219

IP Authentication using Keyed MD5 (RFC 1828), 216

IP Encapsulating Security Payload (ESP) (RFC 1827), 216

The Oakley Key Determination Protocol (RFC 2412), 218

PPTP (Point-to-Point Tunneling Protocol) (RFC 2637), 222

Security Architecture for the Internet Protocol (RFC 1825), 216

SOCKS Protocol Version 5 (RFC 1928), 292

Username/Password Authentication for SOCKS V5 (RFC 1929), 292, 297

.rhosts file, 61-62, 281

rlogin utility, 61

rlogin proxy, 281

rlogin-gw proxy gateway, 281-282

rlogin-qw, 245

rlogin-rw, 267

RMON (Remote Monitoring), 64

root domain, 53

rotating SQUID log files, 308

routers, 35, 94
  access control lists (rules), 126-127
  packet-filtering, 32, 127
  screening routers, 94, 110

routing, 160-161, 314

routing extension header, 389-390

Routing property page, 350

rpcbind daemon, 137

RSA public key encryption, 228

rsh utility, 61

rules. *See also* chains
  attribute valuelist, 272
  creating, 273
  deleting, 327
  ipfwadm, 316, 321
  keywords, 272
  managing, 326-327
  restoring, 330
  routers, 126-127
  saving, 330
  specifying parameters, 327

/rules directory (subdirectories), 251

running
  proxy software on bastion hosts, 153-154
  setup program (CommandView Firewall), 360-364

ruptime utility, 61

rwho utility, 61

rwho command, 186

S

-S *address*[/*mask*][*port...*] parameter, 319

-s command-line parameter, 307

-s *source* parameter, 327

-s *tcp tcpfin udp* command, 318

%s variable, 261

SA encryption, 237

SA public key encryption, 228

SA source address, 218

sacrificial hosts, 18, 104-105

safe finger, 261

SAM (Security Accounts Manager) database, 65

SANS (System Administration, Networking, and Security) Institute, 457

SANS (System Administration, Networking, and Security) Institute Web site, 457

SAPs (Service Access Points), 28

SAs (security associations), length of validity, 218

SATAN (Security Administrator Tool for Analyzing Networks), 250-251, 449

SATAN Web site, 251-252, 449

Save Plan to File command (CommandView File menu), 366

Save Plan to Firewall command (CommandView File menu), 366

saving rules, 330

screened hosts, 100

screened subnet architecture
  demilitarized zone (DMZ), creating, 101-103
  multiple screened subnets, 104

screened subnets, 112

screened-host configuration, 111

screening Internet access, 171-172

screening routers, 94, 110

script (configure), 305

Search button, 192

search engines (altavisa), 456

secondary servers (DNS), 54-55

secure channels, creating, 212

secure connections, ensuring, 82

secure links, 378. *See also* VPNs

secure operating systems, installing from scratch, 133-134

Secure Shell, 136

Secure Sockets Layer (SSL), 373

Secure Sockets Layer (SSL) protocol, 203, 207-209, 212

Secure Sun, 451

Secure Sun Web site, 451

SecureID, 134

security, 10. *See also* firewalls
  application proxies, 17
  benefits of firewalls, 21
  denial-of-service attacks, 69-70
  Destination Unreachable message types, 73
  educating users, 80-81
  home computers, 384-385
  Internet, 12-14
  IP protocols (source routing), 69
  IPSec protocol suite, 216-217
  LANs, 64
    physical safeguards, 67
    resource protections, 66-67
    user authentication, 64-66
  limitations of firewalls, 21-22
  network (firewall appliances), 375
  network protocols, 68
  packet filters, 10, 17
  packet headers, 10
  passwords (password utilities), 446-448
  preventing SYN flooding, 71-72
  Redirect message types, 72-73
  system break-ins, 79-80
  system security check tools, 451-452

TCP/IP, 68
WANS, 67

Security Accounts Manager (SAM) database, 65

security advisories, 68, 106-107

security associations, 217-219

Security button, 341

Security command (Log menu), 194

Security dialog box, 353

security encapsulation extension header, 389

Security event log file, 193-194

Security Parameter Index (SPI), 218

Security Parameters Index (SPI) field, 220

security policies, 12-13, 86-91
  acceptable usage statements, 88-90
  creating, 14-16
  discussing specifics with employees, 90-91
  firewall appliances, 375-376
  incident reporting and response, 105-106
  network connection policy, 87-88

Security Policy Changes event, 190

Security Portal Web site, 459

Security tab, 191

Select Components dialog box, 233

Select Program Folder dialog box, 361

Select User Service for Master Security Plan dialog box, 369

selecting
  PGP components, 233-234
  firewall appliances, 378-379
  firewalls, 18-20

selectors, 182-184

Send SMTP Mail check box, 353

sending messages to other computers (syslog configuration file), 184-185

sendmail, 282-283, 452

sendmail daemon, 256

sendmail *program* command, 285

separating actions and selectors, 184

Sequence Number field, 70, 221

Serial Number field, 59

Server Backup button, 346

Server field, 257, 269

Server Restore button, 346

servers
  cache, 248
    child, 309
    parent, 309
    sibling, 309
    SQUID, 306
  caching, 11, 247-248. *See also* SQUID
  caching proxy, 302
  child, 248
  communicating between child and parent (SQUID), 248
  DNS
    caching-only, 55
    files, 56
    primary, 54-55
    secondary, 54-55
  DNS lookup, 248
  inetd daemon server, 136
  key, 230
  parent, 248
  proxy, 96-97, 158-161, 247, 264, 296
    advantages/disadvantages, 161
    blocking Internet access, 171-172
    blocking IP traffic, 158-159, 163
    built-in proxy servers, 174-175
    configuring, 275
    custom proxies, creating, 166

servers

disabling routing, 160-161
logging, 173
screening Internet access,
171-172
tn-gw, 281
transparent access to net-
work services, 174-175
SOCKS, 246
allocating sockets, 293
configurations, 293
downloading, 299
establishing client server
connections, 292-295
SQUID, 248, 303-304
Telnet, 50
Service dialog box (Windows
NT), 139
service pack downloads Web
site, 335
service packs, 335
Service Properties command
(Properties menu), 340
Service property page, 346
Service tab, 353
services (Windows NT),
139-140
Services Access Points
(SAPs), 28
Services applet (Windows
NT), 139
/services sudirectory (/rules
directory), 251
Session layer, 29
sessions, 29
Set Date/Time command
(CommandView Firewall
menu), 367
Set Group ID (SGID),
144-145
Set Notification Command
dialog box, 363
Set Password command
(CommandView Firewall
menu), 367
Set User ID (SUID),
144-145
setting up
auditing policies, 191
security associations,
218-219

Settings command (File
menu), 195
Setup Complete dialog box,
361
setup program
(CommandView Firewall),
running, 360-364
Setup Type dialog box, 360
severity levels (syslog configuration file), 183
sfingerd, 453
sfingerd Web site, 453
SGID (Set Group ID),
144-145
shadow password files, 65, 134
shareware, 242
shell commands, 260-261
Show Users button, 192, 346
sibling cache servers, 309
signatures (digital), creating,
232
Simple Mail Transport
Protocol (SMTP), 15, 60,
78
Simple Network
Management Protocol
(SNMP), 64, 378
Simple WATCHer
(SWATCH), 448
single key (symmetric)
encryption, 201-202
Skey, 134
slash symbol (/), 327
Slipjack, 202
smap, 245, 267, 282-283
keywords, 284
starting, 285
smapd, 245, 267, 283
keywords, 284-285
starting, 285
smrsh, 452
smrsh Web site, 452
SMTP (Simple Mail
Transport Protocol), 15,
60, 78
SMXP Encryption Key com-
mand (CommandView
Firewall menu), 367
SNMP (Simple Network
Management Protocol), 64,
378

SOA (Start of Authority)
record, 56
SOA field, 58
SOA record, 58-59
SOA record type, 58
social engineering, 22
SOCK-et-S. *See* SOCKS
sockets
/dev/log, 182
allocating, 293
packet filters, 120
SOCKS (SOCK-et-S), 97,
246-247, 292-293
library functions, linking code
to, 298
mailing lists, subscribing to,
299-300
support, 299-300
SOCKS Command Code field
values, 293
SOCKS server, 246
configurations, 293
downloading, 299
establishing client/server connections, 292-295
sockets, allocating, 293
SOCKS V4, 292
BIND requests, 293-294
CONNECT requests,
292-293
SOCKS V5, 296-297
SOCKS V5 Command Code
field values, 297
SOCKS V5 Reference
Implementation, download-
ing, 299
SOCKS Web site, 292
SocksCap, 292, 298
SOCKSifying applications,
247, 298
software (proxy software),
running on bastion hosts,
153-154
software and hardware packet
filters, 126-127
software tools (FWTK),
266-267
Source Address field, 47, 82,
389
source addresses (SA), 218

source code, compiling (UNIX PGP install), 229
Source Quench message type, 35
source quench messages, 124
source routing, 69
  defining, 48
  disadvantages, 69
  loose, 48
  strict, 48
Special Directory Access dialog box (Windows NT), 152
special permissions (Windows NT), 147
specifying
  actions, 184
  addresses, 327
  IP addresses, 327-328
  key size, 229
  network masks, 327
  port numbers, 327-328
  ranges of addresses, 327
  ranges of ports, 328
  rules (parameters), 327
SPI (Security Parameters Index), 218
SPI (Security Parameters Index) field, 220
spoofing
  email, 79, 82-83
  IP addresses, 114
SQUID, 247-248, 302-303
  cache hierarchy, 309
  communicating between child and parent servers, 248
  configuring clients, 310
  downloading, 303
  installing, 303-305
  log files, 308-309
  managing, 305
  servers, 248
    caching, 248
    choosing, 303-304
    DNS lookup, 248
SQUID cache server, 306
squid command, 248, 303-308

squid command-line parameters, 306-308
  -a *port*, 306
  -D, 307
  -d *error-level*, 306
  -f, 306-307
  -h, 306
  -k, 306
  -k check, 307
  -k debug, 307
  -k interrupt, 307
  -k kill, 307
  -k rotate, 306
  -k shutdown, 306
  -N, 307
  -R, 307
  -s, 307
  -u, 307
  -v, 307
  -X, 307
  -Y, 307
  -z, 307
squid user accounts, creating, 303
SQUID Web site, 303, 306
squid.conf file, 248, 305-306
SRA, 453
SRA Web site, 453
ssh, 454
SSH Secure Shell Web site, 136
ssh Web site, 454
SSL (Secure Sockets Layer), 373
SSL (Secure Sockets Layer) handshake protocol, 207-208
SSL (Secure Sockets Layer) protocol, 203, 207-209, 212
SSL (Secure Sockets Layer) record protocol, 207
Stacheldraht, 74
standalone servers (Windows NT Server), 191
standard permissions (Windows NT), 148
Start of Authority record, 56
starting
  plug-gw, 286
  smap, 285
  syslog daemon, 182

stateful inspection, 125
stateful packet filtering, 95, 382
stateless packet filtering, 95
stateless packet filters, 125
static address assignments, 167
stop sign icon, 194
store.log file, 308
storing keys, 230
strategies (firewall strategies), 93-100, 102-105
  application proxy gateway, 96-97
  bastion hosts, 104
  combining, 97-100
    dual-homed hosts, 98-99
    screened hosts, 100
  packet filters, 94-96
  sacrificial hosts, 104-105
  screened subnet architecture, 101-104
stream of data, 117
strict source routing, 48
su command, 187
su dummy program, 454
su dummy program Web site, 454
subdirectories (/rules directory), 251
subdividing addresses (subnet masks), 43
subdomains, 55
subnet addresses, calculating, 43-44
subnet calculators, 43
subnet masks, 41-43
subnet values, calculating, 43
subnets, 41
subnetting, 43
subscribing to mailing lists
  Firewalls, 460
  SOCKS, 299-300
Success check box, 189
success events, logging, 189
successful logins, auditing, 180
SUID (Set User ID), 144-145

support
   authentication, 296
   domain names, 296
   IPv6 addressing, 296
   NAT, 377
   SOCKS, 299-300
swap.state file, 308
SWATCH (Simple WATCHer), 448
SWATCH Web site, 448
symmetric encryption, 201-202
SYN bit, 123
SYN Flag field, 70
SYN flood, 123
SYN flooding, 70-72
synchronizing password files, 65
syslog configuration file
   changing default, 182
   facility names, 183
   reviewing, 184-185
   sending messages to other computers, 184-185
   severity levels, 183
syslog daemon (syslogd), 181-182, 244-246, 256, 267, 289
syslog utility, 181-182
syslogd (syslog daemon), 181-182, 244-246, 256, 267, 289
syslogd.conf file, 256
System Administration, Networking, and Security (SANS) Institute, 457
System Administrator's Tool for Analyzing Networks (SATAN), 250-251, 449
system break-ins, 79-80, 179
System event log file, 193
system security check tools, 451-452
system tools (FWTK), 267

T

-t andmask ormask command-line option, 329
-t andmask xormask command-line option, 320

tables (ARP), 34
tabs
   Alerting, 353
   Certificate Path, 209
   Connections, 310
   Details, 209
   Permissions, 346
   Security, 191
   Service, 353
talkd daemon, 136
targets
   accept, 324
   deny, 324
   masq, 324
   redirect, 324
   reject, 324
   return, 326
TCP (Transmission Control Protocol), 32, 254, 397
TCP header, 70
TCP header information (packet filters), 117-119
TCP port, 49
TCP protocol (three-way handshake connection method), 70-71
TCP Protocol Data Unit, 117
TCP well-known port numbers, 397-443
TCP Wrappers, 136, 242-244, 254-255
   access control, 243, 254-255
   configuring, 256-257
      hosts.allow file, 258-261
      hosts.deny file, 258-261
      inetd.conf file, 257-258
   downloading, 244
   limitations, 261-262
   logging, 244, 255-256
   obtaining, 256
   tcpd daemon, 243, 255
TCP/IP (Transmission Control Protocol/Internet Protocol), 26, 30-32, 50, 62, 254
   security concerns, 68
   Telnet, 50-51
tcpd daemon (TCP Wrappers), 243, 255, 258
tcpdchk, 262

tcpdmatch, 262
tcpdump, 450
tcpdump Web site, 451
Telnet, 15, 50-51, 136, 254, 453
Telnet proxy, 279
Telnet servers, 50
telnetd, 246, 267
testing firewalls, 384
TFN (Tribe Flood Network), 74
TFN2K (Tribe Flood Network 2000), 74
TFTP (Trivial File Transfer Protocol), 52, 127
third-party plug-ins, 345
three-way handshake connection method, 70-71
Tiger, 447-448
Tiger mailing list, 448
Tiger Web site, 447
Time Exceeded message type, 35
Time to Live (TTL) field, 47
timeout *seconds* command, 281, 284, 286
Timeout *seconds* keyword, 275-276
Timestamp Reply message type, 35
Timestamp Request message type, 35
TIS (Trusted Information Systems), 264
TIS (Trusted Information Systems) Firewall Toolkit. *See* FWTK
TLS (Transfer Layer Security) protocol, 209
tn-gw, 267
tn-gw proxy, 279
tn-gw proxy keywords, 280
tn-gw proxy server commands, 281
tn-qw, 245
/todo sudirectory (/rules directory), 251
Toolkit. *See* FWTK

tools
    auditing IP (Argus), 448
    monitoring networks, 448
        Argus, 448
        Courtney, 449
        Gabriel, 449
        ifstatus, 450
        ISS (Internet Security
          Scanner), 448-449
        Merlin, 450
        NID (Network Intrusion
          Detector), 450
        SATAN (Security
          Administrator Tool for
          Analyzing Networks),
          449
        SWATCH (Simple
          WATCHer), 448
        tcpdump, 450
    system security check, 451
        lsof (List Open Files), 452
        MD5, 452
        Secure Sun, 451
        Tripwire, 451
        trojan.pl, 451
Tools menu commands
  (Internet Options), 310
touch command (UNIX), 161
TRACEROUTE command,
  35
traffic (UDP), relaying,
  297-298
Traffic Class field, 388
Transfer Layer Security
  (TLS) protocol, 209
transferring
  files between computers, 51
  packets, 31-32
translating, hardware/IP
  addresses, 33
Transmission Control Pro-
  tocol (TCP), 32, 254, 397
Transmission Control
  Protocol/Internet Protocol.
  See **TCP/IP**
transmitting data (PPTP
  tunnels), 224
transparent proxies, 163-165
Transport layer, 29
transport mode, 221
trial version (CommandView
  firewall), downloading, 358

Tribe Flood Network
  (TFN), 74
Tribe Flood Network 2000
  (TFN2K), 74
Trin00, 74
Tripwire, 105, 451
Tripwire Security Systems
  Web site, 105
Tripwire Web site, 451
Trivial File Transfer
  Protocol (TFTP), 52, 127
Trojan horses, 22, 78
trojan.pl, 451
trojan.pl Web site, 451
/trust sudirectory (/rules
  directory), 251
trusted host, 83
Trusted Information
  Systems Internet Firewall
  Toolkit. *See* **FWTK**
Trusted Information
  Systems (TIS), 264
tunnel mode, 221
tunnels (PPTP), 212,
  222-224. *See also* **VPNs**
TXT record type, 58
Type of Service field, 46
types (ICMP), 322

U

-u command-line parameter,
  307
%u variable, 261
U.S. Department of Energy
  Web site, 461
UDP (User Datagram
  Protocol), 26, 33, 254, 397
UDP ASSOCIATE request
  packet, 297
UDP ASSOCIATE requests
  (SOCKS V5 Command
  Code field), 297
UDP fragmentation, 298
UDP header information
  (packet filters), 120
UDP port 514, 182
UDP ports, 49
UDP proxies, creating,
  296-297
UDP request header, 298

UDP traffic, relaying,
  297-298
UDP well-know port num-
  bers, 397-443
UID (user ID), 257
UID field, 257, 269
unicast addresses, 40, 391
UNIX environment vari-
  ables, defining, 229
UNIX, 181
    auditing (syslog utility),
      181-182
    automating tasks, 187
    commands,
      replacements/patches, 452
    daemon processes, 135-137
        inetd.conf configuration
          file, 135-136
        NFS (Network File
          System), 137
    disabling routing on proxy
      servers, 160
    installing PGP, 229
        compiling source code, 229
        generating public/private
          key pairs, 229-230
        storing keys, 230
    log files, 185
        /etc/utmp, 186
        lastlog, 186
        /usr/adm/wtmp, 186
        /var/adm/aculog, 187
        /var/log/cron, 187
    network configuration files,
      138
    resource permissions,
      142-146
        owner values, changing,
          145-146
        permission values, chang-
          ing, 145-146
        permission values, viewing,
          143-144
        SGID (Set Group ID),
          144-145
        SUID (Set User ID),
          144-145
    shadow password file, 134
    syslogd daemon, 256
    touch command, 161

Unix to Unix Copy Program (uucp), 136
UNKNOWN keyword, 259
Upgrade command (CommandView Firewall menu), 367
URL, 351
URL blocking, 172
Use of User Rights event, 190
user accounts (squid), creating, 303
User and Group Management event, 190
user authentication, 64-66
user databases, centralized, 66
User Datagram Protocol. *See* UDP
User ID field (CONNECT Request), 293
User Manager, 189-191
User Manager command (Administrative Tools menu), 189
user services, managing, 368-369
-user *userid* keyword, 275
user-defined chains, 324-325
userid *user* command, 284-286
userid *user* keyword, 276
userID (UID), 257
usernames, 64
users, educating about security, 80-81
/usr/adm/wtmp file, 186
/usr/local/etc/netperm-table, 272
utilities
    PGP (Pretty Good Privacy), 228
      accessing encrypted files, 232
      configuring, 235-237
      creating digital signatures, 232
      installing, 229-230, 233-234
    r, 60-61
    syslog, 181-182

uucp (Unix to Unix Copy Program), 136

V

-V *address* parameter, 319
-v command-line option, 320, 329
-V command-line parameter, 307
-v option, 330
validity of SAs (security associations), 218
values
    attributes, matching, 273
    policy, 318
    subnet, calculating, 43
/var/adm/aculog file, 187
/var/log/cron file, 187
variables
    %%, 261
    %a, 260
    %c, 260
    %d, 261
    environment, defining, 229
    %h, 261
    %n, 261
    %p, 261
    %s, 261
    shell commands, 260-261
    %u, 261
vectoring addresses, 11
verbose flag, 329
Verbose logging format, 352
Verisign Web site, 207
Version field, 45, 388
Version Number field, 297
    CONNECT Request, 292
    reply code, 293
View button, 310
View menu (CommandView firewall), 366
View menu commands (Internet Options), 354
viewing contents of key rings, 231
Virtual Private Network Consortium (VPNC), 212
Virtual Private Networks. *See* VPNs
virtual security zones, 376
virus scanning, 382

viruses, 22, 78, 173
VPNC (Virtual Private Network Consortium), 212
VPNs (virtual private networks), 66, 82, 212, 228, 373, 378, 385-386
    advantages, 214-215
    authentication, 214
    creating, 212-213
    disadvantages, 215-216
    joining, 213

W

-W *name* parameter, 319
Wait-state field, 257, 268
wakeup *seconds* command, 285
WANs (wide area networks), 64, 67
Web pages, checking for encryption, 209
Web Proxy service, 343
    AutoDial, 343-344
    Proxy server arrays, joining, 345
    third-party plug-ins, 345
Web publishing, 350
Web sites
    altavista, 456
    Argus, 448
    Authd, 454
    Blowfish, 202
    Caldera, 314
    CERT Coordination Center, 458-459
    COAST (Computer Operations, Audit and Security Technology), 461
    Computer Incident Advisory Capability, 75
    COPS, 447
    Courtney, 449
    Crack, 447
    Drawbridge, 250
    Federal Computer Incidence Response Capability, 461-462
    fingerd, 453
    Firewalls mailing list, 460
    Forum of Incident Response and Security Teams, 457

Free Software Foundation, 302
FreeBSD, 250
FWTK, 264, 289
Gabriel, 450
IETF, 209
ifstatus, 450
"Improving the Security of your Site by Breaking Into It" (Dan Farmer & Wietse Venema), 251
ipchains, 322, 330
ipfwadm, 315
IPv6, 386
ISS, 449
L0pht Heavy Industries, 460
lsof, 452
MD5, 452
Merlin, 450
Microsoft, 134, 459
  security, 459
  service pack downloads, 335
National Security Institute's Security Resource Net, 462
Network Associates, 228
NID, 450
NT security, 460
PCERT, 458
Perl COPS, 447
PortMap V3, 453
Red Hat, 314
SANS (System Administration, Networking, and Security) Institute, 457
SATAN, 251-252, 449
Secure Sun, 451
Security Portal, 459
sfingerd, 453
smrsh, 452
SOCKS, 292
SQUID, 303, 306
SRA, 453
ssh, 454
SSH Secure Shell, 136
su dummy program, 454
SWATCH, 448

tcpdump, 451
Tiger, 447
Trip Wire, 451
Tripwire Security Systems, 105
trojan.pl, 451
U.S. Department of Energy, 461
Verisign, 207
World Wide Web Security FAQ, 461
welcome-msg *filename* keyword, 276
well-know port numbers (TCP/UDP), 397-443
well-known ports, 49-50, 396
who command, 186
wide area networks (WANS), 64, 67
windows (PGP), 235
Windows NT
  Add Users and Groups dialog box, 150
  auditing, 188-189
    disabling auditing, 190
    Event Viewer, 188
    setting up events to audit. See events, auditing
  configuring PGP, 235-237
  Directory Permissions dialog box, 149-152
  disabling routing on proxy servers, 160
  Explorer
    modifying permissions, 150-151
    viewing permissions on files/directories, 148-149
  installing PGP, 233-234
  log files
    managing, 195
    reviewing, 193-194
  Network applet, 139
  printers, auditing usage, 193
  resource permissions, 147-152
    modifying, 150-152
    special permissions, 147

  standard permissions, 148
  viewing on files/directories, 148-149
  Service dialog box, 139
  services, 139-140
  Services applet, 139
  Special Directory Access dialog box, 152
Windows NT Explorer, 189-192
Windows NT Explorer command (Programs menu), 191
Windows NT Server, 191
Windows NT Service Packs, 134, 335
WinSock networking functions, intercepting calls, 292, 298
wizards, Key Generation, 235, 238
WKS record type, 58
World Wide Web Security FAQ Web site, 461
WWW (World Wide Web), 15

X-Z

-X *chain* command, 326
-x command-line option, 320, 329
-X command-line parameter, 307
X Windows, 115
x-gw command, 281
Xforwarder *program* keyword, 280
-y command-line option, 320, 329
-Y command-line parameter, 307
Yellow Pages, 65
Z1s, 55
-Z *chain* command, 326
-z command, 317
-z command-line parameter, 307
Zimmerman, Phillip (PGP), 228
zone transfers, 55